# International Legal English

**Second edition**

A course for classroom or self-study use

## Teacher's Book

Jeremy Day

with

Amy Krois-Lindner

and

TransLegal®

**CAMBRIDGE**
UNIVERSITY PRESS

# CAMBRIDGE
### UNIVERSITY PRESS

University Printing House, Cambridge CB2 8BS, United Kingdom

Cambridge University Press is part of the University of Cambridge.

It furthers the University's mission by disseminating knowledge in the pursuit of education, learning and research at the highest international levels of excellence.

www.cambridge.org
Information on this title: www.cambridge.org/9780521279468

© Cambridge University Press 2011

First published 2006
This edition 2011

*A catalogue record for this publication is available from the British Library*

ISBN 978-0-521-27946-8 Teacher's Book
ISBN 978-0-521-27945-1 Student's Book with Audio CDs

# About the authors

## Author of the Teacher's Book

## Jeremy Day

Jeremy Day is Series Editor of *Cambridge English for ...*, a series of ESP courses. The series includes courses on English for *Engineering, Human Resources, Job-hunting, Marketing, Nursing, Scientists* and *the Media*. He has authored or co-authored seven ESP Teacher's Books, including *Introduction to International Legal English, Flightpath* and *Dynamic Presentations*. He is co-author of the advanced level of *Active Grammar*, a CLIL-based grammar book. He currently works for English360 (www.english360.com) as a writer, editor and teacher–trainer. He lives with his wife and children in Warsaw, Poland.

## Authors of the Student's Book

# TransLegal®

**www.translegal.com**

TransLegal is Europe's leading firm of lawyer–linguists, providing the legal community with:

○ online legal English courses;
○ online legal English testing;
○ online legal English dictionary;
○ online legal language resources;
○ live legal English courses and seminars;
○ translations of legal and commercial documents;
○ legal language consultancy services.

TransLegal has collaborated with Cambridge ESOL, a division of the University of Cambridge, in the development of the Cambridge ILEC examination, the world's only internationally recognised test of legal English.

For more information about TransLegal and for online legal language resources, visit www.translegal.com.

## Acknowledgements

Many people have contributed to this book, knowingly or otherwise. I have learned a huge amount about law and legal English from three sources: the anonymous writers behind countless Internet sites (acknowledged throughout this book); my legal-English students at the British Council and elsewhere; and of course the Student's Book authors, Amy Krois-Lindner and TransLegal. For the second edition, I've also benefited enormously from the comments, advice and encouragement from friends in the legal-English teaching community, including the excellent members of the EULETA discussion group (http://groups.yahoo.com/group/euleta).

Clare Sheridan at CUP managed the first edition seamlessly and professionally, and brought together many legal and ELT professionals to review and check the material, especially Dorthe Engelhardt from the University of Griefswald and Robert Houser, William Yeago and Janice Carling from TransLegal. For the second edition, Caroline Thiriau has also done an excellent job. Once again, Catriona Watson-Brown has been outstanding as an editor, adviser and motivator. Above all, I must thank my wife and children, Ania, Emilia and Tomek Day, for their patience and support.

## Amy Krois-Lindner

Amy Krois-Lindner has taught language competence at the English Department of the University of Vienna for many years. She teaches English for Special Purposes and academic writing and is also a teacher-trainer. In addition, she has played a role in the development of a departmental ESP module with certification and has been involved in the curriculum development of several ESP courses at the Vienna University of Applied Sciences and the Vienna University of Technology.

# Contents

# Introduction

## Who is the *ILE Second edition* Teacher's Book for?

The *International Legal English Second edition* (*ILE*) Teacher's Book is aimed at all teachers using *ILE* in the classroom. It is designed to make the *ILE* course as flexible as possible, so that it is suitable for a wide range of teaching situations: from individual students to large groups; from prospective law students to experienced lawyers; from single-nationality groups to international classes; and from upper-intermediate level to advanced and beyond. It is aimed at teachers who may have limited teaching experience or little or no knowledge of legal English or the worlds of law and business. For this reason, more experienced teachers of legal English may find some sections of the book a little obvious, but it is hoped most teachers will appreciate the careful guidance. I myself am a teacher, not a lawyer, and throughout the book I have drawn heavily on my own experience of trying to get to grips with the concepts and language of commercial law.

## What does the course involve?

Teachers are strongly advised to read the introductory sections in the *ILE* Student's Book for guidance on the structure and contents of the course, and how it relates to the Cambridge ILEC (International Legal English Certificate) exam. There is also a section focusing on preparation for the exam on page ix of this book. In addition, you should familiarise yourself with the ILEC exam by looking at www.legalenglishtest.org.

## How is the *ILE* Teacher's Book organised?

At the beginning of this book, there are sections on **Teaching lawyers as a non-lawyer** (general advice for new teachers of legal English), **Writing** (ideas for making the writing activities more varied and interactive), **Games and activities** (to supplement many activities throughout the course) and **Using the Internet for research** (advice for teachers who wish to increase their knowledge in order to prepare for teaching legal English). There is also a section entitled **Preparing students for the ILEC exam**, giving advice on how to best prepare students for all four sections of the exam.

Each unit starts with a **Teacher's brief**, designed to introduce non-lawyers to the legal topic of the unit. Where possible, the Teacher's brief relates the legal concepts to the everyday experiences of non-lawyers. To enable teachers to read the briefs quickly and to scan them for specific information, the most important words and phrases are given in bold. These bold terms include key legal vocabulary (most of which is explained in the Glossary booklet that accompanies the Student's Book) as well as the language skills developed in each unit. The briefings also include some useful Internet sources related to the unit. Inevitably, given the constantly changing nature of the Internet, some of these links may not work or may change.

The teaching notes start with an introductory discussion, designed to get students thinking and talking about the topic from a non-technical perspective. The notes then follow the organisational structure of the Student's Book. The answers to each exercise are included immediately after the notes. (They are also listed at the end of the Student's Book.)

There are also many supplementary activities (**Optional lead-in/extension**), usually designed to exploit the grammar and vocabulary from reading and listening texts more fully. Not all of these activities will be appropriate for all teaching contexts: some classes may find a text so easy that they need no further support or analysis, while others may find a text so difficult and time-consuming that you decide to move on to a new section in the book as soon as possible! However, it is hoped that they will make lesson planning easier, as they offer a good way of using five or ten minutes at the beginning or end of a lesson.

There are also **Language** and **Background notes** throughout the units to explain difficult language (usually vocabulary from reading or listening texts, but also some unusual or difficult grammar structures). IPA pronunciation is often given inside Language/Background notes, or as separate **Pronunciation notes**. The aim of all of these notes is to provide teachers with some background before they start a lesson, or to provide answers to difficult questions from students during lessons. For this reason, the Pronunciation notes contain some non-technical terms which may nonetheless cause you problems.

For each Listening section, there is a reference to both the relevant CD/track number(s) and the page in the Student's Book where the transcript can be found.

Each unit in the Student's Book ends with an online research activity and a self-study **Language focus** section. This book does not provide specific guidance for these (other than answers for the Language focus), as they are self-explanatory, although there are some ideas for doing the online research activities on page xviii. Both activities are ideal for homework, either during the course of the unit or afterwards as revision. They can also be done in class. Needless to say, it is important that you, the teacher, try these activities yourself so that you are ready to deal with any problems students may have with them. The sections on the ILEC exam at the end of the Student's Book (**Exam focus** and **ILEC practice test**) are also an excellent source of ideas for homework.

Each unit contains references to photocopiable worksheets, which can be found at the back of the book. Instructions and answer keys (where applicable) for these activities are included within the notes. In most of the units, one of the worksheets provides notes for a role-play. A few units contain role-plays elsewhere (in the Student's Book or Teacher's Book), in which case there is no separate role-play worksheet.

The Student's Book also contains six case studies, after Units 4, 6, 9, 11, 14 and 16. Notes for these are given at the same positions in this book.

## How can the book be used with different levels?

Although *ILE*, like the ILEC exam, is aimed at upper-intermediate to advanced levels, this does not mean that it cannot be used with lower or higher levels. The notion of 'level' is rather

complicated when it comes to legal English. For example, Student A, an experienced international lawyer, may be fairly fluent and confident in English, but due to his frequent mistakes is classified as 'intermediate'. Conversely, Student B may have technically proficient English, but due to her lack of legal knowledge, may struggle with the course as much as Student A. For both of these students, you should provide plenty of support, including supplementary activities, with the aim of getting them through the course and their exams.

Student C, on the other hand, is already an experienced lawyer with an excellent command of both legal and general English. In her case, your aim should be for her to master most of the language used in the book, with a view to producing it, rather than merely understanding it. The supplementary activities should therefore be used to make the course more challenging.

Even in a mixed-ability group, it is possible for all students to make good progress, whatever their initial level. You should encourage them each to push themselves to use difficult, new or sophisticated language as much as possible in their speaking and writing, and you should provide sensitive feedback and error correction.

## How can the book be used with different class sizes?

At many points in both the Student's Book and the Teacher's Book, there are instructions for the students to work in pairs. Obviously, if you have only one student or an odd number, this will be impossible, but for the most part this should not cause problems. With one-to-one classes, you will have to be the partner in discussions and role-plays. Where a role-play includes a lawyer and a client, you should always play the role of the client. With odd numbers of students, most pairwork exercises will work equally well with groups of three. In both cases, specific advice has been provided where necessary (for example, with role-plays).

There is no upper limit to the class size. For time reasons, some activities (such as individual presentations) may have to be modified for very large groups, but again specific instructions have been provided where necessary.

## Do I have to work through the book in order?

You can work through the units in any order you like, although it's a good idea to start with Unit 1. The three units on company law (Units 2, 3 and 4) are best done in that order, but you may decide to do some other units in between to add a bit of variety. The same goes for the three units on contract law (Units 5, 6 and 7). The Case studies can be done at any point, but of course they will work better after the units which deal with the relevant topics. It is also not a good idea to save all the Case studies for the end of the course. The Exam focus section and ILEC practice test should be used throughout the course – if you leave them to the end, it will be too late.

## How long does the course take?

Whenever I have taught from *International Legal English,* it has taken me around five 90-minute lessons to complete a unit (so around 7.5 hours per unit, 120 hours for the whole course). But I know teachers who have completed units at a much faster rate – as few as three 90-minute lessons per unit (so 72 hours for the whole course). It all depends on your approach, your students and your timetable. Bear the following in mind:

○ Will you use most of the supplementary activities and worksheets?

○ Will you play lots of vocabulary revision games?

○ Will you allow long discussions to develop from the topics in the book (and from students' own professional lives)?

○ Will you supplement the course with materials you have made yourself?

○ If you set a reading task as homework, will you go through it carefully and discuss it in the next lesson (rather than simply checking the answers)?

I tend to do all of these things, and I believe this to be the most appropriate and effective way to work with this book.

# Preparing students for the ILEC exam

The **Exam focus** section and the **ILEC practice test** at the back of the Student's Book are invaluable for students taking the ILEC exam, and you should use the exercises there throughout the course, either as homework tasks or as in-class activities. For example, the text on Partnership on page 241 is ideal as follow-up homework to the topics in Unit 2.

For more exam practice, download past papers from the ILEC website (http://www.legalenglishtest.org/downloads.php). The Course Design Guidelines from the same site will help you create your own supplementary materials: http://www.legalenglishtest.org/downloads/ILEC_Course_Design_Guidelines.pdf.

## Preparing students for the Test of Reading

In addition to the exam practice provided in this course, you can also create your own exam-style tasks quickly and easily. This is an excellent opportunity for you to introduce texts that are directly related to your students' own jurisdictions, or to current stories from news websites. You could also search Google News (http://news.google.com) for recent news stories containing key words of your choice (e.g. *easement*). Law firms' websites are also an excellent source of up-to-date and interesting texts. If you do decide to use a text from the Internet, you should of course be careful to avoid infringements of copyright. At the very least, you should always acknowledge your sources and never claim the text as your own (for example by putting your school's logo on it or selling your materials).

It is extremely easy to make tasks to prepare for Parts 1, 2 and 3 of the Test of Reading, although you need to be ready to explain why the 'correct' answer is as it is, and not another possibility suggested by students. Students can also make such activities for themselves and for their classmates. Of course, if they make the activities for themselves, they are likely to remember many of the answers and score 100% in the test, but this could be taken as evidence of learning! Also, if they keep a copy of their exercises and try them again after a few months, they can check if they really have learned as much as they thought.

Parts 4, 5 and 6 of the exam are more difficult to create activities for. However, make sure when you are working with longer texts (either from the Student's Book or from other sources) that you develop the skills needed for the exam, e.g. reading quickly for general understanding (skimming), hunting through a text to find specific answers (scanning) and guessing meaning from context. For this reason, it is always useful to set a time limit for longer reading tasks.

## Preparing students for the Test of Writing

There is, of course, no substitute for plenty of writing practice. However, it is also vital to introduce students to the marking scheme for the exam (see http://www.legalenglishtest.org/downloads/ilec_handbook.pdf for the full list of criteria). According to the handbook, ILEC writing is judged according to:

○ content (Has the examinee included all the information that he/she needed to include?);

○ organisation and cohesion (Is the text logically organised? Does it fit together naturally?);

○ range and accuracy of vocabulary;

○ range and accuracy of grammatical structures;

○ effect on the target reader (Would the reader consider this a polite, intelligent and professional communication?).

Note that grammatical accuracy is just a small part of the total marking scheme, and students would do well to focus on other aspects of writing in order to maximise their grade. Organisation and cohesion are just as important, and arguably much easier to master (with proper planning, paragraphing and some useful structuring phrases, as studied in some depth in the Student's Book). Content is also easy to get full marks on, as long as examinees plan their writing before they start. This is probably the most important lesson with regard to the Test of Writing: the importance of careful planning. Point out that students can also plan the sophisticated grammar and vocabulary to include in each paragraph before they start writing.

Note also the importance of word counts, which are taken very seriously in the ILEC exam. A key skill that is tested is the ability to express a large amount of information in a limited number of words.

## Preparing students for the Test of Listening

There are two important issues here. Firstly, students need to be given plenty of practice in listening to fluent English, ideally in a legal English context. For this reason, the Student's Book includes CDs containing all the recordings from the course, which students should be encouraged to listen to regularly (but only after they have listened to those recordings in class). They should also watch TV and films in English if possible – most DVDs can be played in the original language, for example. Audiobooks are another good way of developing general listening skills.

Secondly, students need to know the structure of the ILEC Test of Listening, to know what is expected of them in each task. Part 4 of the Test of Listening in particular can be difficult to manage the first time you try it, as there are two separate tasks. You can, of course, use the tasks from the Exam focus section and the ILEC practice test, as well as the downloadable listening tests from the ILEC website. In addition, note that the format of the ILEC Test of Listening is very similar to other exams, such as BEC (Vantage or Higher). You could get hold of some practice-test books for those exams to provide further exam practice for your students.

## Preparing students for the Test of Speaking

As with the Test of Writing, it is important that students are familiar with the marking criteria, so that they know what to pay particular attention to

in their preparation and in the exam itself. The four analytical criteria are:

○ grammar and vocabulary;
○ discourse management;
○ pronunciation;
○ interactive communication.

Students should note that grammar and vocabulary together constitute only one of the four elements, and even this can be divided into accuracy (= how many mistakes), range (= does the examinee just use easy language, or does he/she take risks) and appropriacy (= is the examinee using appropriate grammar and vocabulary for the topic, or just showing off by using fancy structures, for example). In other words, grammatical accuracy makes up only a tiny proportion of the assessment. Students would be well advised to focus instead on improving their discourse management (e.g. the way they structure and build up their arguments, using signposting language, etc., especially in Part 2) and their interactive communication (e.g. the way they listen to and respond to their partner, and how they involve their partner in a discussion, especially in Parts 3 and 4).

Note also that no part of the exam is intended to test examinees' knowledge of the law, and certainly not of British or American law. The examiners in the Test of Speaking are not legal experts; they are experts in assessing language level. It is the job of university exams to assess students' knowledge of law, which is distinct from their level of English.

That said, it would be very difficult for someone with no knowledge of the law to bluff in the Test of Speaking. Candidates need to have a solid knowledge of the issues and vocabulary covered in *International Legal English*[1]. Most obviously, Part 2 of the Test of Speaking requires them to speak for a minute on a legal English topic. This would be extremely stressful for someone who has no idea about that topic.

Students need plenty of practice and guidance in the four parts of the Test of Speaking, including an awareness of how long to speak in each part. In Part 1, where candidates talk about themselves,

[1] Note that the list of topics that could come up in the exam is very similar to the topics covered in this book: see page 4 of the ILEC handbook for a complete list.

a good rule of thumb is around 20 seconds per answer. In Part 2, the examiner will interrupt the talk after a minute, so candidates need to know what it feels like to speak for that long, so that they can structure their talk logically (using plenty of discourse markers). In Parts 3 and 4, examinees are assessed on their ability to work together with a partner, so make sure they know not to dominate the conversation with long answers. Equally, they need to know some strategies for interrupting (or trying to interrupt) a partner who is talking too much, or getting a quiet partner involved. They will not be penalised if their partner is too talkative or too quiet, but they may well lose marks if they don't try to keep the conversation balanced.

The most difficult parts of the Test of Speaking, and arguably of the whole ILEC exam, are Parts 2 and 3. For this reason, there are sample ILEC Speaking tasks for these two parts of the exam for each unit of the Student's Book available for download on the *ILE* resource site (http://www.cambridge.org/elt/ile2).

The following table shows where you can find exercises which are specifically aimed at ILEC exam task practice (other than the Exam focus and ILEC practice test sections) or which contain useful language for the exam. Note that *OE* refers to an Optional extension activity in this book; *PW* refers to a Photocopiable worksheet.

**ILEC tasks in *International Legal English Second edition***

| Test of Reading | |
|---|---|
| **Part 1** | PW11.2; PW12.1; Unit 13, Ex. 9 (OE); PW14.4; PW16.3 |
| **Part 2** | PW2.3; Unit 13, Ex. 9 (OE); PW14.4 |
| **Part 3** | Unit 1, Ex. 2 (OE); PW6.2; PW8.1; PW16.2 |
| **Part 4** | Unit 3, Ex. 11 (OE); PW14.2 |
| **Part 5** | Unit 16, Ex. 1 (OE) |
| **Part 6** | PW2.3 |
| **Test of Listening** | |
| **Parts 1 and 2**[1] | Unit 9, Ex. 4.3; Unit 12, Ex. 9.3; Unit 15, Ex. 10 (OE) |
| **Part 3** | PW7.2 |
| **Part 4** | Unit 1, Ex. 15; PW1.3 |
| **Test of Writing** | |
| **Part 1** | Unit 4, Ex. 12 (OE); Unit 16, Ex. 8 (OE) |
| **Part 2** | Unit 5, Ex. 8 (OE); Unit 6, Ex. 13.4; Unit 7, Ex. 11; Unit 11, Ex. 5 (OE); Unit 16, Ex. 8 (OE) |
| **Test of Speaking** | |
| **Part 1** | PW1.4 |
| **Part 2** | Unit 1, Ex. 11 (OE); Unit 1, Ex. 12; Unit 6, Ex. 7; Unit 10, Ex. 6 (OE); Unit 10, Ex. 7; Unit 13, Ex. 13 (OE); Unit 16, Ex. 6 |
| **Parts 3 and 4**[2] | Unit 11, Ex. 11.1; Unit 11, Ex. 11 (OE); Unit 15, Ex. 13 |

[1] Parts 1 and 2 of the Test of Listening are both multiple-choice tasks, requiring the same skills. The only difference is that Part 1 has three short extracts, while Part 2 has one long extract.
[2] Part 4 of the Test of Speaking is a less-structured continuation of Part 3, and requires the same skills. Every discussion exercise in the book can be considered preparation for Part 4.

# Teaching lawyers as a non-lawyer

Some legal English teachers are fortunate enough to be experts in law as well as language teaching. However, there are many legal English teachers who have had no law training and therefore have limited knowledge of legal systems, procedures and terminology. These teachers may dread the idea of teaching lawyers. Legal English is so full of strange vocabulary and grammar that it seems like a different language. Lawyers themselves can be quite scary: they tend to be highly intelligent, extremely demanding and focused on tiny details. With most other branches of English teaching, it can be enough to be a good teacher with knowledge of English, but with legal English, this is not enough. The problem is that there are very few good teachers who are also knowledgeable about legal matters. This section is aimed at teachers who know very little about law.

My first lesson with lawyers was exhausting and stressful. The vocabulary brainstorm activity I had planned as a warmer ended up taking the whole lesson and left me with a list of over 40 items which either I could not explain or was not sure how to pronounce. I then spent several hours before the next lesson checking all the words on my list (see **Using the Internet for research** on page xviii) and turning them into two simple match-the-words-with-their-definitions worksheets. This hard work convinced my students that a non-lawyer could teach them legal English, and my lessons became increasingly stress-free and even enjoyable. As the course progressed, I noticed more and more that I really did understand what they were talking about, and that my opinions, life experience and ideas were just as valid as those of my students. Through a combination of honesty, hard work and professional confidence, I was able to win over their trust and become accepted as an authority.

## Be honest

It is essential to manage students' expectations. If you pretend to be a lawyer or an expert before or at the beginning of the course, students are likely to be disappointed. But if you admit that you are still learning about law yourself, they may be pleasantly surprised by how much you know.

## Be prepared

This is the key to successful teaching of legal English. It means making sure you have read all the relevant sections of the Student's Book and Teacher's Book before you step into the classroom, and really know what all of the words and phrases mean and how they are pronounced.

## Be armed

Bring a legal English dictionary with you to every lesson. I always have *Osborn's Concise Law Dictionary* (Sweet and Maxwell, 2001) to hand for emergencies.

## Be confident

Remember that, even if you know nothing about law, you can still help students enormously. You can:

○ motivate them (to come to class, to learn in class, to learn at home);

○ be an expert on plain English (the English they need in order to explain things to clients);

○ be an expert on finding things out (using the Internet and dictionaries to answer students' questions – it can be surprising to see how helpless they are when they encounter language problems);

○ be a source of real-life experiences (such as signing employment contracts, buying or renting property, borrowing money, etc.), especially if you come from a different country from your students;

○ be knowledgeable on universal problems such as dependent prepositions, punctuation, spelling, articles, tenses, levels of formality, collocations, paragraphing, etc.

You need to feel positive about why students should be paying for you to teach them.

## Learn from students

Ask lots of questions during lessons. Lawyers need to practise the skill of explaining complicated things to non-lawyers, so you should exploit this opportunity to the full. At times, you can 'act stupid' (ask questions to which you already know the answer) or 'play devil's advocate' (air controversial opinions, even if these are not your own opinions).

Just as good students should take notes and learn from them, so should you as a teacher. Write down everything you learn about what your students do in their jobs and how the law works in their countries, and try to learn from your notes.

As I started teaching more legal English classes, I found my expertise in the subjects covered in this book grew every time I taught them. I filled my copy of the Student's Book with notes taken from discussions with my students, and these notes proved invaluable next time I was teaching the same lesson with a different class.

## Think about what students need

A common mistake made by teachers of legal English is to assume that lawyers spend their time defending or prosecuting criminals in court. In fact, most lawyers deal with contract and company law, rather than criminal law, so they are unlikely to be interested in vocabulary connected with crime, the police and punishment. Most lawyers also spend very little time (if any) in court. Much of their work involves preparing or analysing documents for business clients, and trying to avoid disputes (or at least to resolve them without the need to go to court).

There is also no reason to think that your students are particularly interested in US or UK law. As English is increasingly becoming the international language of business, legal English is rapidly losing its ties with English-speaking countries. The most likely scenario is that your students need legal English to explain aspects of their own legal systems (which they already know about) to international clients (who may well be non-native English speakers). *ILE* uses discussions and language work throughout to encourage students to describe the systems in their own jurisdictions and to constantly compare the different systems. It aims to equip students with the language they need to talk about their own systems, rather than with a complete working knowledge of either UK or US systems. This means that you should try as much as possible to relate the country-specific materials in this book to students' own jurisdictions.

It is important to remember that students can probably already function fairly effectively in legal English. They may have good negotiating and writing skills, which they have developed in their own language, and their English has already reached a good level of general fluency and accuracy. Your job is to help them to function even more effectively.

If you ask students' bosses and clients what sort of English the lawyers need, they might say 'plain English': the language to communicate difficult ideas clearly to non-experts (such as clients). Many lawyers (including native English speakers) struggle to use 'client-friendly' English, with the result that they frequently fail to communicate with their clients. On the other hand, if you ask the lawyers themselves what they need, they might ask for more 'legalese': the jargon that non-lawyers find so incomprehensible. Lawyers like knowing such language because they need to understand it when they encounter it, and they feel they are expected to use it (rather like their formal dress code).

The reality is that lawyers need both types of English (as well as other formal and informal registers for writing and speaking). Your job is to raise awareness of these differences, and to provide plenty of opportunity to practise them.

# Writing

An essential part of the Student's Book is its emphasis on writing, with around two tasks per unit. The problem is that writing does not seem to fit in a communicative classroom. Students complain if they have to write for extended periods during their lessons, but they are often too busy to write at home. An obvious question is whether it is reasonable to expect students to produce 30 pieces of writing during the course, and whether you, as a teacher, have to find the time to mark so many pieces from each student. This section offers a few ideas to get around this dilemma.

Writing is one of the best ways of learning and practising language. It provides the opportunity for individual creative production without the time pressure associated with speaking. It allows students to experiment with new or complicated language structures that they would probably avoid when speaking. In fact, written language is fundamentally different from spoken language in many ways:

○ It includes skills such as spelling and punctuation which are not used in speech;

○ It uses many different grammar and vocabulary structures;

○ Accuracy is far more important than in speech because communication breakdowns cannot be overcome using body language or negotiating the meaning with the listener.

For lawyers, such issues are especially acute. Whether they are drafting contracts, legal opinions, internal memos, case summaries or emails to clients, it is essential to use professional, accurate language. A misspelled word or a misplaced comma may dangerously change the meaning of a legal document, and lawyers need practice before they can get it right.

## Teaching writing skills

Although there is no substitute for writing practice, it is just as important to focus on the sub-skills that students need to develop in order to become better writers. These are presented and practised throughout the Student's Book. Important skills include:

○ writing letters of advice and legal opinions (see Unit 2)

○ contrasting ideas (see Units 3 and 10)

○ summarising (see Unit 3)

○ standard phrases for letters and emails (see Unit 4)

○ checking your writing (see Unit 5 for a writing checklist)

○ levels of formality (see Units 8 and 13)

○ using discourse markers (see Unit 11)

○ paraphrasing in plain language (see Unit 11)

○ planning the contents and structure of a letter (see Unit 16)

○ textual transformation techniques (see Unit 16)

## In-class writing

The advantage of in-class writing over homework is that you can guarantee that all the students produce some work, and that a piece of work is actually written by a given student. Unfortunately, in-class writing is often unpopular with students, who prefer to spend their class time in a more interesting way. With this in mind, in-class writing needs to be quick (e.g. set a time limit of five or ten minutes) and different from the experience of homework writing. The following ideas explore how to achieve this.

### Team writing

There is no reason why writing has to be a solitary activity. A simple trick is to hand out a single sheet of (coloured) paper to each pair or group, and to make them plan and produce their writing together. This means that they have to speak with each other to compare ideas and can correct each other's mistakes. This may even be done with the whole class, where one scribe writes the class's suggestions onto the board.

### Chain writing

Team-writing activities can be spiced up by telling the teams to swap their pieces of paper with another team after a certain amount of time (or number of words). This forces them to read each other's work and can produce some very creative (or funny) texts.

### Oral writing

'Writing' does not have to involve a pen and paper. Students can work with a partner to decide what they would write, and to speak the text as if they were dictating to a secretary. At the end, ask some groups to 'read' their 'writing' aloud to the class.

### Written dialogues

Writing can be more satisfying when it is genuinely communicative, so when students have produced a complete text (e.g. an email request), tell them to pass it on to a different student, who can reply to that text (e.g. a polite refusal). Such dialogues can continue over several turns.

## A last resort

If students cannot (or will not) produce any writing, either in class or as homework, you may offer to correct any authentic writing they do in English (although they will need to edit their writing in order to protect confidentiality). This is an opportunity to remind them to use the useful language and structures from the course, and to check where they are still having problems. From a teacher's point of view, this can also provide an invaluable insight into what real lawyers actually have to write in their day-to-day lives.

## Checking written work

For many students, the value of writing practice is that their work is checked by their teacher. At the very least, this should include practical advice about how to improve. Unfortunately, if every student in a large group completes every written task, with you making written corrections during your free time and handing the work back in a later lesson, the workload for you is enormous.

Checking students' work is an important exercise, and students can learn from their corrected mistakes, but they can also learn from simply writing. For example, in order to practise unusual grammar structures or experiment with new vocabulary, they first need to do some research (e.g. in a dictionary or grammar reference) and then concentrate on how to structure their writing so that it is accurate, sophisticated, appropriate and natural. This process is where the real learning takes place, much more than being corrected by a teacher. In other words, even if you do not have time to mark written work thoroughly, students can still benefit from writing.

An alternative to the traditional way of marking is to put students' work onto photocopies or an overhead transparency so that you can discuss the work with the whole class. This can take up a lot of class time and be very teacher-focused, but it is also very useful for students to see and learn from others' strengths and weaknesses. This works best if the work is anonymous (and written on a computer).

## Grading

It can be very motivating for students to have their writing graded, especially if they can see their grades improve as the course progresses. Grading should be based on task fulfilment (i.e. does the writing communicate the necessary message concisely and in a way that creates the right impression on the target reader?), rather than simple accuracy.

# Games and activities

It is strange that two of the elements that seem so central to teaching younger students – humour and competitive games – are often completely absent from the teaching of 'serious' subjects such as legal English. Lawyers and law students are no different from any other type of learner: they respond to activities which are enjoyable, stimulating and memorable. A game can be a good way to start a lesson, to fill a spare five minutes at the end, or simply to change the pace whenever students are looking tired. It can introduce new language, practise recently taught language or recycle old language. Of course, not all students will enjoy (or see the point of) games – or they may prefer collaborative games to competitive ones – so you will need to find the right balance for your particular class.

This section outlines some games and activities which can be applied to many of the exercises in the Student's Book, either as supplementary activities or as replacements. They usually require little or no preparation.

## Snake game

Write a grid of numbers (say, 1–20) on the board in a honeycomb pattern. Each number represents something that may be tested (e.g. the first 20 vocabulary items from the Glossary booklet, or 20

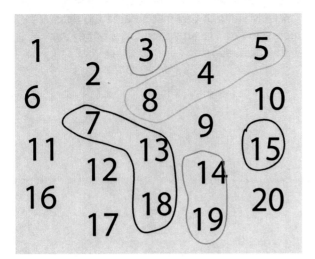

comprehension questions based on a text). Divide the class into teams and use a different-colour marker for each team. Tell the first team to choose a number. Then ask the question for that number (e.g. read the definition for the corresponding Glossary item). Allow that team five seconds to supply the answer, before handing over the question to the next team. When a team answers a question correctly, draw a circle around the number in that team's colour. The aim is to make a chain (= a snake) of adjacent numbers, and to block the other teams' snakes. At the end, the team with the longest continuous snake is the winner.

## Stake game

This game works best with an exercise containing around eight or ten challenging questions (e.g. reading/listening comprehension questions or grammar questions). Tell students to work in teams to answer the questions, perhaps with a time limit. Draw a grid on the board, with the question numbers down the first column and the team names along the first row. Before checking the answer to the first question, ask each team to place a stake of between €10 and €100 on the question, depending on how sure they are of their answer. Write the stake in the appropriate place in the grid. Then elicit an answer from each team for the question. For those teams which answer correctly, write '+' next to their stake, and for those answering incorrectly, write '–'. Repeat the procedure for each of the remaining questions. At the end, add together all the winnings for each team (i.e. those marked '+'), and subtract any losses (i.e. those marked '–') to find out which team has won the most money.

This game is useful for teaching new language points, as students are generally interested in why a particular answer is right or wrong, and try to learn from their own mistakes when answering later questions.

## First-use game

When you set up role-plays, it is important to encourage students to use new target language (e.g. the useful functional phrases studied in a particular unit). One way to do this is to award a point for the first student to use each phrase from a list (either on the board or on cards). It is essential that the phrase is used naturally and appropriately, so you should not award points if students use several phrases simply to get points. After the first good use of a particular phrase, cross it off the list and write the student's initial next to it (or give that student the card). This phrase may no longer be used during the role-play. At the end of the role-play, the student who has used the most phrases is the winner.

## Buzz game

This can be done with any text that has already been studied. Read the text aloud slowly, pausing after each line. In each line substitute a 'buzz' for one of the words. Students should work in teams to remember/work out what the missing word should be. The team with the most correct answers at the end is the winner.

## Easy-first procedure

This technique is surprisingly useful for turning any exercise into a game, especially those with a large number of questions. It also works if you join several short exercises together. Tell students to complete an exercise in teams. Write the question numbers on the board. When students have finished answering the questions, ask the first team to choose the number of a question they are sure they know the answer of. If they supply the correct answer, draw a circle around that number in that team's colour, and move on to the next team. If they are wrong, move on to the next team. They may choose the same number or a different one. Keep going until all the questions have been answered correctly. The team with the most numbers at the end is the winner.

The procedure is called 'easy first' because the best strategy is to answer the easy questions (which other teams are also likely to know) as early in the game as possible, and to leave tricky ones until the end of the game.

See also this article on my blog for ideas on how to exploit the Glossary booklet: http://specific-english. blogspot.com/2010/01/wordlists-in-esp.html.

# Using the Internet for research

As a teacher of legal English, it is important that you and your students accept that you cannot be an expert on all aspects of law in students' jurisdiction(s). In fact, it can sometimes be useful for both you and your students if you claim to be ignorant of their legal systems in order to make them explain things to you in everyday English.

However, you may feel dissatisfied with this situation. If you conduct some research before your lessons, you can increase your self-confidence, improve your teaching and impress students. An obvious source for research is books, either bought or borrowed from a library. The problem is that they can be very expensive, difficult to get hold of, or written in a foreign language.

The alternative source, the Internet, also has flaws as a research tool: there is often too much material available, with no way of easily telling what is reliable and useful and what is not; most of the English-language content relates to the USA (and, to a lesser extent, the UK), while most other jurisdictions are poorly represented; and it is constantly changing, which means that printed guides, such as this one, go out of date quickly.

That said, as long as you are patient and careful to check information from unreliable sites, the Internet can be an invaluable resource. Below are ten sites which I have found especially useful while writing this book.

1   **Wikipedia** (http://en.wikipedia.org/wiki/Main_Page): This encyclopaedia is an impressive source of knowledge on virtually any subject. Many of the key terms from this course have their own sections, with countless links to other related articles. It is written by members of the public, which means that it is constantly growing. Unfortunately, it also means that information may be unreliable or biased. It is therefore important to double-check its accuracy with other sources. For me, the best thing about Wikipedia are the links to external sources, usually given at the end of an article.

2   **TransLegal** has an ever-growing bank of resources at http://www.translegal.com/resources. These include the world's first learner's dictionary of legal English, a legal English blog, LETS (Legal English Teaching Support) and many other excellent tools for legal English teachers. In addition to the free resources, TransLegal also has many courses to buy, including PLEAD, a distance-learning course designed to accompany this book: http://www.translegal.com/online-courses/plead.

3   **Law.com** (http://www.law.com): The best thing about this site is its dictionary (http://dictionary.law.com), which offers clear definitions of most of the key terms from this book. Other useful sources of legal terms and legalese include http://www.law.ucla.edu/volokh/legalese.htm and http://www.uchelp.com/law/glossary.htm.

4   **OneLook** (http://www.onelook.com): This site is a collection of dozens of online dictionaries. If you type in a query, it will generate links to all the online dictionaries which contain definitions, including Wikipedia and Law.com. This is especially useful for the financial/business terminology used in this book. OneLook also links to the **Cambridge Advanced Learner's Dictionary** (http://dictionary.cambridge.org), an excellent all-round guide to all but the most specialised vocabulary, which also has a useful pronunciation guide. There is also the interesting **Online Etymology Dictionary** (http://www.etymonline.com), which can provide interesting background information on strange legal words such as *usufruct* and *chattel*.

5   **Google** (http://www.google.com): Like all good search engines, Google is an extremely useful tool when searching for obscure or very specific information (i.e. information which no encyclopaedia or dictionary provides). It is important to know a few tricks to limit the number of sites generated. For example, if you search for [intellectual property] you will find sites on intellectuals and sites on property, as well as those on

intellectual property, but if you search for ["intellectual property"], using quotation marks, or [intellectual_property], using a baseline rule, you will find only those sites which include the complete phrase *intellectual property*. If you use several keywords in your search (e.g. ["intellectual property" + korea + law]) you may find very specific information. Searches can also be refined by using the Language Tools option to search for pages written in a particular language or country.

6 **Onecle** (http://www.onecle.com): This is a collection of thousands of authentic contracts and other legal documents, including employment agreements, promissory notes, credit agreements and merger agreements. If you have the time and patience to read through and try to understand some of these documents, you will gain a tremendous insight into both what lawyers need to think about and how to read and write such documents. See also **Hoover Web Design** (http://www.hooverwebdesign.com/business/menu_legal.php) for an incredible bank of free sample legal documents.

7 **Lexmercatoria.org** (http://www.jus.uio.no/lm): This site is particularly useful for finding articles and links for a wide range of legal subjects in many countries.

8 **Encyclopedia of Law and Economics** (http://encyclo.findlaw.com/index.html): A huge resource, with detailed articles on aspects of law in many countries.

9 **LawGuru** (http://www.lawguru.com/ilawlib/index.php?id=52) has links to English-language versions of the laws of almost every country in the world. Similarly, **Constitution Finder** (http://confinder.richmond.edu) provides links to constitutions and related documents, usually in English, for virtually every country in the world.

10 **Wex** (http://topics.law.cornell.edu/wex/all): This encyclopaedia from Cornell University Law School is more reliable than Wikipedia. Also available from the Cornell site is the complete text of the Uniform Commercial Code (UCC), an invaluable guide to US commercial law: http://www.law.cornell.edu/ucc/ucc.table.html.

# Other useful sites

○ Another essential website for teachers of legal English is **EULETA** (the European Legal English Teachers' Association): http://www.euleta.de. For me, the most useful thing about EULETA is its online discussion group (http://groups.yahoo.com/group/euleta), where legal English teachers around the world engage in interesting discussions and offer support and advice to other teachers.

○ For anyone teaching students for the ILEC exam, the **ILEC handbook** (http://www.legalenglishtest.org/downloads/ilec_handbook.pdf) is essential reading. The **ILEC website** (http://www.legalenglishtest.org) also contains many useful links, including past ILEC papers to download.

○ I have written quite a few articles on legal English on my blog, **Specific English**, which is aimed at teachers of ESP: http://specific-english.blogspot.com.

○ Finally, the **resource site** for this book (http://www.cambridge.org/elt/ile2) contains many useful resources to develop the topics covered in the book, including vocabulary games and a series of online research tasks. Each of these research tasks contains a learning synopsis, a case study and a series of exercises. The strength of these tasks, however, is in the answer keys, which offer clear step-by-step guidance in finding the solution. More importantly, however, they introduce students and teachers of legal English to surprisingly useful research techniques that can be applied much more widely. When you set these tasks as homework, encourage students to try to complete them first without looking at the solution, but then to work through the solution afterwards to check their ideas. Point out that the lessons they learn by working through the solution are more valuable than the information they find in order to complete the tasks.

# 1 The practice of law

This unit covers a lot of important ground, but does not go very deeply into any one area. Many of the areas mentioned in this unit will be addressed much more fully in subsequent units.

Part I deals with **bodies of law**, and focuses on the two most internationally important bodies: **common law** and **civil law**. This distinction will be well known to all lawyers and even to most beginner law students. In common-law jurisdictions, such as England, Wales and Northern Ireland and the USA, laws come primarily from customs, usage and earlier court decisions. In civil-law jurisdictions (e.g. much of continental Europe), laws come from written legal codes. Much of the world can be neatly divided between these two bodies of law, but there are many **mixed systems** (e.g. India, Israel, Iran, China and South Africa). Note that the term **jurisdiction** is preferred to 'country': the countries of the UK, the USA and Canada are all mostly common law, but all contain several jurisdictions, some of which have rather different bodies of law (e.g. Scotland, the Channel Islands, Louisiana and Quebec).

Another important difference between common-law and civil-law jurisdictions is their approach to court **proceedings** (e.g. criminal trials). Common-law jurisdictions tend to use an **adversarial** system, pitting one side against the other, while some civil-law jurisdictions (e.g. France) use an **inquisitorial** system, where the proceedings are seen as a search for the truth rather than a battle between opposing sides. The match between civil law and the inquisitorial system on the one hand and between common law and the adversarial system on the other is far from perfect – some civil-law jurisdictions use an adversarial system, for example, and common-law jurisdictions may use an inquisitorial system for certain types of proceedings (e.g. for minor traffic violations).

Part I goes on to describe five **types of laws**: the most important of these are **statutes**, which are the documents issued by sovereign states (i.e. independent countries). Note that each state in a federation (such as the USA and Brazil) also has its own statutes and **codes**. Non-sovereign bodies (e.g. colonies and county, city or local governments) issue **by-laws** (UK) or **ordinances** (USA). Non-governmental agencies, such as (in the UK) Companies House, the Driver and Vehicle Licensing Agency (DVLA) and HM Prison Service, have sets of **regulations**, which have the force of law. Not all countries have such agencies, which must be authorised by statutes to issue such rules and regulations. There is a type of law which is specific to the EU: **directives**. These devices commit the member states to meeting certain obligations in their own legislatures (parliaments). Finally, **bills** are proposed laws which have not yet been ratified or adopted. When they have been passed, they are known as **Acts of Parliament** (in the UK, Canada, New Zealand, Australia, etc.) or **Acts of Congress** (in the USA), but of course can be more generally described as **statutes**.

The section on **types of courts** is inevitably country-specific: countries will vary in terms of the types of court that exist and the names given to each. All jurisdictions tend to have **lower courts**, **appeals courts** and **high courts/supreme courts**, but they may not have anything like the UK's distinction between **small claims courts**, **crown courts** and **magistrates' courts**. Note that in the UK, **magistrates** are usually volunteer non-lawyers (**Justices of the Peace (JPs)**) who preside over minor cases, and who are advised on legal matters by a **Court Clerk**. This is different from the magistrates in mainland Europe, where the term is commonly used to refer to **public prosecutors**.

Part I goes on to describe some persons and documents in court. In a typical **lawsuit** (case), the most important persons are the **plaintiff**[1], who initiates the case by **filing a complaint**, and the **defendant**, who has to **answer** that complaint. However, when the case is a **petition** (request) for a **court order** (an official proclamation by a court), rather than a complaint, the two parties are known as the **petitioner** and the **respondent** respectively. An important type of court order is an **injunction** for a person to refrain from doing something or be obliged to do something. The lawyers for both parties and in both types of case are known as **advocates**, a general term for anyone who speaks on behalf of someone else. The general name for **complaints**, **answers**, **petitions** and **motions** is

---

[1] In the UK (except Scotland), the plaintiff is known as the **claimant**.

**pleadings**, a term which covers all documents filed by lawyers in a lawsuit. The legal claims made in these documents are called **causes of action**. More details about specific points in a pleading are given in **briefs** or **written submissions**.

The last section on the legal system focuses on **Latin** expressions used in legal English. (Many are also common in general English.) Latin borrowings (such as *versus*) have been a feature of legal English throughout the history of English, but Latin became the language of legal documents in England after 1066. It was replaced by French around 1275, which in turn was replaced by English in 1362 under the **Statute of Pleading**. French's influence on legal English is far greater than that of Latin, giving us most of the vocabulary mentioned in this unit.

Part II of the unit focuses on lawyers. The general term **lawyer** covers anyone who has been trained in the law and certified to give legal advice. In some jurisdictions, such as England, clients typically engage the services of a **solicitor** for legal advice, who may in turn engage a **barrister** to carry out a specific job, such as pleading in court. Solicitors may appear in lower courts, but require a **certificate of advocacy** if they wish to contest a case in a higher court. Both types of lawyer deal with both criminal and civil cases. In other jurisdictions, such as Canada, the two roles are not kept separate (so a lawyer is known as a **barrister and solicitor**). The same is true in the USA, where such a lawyer is called an **attorney**. In many civil-law countries, **notaries** play an important role in drafting contracts and giving legal advice to private individuals. These civil-law notaries should not be confused with the US term **notary public**, which refers to people who witness and certify the legal validity of documents, take **affidavits** (sworn statements), etc. Notaries public are not necessarily trained lawyers. Finally, a **corporate counsel** works exclusively for a corporation, and both advises and represents that corporation in all legal matters.

The section on **legal education** focuses on the stages involved in becoming a barrister or solicitor in the UK, or a lawyer in the USA. Different countries around the world all have their own systems for preparing lawyers, but lawyers everywhere have to study formally (typically at a **university** or **law school**) before undertaking some sort of **work experience**, which involves **shadowing** fully qualified lawyers. There is usually some kind of **exam** and **ceremony** to mark the end of this process. For example, in the UK, new barristers are **called to the Bar** (invited into the profession).

The section goes on to look at an organigram (organisational hierarchy) of a **typical law firm**, and introduces the various levels within the hierarchy: **senior partners**, **full partners**, **salaried partners**, **associates**, **paralegals** and **clerks**.

The unit ends with a non-technical look at the advantages and disadvantages of large and small law firms.

**Further information**

- For a comprehensive list of **bodies of law** throughout the world, see http://www.droitcivil. uottawa.ca/world-legal-systems/eng-tableau. html. For more detailed information, see http:// en.wikipedia.org/wiki/Common_law.
- There is a useful analysis of the advantages and disadvantages of the **adversarial and inquisitorial systems** at http://en.wikipedia. org/wiki/Adversarial_system.
- For information on **magistrates' courts**, see http://en.wikipedia.org/wiki/Magistrate.
- For more on **legal Latin**, see http://en. wikipedia.org/wiki/List_of_legal_Latin_terms.
- There is some fascinating background to the **history and nature of legal language** at http:// www.languageandlaw.org.
- The **difference between solicitors and barristers** is explained fully at http://en. wikipedia.org/wiki/Barrister.
- There is a very clear description of the stages involved in **becoming a UK barrister** at http:// www.barcouncil.org.uk.
- The Law Society's Junior Lawyers Division offers similar insight into the process of **becoming a solicitor**: http://juniorlawyers.lawsociety.org.uk/.

# PART I: THE LEGAL SYSTEM

## Discussion

With the whole class, brainstorm the differences between *common law* and *civil law*. Use these questions to generate ideas.

a   Which jurisdictions around the world use which body of law?

b   What do you know about the histories of the two bodies?

c   What is the primary source of laws under each body?

d   Are there any jurisdictions which use a different body of law?

a Common law is used in England, Wales and Northern Ireland, most of the USA (except Louisiana), most of Canada (except Quebec) and most of the former British Empire / Commonwealth. Civil law is used in most of continental Europe. Much of the rest of the world uses either civil law or a mixture (e.g. civil law with Muslim law, etc.).

b Common law originated in England. It was institutionalised by King Henry II, who created a unified system of law which was 'common' to the country. Civil law is based on Roman law, especially Emperor Justinian's *Corpus Juris Civilis*.

c Under civil law, they come from legislation. Courts base their decisions on codes and statutes. By contrast, under common law, they are based primarily on customs, usage and court decisions. Of course, some laws do come from legislation, but such laws are seen as incursions into the common law. See http://en.wikipedia.org/wiki/Civil_law.

d There are many jurisdictions which use a mixture, including mixtures of common or civil law with Islamic (Sharia) law or customary law. See http://www.droitcivil.uottawa.ca/world-legal-systems/eng-tableau.html. You could use a list such as this for a light-hearted quiz: *Which system do they use in Argentina/Hungary/Israel/China (etc.)?*

1 ## Reading A: Bodies of law

**1.1** Tell students to read the two excerpts quickly to answer the three questions. Allow one minute for strong classes or two minutes for weaker classes. Check the answers with the whole class. Do not analyse the texts in any detail, although you may decide to ask students what they understand by the term *law of torts* (see Background note in the next column).

 **Answers**

1 A international students who will be studying at English universities

 B students who are going to study law in a foreign university

2 A

3 B

 **Background note**

The *law of torts* is a major branch of common law. *Tort* means 'civil wrong', and covers all cases of damage or injury, either through negligence or through wilful misconduct. It is usually taken to exclude criminal wrongs, although the same event may be covered by both branches (e.g. if somebody crashes into someone else's car, a civil wrong has occurred, but if the driver was drunk at the time, a criminal wrong has also occurred). The law of torts excludes breaches of contract, which are covered by contract law.

**1.2** Do this quickly with the whole class. Point out that the term *civil law* has two distinct meanings: it contrasts with *common law* in terms of bodies of law, but with *criminal law* within the common-law jurisdictions. You may need to check the pronunciation of *penal* /ˈpiːnəl/.

 **Answers**

**1** b **2** c **3** a

**1.3** Tell students to work alone or in small groups to complete the extract. When most groups have finished, check the answers with the class.

 **Answers**

**1** based on **2** disputes **3** legislation
**4** bound by **5** provisions **6** custom
**7** precedents **8** rulings **9** codified
**10** non-criminal

**Background notes**

○ *Normative principles* prescribe the way something ought to be, rather than describe the way it actually is.

○ If you are *bound* /baʊnd/ by a particular law, you must act according to that law.

○ *Precedents* /ˈpresɪdənts/ are previous court decisions which are used as the base for later decisions.

**1.4** Discuss this with the whole class, focusing especially on any interesting differences between students' jurisdictions and those mentioned.

## 2 Reading B: The adversarial and inquisitorial systems

**2.1** Elicit from the class the meanings of the words *adversarial* /ˌædvəˈseəriəl/ and *inquisitorial* /ɪŋˌkwɪzɪˈtɔːriəl/. It may help to focus on related words such as *an adversary* (= an opponent) and *an inquiry* (= an investigation to find the truth). Make sure students also know what the term *proceedings* refers to (see Background note below), and elicit how proceedings might be adversarial or inquisitorial. Students then read the text to find the answers to the four questions. When they have discussed their answers in pairs, open up the discussion to include the whole class.

**Answers**

1 The adversarial system is characteristic of common-law countries.

2 In the adversarial system, the two opposing parties gather evidence to present to the judge and jury. In the inquisitorial system, the gathering of evidence is supervised by the judge.

3 In the adversarial system, the role of the attorney is to gather evidence and present arguments to the judge and jury; in the inquisitorial system, the attorney suggests routes of enquiry to the judge and follows the judge's questioning with their own questions.

**Background notes**

○ *Proceedings* is a general term to cover all types of *legal action* events/ processes, including *lawsuits* and *criminal prosecutions*.

○ *Litigation* is another general term for *legal action*, referring to the activity of arguing a case in court.

○ The *respondent* is the party in a lawsuit who is being sued. The *defendant* is the party being prosecuted in a criminal prosecution, also referred to as *the accused*.

**Optional extension**
**ILEC preparation: Test of Reading Part 3**

If your students are planning to take the ILEC exam, point out that Part 3 of the Test of Reading focuses on word building: forming the correct word from a simpler form. For example, students may be given the word *adversary* and be expected to use the context of a text such as Reading B to transform this word into *adversarial*.

Elicit from the class more words from Reading B which could be tested in this part of the exam, and write the simpler form onto the board, together with the grammatical form of the target word (e.g. for the word *inquisitorial*, you would write *inquiry* – adjective). Focus especially on words which are important for legal English, such as those below (with answers in brackets, which should not be written on the board):

*inquiry* – adjective (*inquisitorial*)
*adversary* – adjective (*adversarial*)
*oppose* – adjective (*opposing*)
*litigate* – noun (*litigation*)
*try* – noun (*trial*)
*defend* – noun, person (*defendant*)
*preside* – adjective (*presiding*)
*receive* – noun, person (*recipient*)
*respond* – noun, person (*respondent*)
*accuse* – noun, person (*accused*)

Students then close their books and test each other in pairs by reading an item from the board for their partner to supply the original word. You could also read the text aloud, substituting a number for each target word. Students write down the correct word for each number.

Point out that simple word-building exercises such as this are not only useful preparation for the ILEC exam; they are also important for building a large vocabulary for professional use.

**2.2** Students work in pairs to complete the two tasks. You may need to check the meaning of *recant* (= to announce that you no longer stand by your earlier statement).

**2.2 1** evidence: gather, present
**2** testimony: give
**3** arguments: present
○ dismiss, gather, hear, present, provide, reject, uncover evidence
○ dismiss, give, hear, present, provide, recant, reject, support testimony
○ dismiss, hear, present, provide, reject, support arguments

---

**Optional extension**
Ask students to find more verb–noun collocations in the text. Write these on the board in two columns, but in a mixed-up order, together with those from Exercise 2.2. Students then test each other in pairs by reading a verb to elicit from their partner a suitable collocation.

**Suggested answers** (not mixed up)

| | |
|---|---|
| employ/define/use | a system |
| present/resolve | a case |
| steer | a search |
| question | witnesses / the respondent / the defendant |
| play | a passive role |
| suggest | a route of enquiry |
| find/seek/reveal | the truth |
| pit | the parties against each other |
| place | a premium on something |

---

**2.3** Students work in pairs to use the collocations to make as many sentences as possible. They may also make sentences about attorneys in the two systems. Afterwards, go through the answers with the class.

→ **Suggested answers**
○ The role of the judge in the inquisitorial system: The judge gathers evidence. The judge uncovers evidence. The judge hears testimony. The judge dismisses arguments.
○ The role of the attorney in the adversarial system: The attorney gathers evidence. The attorney presents testimony. The attorney presents arguments. The attorney rejects arguments.

---

# 3 Reading C: Types of law

**3.1** Tell students to close their books. Elicit from the whole class some institutions which might issue laws. Avoid providing the answers, as these will come up in Exercises 3.2 and 3.3.

 **Suggested answer**
National governments, local authorities, state governments, government agencies, super-national institutions such as the EU and the UN.

Tell students to read the five texts quickly and then discuss in small groups which came from which source. Then go through the answers with the class.

 **Answers**
**1** c **2** a **3** b **4** e **5** d

---

**Background notes**
○ If a statute is *unambiguous* /ˌʌnæmˈbɪɡjʊəs/, it has only one possible interpretation, so it is not likely to be misunderstood.
○ If the court *gives effect to* the intention of the legislature, it enforces the legislature's intention. This use of *effect* is related to the phrase *to come into effect*: if a law *comes into effect*, it starts being valid.

---

**3.2** Point out that the five definitions refer to the words in bold in Exercise 3.1. Tell students to work in small groups to match the words with the definitions. They may need to consult the Glossary booklet. Then check the answers with the class. You may need to elicit or provide some examples of *government agencies* (see Teacher's brief, page 20). Discuss with the class if the same five words apply to their own jurisdictions. This will depend on a) whether their jurisdiction is a part of the EU, otherwise *directive* will not apply, and b) whether their jurisdiction has government agencies authorised by statute to issue *regulations*.

→ **Answers**
**1** regulations **2** ordinance/by-law **3** bill
**4** directive **5** statute

**3.3** Tell students to work alone to answer the questions quickly. Go through the answers with the class.

## 4   Speaking A: Explaining what a law says

Tell students to close their books. Ask them to think of a more sophisticated way of saying the following sentence: *The law says that all dogs must be registered and licensed.* Focus especially on the word *says*, and try to elicit as many alternatives as possible, such as the eight verbs from the box on SB page 11. You might give clues, such as writing the first letters of the verbs on the board, together with the number of letters (e.g. *The law s _ _ _ _ _ _ _ _ s that ...*), but avoid giving the answers. Tell students to check their predictions in the box on SB page 11.

> **Language note**
> There are no significant differences between the eight verbs in terms of meaning, although several are more natural when followed by a clause (e.g. *to provide that ...*) and others by a noun phrase (*to set something forth / to lay something down*). Note that these last two are separable phrasal verbs (i.e. a pronoun can separate the verb from the particle), but in practice they tend not to be separated.

If students are experienced, tell them to choose their 'favourite' law and describe it to a partner using as many of the eight verbs as possible. You might suggest that they choose a particularly pointless law that they have come across, whether real or not (such as the mythical EU directive on straight bananas). With less experienced (or more creative) classes, you could ask them to work in small groups to invent their own ridiculous laws, and then to present their stipulations to the rest of the class. See http://ec.europa.eu/unitedkingdom/blog/index_en.htm for some so-called euromyths.

## 5   Reading D: Types of court

Tell students to work in small groups to match the types of court with their explanations. When you go through the answers as a class, discuss whether the same types of court exist in students' jurisdictions, and any important differences (e.g. up to what age someone is tried in a juvenile court). See Teacher's brief (page 20) for information on magistrates.

> **Pronunciation notes**
> appellate /əˈpelət/
> juvenile /ˈdʒuːvənaɪl/
> magistrate /ˈmædʒɪstreɪt/
> tribunal /traɪˈbjuːnəl/

## 6   Speaking B: Civil-court systems

Elicit from students the verbs used in Exercise 5 and write them on the board: *to try a person; to hear/argue/review/handle a case; to examine a legal problem.* You could now elicit more such 'court verbs': *to find a person guilty; to question/examine/grill/convict a person; to win/lose a case.* This vocabulary will be essential to describe the types of courts in students' jurisdictions.

If your students come from different jurisdictions, this can be a nice communicative discussion, either in groups or with the whole class. With groups of students from the same jurisdiction, you could turn it into a mini role-play, where they have to present their systems to a client from another country. Students could take turns to explain one type of court to the others, using the vocabulary on the board.

## 7   Reading E: Persons in court

Brainstorm with the class all the persons who are associated with courts. Then tell students to compare their ideas with those in the diagram. Tell them to work alone or in small groups to complete the diagram. When they have finished, check the answers with the class.

**Language note**

The normal plural of *person* is *people*, but the alternative plural, *persons*, is often used to treat the people as items or objects rather than as individuals. In a lift we might see *maximum five persons*, where their individual identity is not relevant. For this reason, we refer to *persons in court* (i.e. certain jobs), where *people in court* might suggest the individuals who do these jobs in a particular court.

**Pronunciation notes**

advocate (*noun*) /ˈædvəkət/
advocate (*verb*) /ˈædvəkeɪt/
appellant /əˈpelənt/
juror /ˈdʒʊərəʳ/

##  8 Listening A: Documents in court

**8.1** Tell students to read the task and questions. Play the recording and then tell them to discuss the answers, as well as any other details they remember, with a partner. Then go through the answers with the class. Point out to students that they will have a second chance to listen later.

**Transcript »** STUDENT'S BOOK **page 278**

 **Answers**

1 an action for breach of contract
2 The lawyer says he needs information and documents from the client.
3 The lawyer is unable to say whether the case will go to trial or not.

**8.2** Tell students to close their books. Elicit from the class a range of documents connected with courts. This should include the documents listed on SB page 13, but you should avoid giving them the answers. If they don't know the names of some documents in English, ask them to try to explain their functions. Then tell them to check the list on SB page 13 to see if their list is the same, and if they can find the names of any of the documents they were trying to describe.

Ask students to work in pairs to complete the exercise. Go through the answers with the class, making sure they have understood all the definitions.

 **Answers**

**1** e  **2** i  **3** b  **4** h  **5** g  **6** f  **7** c
**8** d  **9** a

 **Pronunciation notes**

affidavit /ˌæfɪˈdeɪvɪt/
writ /rɪt/

 **Background notes**

(See Teacher's brief on page 20 for information on many of the documents.)

○ A *claim* is a demand for money, property or enforcement of a right. It may lead to a lawsuit (in the form of a *complaint* or other *pleading*), but may be settled out of court.

○ An *order* is an official proclamation by a court, and results from a *petition* (a formal written request, which may initiate a court case) or a *motion* (a more general term for any formal request during a court case).

○ A *ruling* is a court decision on a case (e.g. to award damages) and results from a *complaint*.

○ A *proceeding* is a court case.

○ A *cause of action* is an individual legal claim. A *complaint* will typically include several causes of action.

○ An *action* is a general name for a lawsuit which involves one person suing another.

**8.3** Tell students to listen to the conversation again to identify the documents mentioned. When you have played the recording, tell them to work in pairs to discuss which documents were mentioned, and, if they remember, what was said about each.

 **Answers**

1, 2, 3, 4, 6, 7, 9

**Optional extension**

When you check the answers with the class, you could also ask some further content-based questions. If there are any that students are unsure of, play the recording again.

1 What did the client receive yesterday?
2 Who might they get affidavits from?

**3** What will they hope to achieve by filing motions?

**4** When will the trial take place?

**Answers**

**1** A writ

**2** Potential witnesses

**3** They might get the case dismissed.

**4** We don't know yet even whether there will be a trial. If there will be a trial, the date will be included in the notice.

**8.4** Tell students to work in pairs to match the verbs with the definitions. The difference between *submit* and *file* is very subtle, so make sure you read the definitions carefully before you attempt to discuss them with students.

 **Answers**

    **1** b  **2** e  **3** d  **4** a  **5** c

**8.5** Tell students to note which documents were used with which verb. If necessary, tell students to check in the transcript (SB page 278). Then check the answers with the class, including the prepositions used.

 **Answers**

  **1** to draft an answer (*our next step will be to draft an answer to this complaint*); briefs (*we will also have to draft briefs*)

  **2** to issue a notice (*the court will issue a notice*)

  **3** to file an action (*an action has been filed against you*); a complaint (*a complaint against you has already been filed*); motions (*this will require filing motions*)

  **4** to serve a writ (*a writ has been served on you*)

  **5** to submit briefs (*briefs ... which we will then submit to the court*)

Tell students to work in teams of four or five to brainstorm as many collocations as possible. When they have finished, go through the answers with the class, perhaps using the 'Easy first' procedure (see Games and activities section, page xvi).

 **Answers**

  **1** draft: an answer, a brief, a complaint, a motion, a pleading

  **2** issue: an injunction, a notice, a writ

  **3** file: an affidavit, an answer, a brief, a complaint, a motion, a notice, a pleading (with)

  **4** serve: a complaint, an injunction, a notice, a pleading, a writ (on someone)

  **5** submit: an affidavit, an answer, a brief, a complaint, a motion, a notice, a pleading, a writ

## 9 Reading F: Legal Latin

Elicit from the class any Latin phrases they know which are used in legal English, or in a legal context in their own languages. This list could include any of the 18 mentioned in Exercises 9.2 and 9.3, but it may also generate some that you are not familiar with. If this happens, make a note and check them in a legal dictionary (e.g. http://dictionary.law.com) after the lesson.

**9.1** Tell students to read the text quickly to find four Latin phrases. As you go through the answers with the class, check that students understand the meanings of the Latin words. Note that *sic* is used because the complaint misspelled *party* as *part*. This makes the plaintiffs seem especially incompetent, and thus may help the defendants' case. (See also Language notes below.)

 **Answers**

  inter alia (line 1); sic (line 5); e.g. (line 9); v. (line 10)

**Optional extension**

You could make the reading slightly more challenging by asking comprehension questions:

**1** Who is suing whom?

**2** What is the complaint?

**3** What is the answer?

**Suggested answers**

**1** The plaintiff, probably a property developer, or possibly a private individual, is suing LongCo, some sort of company involved in building a house for the plaintiff.

**2** Breach of contract specifically the 'Construction Contract'.

**3** Although LongCo may (or may not) be party to a written, oral or implied contract, it is not a party to the Construction Contract identified in the complaint.

### Language notes

○ A contract can be *written*, *oral* or *implied*. Written contracts are obviously more reliable and easier to prove than oral or implied contracts, but any agreement which involves an offer, an acceptance of that offer, a promise to perform and a valuable consideration (typically, a promise of money), can be classed as a contract, and can be used as a basis of a lawsuit. This may be a single document, a series of letters or emails, or a conversation (although this is much more difficult to prove). An *implied contract* is based on circumstances, rather than specific facts, and has to be interpreted by a court. For example, A asks B to estimate how much a particular job would cost. B provides an estimate by email. A then asks B (orally) to carry out that job. When the job has been half done, B invoices A for significantly more than the estimate, arguing that it was an estimate, not an offer. A could then argue that there was an understanding that the estimate constituted an offer, and sues B for breach of (implied) contract.

○ A *sub-contract* /ˈsʌbˌkɒntrækt/ is a contract with a contractor. It is common in the construction industry: the contractor might be a building firm, but may *sub-contract* /ˌsʌbkənˈtrækt/ work such as plumbing and electrical work to a *sub-contractor* /ˌsʌbkənˈtræktəʳ/.

○ A *beneficiary* /benəˈfɪʃərɪ/ is somebody who receives money or other benefits. In this case, the beneficiary to each sub-contract is the sub-contractor (e.g. the plumber or electrician), because they receive money in the contract.

**9.2** Tell students to work alone or in small groups to match the Latin expressions with their meanings. Then check the answers with the

class, paying attention to the (English) pronunciation of the Latin. NB *et al.*, *e.g.* and *i.e.* are rarely pronounced as full words, so there is no need to teach their full pronunciation.

 **Answers**
**1** c **2** e **3** f **4** b **5** h **6** g **7** a **8** d

### Pronunciation notes

ad hoc /æd ˈhɒk/
et al. /et ˈæl/
et cetera /et ˈsetrə/
per se /pɜː ˈseɪ/
sic /sɪk/
versus /ˈvɜːsəs/

### Language notes

○ Latin phrases are often *italicised* when used in legal English, apart from those which are in common use in general English (*v(s).*, *N.B.*, *e.g.*, *i.e.* and *etc.*).

○ In everyday English, there is a fashion for abbreviations to be written without full-stops (*v*, *NB*, *eg*, *ie* and *etc*), especially in emails, but legal English is rather conservative in this matter, and usually keeps the full punctuation.

○ Many people, including native speakers of English, often confuse *i.e.* with *e.g.* *I.e.* may be used to introduce an explanation: *There needs to be a quorum of directors, i.e. at least six of them.* *E.g.* introduces some, but not all, examples: *I have written all types of pleading, e.g. complaints and answers.* *I.e.* can also introduce examples, but if the list is not complete, we would expect it to be completed with *etc.*: *I have worked in a wide variety of legal settings, i.e. crown courts, magistrates' courts, etc.*

**9.3** Repeat the same procedure as in Exercise 9.2. There is no need to teach the pronunciation of *videlicet*, as it is always shortened to *viz.* Your students may struggle to understand definition g): *by that very fact itself*, which means *precisely by that fact*.

 **Answers**
**1** d **2** g **3** a **4** b **5** h **6** f **7** c
**8** e **9** j **10** i

**Pronunciation notes**

de facto /deɪ ˈfæktəʊ/
inter alia /ˌɪntər ˈɑːlɪə/
ipso facto /ˌɪpsəʊ ˈfæktəʊ/
per annum /ˌpɜːr ˈænəm/
pro forma /ˌprəʊ ˈfɔːmə/
pro rata /ˌprəʊ ˈrɑːtə/
quorum /ˈkwɔːrəm/
sui juris /ˌsuːɪ ˈdʒʊərɪs/
ultra vires /ˌʌltrə ˈvɪərɪz/

---

**Optional extension**
**Photocopiable worksheet 1.1**

To reinforce the meanings of these Latin expressions, hand out Photocopiable worksheet 1.1. Tell students to work alone or in small groups to put the 18 Latin phrases into the sentences given. The number of words in each answer has been given. When they have finished, check the answers with the class.

**Answers**

**1** ad hoc   **2** pro rata   **3** inter alia
**4** i.e.; etc.   **5** per annum   **6** v.; et al.
**7** per se   **8** viz.   **9** de facto   **10** quorum
**11** ipso facto   **12** sic; e.g.   **13** sui juris
**14** ultra vires   **15** pro-forma

**Language note**

Question 12 includes a deliberate misspelling of *ordinance*. *Ordnance* is in fact a military term, meaning weapons and equipment. Question 15 mentions a pro-forma invoice, which is a price quote in the form of an invoice, often issued to accompany goods which will be invoiced later.

# PART II: A CAREER IN THE LAW

**10  Listening B: Lawyers**

**10.1** Tell students to close their books and elicit from the class as many different alternative words for *lawyer* as they know. Discuss the differences between the various words (see Teacher's brief, page 20), but avoid confirming or rejecting students' ideas. Then tell students to open their books and work in pairs to try to guess / work out which words go with which definitions and usage notes.

Then play the recording for them to complete the task. After they have checked in pairs, you may want to play the recording a second time for them to check. Finally, go through the answers with the class. Remind students that some of the words are typically used only in certain jurisdictions.

**Transcript »** STUDENT'S BOOK **page 278**

 **Answers**

**1** advocate a, e   **2** attorney a, d
**3** barrister c, f   **4** lawyer a, d
**5** solicitor b, f

**Background note**

As suggested in the recording, it is an oversimplification to assume that only solicitors /səˈlɪsɪtəz/ give legal advice and draw up legal documents while only barristers /ˈbærɪstəz/ plead in court. In fact, there is some overlap in what the two professions actually do (see http://en.wikipedia.org/wiki/Barrister).

---

**Optional extension**

Discuss these questions with the class. Note that each pair of questions includes one based on the recording and one discussion question.

**1**  What is on the sign outside the office of the lawyer in Virginia? What would this sign say in your country?
**2**  Who is the Head of the Justice Department in the US? What is the equivalent in your country?
**3**  Which three UK jurisdictions are mentioned? Does your country have a similar range of jurisdictions?
**4**  What, according to Robert, is as important as knowing definitions? Do you agree?

**Answers**

**1**  Attorney-at-Law
**2**  Attorney General
**3**  Scotland, the Channel Islands and the Isle of Man
**4**  Knowing about usage

**10.2** Go through the example with the class, drawing attention to the fact that *counsel* can be used as a noun and as a verb. Elicit who might say the example sentence from the usage notes (Answer: A judge). See Using the Internet for research on page xviii for some good online dictionaries. If students have access to dictionaries / the Internet in the classroom, ask them to work in small groups to research one or both of the other terms, and especially to find unusual or interesting usage notes about them. You could expand this exercise to include other terms from this unit (e.g. *advocate*, *draft*, *brief*, *pleading*). If you don't have access to dictionaries, you could set this task as homework. Afterwards, discuss students' findings with the class, as well as the usefulness of this type of analysis.

**10.3** Elicit from the class a brief definition of the word *notary*, but avoid confirming or rejecting students' ideas at this stage. Students then read the text briefly to compare it with their ideas. Students work alone to complete the exercise and then compare their answers in pairs. Then go through the answers with the class.

 **Answers**
**1** performs **2** drafting **3** authenticating
**4** serving **5** administer **6** take
**7** verify **8** executes

---

**Optional extension**
Use these questions to focus on the useful vocabulary from the text and generate some discussion.
**1** What would be a simpler way of saying 'to undergo training'?
**2** What is the difference between a will, a contract and a deed?
**3** What are legal instruments?
**4** What is the difference between an oath and a sworn statement?
**5** What is the difference between authenticating and verifying?
**6** What exactly is involved in executing a legal document?

---

**Suggested answers**
**1** to be trained
**2** A contract (under common law) has three essential requirements: there must be an offer, acceptance of that offer by the other party, and some form of consideration from both parties (= something of value, such as money). A will (= a declaration providing for the transfer of a person's property after death) does not require acceptance or consideration. A deed (= a legal instrument conferring a right on another party) requires acceptance but does not require the transfer of consideration.
**3** *Legal instrument* is a general term for contracts, deeds, wills and similar documents, etc. which have legal force. Not all legal instruments need to be in written form.
**4** An oath is a legally binding promise to tell the truth. A sworn statement is a statement made after an oath. (In practice, a sworn statement may also be described as an oath.)
**5** Authentication involves establishing that something is authentic, i.e. what it purports to be. Verification involves establishing that a statement is true.
**6** Executing a document means signing it in order to make it legally binding.

**10.4** Tell students to discuss the four questions in small groups. You may need to check the meaning of *render* (= provide, conduct). If the discussions generate some interesting differences, or if some students are not sure of the various concepts and duties in their jurisdictions, open up the discussion to include the whole class. If you have students from several jurisdictions in your class, you could ask them to give mini-presentations to the class on the questions.

**10.5** Tell students to work in small groups to come up with as many combinations as possible. When they have finished, check the answers with the class, perhaps following the 'Easy first' procedure (see Games and activities section, page xvi).

**Answers**

1  advise: clients, corporations, defendants
2  draft: contracts, decisions, law*,
   legislation*
3  litigate: cases, disputes
4  practise: law
5  represent: clients, corporations,
   defendants
6  research: cases, decisions, law,
   legislation
\* Note that in general, lawyers can draft
laws, but only legislators (e.g. politicians)
can draft legislation.

**10.6** Have students write their sentences alone
and then swap with another student to check
their answers. Elicit one sentence from the
class as an example (e.g. *It's important to
advise defendants on what they are supposed
to do during their court case*).

**Background notes**

○ If you *litigate*, you take legal action to
  settle a dispute in a court of law.
○ You may need to point out that in
  British English, *practice* is a noun, while
  *practise* is a verb (following the pattern
  of *advice /advise*, but without the
  change in pronunciation). In American
  English, both the noun and verb are
  spelled *practise*.

**10.7** Tell students to work in small groups to
discuss which of the words can be combined
with the word *lawyer*. Point out that in all the
answers, the word *lawyer* is at the end. When
they have finished, go through the answers
with the class. Ask students what each type
of lawyer does, and encourage the use of the
verbs from Exercise 10.5 (e.g. *A corporate
lawyer advises corporations and spends a lot
of time drafting contracts*).

**Answers**

corporate lawyer, defence lawyer,
government lawyer, patent lawyer, public-
sector lawyer, tax lawyer, trial lawyer

**Background notes**

○ There is no need for an expression
  such as *bar lawyer*, as this concept is
  covered by the word *barrister*.
○ A lawyer who works alone is called a
  *sole practitioner*, and his/her firm is
  often called a *solo practice*.
○ Note that *defence* is spelled *defense* in
  American English.
○ A *corporate lawyer* works with corporate
  law, either as corporate counsel (within
  a company) or as an independent
  lawyer advising and representing
  various companies.
○ A *government lawyer* advises the
  government (e.g. drafting legislation),
  representing it in court, etc.
○ A *public-sector lawyer's* job is similar to
  that of a corporate lawyer, although he/
  she may advise or represent government
  agencies such as a Patent Office,
  institutions such as hospitals, etc.
○ *Tax lawyers* and *patent lawyers* are
  examples of specialists, who may also
  be corporate/government/public-sector
  lawyers.
○ Unlike a *patent lawyer*, a *patent attorney*
  may or may not be a lawyer, depending
  on the rules in the individual country. In
  many countries, patent attorneys have
  technical/scientific backgrounds rather
  than law qualifications.

**Pronunciation note**

*Patent* has two pronunciations: /ˈpeɪtənt/
and /ˈpætənt/. The former pronunciation is
more widespread, but the latter is
preferred by many patent attorneys.

**CD1 T4**  **11  Listening C: Legal
education**

**11.1** Tell students to read the introduction on page
16 to find four expressions with the word *bar*
(Answers: the Bar, a bar association,
admitted to the Bar, the bar examination).
Discuss briefly with the class whether
equivalents exist for the four terms in
students' countries. Elicit what (if anything)
students know / can guess about legal
education in Germany, using the four true/

false statements to predict what the answers might be. Then play the recording for students to complete the task. After they have checked in pairs, play the recording a second time if necessary. Then go through the answers with the class.

**Transcript »** STUDENT'S BOOK **page 278**

 **Answers**
1 False   2 False   3 True   4 True

---

**Optional extension**
**ILEC preparation: Test of Speaking Part 2**

If your students are planning to take the ILEC exam, point out that Part 2 of the Test of Speaking focuses on the ability to organise a short presentation, similar to the one in Listening C. Tell students to listen again, this time looking at the transcript on page 278 to underline useful phrases and techniques for organising a presentation and showing contrasts. When you go through the answers with the class, elicit ways of using the same phrases and techniques to describe legal education in students' own countries.

**Suggested answers**
Studying law in X is quite different from Y. In the Y, you … . The only prerequisite for X is … (which means … , a rough equivalent of …).

… is divided into three types of course and deals with the following three subjects: …

First, there are … . Here, there is … (unlike … , when …).

The second type includes …

This is certainly different from … , where emphasis is placed … . Specifically, …

The third type of course involves … in which …

… the X equivalent of …

Finally, …, which is …

The exam consists of seven … : four in … , two in … and one … .

It's …, but I guess you would say that about Y, too.

(This is also different from Y, where you … .)

**11.2** Students discuss the two questions in small groups and then share their ideas with the class.

---

 **Suggested answer**
2   The Socratic method refers to a method of instruction common in law schools in the US. It involves the practice of posing questions to encourage students to think critically. Typically, students are called on at random and asked to paraphrase the argument of the court in an assigned case. The student is then asked to defend the argument, refuting objections raised by the professor.

---

**Background note**
For more on the Socratic method, see http://en.wikipedia.org/wiki/Socratic_method.

---

## 12  Speaking C: Legal education

Students work in small groups to discuss the questions, then feed back to the class. You may need to check the pronunciation of *prerequisite* /ˌpriːˈrekwɪzɪt/ and *clerkship* /ˈklɑːkʃɪp, ˈklɜːrkʃɪp/. Alternatively, if your students are preparing for the ILEC exam, you could ask each student to use the prompts to prepare a short presentation (about one minute each) on legal education in their country or in a country they know. They can then give their presentations either to their groups or to the whole class. After each presentation, a member of the audience should ask a question based on the presentation, which the presenter should answer.

##  13  Listening D: Law-firm structure

**13.1** Tell students to listen to the extract, which comes from the end of a job interview, and to answer the three questions. If you have a particularly strong group, you could ask students to count the number of employees as they listen. When you check the answers with the class, discuss the atmosphere of the law firm to see what students think about the dress code and the policy of calling the senior partners *Mr*. Avoid going into too much detail about the structure of the law firm, as this will come up in Exercise 13.2.

**Transcript »** STUDENT'S BOOK **page 279**

**Answers**

1 He says that the firm is traditional, and people are hard-working, serious, but friendly.
2 The full partners are responsible for the day-to-day affairs and the finances of the firm, and oversee the two departments.
3 He says that the size sounds ideal, that it is not as small as the firm he worked for in Cambridge, but not too big either (unlike the EU Commission).

**Background notes**

○ A *law boutique* /'lɔː ˌbuːˈtiːk/ is a law firm which specialises in a small number of areas.
○ *Real property* refers to land, buildings and other installations, anything growing on that land, minerals under the land, etc., together with the rights associated with these things.
○ A *debtor* /'detər/ owes money to a *creditor*. For example, most day-to-day commercial transactions involve a delay between delivery of goods and paying for them. The Debtor–Creditor department will deal with any financial disputes arising from such transactions.
○ Most law firms are *partnerships*, and are owned by the lawyers themselves. Within a partnership, some partners may have more rights and responsibilities than other partners, probably because they have invested more money. These partners are the *senior partners*. *Full partners* are also fully liable for the partnership (in the sense that their share of the partnership's financial successes or problems are their own personal successes or problems), but their share is smaller than that of the senior partners. *Salaried partners* have limited liability, and are thus less exposed than full partners, although they are also likely to have less power within the partnership.
○ An *associate* /əˈsəʊsɪət/ is likely to be a relatively newly qualified lawyer who is a member of the partnership, but does not yet have the full rights of a partner.

A *summer associate* works in the law firm during a summer holiday, typically before the final year of a law degree.
○ A *paralegal* /ˌpærəˈliːgəl/ is usually not a lawyer, but has some training in and knowledge of the law, and helps the lawyers in a law firm by dealing with routine tasks.
○ The term *clerk* /klɑːk/ (British English), /klɜːrk/ (American English) sometimes refers to a young lawyer who assists in a court, but here it refers to a person who performs relatively simple work such as filing and typing in an office.

**13.2** Tell students to work in pairs to complete the organigram. Then play the recording a second time so they can check. Go through the answers with the class.

**Answers**
1 Mr Robertson   2 Full Partners
3 Real Property   4 Salaried Lawyer
5 Associate   6 Paralegal

**Optional extension**
**Photocopiable worksheet 1.2**

Tell students that they are going to look at the CV that Linus sent in to the law firm when he applied for the job. Ask them to scan it quickly, then discuss with the class whether a) he is well qualified, and b) the format of the CV is the same as they would use. Then tell them to read the CV to answer the five questions, and discuss them with a partner. When they have finished, go through the answers quickly with the class.

**Answers**
1 He worked at G.R. Foster & Co. Solicitors, Cambridge, UK.
2 He speaks English, French and Swedish.
3 He did his first degree at the University of Essex, Colchester, UK.
4 His main duty at the European Commission was drafting opinions in English and French dealing with contracts awarded for projects.
5 He is presently enrolled in a Master's Programme in Law and Information Technology at the University of Stockholm, Sweden.

**Pronunciation notes**
curriculum vitae /kəˈrɪkjʊləm ˈviːtaɪ/
liaison /liˈeɪzən/
résumé /ˈrezʊmeɪ/

**Background note**
○ In most jurisdictions, *penal law* is the same as criminal law.

If your students are studying to be lawyers, you could ask them to write their own CVs in English. Point out that they should mainly follow the format of the example given.

## 14 Speaking D: Describing a law firm

**14.1** Go through the phrases with the whole class. Elicit examples for each structure, based on the organigram. Then tell students to work in small groups to describe the whole organigram using the phrases given.

**Answers**
Department/Company: *is/are headed by,*
   *(is/are in charge of)*
Person: *is/are assisted by, is/are*
   *responsible for, is/are in charge of, is/*
   *are assigned to, report to*
Both: *is/are managed by*

**Pronunciation note**
assigned /əˈsaɪnd/

**14.2** Tell students to work in pairs to draw an organigram of a firm one of them knows well. If there are no experienced lawyers in a group, they could invent their own organigram. When they have finished drawing, they should change partners and describe their law firm to their new partners, using the phrases from Exercise 14.1.

(CD1
T6–10) **15 Listening E: Practice areas**

**15.1** Tell students to read through the statements about the five lawyers to check that they understand all the words. Then play the

recording once for them to tick the information they hear. Tell them to discuss their answers in small groups. Play the recording a second time for them to check their answers. Finally, go through the answers with the class. With weaker classes, you could divide the exercise into five short exercises and check each part before moving on to the next.

**Transcript »** STUDENT'S BOOK **page 279**

**Answers**
Speaker 1: 3, 4, 5
Speaker 2: 1, 2, 3, 4
Speaker 3: 2, 3, 4
Speaker 4: 2, 4, 5
Speaker 5: 1, 2, 3

**Background notes**
○ A *litigator* is a lawyer who specialises in litigation (= lawsuits).
○ Speaker 2 says she *provides advocacy* /prəˌvaɪdz ˈædvəkəsi/ for her clients, which means that she represents them in court and in similar adversarial situations.
○ *Copyright infringement suits* /ˌkɒpɪraɪt ɪnˈfrɪndʒmənt ˌsuːts/ involve any alleged illegal use of copyrighted material.
○ *Domain-name disputes* refer to multiple claims to certain Internet addresses.
○ *Clearances of (trade) marks* involve checking that planned trade marks are not already owned by another party, and are not going to result in litigation.
○ *IP* stands for 'intellectual property'. An IP firm therefore deals with issues such as copyright, patents and trade marks.
○ A *retainer agreement* is a written agreement between a client and a lawyer, setting out the details of their (long-term) relationship.
○ A *cartel* /kɑːˈtel/ is a group of organisations which work together to fix prices in the industry they control. In most countries, they are illegal, as they exploit consumers and distort free trade. The most famous (legal) cartel is OPEC, which tries to manipulate the international price of oil.

○ *Restrictive trade practices* are any that interfere with the free market, usually by conspiring with 'competitors' to manipulate prices. Some such practices are endorsed by law (such as the EU's Common Agricultural Policy), but many are illegal.

○ Under a property *lease* agreement, a *landlord* (property owner) rents all or part of a property to a tenant.

○ A *mortgage* /ˈmɔːgɪdʒ/ is a loan to buy property, which uses the property as security. If the property owner fails to keep up with regular mortgage repayments, the lender has the right to recover the money loaned by forcing the sale of the property. This is known as a *foreclosure* /fɔːˈkləʊʒəʳ/.

**Optional extension**
**ILEC preparation: Test of Listening Part 4**
**Photocopiable worksheet 1.3**

If your students are planning to take the ILEC exam, point out that Part 4 of the Test of Listening involves listening to five short extracts, similar to the ones in Exercise 15.1, in order to complete two matching tasks. Photocopiable worksheet 1.3 provides practice of this type of exercise. Of course, this means that students will have listened at least three times (once or twice for Exercise 15.1 and twice for this worksheet), rather than only twice as in the exam, but it will still serve as good practice.

Go through the instructions carefully with the class. Point out that it is a good idea to complete Task 1 the first time they listen and Task 2 the second time, but they could try to do both at the same time if they prefer. Make sure they also understand the numbering system, so that, for example, answer 7 refers to Speaker 2 and so on.

Play the recording twice for students to complete the two tasks. Afterwards, allow them to discuss their answers in pairs but not to change their answers. Then go through the answers with the class, focusing on the phrases in the recording that gave them the answers.

**Answers**
**1** D    At present, I am working in commercial litigation and am enjoying it.

**2** B    Two paralegals assist me in my work at my office.

**3** E    I represent both plaintiffs and defendants in trade-mark, trade-secret and copyright infringement suits.

**4** A    I advise clients on a regular basis with respect to restrictive trade practices.

**5** C    I […] have tried many cases (mostly to successful conclusion).

**6** D    Our lawyers provide advice on many different legal areas, including […] corporate tax …

**7** A    My clients are primarily individuals.

**8** C    For bigger cases […], I […] can arrange representation under this firm if a client requests it.

**9** E    I advise domestic and international clients.

**10** B    I assist clients with all types of real-estate-related litigation […] My practice also involves all types of real-estate transactions.

**Optional extension**
**Photocopiable worksheet 1.4**

Listening E contains many useful phrases for talking about one's job. Photocopiable worksheet 1.4 highlights these phrases (in bold). Tell students to work in pairs to match the beginnings and endings of each extract. When most groups have finished, go through the answers with the class. Afterwards, students work in pairs to describe their own work (or planned work), using as many of the phrases in bold as possible.

Note that these phrases are all useful for Part 1 of the ILEC Test of Speaking, where candidates have to answer questions about their work or studies.

**Answers**
**1** e    **2** c    **3** d    **4** a    **5** b    **6** g    **7** j    **8** h
**9** f    **10** i    **11** m    **12** l    **13** n    **14** o
**15** k    **16** s    **17** p    **18** t    **19** q    **20** r
**21** x    **22** w    **23** y    **24** v    **25** u

**15.2** Tell students to work in small groups. Experienced lawyers should tell their partners about their current jobs. Law students should talk about their plans. Tell them to use the language from the listening exercise to give them ideas.

# 16 Listening F: Law-firm culture

**16.1** Tell students to read the text quickly to find five types of law firm. When they have found all five (solo practice, global firm, small law firm (boutique), mid-size law firm and large law firm), tell them to discuss the question in small groups. You could make this more structured by asking them to identify advantages and disadvantages (from a lawyer's perspective) of each type. When they have finished, discuss their answers briefly as a class. Do not go into too much detail, as this issue is raised again in Exercise 16.3.

**16.2** Tell students to read the task to find out who they are going to be listening to. Check that they know what a *clerk* is (see Background note, page 33) and tell them to listen and answer the four questions. Play the recording, and then tell students to discuss their answers in small groups. Then discuss the answers with the class.

**Transcript »** STUDENT'S BOOK **page 279**

 **Answers**
1 Because it will improve future job opportunities, be a good learning experience, will enable students to meet new people.
2 Four weeks
3 At the larger firms, Richard worked on bigger cases, moving between groups in the different practice areas and helping out where needed.
4 He advises the students to do clerkships and to get to know as many different law firms as possible.

**16.3** Tell students to work in small groups and to look at the table to try to remember what Richard said about each advantage. When they have spent a few minutes discussing this, play the recording a second time for them to check. Then go through the answers with the whole class.

 **Answers**

| Advantages | Small firms | Large firms |
|---|---|---|
| more autonomy and responsibility | ✓ | |
| opportunity to work on prestigious cases | | ✓ |
| chance to rotate through different practice areas | | ✓ |
| asked to write briefs and letters | ✓ | |
| allowed to conduct research and manage court books | | ✓ |
| opportunity to make many contacts | | ✓ |
| more training offered | | ✓ |
| made to feel part of a team | ✓ | ✓ |
| invited to participate in social events | | ✓ |
| family-like atmosphere | ✓ | |
| made good use of time | ✓ | ✓ |

**16.4** Tell students to discuss the three questions in small groups. If this generates some interesting discussion, open it up to include the whole class.

 Tell students to do the Internet activity as homework. See Using the Internet for research on page xviii.

# 2) Company law: company formation and management

## Teacher's brief

This unit begins with the documentation and procedures associated with **setting up various types of new companies**. Examples are given from the UK and the USA, including procedures specific to the state of Delaware. Many US corporations choose to set up in this state because Delaware corporations are not taxed on activities outside the state.

It is important to realise that although the details may vary from country to country, the general picture for most countries will be sufficiently similar to these examples to allow comparisons. Your students should have thorough knowledge of this sort of information about their own countries, as this is central to all company law, and they will often need to explain the details to their clients. An important purpose of this unit is therefore to give them the language to **explain to clients** the situation in their own countries, and to compare this with the situation in other countries.

An important concept in company formation is **liability**. Liability is legal responsibility for what you do (such as causing an accident) and what you fail to do (such as paying your bills). If something goes wrong, the person who is liable may be sued. As Reading A explains, the main difference between a **company** and a **partnership** is that a company can be liable (rather than its owners, who are insulated from this threat), while a partnership usually cannot be liable (and therefore does not insulate the partners from liability). Much of the variation between different types of companies around the world concerns the extent to which owners are liable. For example, in a **limited liability company**, investors may lose their investment, but they are otherwise not liable for the company's financial problems.

Another important distinction is between companies whose shares are traded **publicly** (i.e. in a stock exchange) and those which are **privately** traded. Both types of company have **shareholders**, but the way those shares are bought and sold affects the legal requirements for each type of company. For example, many countries have a requirement for the **share capital** (i.e. money invested by shareholders) of publicly traded companies to be above a given threshold. Privately traded companies may be limited to a given number of shareholders.

Listening A introduces the five most important **types of company** in the USA and UK. In both countries, a **sole proprietorship** has one owner ('the sole proprietor'), who is responsible for managing the business. A **partnership** has more than one owner, who all tend to be responsible for management. In a **general partnership**, the individual partners share rights and responsibilities, but in a **limited partnership** there are both limited partners, who have no liability, and one or more general partners, who are liable for the obligations of the business. Most large corporations in the USA (including all publicly traded corporations) are **C corporations**, which pay corporate taxes. **S corporations**, which tend to be smaller, are taxed through their owners (i.e. profits and losses are passed directly to the owners, who declare them as part of their personal taxable income). Note that 'S' and 'C' simply refer to sub-chapters in the US Internal Revenue Code. The UK makes no such distinction, although it does distinguish between **private limited companies** (Ltd), which are privately owned, and **public limited companies** (plc), which are publicly traded.

Reading C focuses on Russia, where there is an important distinction between **Wholly Foreign-Owned Entities** (WFOE) and **representative offices**. This is always a key issue for foreign investors: whether to set up a new company, a **joint venture** with a local partner or simply an office in the new country. In many countries, including Russia and China, the first option was not available until recently.

The last sections of the unit deal with the **management of a company**, and highlight how the initial documents which were used to set up the company (in this case, the **bylaws**) affect its later management (in this case, the legality or otherwise of an election of directors at a shareholders' meeting). The text in this section (Reading D) is a **letter of advice**, which is a common type of legal writing. It is similar in function to a **legal opinion**, although legal opinions tend to be much longer and more complicated. The function of a letter of advice (as well as of a legal opinion) is to provide an analysis of a legal problem so that the client can make an informed decision concerning a course of action.

**Further information**

○ For descriptions of **types of companies** in many countries, see http://www. corporateinformation.com/defext.asp. See also http://en.wikipedia.org/wiki/Types_of_ business_entity for links to articles on business entities around the world.

○ For full, authentic samples of a wide range of **legal documents** (including legal opinions, partnership agreements, articles of association, and many others mentioned in this unit), see http://contracts.onecle.com/type/index.shtml.

○ For some detailed background to **letters of advice** and **legal opinions**, see the articles recommended at http://www.abanet.org/ buslaw/tribar/home.shtml. There are also many examples of legal opinions available online (search for 'legal opinions'), but few collections. See, for example, http://ag.ca.gov/ opinions.php, for a collection relating to the State of California.

## Discussion

Use these questions to generate a discussion with the whole class.

a   What are the most important companies and partnerships in your country? (The word *important* is deliberately vague, so allow students to interpret it as they choose. If students are not lawyers, there is a chance that they will not know the difference between companies and partnerships. At this stage, it is more important that they use their common sense to work out what the difference might be rather than their expert knowledge. Try to avoid simply collecting a list of company names, but instead try to elicit a range of types of companies, e.g. both public companies and private companies, or specific types of company in students' jurisdictions. They may struggle to come up with famous private companies and partnerships because these tend to be smaller than public companies. Note that law firms and accountancy practices tend to be partnerships.)

b   What is the difference between a company and a partnership? (This is answered in Reading A, so avoid confirming or rejecting students' answers at this stage.)

c   What sorts of documents are required when forming a company in your jurisdictions? (This is partially answered in Reading A for British and American companies, but obviously students' jurisdictions will require different types of documents. Avoid going too deeply into this question, as it will be covered later in the unit.)

## 1   Reading A: Introduction to company law

Tell students that they are going to read a text related to the above discussion. Tell them to read through the text quickly to match the six topics to the paragraphs. Set a time limit (e.g. two minutes for strong classes, four minutes for weak classes). At the end of the time, ask students to check their answers in pairs and to discuss what they remember about each of the six topics. Then go through the answers as a class.

   **Answers**
   **a** 5   **b** 4   **c** 1   **d** 6   **e** 2   **f** 3

   **Pronunciation notes**
   fiduciary /fɪˈdjuːʃəri/
   ultra vires /ˌʌltrə ˈvɪərɪz/
   veil /veɪl/

**Optional extension**
To check comprehension and reinforce the vocabulary and concepts from the text, use the following questions either as a straightforward comprehension quiz or as a 'Snake game' (see Games and activities section, page xvi). Students should try to answer the questions without looking back at the text, but if they struggle you may allow them to scan the text for the answers.

**Questions**
1   Are partners insulated against personal liability?

38

**2** Can the company secretary be a director of the company?

**3** Do the courts like to interfere in matters connected with fiduciary duty?

**4** May a partnership cease to exist when a partner dies?

**5** What are the owners of a company insulated against?

**6** What are the two accounting tools mentioned in the text?

**7** What are the two types of duty owed by directors of a company?

**8** What can a company own in its own name?

**9** What does *AGM* stand for?

**10** What is another name for *authorised capital*?

**11** What is the general term for directors, managers and secretaries who carry out the management of a company?

**12** What may be lifted if the company is used to perpetrate fraud or act ultra vires?

**13** What might be issued to shareholders if profits are healthy?

**14** What sort of business association is merely an association of owners, rather than a legal entity?

**15** What two documents constitute the *constitution* of a company?

**16** What two things must happen before a certificate of incorporation is issued?

**17** Which document determines the structure, procedures and work of the board of directors?

**18** Which document states the aims of the company?

**19** Who do the auditors owe a duty to?

**20** Who issues a certificate of incorporation?

**Answers**

**1** No (para. 2)   **2** Yes, but not the sole director (para. 4)   **3** No, they are reluctant (para. 5)   **4** Yes (para. 2)   **5** Personal liability (para. 1)   **6** Balance sheet; profit and loss account (para. 6)   **7** Duty of care; fiduciary duty (para. 5)   **8** Property (para. 1)   **9** Annual general meeting (para. 3)   **10** Nominal capital (para. 3)   **11** Officers (para. 4)   **12** The corporate veil (para. 1)   **13** A bonus or capitalisation issue (para. 6)   **14** Partnership (para. 2)   **15** Memorandum of association; articles of association (para. 3)   **16** Filing of

constitutional documents and statutory forms; payment of filing fee (para. 3)   **17** Articles of association (para. 4)   **18** Memorandum of association (para. 3)   **19** Shareholders (para. 4)   **20** Governmental authority (para. 3)

**Optional extension**
**Photocopiable worksheet 2.1**

This activity highlights (in bold) the legal terminology, rich vocabulary and collocations from Reading A. Tell students to work in small groups to match the beginnings and endings of extracts from the text. When they have finished, go through the answers and deal with any problems. As a final consolidation, students may test each other by folding the worksheet in half and trying to remember the end of each extract. Point out that they can also use this technique by themselves to learn vocabulary.

**Answers**

**1** e   **2** h   **3** d   **4** i   **5** b   **6** f   **7** g   **8** a
**9** c   **10** r   **11** o   **12** q   **13** n   **14** p
**15** l   **16** k   **17** m   **18** j   **19** z   **20** zz
**21** s   **22** v   **23** w   **24** x   **25** u   **26** y   **27** t

## 2   Key terms: Roles in company management

**2.1** Do this exercise quickly with the whole class. Ask students for more roles in companies. Encourage discussion of how each role could be defined, and any crossover between the various roles (e.g. can a managing director be a shareholder?). The roles and definitions may vary from country to country, and this could lead to some interesting discussion.

➡ **Answers**

officers, partners, directors, managers, company secretary, auditor
For additional roles, see Exercise 2.2.

**2.2** Tell students to work alone or in small groups to match the roles with their definitions. When most of the groups have finished the exercise, check the answers as a class. As you go through the answers, check students have understood the vocabulary.

🖊️ **Language notes**

○ *to take the initiative to do something*
(d) = to do something without anyone
else telling you to do it

○ *compliance with something* (f) = doing
everything necessary to obey something
(e.g. rules, laws)

○ *by virtue of something* (g) = thanks to,
as a result of

○ *to wind* /waɪnd/ *up a company's affairs*
(j) = to deal with all a company's affairs
after it ceases to operate

○ *to be wound* /waʊnd/ *up by a court*
(h) = passive form of 'to wind up'

If you feel students need to practise the
vocabulary, tell them to work in pairs.
Students should take turns to read one of the
roles (or definitions) aloud. The other student
should supply the corresponding definition (or
role) without looking at the book.

## (CD1 T12) 3 Listening A: Company formation

As a group, elicit some ways that a lawyer can be
useful in the formation of a company. Then tell
students to read the introduction to see if it
mentions any of the ways they have given. Note that
*duly* means 'properly and at the expected time'.

**3.1** Go through the list of documents with the class
to see if anyone knows what they are, or to
give them a chance to guess. Avoid giving
answers at this stage, as these will come up in
subsequent exercises. Tell students to listen to
the conversation and tick the documents
mentioned by the lawyer. Play the recording
once, then tell students to discuss in small
groups which documents were mentioned and
what the lawyer said about each of them.
Check briefly with the whole group.

**Transcript »** STUDENT'S BOOK **page 280**

➡️ **Answers**

Documents 2, 3, 5, 7 and 8 were
mentioned.

🖊️ **Background notes**

○ A *DBA* ('doing business as') *filing* is a
document which states the name of a
company. It must be filed by all US sole
proprietorships, apart from persons
doing business under their own name.

○ A *stock ledger* is a record of each
shareholder's ownership.

○ *Bylaws* (in the USA) are a company's (or
partnership's) written rules for conduct
(e.g. how directors are elected, who is
responsible for what, etc.). They must
be formally adopted and/or amended.
In the UK, they are known as 'Articles of
Association' and a by-law (or bylaw) is a
law issued by a local government (US:
ordinance).

○ A *general partnership agreement* is a
contract between the partners in a
general partnership, outlining the rights
and responsibilities of each.

○ *IRS & state S corporation election*: IRS
stands for Internal Revenue Service (i.e.
the US tax office). In the USA, an S
corporation is one with 75 or fewer
shareholders, which is taxed as if it
were a partnership. In order to become
an S corporation, it is necessary to hold
an election of all shareholders, and to
file details of this election with the IRS
and the appropriate state. See http://
www.irs.gov/pub/irs-pdf/f2553.pdf for
the IRS form.

○ *Stock certificates* (in the USA) are the
same as share certificates (in the UK).

---

**Optional extension**
**Photocopiable worksheet 2.2**

**1** Hand out Photocopiable worksheet 2.2. Tell
students to discuss the statements in
Exercise 1 in pairs or small groups to
decide whether they are true or false. Play
the recording again so that students can
check their answers. Tell them to discuss
their answers briefly in their groups and
then go through them with the whole class.

**Answers**

1 True  2 True  3 False  4 False  5 False
6 True  7 False  8 True  9 True  10 True

**2** Point out that the extracts from the transcript all contain useful expressions for explaining legal terms to clients. This is an extremely important skill for lawyers which needs to be practised. Tell students to work in pairs or small groups to identify the wrong word in each extract. The useful expressions are in bold, but obviously the extra word must be deleted.

**Answers**

**1** to (1ˢᵗ)  **2** to  **3** what  **4** it  **5** in  **6** who
**7** an  **8** is (1ˢᵗ)  **9** be  **10** a

When you have checked the answers with the class, you might point out that the most common device in the extract is the formula:

| *That's* | + noun phrase | + relative clause (or reduced relative clause) |
|---|---|---|
| That's | the person | who prepares ... |
| That's | something | (that) I could do for you. |
| That's | the first document | that needs to be filed. |
| That's | the person | (who is) to be served if the corporation is sued. |
| That's | the time | when the first meeting will take place. |

There will be an opportunity to use the useful language later in the role-plays, but for more controlled (and less serious) practice, tell students to work in teams to come up with a dialogue to explain an everyday process (such as taking a shower) to a client, using all the useful expressions. The dialogues should be funny (as this will make the useful expressions more memorable). Elicit an example for the first expression to illustrate, e.g. *So, based on all the background information you have provided me, my strongest recommendation is for you to* take a shower rather than a bath ... *The first thing you have to do is ...*

**3.2** Students discuss the questions in pairs to see if they remember the answers, then listen again to check. Afterwards, discuss the answers with the whole group.

 **Answers**

**1** The advantage of incorporating in Delaware is that the state has a highly developed corporate legal system.

**2** The articles of incorporation include the name of the corporation, the address of the corporation and of the corporation's registered office, and the name of the registered agent at that office. They also include the purpose of the corporation and the length of time that the corporation is to exist, which can be either perpetual or renewable. Finally, they provide information about the capital structure of the corporation.

**3** At the first organisational meeting of a corporation, the bylaws are approved and adopted, officers are elected, and directors are appointed.

**3.3** Tell students to read through the question and the information in the table quickly, and then elicit the answer from the class.

 **Answer**
C corporation

 **Pronunciation note**
proprietorship /prəˈpraɪətəʃɪp/

As a follow-up, tell students to discuss briefly the five US entities in small groups. Tell them to think about a) what the difference might be between the five entities, and b) whether the paperwork for each entity looks simple or complicated/time-consuming.

 **Suggested answers**
a See Teacher's brief (page 37).
b The paperwork for the various entities seems to become more complicated in the order they are given. The documents for the first three entities should be fairly simple forms and contracts, but for C and S corporations, the documents are likely to be much longer and more complicated.

**3.4** Tell students to read the introduction and then match the five types of business association with the descriptions. This should be fairly easy, as they will be able to work out the answers by scanning the table quickly. As you go through the answers with the class, elicit some similarities and differences between the USA and UK.

 **Answers**

**1** e  **2** a  **3** c  **4** b  **5** d

Three of the entities have the same names in both jurisdictions. The US *S corporation*, which cannot have more than 100 shareholders, is broadly similar to the UK *private limited company* (Ltd), while the *C corporation* (Inc.) is comparable to a *public limited company* (PLC).

As a follow-up, tell students to take turns to test each other in small groups. For example, one student could ask, 'Tell me about management in a general partnership.' The other students in the group have to remember the information in the table without looking, or bluff and try to invent a plausible answer.

## 4 Reading B: Memorandum of association

Ask students what they remember/know about a memorandum of association. (This document was mentioned in Reading A.) Then tell them to read the introduction for Reading B to see if they were right. You may need to check that they understand some words from the introduction, e.g. *to set forth*, *objects*, *legally binding* and *to adhere*.

**4.1** Tell students to read the four issues and the text, and to tick those addressed in the extract. Even though the language of the extract is very complicated, the task is not difficult, so allow only about 60–90 seconds. Tell them that they will have a chance to read more slowly later. At the end of the time limit, tell students to stop reading and to check in pairs or groups of three. Check the answers with the class.

 **Answers**

2 (paragraph 1) and 4 (paragraph 2)

---

 **Background notes**

○ *Objects* here mean the company's objectives.
○ Breach of any *legally binding* /ˈliːgəli ˈbaɪndɪŋ/ agreement or declaration may result in legal action.
○ *Stipulations* are the terms or conditions in an agreement.
○ *In lieu thereof* is pronounced /ɪn ˈluː ðeəˈrɒv/.
○ If a bylaw is *amended*, it is changed by adding an amendment, but it is still essentially the same bylaw. If it is *altered*, the changes are to the main body of the bylaw, and it effectively becomes a new bylaw.
○ An *agent* is a person authorised (e.g. by contract) to act for another.
○ The text refers to *classes of shares*. There are two main kinds: preference shares (US: preferred shares) and ordinary shares (US: common shares). Preference shareholders are often entitled to a fixed dividend even when ordinary shareholders are not. Ordinary shareholders are allowed to vote at general meetings, while preference shareholders normally cannot. (Source: http://www.bized.ac.uk)

**4.2** Tell students to discuss in the same groups whether the four statements are true or false. This is rather difficult, so allow them to re-read the text slowly and to work out the answers with their partners. When most groups have finished, discuss the answers with the class.

 **Answers**

**1** True
**2** False (They are permitted to change such bylaws, but only after two years have passed since the shareholders' vote.)
**3** False (Other records must also be kept: minutes of all meetings, records of all actions taken by shareholders or directors, accounting records, and records of shareholders.)
**4** True

**4.3** Tell students to work in the same groups to match the words and phrases with their synonyms. Point out that *passed* here refers to *time* passing. When most groups have finished, check the answers with the class.

**Answers**
**1** expired   **2** entitled to   **3** in lieu thereof
**4** provided   **5** repealed   **6** amended
**7** vested in

As a further check, ask students what the following words refer back to:
**1** *thereto* (line 2)   **2** *thereof* (line 4)   **3** *such* (line 5a)   **4** *such* (line 5b)   **5** *such* (line 7a)   **6** *such* (line 7b)   **7** *each* (line 15)

**Answers**
**1** ... any amendment *to any bylaw*
**2** ... in lieu *of any bylaw or amendment which has been adopted by the board of directors*
**3** ... shareholders *who are entitled to vote for the election of directors*
**4** ... a vote *to adopt a new bylaw*
**5** ... *alteration, amendment or adoption of a new bylaw*
**6** ... shareholders *who are entitled to vote for the election of directors*
**7** ... each *shareholder*

## 5   Language use: *shall* and *may*

Elicit from the class how *shall* and *may* are used in everyday English. Then ask them if they are aware of any special uses of these verbs in legal English. Avoid providing answers yourself, as these will come up in the exercise and the box on SB page 24.

**Language note**
In everyday English, *shall* is used to ask for a suggestion. It is almost always used in questions with *I* or *we*: *Where shall we go?*; *What shall I bring?* It is more direct than *should*, which is a rather tentative way of asking for advice. Note that *shall* does not normally mean the same as *will*: *Where will we go?* is asking for a prediction, not a suggestion.
*May* is used to ask for, and occasionally to give, permission: *May I smoke?*; *Yes, you*

*may*, a usage which is often replaced by *can*. *May* is also used to show probability: *She may arrive tonight, or she may not*, a usage which is often replaced by the slightly more tentative *might*.
Lawyers need to be aware of the differences between these everyday uses and legal English uses (see SB page 24), and to avoid the legal uses when explaining legal issues to a client.

Tell students to work in pairs or small groups to decide which of the three alternatives could be substituted for each instance of *shall* and *may*. When you collect the answers, allow some discussion of the answers, including the possibility that *shall* and *may* are ambiguous and should therefore be replaced in the text. A further issue is the sentence *No bylaw ... may be altered* (lines 5–6), which might be clearer as *A bylaw ... must not be altered*.

**Answers**
**1** a (*will*): lines 1, 6
   b (*must*): lines 8, 11 and 12
**2** It can be deleted without changing the meaning of the sentence.
**3** a (*can*)

Tell students to read the information in the box about *shall* and *may* quickly and then close their books. Check their understanding by eliciting the three uses of *shall* and the main use of *may*, ideally with the sample sentences from the box. Elicit also some of the problems with the overuse of *shall*, as described in the Language use box, and use these to generate some discussion (e.g. Is it good to give a text a 'legal feel', even if it may lead to confusion or disputes? Are there any other structures (in English or in students' own languages) which are overused to give a 'legal feel'?).

**Optional extension**
Tell students to work in small groups. Each group should write a paragraph for the memorandum of association in Reading B.

It should cover either appointing members of the board of directors or procedures for holding a vote of the shareholders. Only one person in each group should write; the others should tell that person what to write. Make sure that they understand that the purpose is to practise the various uses of *shall* and *may* in legal documents, so their sentences do not have to be legally accurate. They may even be humorous. Encourage them to write their paragraphs quickly, and then tell them to pass their writing on to another group. They should read other groups' paragraphs to try to spot any mistakes (see Writing section, page xiv).

## CD1 T13   6   Listening B: Forming a business in the UK

**6.1** Tell students to read the statements to see if they can work out the answers to any of them (e.g. questions 4 and 7) before listening. Then play the recording for students to decide if the statements are true or false. They discuss their answers in pairs before feeding back to the class.

 **Answers**
1 False (He has decided on a private company limited by shares.)
2 False (He says he already has some experience with company formation, but only in the United States.)
3 False (He says they are similar in many ways, particularly in respect of liability.)
4 True
5 True
6 False (There is no restriction.)
7 False (This method can take 'a couple of weeks'. The fastest way is through a company formation agent.)

**Transcript »** STUDENT'S BOOK **page 280**

**Optional extension**
Write the following on the board:

| 1 | But if I'm not ... | a | ... counter. |
| 2 | To buy shares over the ... | b | ... hand ... |
| 3 | As I ... | c | ... easy to form. |

4   On the other ...    d   ... mistaken ...
5   A limited company   e   ... recall ... is comparatively ...

Ask the class to match the two halves of each fragment, and to remember who said each. This should be very easy, but will at least draw attention to this useful language. You may need to check the meaning of some words (e.g. *comparatively*).

**Answers**
**1** d   **2** a   **3** e   **4** b   **5** c
All comments were made by the lawyer, Mr Larsen.

**6.2** Tell students to work alone to put the phrases into the spaces. Allow them to check with their neighbours. Either play the recording or simply go through the answers with the class, pointing out useful phrases such as *in respect of* (1), *in this respect* (3), *need not* (4) and *not more than* (6).

 **Answers**
**1** b   **2** d   **3** c   **4** a

**6.3** Students work in pairs to take turns to make as many sentences as they can. When they have finished, elicit a range of sentences from the class.

## 7   Speaking: An informal presentation: a type of company

Tell students to close their books. Use these questions to generate a short discussion. Avoid supplying answers.
a   Have you ever had to give a presentation in English?
b   Do you know any rules for the structure of a presentation?
c   How many sections should there be?
d   How many main points should you make?

 **Suggested answers**
   b   See SB page 26.
   c   Three: introductory remarks, main points and concluding remarks.
   d   Three

Then tell students to read through the box on SB page 26 to see if the advice agrees with their suggestions.

Tell students to read through the task. Use these questions to make sure they know what they have to do.

a   What do you have to write?
b   Who is the presentation for?
c   What do you have to compare?

**Answers**

a   Something similar to the example framework from the box (three parts, three main points), using a type of company from the student's jurisdiction to replace those of Sweden in the example. They should not write a script for their presentation, only brief notes.

b   Somebody from another country planning to form such a company in the student's country.

c   The company type in the student's country with its nearest equivalent(s) in the UK.

Encourage as much variety as possible, both in terms of countries and types of company. You will also need to decide whether students should:

○ plan their presentations alone or in groups (if they are from the same jurisdiction);

○ plan at home (if they need to conduct research) or in class;

○ conduct some research or invent any information they are not sure about.

It might also be fairer to give them an opportunity to practise their presentations (silently) before they have to give them.

Note that they will work on the language of presentations in later units, so you should not need to provide much language input at this stage. However, encourage them to use the phrases for comparing and contrasting from Exercise 6.2, as well as the language of approximation (see below).

When students have prepared their presentations, they could work in small groups and take turns to be the presenter and the clients. Tell them that the clients may ask questions after the presentations. Alternatively, you could invite each student to present their company type to the whole class, who will act as clients. This is more stressful for students, and rather time-consuming, but it will allow you to give useful feedback on the presentations, and students will learn some interesting facts about a range of company types.

**Optional extension**
The language of approximation (e.g. *X is rather similar to Y*) is useful for describing the extent to which two entities are similar or different. Lawyers need this language for describing legal terms from their own jurisdictions which have no exact equivalent in English.

Learners of English often know the phrases when others use them, but avoid using them themselves. With this area of language, the question of collocation is very important: certain combinations sound natural, while others do not, even if their meanings are very similar.

Draw the following grid on the board (without the ✓ symbols). Elicit from the class which two phrases from the top row collocate (= sound natural) with the word *completely*. In the second row, mark good collocations with a tick (✓). Then divide the class into teams and allocate a different colour to each team. Ask each team in turn to suggest a good collocation from the rest of the grid, and if you agree with their suggestion, mark a tick in the grid in that team's colour. Continue until there are no more good collocations to find. The winning team is the one with the most ticks in their colour. (Note: The grid contains suggested answers only. You as teacher should use your own judgment as to whether a given combination is really a collocation.)

| | ... similar to ... | ... different from ... | ... like ... | ... unlike ... | ... the same as ... | ... equivalent to ... |
|---|---|---|---|---|---|---|
| completely ... | | ✓ | | ✓ | | |
| exactly ... | | | ✓ | | ✓ | |
| more or less ... | | | | | ✓ | ✓ |
| basically ... | | | | | ✓ | ✓ |
| in many ways ... | ✓ | | ✓ | | ✓ | |
| rather ... | ✓ | ✓ | ✓ | | | |
| slightly ... | ✓ | ✓ | | | | |
| quite ... | ✓ | ✓ | ✓ | ✓ | | |

As a follow-up, you could elicit some more collocations not in the grid (e.g. *a bit like ...*, *broadly the same as ...*, *somewhat similar to ...*, *the exact equivalent of ...*). You could also elicit some patterns (e.g. *completely* goes only with negative expressions such as *unlike* and *different from*; most other structures cannot go with these negative expressions; *quite* changes its meaning with the negative expressions: *quite unlike = totally unlike*). However, the most important 'pattern' is that there is no pattern: collocations have a logic of their own, and simply have to be learnt as chunks of language.

Encourage students to use these phrases, especially the ones they are less familiar with, in their presentations (e.g. *an aktiebolag is basically the same as a public limited company, except for the fact that ...*).

**Language note**
Many English speakers say *different to* or *different than*, but *different from* is the most common of the three alternatives and the least likely to be treated as a mistake.

## 8 Reading C: Russian entity formation

Elicit from the class what sort of articles law firms put onto their websites and why. Students then read the introduction on page 26 to compare it with their ideas and to find out what the text will be about.

**8.1** Tell students to read the first paragraph to find the answer to the question. Allow 30–40 seconds. Discuss the answer as a class. You may want to check students understand the meaning of *enmeshed* (= tied together, intertwined, entangled).

**Answers**
joint venture, representative office, WFOE

**Background notes**
○ A *joint venture* is a business entity set up and owned by two or more partners for a particular purpose.
○ A *representative office* is simply an office where a representative (or team of representatives) of a company works. It has no distinct legal status from the company that employs the representatives.

**8.2** Tell students to read the rest of the article carefully to decide whether the statements are true or false. After three or four minutes, tell students to discuss their answers in pairs and then feed back to the class, focusing on why each false statement is false.

**Answers**
**1** False  **2** True  **3** True  **4** True  **5** True

**8.3** Students discuss the question in small groups, focusing on each row of the table. Afterwards, open up the discussion to include the whole class.

**Optional extension**
You could ask students to research and write a similar article about forming a new company in their own country, using Reading C as a model.

**Optional extension**
**ILEC preparation: Test of Reading Parts 2 and 6**
**Photocopiable worksheet 2.3**
**1** If your students are planning to take the ILEC exam, point out that Part 2 of the Test of Reading focuses on short grammatical words such as *it*, *by* and *unless*. These words are often overlooked by advanced learners who are keen to build their vocabulary, but they are crucial to high-quality writing. Focusing on these words is therefore not only a useful exam skill but also important for real life.

Tell students to close their books and to work alone to complete Exercise 1 on

Photocopiable worksheet 2.3. Tell them not to look at Exercise 2 until you have checked the answers to Exercise 1.

When you go through the answers carefully with the class, award a point for each correct answer. The student with the most points at the end is the winner.

Afterwards, students work in small groups to find similar words that could be gapped from the rest of the text. They then read their sentences aloud for students from other groups to work out the missing words.

**Answers**

**1** up  **2** in  **3** does  **4** with  **5** how
**6** they  **7** with  **8** over

**2**  Point out that Part 6 of the ILEC Test of Reading is a multiple-choice test, where students must choose one of four possible answers. Tell students to open their books and to work alone to choose the best answer, A, B, C or D, for each question. After about five minutes, allow students to discuss their answers with a partner but not to change their answers. When you go through the answers with the class, discuss why the incorrect statements are wrong.

**Answers**

**1** D  **2** B  **3** C  **4** A

## 9  Reading D: Corporate governance

Ask the class what they understand by the term *corporate governance* (Suggested answer: the ways in which rights and responsibilities are shared, typically between the management and the shareholders).

**9.1**  Tell students to read the first three paragraphs to find the answer to the question. They should be able to do this very quickly, so only allow a minute or so. Discuss the answer as a class.

 **Answer**

The dispute involves whether the directors were acting lawfully when they called the annual shareholders' meeting early.

**9.2**  Tell students to read the whole letter to answer the four multiple-choice questions. Tell them to discuss their answers with a partner when they have finished. Avoid helping with vocabulary at this stage; point out that they should be able to work out the answers without understanding every word. Finally, discuss the answers as a class.

 **Answers**

**1** b  **2** c  **3** d  **4** b

---

**Background notes**

(NB Several terms are also explained in Exercise 9.3.)

○ If somebody *files an action* (or *files suit*), they deposit it with the clerk of the court as the first step in a lawsuit. An *action* is a lawsuit in which one party sues another; a *suit* /suːt/ (= lawsuit) is a more general term for a request for judicial action, and may include court orders for action as well as money judgments.

○ In a *proxy fight*, an acquiring company attempts to persuade the shareholders of a target company to replace the present management with new directors who are favourable to the acquirer. This is a cheap way for an acquiring company to gain control of the company. (Source: http://www.money glossary.com)

○ To *allege* is pronounced /əˈledʒ/.

○ If a court *holds that* a statute was violated, this is its legal judgment.

○ If something is *invalid* /ɪnˈvælɪd/, it is in breach of some statutes or bylaws, and therefore has no legal status.

○ If you *second-guess* somebody, you try to guess what they intend, often with little evidence.

○ An *appellate* /əˈpelət/ *body* is usually a court, and has the power to hear court appeals and to review court decisions.

○ To *warrant* /ˈwɒrənt/ has several meanings, but here it means 'to justify something' or 'to provide adequate grounds for something'.

○ To *prevail* means 'to win in a lawsuit'.

**9.3** Tell students to work alone or in small groups to work out the meanings of the words and phrases. When they have finished, go through the answers with the class.

 **Answers**

**1** b **2** a **3** c **4** b **5** a **6** b

**9.4** Tell students to discuss these questions in small groups, perhaps with Exercise 9.5 at the same time. Then discuss the answers as a class.

 **Answers**

**1** They stipulate a deadline before which the directors must, at their discretion, determine when to hold the shareholders' meeting for elections of the board.

**2** The shareholders claim that the board held the annual shareholders' meeting early to strategically circumvent an anticipated proxy fight in order to perpetuate their control of the company.

**3** It might be used to define the board's duty to act and, depending upon the severity of the potential breach of such duty, the court might step in and overturn the board's decision.

**9.5** This can be discussed in small groups or as a whole class. The answers will vary depending on students' interpretation of the facts.

---

**Optional extension**

Tell students to read through the letter again slowly a) to identify and underline typical expressions which are used in legal English but rarely in everyday English, and b) to circle any useful formulas for letters to clients. Then go through the letter with the whole group to collect all the answers. Point out that this is a very effective way of building their legal English vocabulary, as long as they take steps to learn the useful language.

**Suggested answer**

Some important legal English expressions are in bold. Students may find many more. Formulas for writing are boxed. Note that

---

there is also an example of inversion[1] (*Only where there is a clear and serious breach of the directors' duty to act in good faith will a court step in*), which you may draw attention to.

**Re: Special shareholders' meeting of Longfellow Inc.**

I have now had an opportunity to research **the law on this point** and I can provide you with the following advice.

Firstly, to summarise the facts of the case, a group of shareholders of Longfellow Inc. has **filed an action** in the district court **seeking to set aside** the election of the board of directors **on the grounds that** the shareholders' meeting at which they were elected was held less than a year after the last **such** meeting.

The bylaws of the company state that the annual shareholders' meeting for the election of directors **be held** at **such time** each year **as** the board of directors determines, but **not later than** the fourth Wednesday in July. In 2009, the meeting was held on July 17th. **At the discretion of** the board, in 2010 the meeting was held on March 19th. The issue in this case is whether the **provision** for annual election of directors for **the ensuing year** means that no election can be held unless a full year has passed since the previous annual election meeting.

The law in this **jurisdiction** requires an 'annual' election of the directors for the ensuing 'year'. However, we have not found any **cases or interpretation of this law** which determine the issue of whether the law **precludes the holding of** an election until a full year has passed. The statutes **give wide leeway** to the board of directors in conducting the affairs of the company. I believe that it is unlikely that a court will create **such** a restriction **where** the legislature has not specifically **done so**.

[1] Where certain expressions (such as *Only where* + a clause, *Hardly*, *Under no circumstances* or *Not only*) are used at the beginning of a sentence, the subject and auxiliary verb are reversed, in exactly the same way as with questions: *Under what circumstances **will a court** step in? Only where is a clear and serious breach of the directors' duty to act in good faith **will a court** step in.* There is another example of inversion in Reading 3, paragraph 3: *Not only are these rules some of the most demanding in Europe, ...*

However, this matter is complicated somewhat by the fact that there is currently a **proxy fight underway** in the company. The shareholders who **filed suit** are also **alleging** that the early meeting was part of a strategy **on the part of** the directors to obstruct the anticipated proxy contest and to keep these shareholders from **gaining representation** on the board of directors. It is possible that the court will **take this into consideration** and **hold that** the purpose in calling an early meeting was to improperly keep themselves in office. The court might then hold that, despite the fact that no **statute or bylaw** was **violated**, the election is **invalid** on a general legal theory that the directors have **an obligation to act in good faith**. Nevertheless, courts are usually reluctant to second-guess the actions of boards of directors or to play the role of **an appellate body** for shareholders unhappy with the business decisions of the board. Only where there is a clear and serious breach of the directors' **duty to act in good faith** will a court **step in and overturn the decision**. The facts in this **case** simply do not **justify such court action** and I therefore conclude that it is unlikely that the shareholders will **prevail**.

**9.6** Do this activity quickly with the whole class. Encourage students to predict the answers before checking back in the text.

➡ **Answers**
   **1** state   **2** requires   **3** precludes

## 10 Text analysis: A letter of advice

**10.1** Tell students to discuss these questions in pairs. These are important and useful questions, but students might find it difficult to analyse a text in this way. When they have finished, discuss the answers carefully with the class.

➡ **Suggested answers**
   **1** The purpose of the text is to provide the lawyer's client with an understanding of the legal aspects of the case in which the client is involved.
   **2** It was probably written at the client's request so that he/she could make an informed decision about how to proceed regarding the matter.
   **3** Paragraph 1: Referring to the subject matter
   Paragraph 2: Summarising facts
   Paragraph 3: Summarising facts; Identifying legal issue
   Paragraph 4: Referring to relevant legislation/regulations; (Referring to previous court decisions)
   Paragraph 5: Summarising facts; Referring to previous court decisions; Drawing conclusions

Briefly discuss with the class a) what the function of a letter of advice is, b) what it should contain, and c) what its structure should be. Then tell them to compare their suggestions with the guidelines in the box on SB page 30. When they have finished reading, discuss any differences they found.

**10.2** This should be easier if students have already done the optional extension after Exercise 9.5. Tell them to work alone to find the 11 phrases from the letter and to add them to the table. Tell them to compare their answers with a partner, and then discuss the answers with the class. Use this opportunity to elicit any similar useful phrases that students know but which are not on the list. Discuss which of the options students prefer for each of the eight functions.

➡ **Answers**
   **1** I have now had an opportunity to research the law on this point and I can provide you with the following advice.
   **2** To summarise the facts of the case, ...
   **3** The issue in this case is whether the ...
   **4** The bylaws of the company state that ...
   **5** The law in this jurisdiction requires ...
   **6** The statutes give wide leeway ...

**7** It is possible that the court will take this into consideration and hold that ...

**8** The court might then hold that ...

**9** Courts are usually reluctant to ...

**10** The facts in this case simply do not justify ...

**11** I therefore conclude that ...

## 11 Writing: A letter of advice

Tell students to read through the instructions and then discuss in small groups what they should mention about each bullet point, as well as the function, contents and structure of a letter of advice. The writing can be set for homework or done in class. (See Writing section, page xiv.) Encourage students to use the useful phrases from this unit in their writing.

 **Suggested answer**

Dear Mr Rodríguez

**Subject: Establishing a business presence in Russia**

Thank you for instructing us in relation to the above matter. You have requested advice concerning establishing a business presence in Russia. In the following, I would like to outline the present situation in Russia and to indicate your options.

Based on the information provided to us, we understand that your company is seeking to introduce its product, the chocolate-flavoured energy drink Xocoatl, into the Russian market next year and to conduct the full range of commercial activities throughout Russia. You are considering whether to establish a representative office in Moscow or to form a legal entity, and would like to know which option would be the most advantageous for your firm.

I have now had an opportunity to research the law on this point and I can provide you with the following advice. Due to a recent change in legislation, Russia now allows the formation of Wholly Foreign-Owned Entities (WFOEs), which would have significant advantages over a representative office.

The two options can be compared as follows:

○ **Formation**: A representative office in Russia can be opened and closed with relatively little formality; a WFOE must adhere to the more extensive procedures prescribed for company formation.

○ **Liability**: The foreign entity is liable for acts of its representative office done pursuant to the power of attorney, while the WFOE is liable for its own obligations.

○ **Tax and reporting requirements**: Since a representative office is not a Russian legal person, it is not subject to many of the regulations that apply to legally established Russian companies, such as tax and reporting requirements, which are more extensive and burdensome.

○ **Ability to conduct business**: A representative office is not allowed to conduct commercial activity; it is limited to negotiating contracts, marketing or conducting other supporting activities for the foreign entity it represents. A WFOE, in contrast, possesses all the rights of a Russian company.

Based on these considerations, and the instructions you have provided regarding the goals of your company in Russia, we therefore believe that, although a WFOE is subject to the same taxation, reporting and company regulation requirements of any Russian company, it enjoys both the rights and obligations of any other Russian company, and thus would be better suited to your company's needs.

I await further instructions at your earliest convenience.

Yours sincerely

Bruno Martenson

 Tell students to do the Internet activity as homework. See Using the Internet for research on page xviii.

# Language focus

## Answers

### 1 Vocabulary: distinguishing meaning

**1** *proscribe*: The others mean 'to set out the details of something'; *proscribe* means 'to forbid'.

**2** *elapsing*: The others mean 'following'; *elapsing* means 'passing'.

**3** *discretion* /dɪsˈkreʃən/: The others refer to things one must do; *discretion* refers to a choice.

**4** *prerequisite* /ˌpriːˈrekwɪzɪt/: The others refer to events which happened earlier; *prerequisite* means 'required'.

**5** *interpretation*: The others refer to freedom within certain limits.

**6** *permit* /pəˈmɪt/: The others mean 'prevent'.

### 2 Vocabulary: word choice

**2** states **3** provisions **4** to **5** make
**6** on behalf of

### 3 Word formation

| Verb | Abstract noun | Personal noun |
|---|---|---|
| ad<u>mi</u>nistrate | adminis<u>tra</u>tion | ad<u>mi</u>nistrator |
| <u>au</u>dit | <u>au</u>dit | <u>au</u>ditor |
| <u>li</u>quidate | liqui<u>da</u>tion | <u>li</u>quidator |
| <u>per</u>petrate | perpe<u>tra</u>tion | <u>per</u>petrator |
| ap<u>poin</u>t | ap<u>poin</u>tment | |
| as<u>sume</u> | as<u>sum</u>ption | |
| <u>au</u>thorise | authori<u>sa</u>tion | |
| form | for<u>ma</u>tion | |
| <u>is</u>sue | <u>is</u>suance/<br><u>is</u>suing | <u>is</u>suer |
| o<u>mit</u> | o<u>mi</u>ssion | |
| pro<u>vide</u> | pro<u>vi</u>sion | pro<u>vi</u>der |
| re<u>deem</u> | re<u>dem</u>ption | re<u>dee</u>mer |
| re<u>quire</u> | re<u>quire</u>ment | |
| re<u>solve</u> | reso<u>lu</u>tion | |
| trans<u>mit</u> | trans<u>mi</u>ssion | trans<u>mit</u>ter |

**Note:** Some of the shaded boxes could be filled in (e.g. *an appointee*, *an author*), but these all require a change of meaning, and are probably not relevant.

### 4 Vocabulary: prepositional phrases

**2** d **3** a **4** b

**Note:** It might be a good idea to do this together with Exercise 5, as the sample sentences may be easier to understand than the paraphrases in this exercise.

### 5 Vocabulary: prepositional phrases

**2** in the course of / by way of **3** by way of
**4** in terms of **5** in response to **6** in response to **7** in terms of **8** by way of

### 6 Verb–noun collocations

**2** c **3** d **4** b **5** a

### 7 Collocations with *file*

an action, an amendment, an appeal, a brief, charges, a claim, a complaint, a defence, a document, an injunction, a motion, a suit

# 3 ) Company law: capitalisation

**Capitalisation** is the process of raising capital for a business (although there are other meanings – see http://dictionary.law.com). The term **capital** (= wealth) includes both money and property, but typically refers to the money that is needed to set up and maintain a business.

For companies, there are two external **sources of capital**: borrowing money (**loans**) and selling ownership rights in the company (**shares**). Both sources involve issuing **securities** (typically legally binding certificates): **debt securities** for loans and **equity securities** for shares. Loans are mentioned briefly in this unit, but covered thoroughly in Unit 13 (Secured transactions). This unit is mainly concerned with shares.

To understand how shares work, it helps to use a simplistic example. An entrepreneur wants to raise some money for investment in her company, so she divides her company into ten parts (**shares**), each with a **nominal value** (= face value, par value) of €100. She sells one share each to three investors, who may in fact pay more (or less) than the nominal value, depending on what they can negotiate. She awards three to herself (having already invested €300 of her own money in setting up the company). The other four are not sold, but may be sold later. The company's **authorised capital** (that which it may issue) is €1,000, but its **issued capital** (that which has been issued) is only €600.

The investors' incentive for investing in the enterprise is the prospect of receiving a proportion (in this case, 10% per share) of the company's profits every year (**dividend**), although often a proportion of the company's profits will be reinvested, so in practice they may well receive less than 10%.

The investors in this company (**shareholders**) also have **rights** to influence all company decisions (one vote per share). In practice, however, there is likely to be an election to choose a **board of directors**, who are then authorised to make day-to-day decisions for the good of the shareholders. The entrepreneur, with a 50% share of the issued capital, is likely to remain a powerful influence, but can no longer dictate what the company does. For the other investors, their voting rights might be less important than the chance to make money, either by receiving dividends or by selling the shares when they go up in value.

As Reading A explains, there are two types of shares. Holders of **ordinary shares** have voting rights, but are not guaranteed dividends; owners of **preference shares** receive fixed dividends, but normally cannot vote.

Reading B deals with the question of **shareholders' rights**. In countries such as the USA and UK, most shareholders have very few powers to influence management of the companies they own. In Germany and other countries, there exist **supervisory boards** to oversee and scrutinise the work of the **executive board** (senior managers), which are supposed to ensure co-operation between managers, shareholders and employees. Shareholders do not control the supervisory board, but they may appreciate the fact that the executive board is being monitored in their interest.

A board of directors might decide to issue more shares (in the above example, four shares remained unsold). Issuing more shares dilutes the power and value of existing shares, so to compensate existing shareholders for this potential loss of power, in the UK they have a **right of first refusal** to buy new shares, in proportion to their existing holdings, before the shares can be offered to new shareholders. In many countries, it is normal practice to sell shares to existing shareholders in such a **rights issue**. Listening A deals with such questions.

Reading C introduces the concept of **minimal share capital requirement**. In many countries, there are strict rules about how much capital must be invested and held by the company, and under what circumstances (if any) shareholders can take money back out of the company. Historically, the purpose of such rules was to secure creditors (= lenders) by ensuring that the company had enough money to pay its debts in the event of liquidation. In practice, however, creditors now have more effective ways of securing loans, so the usefulness of the minimum share capital requirement has been questioned, especially as it may discourage entrepreneurs from starting a business in the first place.

As discussed in Unit 2, there is an important difference between **private companies** and **public companies**. The shares of public companies are traded publicly, and are subject to much stricter legal and financial controls. For example, in Bulgaria, the minimum share capital requirement has been virtually eliminated for **limited companies** (= privately owned companies) but remains high for **joint stock companies** (= publicly traded companies).

Listening B introduces the concepts of **plain English** and **legalese**. Traditionally, lawyers have used a style of language which is impenetrable to non-lawyers, with long sentences, unusual grammar and obscure words. In recent decades, there has been a movement towards making legal English more accessible. This has obvious benefits for clients wishing to understand what they are signing, but can also help lawyers by making their language less prone to misinterpretation. In practice, lawyers need to be skilled in both legalese (e.g. in order to understand legal documents) and plain English (in order to communicate with clients). This is a recurrent theme throughout this book.

The unit also deals with other important skills for lawyers: **contrasting information** (with structures such as *as opposed to*), **summarising** a long or complex text for a client, **paraphrasing** legalese into plain English for a client, and **expressing opinions**.

**Further information**

○ For a very clear guide to **shares**, including sample share certificates, see http://www.offshore-fox.com/offshore-corporations/offshore_corporations_010408.html. For hundreds of **shareholders' agreements**, see http://contracts.onecle.com/type/68.shtml.
○ There is a thorough guide to **securities**, including many of the topics mentioned in this unit, at http://en.wikipedia.org/wiki/Securities. There is an excellent dictionary of vocabulary connected with **shares** at http://www.investorwords.com.
○ There is a good article on the **two-tier board** at http://www.socius.si/media/uploads/file/article_4132.pdf.
○ An excellent list of **legalese expressions**, with their plain English equivalents, is at http://www.law.ucla.edu/volokh/legalese.htm. There is also a 'legalese glossary' at http://www.uchelp.com/law/glossary.htm.
○ An invaluable resource on **plain English** is the US Securities and Exchange Commission's Plain English Handbook (http://www.sec.gov/pdf/handbook.pdf). There is also a wealth of material at www.plainlanguagenetwork.org and www.plainenglish.co.uk.
○ A rare article in defence of **legalese** can be found at http://www.utexas.edu/law/faculty/wschiess/legalwriting/2005/06/bringing-back-some-classic-legalese.html.

## Discussion

Use these questions to generate a discussion on capitalisation.

a What is capitalisation? (If students struggle, rephrase the question as 'How can companies raise capital?' This should make them think of shares and other forms of finance, such as loans. Encourage discussion of any differences in capitalisation between your students' jurisdictions.)

b Have you ever bought or sold any shares? (This may include buying on behalf of a client. Encourage discussion of what is involved in buying and selling shares, and again any differences between jurisdictions.)

c Why do lawyers need to know about capitalisation?

➡ **Suggested answer**

c Since shareholders actually own their companies, there is plenty of potential for conflict with other shareholders, managers, etc. and therefore plenty of work for lawyers. For example, lawyers might:

○ work closely with their client companies before the shares are issued, to ensure the right balance between shareholder rights and responsibilities;
○ advise their clients on the legal procedures for issuing, buying or selling shares;
○ draft a shareholders' agreement (a contract among shareholders) and share certificates;
○ advise potential shareholders before they invest in a company;
○ be called on by both sides in the event of any conflict or misunderstanding between one shareholder and another, or between shareholders and the company's management.

# 1  Reading A: Introduction to company capitalisation

Read through the true/false statements first as a class, in order to a) generate some interest in the text, and b) check some vocabulary items from the statements (e.g. *the right of first refusal*, *a means of doing something*). Avoid confirming or rejecting students' suggestions.

Tell students to read the text to find out if the statements are true or false. When they have finished reading, tell them to check their answers in pairs, and to make sure their partners understand all the key terms (in bold). Tell them to refer to the Glossary booklet for help with key terms if necessary. Then go through the answers with the whole class, paying attention to the key vocabulary.

**Answers**
**1** False (They are known as issued capital)
**2** True  **3** True  **4** True

**Pronunciation notes**
debenture /dəˈbentʃəʳ/
issuance /ˈɪʃʊəns/
mandatory /ˈmændətəri/
pre-emption /ˌpriːˈempʃən/
waive /weɪv/
whereby /ˈweəˌbaɪ/

**Optional extension**
Discuss these questions with the class.
**1** Apart from shares, what other types of securities are there?
**2** Why might a company refrain from issuing all of the authorised capital until a later date?
**3** Why would it increase marketability to split one ten-pound share into ten one-pound shares?
**4** What sort of group or individual might obtain shares through a directed placement?
**5** What are *debentures*?
**6** What is *stock in trade*?

**Possible answers**
**1** There are two types of security: debt (e.g. government bonds, certificates of deposit and commercial papers) and equity (e.g. shares). There are also hybrids between these two types, such as convertibles and equity warrants. See http://en.wikipedia.org/wiki/Securities for detailed information.
**2** To keep available the option of issuing more capital later, perhaps when the market is willing to pay more for the shares.
**3** Investors prefer to invest a specific amount of money, and lower-value shares allow much greater precision.
**4** Corporate investors such as pension funds, insurance companies, equity funds, trusts, etc.
**5** They are used by governments and large companies as instruments to raise long-term finance. They are similar to bonds. See http://en.wikipedia.org/wiki/Debenture.
**6** The merchandise, materials and equipment which a company uses in its operations.

**Optional extension**
**Photocopiable worksheet 3.1**

Photocopiable worksheet 3.1 focuses on prepositions used in the text. Tell students to close their books and to work in small teams to put prepositions into the extracts from the text. Point out that sometimes several different prepositions are possible, but that there is only one solution which uses each preposition in the box once. To add a competitive element, you may turn this activity into a 'Stake game' (see Games and activities section, page xvi), in which case every preposition in a sentence must be correct for it to 'win'.

**Answers**
**1** through  **2** with; into; of  **3** as; to; to; by
**4** in; of; from; at  **5** of; upon; of  **6** on; of
**7** for; into; in  **8** in; to; to  **9** in; to; to; by
**10** of  **11** of; for; from  **12** by; in

## 2  Key terms: Shares

**2.1** Tell students to cover the text and work alone or in small groups to match the key terms with their definitions. When most students have finished, check the answers with the class.

**Answers**
**1** e  **2** h  **3** f  **4** c  **5** d  **6** g  **7** b  **8** a

**2.2** Do the matching exercise quickly as a class.

**Answers**

**1** c  **2** e  **3** b  **4** a  **5** d

Elicit from the class how the five verbs were used in the text. Make sure all students have understood all the vocabulary by asking concept-checking questions, such as:

**a**  What sort of activities does your job entail?

**b**  When might you waive your right of first refusal?

**c**  How could a creditor recover his capital sum?

 **Suggested answers**

**a**  Dealing with clients, writing legal opinions, etc.

**b**  As part of the give-and-take process in a negotiation.

**c**  He might appoint an administrative receiver to get the money back.

**Optional extension**

Tell students to look back to the first line of Reading A. Elicit some alternatives to the structure *the term x refers to y*. Then tell them to scan the text for more of these 'referring devices'. Collect all the examples on the board.

**Suggested answers**

| | |
|---|---|
| x refers to y | The term capitalisation refers to ... |
| | Issued capital ... refers to ... |
| x means y | Accordingly, this means that ... |
| x entails y | The division of share capital usually entails ... |
| There is x, whereby y happens | There is also the possibility of share subdivision, whereby ... |
| | Shares ... are subject to pre-emption rights, whereby ... |
| x is termed y | The reverse process is ... , termed ... |
| | The grant of security for a loan ... is termed ... |
| x is typified by y | The other is loan capital, typified by debentures. |
| x is known as y | This arrangement is known as a floating charge. |

Then set up a mini role-play between a lawyer (or two lawyers) and a client. The client has to ask the lawyer(s) to explain one of the key

terms. The lawyer(s) should then explain the key terms using a wide range of referring devices (e.g. *There are also preference shares, whereby shareholders are given priority as to dividends and voting / Subscribers are typified by corporate investors rather than private individuals*). Tell students to swap roles halfway through.

**2.3**  If students are all from the same jurisdiction, this question is best done quickly as a class. Ask if there are any other restrictions, such as a minimum number of shares or shareholders. If students are from a range of jurisdictions, ask them to compare the restrictions in each of their jurisdictions, and then present any similarities and differences to the class at the end. If students do not know the restrictions, you could ask them to research the question and report back later. An excellent website for this information is http://www.corporate information.com/defext.asp.

## 3  Language use A: Contrasting information

Tell students to read through the information in the box to find three phrases for contrasting information, and three uses for these phrases.

 **Suggested answer**

The three phrases (*as opposed to*, *unlike* and *in contrast to*) can be used a) after an unfamiliar term and before a familiar term, b) at the beginning of a sentence before a familiar term, and c) with *which* to define two new terms.

 **Language notes**

○  *Unlike* is used around twice as often as *as opposed to*, which in turn is about twice as popular as *in contrast to*.

○  The conjunctions *while* and *whereas* have a similar function, but are followed by whole clauses rather than noun phrases. *On the other hand* and *In contrast* are sentence adverbials, usually separated from a whole sentence by commas. These other ways of contrasting information are covered in later units.

Tell students to cover the examples and to look only at the table. Elicit some ways of contrasting the first pair of facts using the three prepositions. Then compare students' suggestions with the examples given. Draw attention to the phrases used in the examples to expand the notes (*do not entitle*, *such a right*). Check the vocabulary in the remaining rows of the table.

 **Background notes**

○ *pro-rata* /ˌprəʊ 'rɑːtə/ = proportional; in this case, shareholders receive a share of the total dividends proportional to the number of shares they hold.

○ *to bear* a risk = to carry a risk.

○ *to be wound up* /ˌwaʊnd 'ʌp/ = to be closed down as a business; for example, when a company goes bankrupt, an official receiver may be appointed to wind up the company's affairs, which includes attempting to recover creditors' money.

○ *par value* = nominal value or face value: the value printed on a security (e.g. share or bond), which is used to calculate dividends. The market value of the security will rise and fall, but the par value remains constant.

Tell students to work in pairs to come up with sentences for the remaining three pairs of facts. When they have finished, elicit several sentences for each pair of facts.

 **Suggested answers**

2 Ordinary shares have the potential to give the highest financial gains, as they give a pro-rata right to dividends, as opposed to preference shares, which have a fixed dividend and do not give an increased return in relation to the business's profits.

3 In contrast to ordinary shares, preference shares are relatively low risk, as the shareholder has the right to a dividend ahead of ordinary shareholders.

4 Ordinary shareholders are the last to be paid if the company is wound up, as opposed to preference shareholders, who are repaid the par value of their shares first.

If you feel students need further practice of these structures, tell them to make further sentences based on their discussion in Exercise 2.3.

 **4   Listening A: A rights issue**

Tell students to read the introduction (SB page 37) to find out who the two speakers in the dialogue are, and what they are going to be discussing.

**4.1** Tell students to read the eight points and then listen to the dialogue to check which ones Ms Siebert asks about. After the recording, tell them to discuss the answers with a partner. Tell them also to discuss anything else they remember from the dialogue. When they have finished, go through the answers with the class.

**Transcript »** STUDENT'S BOOK **page 281**

 **Answer**
Ms Siebert asks about points 1, 3, 5, 6 and 7.

**4.2** Tell students to discuss the questions in pairs to try to remember the answers. Then play the recording for them to check (but see the optional extension activity below). Allow them to compare answers with a partner before checking with the whole class.

**Answers**
1 The new shares are offered in proportion to the number of shares the shareholders already hold.

2 The speaker says that shareholders want to take up their pre-emption right to maintain the proportion of shares they own.

3 New shares are issued at a price that is lower than the market price to increase the likelihood that the issue is fully subscribed.

4 A share issue is said to be fully subscribed when all of the shares have been agreed to be purchased.

5 They can be unhappy about having to decide whether to buy shares or sell rights.

**Optional extension**
Tell students to work in small teams to remember Ms Siebert's six questions. While they are discussing, write on the board the

first and last words of each question, plus spaces for the missing words:

1 Could ...... ...... ...... ...... ...... ...... ...... ...... ...... ...... is?
2 But ...... ...... ...... ...... ...... shareholders?
3 What ...... ...... ...... ...... ...... shares?
4 Why ...... ...... ...... ...... ...... ...... ...... ...... ...... ...... ...... ...... ...... ...... ...... ...... ...... ...... ...... shares?
5 You ...... ...... ...... ...... ...... ...... ...... ...... ...... ...... ...... ...... ...... ...... ...... , ...... ...... right?
6 Are ...... ...... ...... ...... ...... ...... ...... ...... ...... ...... ...... ...... about?

When students listen to the recording the second time (see Exercise 4.2), tell them to write the six questions word for word, and to try to remember as much as they can about the answers. After the recording, tell them to compare their answers with their teams. Then collect the six questions on the board. You could make this competitive by going round the teams in turn and writing the correct words they supply until they make a mistake, and then going to the next team. Award a point for the team which completes each question. When all the questions are on the board, set up a mini role-play. Students should work in pairs to re-enact the dialogue between Ms Siebert and Mr Young. Halfway through, they should change roles.

### Answers

1 Could you explain to me in detail what a rights issue is?
2 But why issue shares to existing shareholders?
3 What about the price of these shares?
4 Why would a business offer new shares at a price that's significantly lower than the current market price of the shares?
5 You said that existing shareholders don't have to take up their rights to buy new shares, is that right?
6 Are there any other matters connected to rights issues that I should know about?

## 5 Reading B: Shareholders and supervisory boards

**5.1** Tell students to discuss the three questions in small groups to predict the answers. Do not

confirm or reject their suggestions at this stage. As this is a long text, it may be best to do it as a jigsaw reading, especially with weaker groups. Divide the class into pairs or groups of three. In each pair, one student should read paragraphs A, B, C and D, while the other should read paragraphs E, F and G. (In groups of three, divide the text as follows: ABC / DE / FG.) Tell students to read their sections very quickly (e.g. set a one-minute limit), and then work together with their partner(s) to answer the questions. When they have finished, check the answers with the class.

### Answers

1 The right to receive the residual income based on shares owned in the company, and the right to transfer ownership of the shares to others.
2 Shareholders can express their disappointment with the company's performance by either getting rid of their shares or in some way exercising their voice by communicating their concerns to the company's board.
3 The one-tier board consists of directors, executive as well as non-executive, who are appointed by the controlling shareholders and who must answer to the annual meeting. A two-tier board consists of an executive board and a supervisory board. The executive board includes the top-level management team, whereas the supervisory board is made up of outside experts, such as bankers and executives from other corporations, along with employee-related representatives.

### Background notes

○ *Residual* /rə'zɪdjʊəl/ *income* (paragraph A) refers to income which continues to be generated without any additional input (e.g. an author may continue to receive royalties for decades after the initial effort of writing the book).
○ *Proxy votes* (paragraph B) are cast by one person on behalf of another. In the text, the suggestion is that the chairman has enough influence to determine how other shareholders will vote (or may cast those votes himself).

○ *Germanic countries* (paragraph E) refers to Germany and Austria. *Anglo-Saxon* refers primarily to the UK and US (but also Ireland, Canada, Australia and New Zealand).

○ *Co-determination* (paragraph F) is where management and workers (or their representatives) make decisions jointly.

### 💬 Pronunciation notes

awkward /ˈɔːkwəd/
cosiness /ˈkəʊzinəs/
crises /ˈkraɪsiːz/
dichotomy /ˌdaɪˈkɒtəmi/
tier /ˈtɪəʳ/
whereas /ˌweərˈæz/

**5.2** Tell students to work in the same groups. They should a) work out between them which paragraph mentions each issue, and b) try to explain to their partners what was said about each issue in the paragraphs that they read. You may need to check the word *stipulations* from question 1. The questions should generate quite a lot of discussion.

Before discussing the questions as a class, tell students to read the sections of the text which they have not already read, in order to a) check that their partners were correct, and b) underline any difficult or interesting vocabulary.

When most students have finished, go through the questions as a whole class. You may also ask students if they have any experience of a two-tier board, and whether they think it is better or worse than a one-tier board. Also try to relate the discussion to students' own jurisdictions: are they more similar to the Anglo-Saxon countries or the Germanic countries?

### Answers

**1** F  **2** E, F, (G)  **3** C, D  **4** B  **5** G
**6** C  **7** A  **8** E

Point out that most of the vocabulary they have underlined will come up in the following exercises, so they should ask about any outstanding questions after Exercise 6.3.

**5.3** Tell students to discuss in small groups what they understand by each of the expressions. Encourage them to think of real-life examples. When they have finished, go through the answers with the class.

### Suggested answers

1. **risk diversification**: the division of investments among various assets such that the failure of or loss in one investment will not necessarily financially devastate the company, since other investments remain viable

2. **awkward questions**: questions which the respondent would prefer not to answer. Simply asking them may cause the respondent some embarrassment. For example, *How can you justify the award of a 15% pay rise for the CEO when dividends have fallen by 50%?*

3. **flow of information**: the communication or sharing of knowledge between parties

4. **face ... obstacles**: encounter negative factors that prevent or hinder one from obtaining one's goal

5. **the free-rider issue**: the well-known philosophical problem that there are some things which may be in everybody's collective interest, but which are not worth anybody's individual effort. For example, I might benefit from the construction of a new bridge, but not enough to justify building it by myself. Even if I could assemble a large team of friends to help me build it, there would still be some potential beneficiaries who have not contributed (free-riders). The problem is how to persuade individuals to be contributors rather than free-riders.

6. **vote with one's feet**: If I don't like the way I am treated in a shop, I can 'vote with my feet' by leaving the shop and not returning. If enough 'voters' do the same, either the service will have to improve or the shop will fail. In this context, it means showing your dissatisfaction by selling your shares and leaving the company.

7. **answer to the annual meeting**: be accountable for one's actions to the shareholders at the yearly shareholders' general meeting

8. **co-operative conflict resolution**: collaborating or working together to resolve any disputes or disagreements

**9 participatory framework**: a regulatory framework or structure in which the employees are granted the right to participate in the management of the company

**10 subjected to the public gaze**: in the public eye, subject to public scrutiny, for example by the media

# 6 Language use B: Common collocations (verb plus noun)

**Optional lead-in**
Tell students to close their books. Write on the board the words *benefits*, *capital*, *control*, *employees*, *members*, *powers* and *shareholders*. Read the following sentences from the box aloud, and ask students if they can remember which words were used instead of *blank* (or *blanks*). Point out that three of the words on the board are not used.

1 Can shareholders exercise [*blank*] if the directors fail to protect their interests?
2 In return for the privilege of limited liability under law, shareholders' [*blanks*] are generally restricted.
3 Any one small shareholder investing in the information needed to monitor management will bear all of the costs, whereas shareholders accrue [*blanks*] as a group.
4 Co-determination rules cover the supervisory board, the functions of which are to control and monitor the management, to appoint and dismiss [*blanks*] of the management board, ...

**Answers**
**1** control  **2** powers  **3** benefits  **4** members

**6.1** Do this quickly with the class. To check that all students have understood, ask for some more nouns which could go with the four verbs. This should generate some of the nouns in Exercise 6.2, as well as some non-collocations (i.e. those which make logical sense according to the definitions but which simply sound wrong because they collocate with a different verb, e.g. the government might want to reduce the size of unemployment and prevent it from increasing, but we would not say *they*

*are trying to restrict unemployment*, but rather *control* or *cut* it). Point out that the key to sophisticated and accurate communication is to know the right collocations.

 **Answers**
**1** c  **2** d  **3** b  **4** a

**6.2** Tell students to work in small groups to match the nouns with the verbs, and write the appropriate number next to each noun. When you check the answers, you could add a competitive element by playing 'Easy first' (see Games and activities section, page xvi). Note that there may be several possible collocations for each noun, and students may be able to justify some not listed here.

 **Suggested answers**
**1** exercise: authority, caution, control, force, influence, power, pressure, restraint, rights
**2** restrict: access, authority, benefits, capital, control, freedom, power, rights, sales, spending
**3** accrue: benefits, capital, interest, profits, revenue
**4** dismiss: a case, a charge, a claim, an employee

**6.3** Tell students to work in the same groups to put one of the four verbs from Exercise 6.1 into each sentence. Sentence 5 might cause problems: rather than having somebody accruing something, here we have something accruing to somebody.

 **Answers**
**1** dismiss  **2** exercise  **3** exercise
**4** restrict  **5** accrue(d)  **6** exercise
**7** restrict  **8** dismiss

You could make this more challenging by telling students to close their books before you collect their answers, thus forcing them to remember what they wrote. You could also develop the eight sentences into a discussion by asking students to imagine the background to each event:

1 What sort of case did the Board of Directors want to be dismissed?
2 Why did the chairman make this warning?

**3** Why did the board want greater control over the company's bankruptcy plan?

**4** What would happen if the company increased its spending?

**5** Why might some owners not be shareholders?

**6** Why did the spokeswoman give this advice?

**7** What is the point of such a provision?

**8** When might the annual general meeting dismiss directors of the board?

---

**Optional extension**
**Photocopiable worksheet 3.2**

There is a further exercise on collocations from the text in Photocopiable worksheet 3.2. Tell students to work in pairs to match the two halves of each sentence (which have been split in the middle of useful collocations). As a follow-up, students can test themselves (or each other) by folding the worksheet vertically so that only the left-hand column is visible. The challenge is then to remember the rest of the sentence.

**Answers**
**1** b  **2** d  **3** a  **4** g  **5** c  **6** e  **7** f  **8** m
**9** i  **10** l  **11** h  **12** j  **13** n  **14** k  **15** q
**16** r  **17** o  **18** u  **19** p  **20** t  **21** s

---

## 7 Writing: Summarising

Ask students if they have ever had to write a summary as a lawyer. Discuss with them a) why lawyers need to be able to write summaries, and b) if there are any techniques for writing an effective summary. Make a note of any such techniques on the board. Then tell them to read the information in the box to compare it with their ideas. When they have read the information, ask them if they agree with it.

---

**Optional extension**
To practise finding the main sentence in a paragraph, tell students to work in pairs to find the main sentence in some of the paragraphs in Reading 2. Each pair can work on two or three paragraphs. Point out that there is not always a clear answer, but that simply hunting for the main sentence can be a good starting point in writing a summary.

---

**Suggested answers**
Paragraph A  *Can shareholders exercise ... ?*
Paragraph B  *They have no right ... company.*
Paragraph C  *As outsiders, ... information.*
Paragraph D  *Where there are obstacles ... ownership rights.*
Paragraph E  *In Germany, ... (supervisory tier).*
Paragraph F  *Co-determination rules ... management board.*
Paragraph G  *Obviously, it allows ... constraining management.*

Go through the answers from each pair, and then ask the whole class to identify any important distinctions or contrasts which form the framework of the ideas.

**Suggested answers**
The important distinctions can be summarised in this table:

| Anglo-Saxon system | Germanic system |
| --- | --- |
| One-tier board (includes managers, appointed by controlling shareholders) | Two-tier board (executive board plus supervisory board) |
| Shareholders (other than controlling shareholders) effectively prevented from influencing management. | Supervisory board oversees and disciplines management and resolves conflict with shareholders. |
| Bad strategic decisions subjected to the public gaze. | Bad strategic decisions internalised. |

The writing can be set as homework or done in class. See Writing section, page xiv.

 **Suggested answer**
Dear Mr Fraser
Thank you for your email of 26 September, in which you request information concerning the two-tier corporate management system found in German-speaking countries.
I understand you are interested in investing in a German company and would therefore like to have a clearer idea about how this system differs from the one you are familiar with here in England.

Allow me to provide a brief explanation of how the two systems differ. In the German two-tier system, in contrast to the Anglo-Saxon one-tier system, there is an executive board and a supervisory board. The executive board consists of the top management, and the supervisory board includes outside experts and executives from other corporations, as well as employee-related representatives. The supervisory board serves to oversee the management and resolve conflicts between shareholders, managers and employees. Unlike in Anglo-Saxon countries, employees of large corporations in Germanic countries are entitled to elect half of the members of the supervisory board, and so employees have greater representation on the board.

I hope these remarks were of use to you. Please do not hesitate to contact me should you have any further questions.

Yours sincerely

Max Appleby

## 8 Listening B: Plain language

(CD1 T15)

**8.1** Tell students to read the introduction (SB page 41) to find out who the two speakers are and predict what they are going to be discussing. Have students discuss the two questions in pairs or small groups before opening up the discussion to the whole class.

**8.2** Tell students to listen to the recording to answer the questions. After the recording, tell them to check their answers with a partner and then go through them with the class.

**Transcript »** STUDENT'S BOOK **page 281**

 **Answers**
1 False
2 True
3 True
4 False (He says that he has come to see that the fears expressed about plain language and the arguments raised against it are just myths.)

**8.3** Ask students to discuss the three questions with a partner to see what they can remember. Then play the recording for them to check, and go through the answers with the class.

 **Answers**
1 A school of thought that believes that (legal) documents should be written so that they can be understood the first time they are read.
2 Because the language of law is conservative and text based, and has a tendency to stick to tradition.
3 Mr Mansfield says that writing in plain language does not involve abandoning legal concepts and legal terms and replacing them with colloquial expressions, and points out that such terms only form a small percentage of any legal document.

**Optional extension**
Use these questions to generate a group discussion.
a What are the features of legalese?
b What do you think of the Plain Language Movement?
c Will plain English ever replace legalese?
d What are the advantages of legalese?
e What are its disadvantages?

**Possible answers**
a See box on SB page 41. Write students' suggestions onto the board, as this will serve as a reference for the rest of the discussion.
c Perhaps plain English will take over from legalese in many situations, but lawyers are unlikely to give up legalese completely.
d Most importantly, it is respected as 'correct' by many lawyers and non-lawyers. From a cynical point of view, it creates the illusion that non-lawyers can never understand the law, and this gives lawyers (and others who use legalese) immense power.
e It is difficult to read and understand, thus preventing non-lawyers (and occasionally lawyers too) from understanding what they are signing. From a client's point of view, this is increasingly unacceptable.

# 9 Text analysis: Understanding legalese

Tell students to look at the box on SB page 41 to compare it with their ideas. For each bullet point, ask a discussion question:

**a** Are lengthy/complex questions essential for legal writing?

**b** What do each of the archaic words and expressions mean? Can you think of any more?

**c** What are the advantages and disadvantages of using passive rather than active voice?

➡ **Suggested answers**

**a** Defenders of legalese argue that paragraph-length sentences are less likely to be ambiguous, and referring devices within a sentence (such as *therein*) are more specific than referring devices between sentences (such as *this*). However, a skilful writer should still be able to construct unambiguous short sentences. What is more, a badly constructed long sentence is likely to be much more ambiguous than a short one. For example, in the sentence *The basis of the conversion and the terms upon which such conversion may be made, which must be approved by a majority of shareholders, may be changed by the Corporation*, it is not clear whether the relative clause (underlined) refers to both *the basis* and *the terms*, or to *the terms* alone.

**b** See language note below.

**c** The advantage is that there is no need to mention the agent (= the person or thing which did the action), perhaps because the agent is unknown, irrelevant or concealed. The passive also allows the agent to be moved away from the beginning of a sentence, which is especially useful if it is long or complicated. The disadvantage is that passive is less natural than active, and can be more difficult to understand. It is also longer.

🖊 **Language notes**

○ Words formed with *here–* refer directly to the piece of writing (e.g. *Unless otherwise provided for herein* (= in this contract)) or to the time of writing (e.g. *Access will hereafter* (= after now) *be denied to unauthorised persons*).

○ Words formed with *there-* refer to any other document, action, event, etc. (e.g. *He has missed the deadline and thereby* (= by doing that) *forfeited his right of first refusal.*).

○ Words formed with *where–* are used in relative clauses (e.g. *They were not guilty of the crime whereof* (= of which) *they had been accused.*).

○ *Such* means 'of that kind' (e.g. *You are not permitted to disclose any confidential information, and any such action* (= any action of that kind) *shall result in immediate dismissal.*)

○ *Said* and *same* both mean 'the one just mentioned', but *said* is used as an adjective (i.e. modifying a noun), while *same* is used as a pronoun (i.e. replacing a noun): *The document was drafted by a lawyer. Said document is therefore the work product of such lawyer and can be withheld by same.* (Source: http://www.utexas.edu/law/ faculty/ wschiess/legalwriting/2005/06/bringing-back-some-classic-legalese.html). Note that there is no *the* before *same*.

○ *Aforesaid* is similar to *said*, but it means 'the one mentioned earlier'.

**9.1** Before students read the excerpt in legalese, discuss the meanings of the words in these Language notes.

🖊 **Background notes**

○ *provisions* = clauses or stipulations in an agreement

○ *stated capital* = Also known as the legal capital, this is the capital that, by law, must remain in the company. It is generally equal to the par value of all issued shares.

○ *aggregate par value* = the sum of all the par values

○ *consideration* = in common law (contracts), something of value given in exchange for an act or promise. In this case, the consideration is likely to be money. See page 83 for more information on consideration.

○ *cumulative dividends* = dividends which are accumulated if the company fails to pay the necessary dividends for a given payment period (e.g. a financial year)

Tell students to work in pairs or small groups to read and discuss the excerpt. Point out that they have to identify two things: passive verbs and archaic words. You could also ask them to identify examples of lengthy/complex sentences. In this exercise, they do not need to find other features of legal English (e.g. *shall*) or financial English (e.g. *par value*).

 **Suggested answer**

NB Passive constructions, including reduced forms (e.g. *issued shares = shares which have been issued*) are underlined. Archaic words and expressions are *italicised*. Especially lengthy or complex sentences are boxed.
(1) The maximum number of shares of stock of the Corporation that may be issued is 25,000 of which 5,000 shares shall have a par value of $50 each and 20,000 shares shall be without par value.
(2) The stated capital of the Corporation shall be at least equal to the sum of the aggregate par value of all issued shares having par value, plus the aggregate amount of consideration received by the Corporation for the issuance of shares without par value, plus *such* amounts as, from time to time, by resolution of the Board of Directors may be transferred *thereto*.
(3) The shares shall be divided into preferred, to consist of 5,000 shares having a par value, and common, to consist of 20,000 shares without par value.
(4) The holders of the preferred shares shall be entitled to cumulative dividends *thereon* at the rate of 6 per cent *per annum* on the par value *thereof*, and no more, when and as declared by the directors of the Corporation, payable semi-annually on the first days of January and July in each year.
(5) *Such* dividends shall cumulate on *such* payment dates and no dividends shall be paid to, or set apart for payment to, common shareholders unless all past cumulated dividends on the preferred shares shall first have been paid, or declared and set apart for payment.

(6) All remaining profits which the directors may determine to apply in payment of dividends shall be distributed among the holders of common shares exclusively.

---

**Optional extension**
As you go through the answers with the whole group, discuss ways of making the legalese plainer.
a  Could the passive verbs become active (in which case, what would be the subject)?
b  What do the archaic terms mean/refer to?
c  Could the long/complex sentences be split into shorter/less complex sentences?

**Suggested answers**
a  In some cases (e.g. *the stock that may be issued*), active voice would be possible (i.e. *the stock which the corporation may issue*), but the sentence is not necessarily clearer or more accurate. In other cases (e.g. *the holders of the preferred shares shall be entitled to cumulative dividends*), there is no logical agent who grants this entitlement, so active voice would not really work.
b  *such amounts* = the amounts specified in the rest of the sentence; *transferred thereto* = transferred to this total; *dividends thereon* = dividends on these shares; *the par value thereof* = the par value of these shares; *such dividends/such payment dates* = those stated in paragraph 4.
c  In a contract there would seem to be little to be gained from splitting these lengthy sentences. They could certainly be simplified, however, especially if the aim is to explain them to a client (see Exercise 10 on the next page).

---

**9.2**  Do this quickly as a whole class.

 **Answers**
○ *such amounts*: those amounts or any amounts
○ *such dividends*: these dividends or dividends of this kind
○ *such payment dates*: these payment dates or the payment dates mentioned

**9.3**  Again, do this quickly as a whole group. Point out that the answers use a mixture of *them*, *it*, *that* and *a particular place or thing*.

This has nothing to do with the actual *there-* words, but will vary according to context.

**Answers**
**1** c  **2** b  **3** a  **4** e  **5** d  **6** f

**Language note**
*There-* words almost always immediately follow the noun phrase which they refer to. The choice of *there-* word is usually simply a question of knowing which nouns have which dependent prepositions (if any). For this reason, students of legal English need to be aware of noun + preposition patterns (e.g. *an amendment to something, an increase in something*). This information should be included in any good dictionary. To give a simple example, the sentence *All agreements and any amendments to those agreements must be approved by a majority of shareholders* can be shortened to *All agreements and any amendments thereto must be approved ...*
Occasionally *there-* words are not formed from dependent prepositions, but from ordinary prepositions of place/time, etc. For example, the sentence *She returned the wallet and the money and credit cards which were in the wallet* could be transformed into *She returned the wallet and the money and credit cards therein*. As the following exercise shows, often the correct *there-* word is far from obvious, and a dictionary is sometimes of limited use. For this reason, there is no substitute for experience and practice. This can be facilitated by keeping notes of unusual constructions whenever students come across them.

**9.4** This exercise would be extremely challenging even for most native speakers, so you should expect some problems. The key is usually to work out the dependent preposition of the preceding noun. You could focus students' attention on the preceding nouns in the exercise by writing them on the board (*increases, deadlines, connection, agenda, conduct, interest*) and telling students to find out their dependent prepositions using a dictionary. The problem is that some of the nouns can have different dependent

prepositions for different functions (*an increase in capitalisation* = the fact that it has increased; *an increase to capitalisation* = the amount by which it has increased; *an increase of 25%; interest on an investment; an interest in sport*). A further problem is that sentence 2 does not require a dependent preposition for *deadlines*, but simply a preposition of place (*deadlines located in the provisions*). Tell students to work alone or in small groups, and then discuss the answers carefully as a whole group.

**Answers**
**1** thereto  **2** therein  **3** therewith
**4** therefor; thereof  **5** thereon  **6** thereof

## 10 Speaking: Paraphrasing and expressing opinions

**10.1** Tell students to cover the example after the exercise. Then go through the instructions to the exercise with the class, using the first sentence from the text in Exercise 9.1 as an example. Focus on the techniques that they might use (e.g. changing passive *shares may be issued* into active *a corporation may issue*, separating the relative clause into a separate sentence with *of these*, etc.). Ask students to predict the sort of problems a client might have with the vocabulary (e.g. *par value*), and how a lawyer could explain such terms. Tell them to compare their suggestion with the example given. Also discuss what sort of client might need to understand this sort of information (e.g. a potential investor or a company planning to issue shares).

Tell students to work in pairs. One should be a client and the other should be a lawyer. If you have an odd number of students, there should be two lawyers in one group. Make sure they agree together who the client is and why he/she needs to understand the excerpt. Tell them to simulate a natural client–lawyer conversation about the excerpt. They should swap roles halfway through (or earlier in groups of three). As a follow-up, you could ask students to write their client-friendly transformation of the excerpt as an email.

**Suggested answers**
NB These explanations would be part of a dialogue, but are given here as a monologue for simplicity.

1 The corporation is allowed to issue up to 25,000 shares. Five thousand of these have a par value of $50. The other 20,000 don't have a par value. (In other words, they're treated as if they were free, but in practice they're worth what the market will pay for them.)

2 The stated capital of the corporation is the capital that, by law, must remain in the company. It's calculated by adding the value of all the shares. For the shares with a par value, that's 5,000 times $50, or $250,000. For the shares without par value, it's simply the money which they were sold for. This is the minimum stated capital, but the Board of Directors can transfer more money if they make a formal resolution.

3 The 5,000 shares with a par value are preferred shares. The other 20,000, which don't have a par value, are common shares.

4 Holders of the preferred shares can receive cumulative dividends of 6% of the par value of their shares every year. In other words, $3 per share per year. They will receive this as long as the corporation's directors declare that the dividends can be paid, half on January 1st and half on July 1st every year.

5 If the payments aren't made on those dates, they cumulate, so they have to be paid off sooner or later. The corporation isn't allowed to make any dividend payments to common shareholders until they've paid all the dividends for preferred shares, or at least set money aside to pay them.

6 Only after paying all the preferred shareholders' dividends can the directors decide to distribute any remaining profits to common shareholders.

**10.2** Tell students to do this alone. You may need to find the first signalling phrase with the whole class as an example. Then go through the answers with the class.

**Answers**
as far as I'm concerned, The way they see it, I think, To my mind

**10.3** Tell students to work alone to complete the phrases. When they have finished, go through the answers with the class.

**Answers**
1 opinion   2 see   3 mind   4 my
5 ask   6 point   7 concerned   8 think
9 seems   10 firmly   11 me   12 would

**10.4** Tell students to work in small groups to discuss the question. Make sure they understand that the purpose of the exercise is to practise the phrases from Exercise 10.3, especially the ones which they do not already use habitually, but they should nonetheless try to speak naturally. Allow around five minutes for the discussion, perhaps using the 'First use' rule (see Games and activities section, page xvi).

## 11 Reading C: New legislation – share capital developments in Bulgaria

Tell students to read through the introduction. Ask them what they understand by the term *share capital* (Suggested answer: the total nominal value of all issued shares – see Teacher's brief page 52).

**11.1** The purpose of this exercise is to read quickly for specific information, a task which lawyers have to do often. You should therefore avoid pre-teaching vocabulary. Tell students to read the text to answer the two questions. Set a time limit (e.g. two minutes). At the end of the time limit, ask students to discuss the questions in pairs, and then check with the whole class.

**Answers**
1 The new law specifies that limited companies only need to have a minimum share capital of BGN 2 (approx. EUR 1).
2 It applies only to limited companies.

**Background notes**
○ In some countries (including Bulgaria), *registered capital* is the total capital contribution of the shareholders that is registered with the relevant government agency.

- The term *liquidation quota* is used in Bulgaria to refer to the share of capital that a shareholder may recover from a company when it is wound up. It is not a recognised legal term in most other countries.
- In many countries, the term *joint stock company* is used as an English translation for publicly traded companies. The actual definition varies from country to country, but in Bulgaria, it contrasts with *limited liability companies*.
- *BGN* is the abbreviation for the Bulgarian currency, the lev.
- *Entrepreneurial* /ˌɒntrəprəˈnɜːrɪəl/ activity here refers to the creation of new businesses. An entrepreneur /ˌɒntrəprəˈnɜːr/ is a person who starts his/her own business or invests in businesses. The concept of entrepreneurship often includes the ideas of creativity, risk-taking and seeing new business opportunities.
- When a creditor lends money to a company, it often requires *security in the company's assets*, i.e. concrete rights in the company's property as a guarantee that the loan will be repaid. See Unit 13.
- *Capital maintenance rules* state that investors may not take their money out of a company again except under certain circumstances. The rules vary from country to country.
- If a rule can be *construed*, it is implied but not stated directly.

**11.2** Go through the five statements with the class to make sure they understand all the words, including *entrepreneur* (see Background note above). Tell students to read the text carefully to decide if the five statements are true or false. Allow at least four minutes for this. After students have discussed their answers in pairs, check the answers with the whole class.

➠ **Answers**
**1** True
**2** False (The study showed that the average sum recovered by a creditor is not dependent on the level of minimum share capital requirement in the country.)
**3** False (It is not possible, because it is mandated by the Second EU Company Law Directive.)
**4** True
**5** True

**11.3** Tell students to discuss the questions in small groups. If this generates some interesting discussion, you could open it up to include the whole class.

**11.4** Students discuss the phrases in pairs and then feed back to the class.

➠ **Suggested answers**
**1** measure of creditworthiness: an indicator of a person's (or in this case, a company's) suitability to borrow money
**2** pecuniary benefits: monetary benefits
**3** is something of an anachronism: in some way seems to belong to another time
**4** the prohibition was relaxed: the prohibition was made less severe or strict
**5** a going concern: a business that is not in danger of going into liquidation in the near future, which is usually considered to be within the next year

**11.5** Tell students to do this alone or in pairs. Then go through the answers with the class.

➠ **Answers**
**1** to **2** from; to **3** by; under **4** in
**5** on **6** by **7** on

---

**Optional extension**
**ILEC preparation: Test of Reading Part 4**
If your students are planning to take the ILEC exam, point out that Part 4 of the Test of Reading requires students to match sentences with paragraphs from a longer text. The sentences contain paraphrases of information included in the paragraphs. While students are doing Exercises 11.1 to 11.5, write these sentences on the board:
**1** Investors may only try to recover the money they have invested if the company is liquidated.
**2** On average, the level of minimum share capital requirement does not affect the amount of money that can be recovered when a company becomes insolvent.

**3** Investors may wrongly believe that a company with high registered capital is more valuable than it really is.

**4** The Bulgarian government is no longer obliged to impose such strict rules on financial assistance.

**5** A high level of minimum share capital requirement discouraged some people from starting new businesses.

**6** The Bulgarian government is not allowed to remove the high minimum share capital requirement for joint stock companies.

Tell students to divide the main part of the text (i.e. excluding the introductory paragraphs) into four sections: Section A (Share capital requirements: paragraph 1), Section B (Share capital requirements: paragraphs 2 and 3), Section C (Prohibition on financial assistance and capital maintenance rules: paragraph 1) and Section D (the remainder of the text). Tell students to work alone to identify which section of the text contains the information in the six sentences on the board. Point out that some sections correspond to more than one sentence from the board. Students discuss their answers in pairs before feeding back to the class.

**Answers**

**1D** (... provisions ... prohibit shareholders from claiming back their capital contributions ... and limit the rights of shareholders ... to dividends and liquidations quotas ...)

**2A** (... the average sum a creditor actually recovers ... is not dependent on ...)

**3B** (... may even be misleading if ... the debtor company has no valuable assets.)

**4C** (... the prohibition was relaxed ... Bulgaria has not yet availed itself ...)

**5A** (This threshold was regarded ... as hindering entrepreneurial activity ...)

**6B** (... it is not possible to abandon this ... because it is mandated ...)

 Tell students to do the Internet activity as homework. See Using the Internet for research on page xviii.

# Language focus

## Answers

**1 Vocabulary: distinguishing meaning**

**1** *dividend*: The others are owned, whereas a *dividend* is a payment.

**2** *conversely*: The others are prepositions; *conversely* is a sentence adverbial (i.e. it links two sentences together).

**3** *discretionary*: The others mean 'compulsory'; *discretionary* means 'optional'.

**4** *suggest*: The others convey a factual relationship; *suggest* is used to present an opinion.

**5** *therefor*: The others are near-synonyms; *therefor* means 'for that'.

**6** *postpone*: The others are permanent cancellations; *postpone* means 'to move to a later date'.

**2 Use of prepositions**

**2** of; from   **3** for; under   **4** in; with
**5** on; by; to   **6** into

**3 Adjective formation**

**2** unlikely   **3** irrespective   **4** illegal
**5** abnormal   **6** unlimited   **7** unrestricted
**8** indirect   **9** informal   **10** incomparable

**4 Word formation and meaning**

**2** f pre-emption   **3** i refusal
**4** d consolidation   **5** g division
**6** c resolution   **7** a diversification
**8** b amendment   **9** h reliance

**5 Understanding legalese**

We wish you a Merry Christmas and a Happy New Year!

Try to avoid analysing the language used as this will spoil the joke. As a follow-up, you could ask students to write a similar paragraph for other well-known phrases such as 'Happy birthday!', 'Wish you were here' or 'I love you'.

**Optional extension**
**Photocopiable worksheet 3.3**
Divide the class into two groups, the lawyers and the clients. Hand out the role cards on Photocopiable worksheet 3.3. Give students time to work in their groups to prepare for a major meeting, and then put the two groups together for the meeting. Set a time limit in advance (e.g. 15 minutes). Take notes of any interesting language problems, but make sure you also give feedback on the effectiveness of the meeting in terms of successful and appropriate communication.

# 4) Company law: fundamental changes in a company

## Teacher's brief

This unit deals with those changes in company structure which are of particular relevance to lawyers, as they are potentially controversial and tend to be tightly regulated by law. These include **liquidation** (whether ordered by a court or instigated voluntarily by the company itself) and **constitutional amendments** (such as an amendment to change the company's name or its capital structure). One such constitutional amendment is the focus of Listening B and Reading C: increasing the **authorised share capital** of a company, which must be approved by the company's existing shareholders.

The most important fundamental changes to companies involve buying other companies (or being bought). Three ways of buying a company are mentioned in Reading A: acquisition of controlling shares, merger, and sale of substantially all assets. In an **acquisition of controlling shares**, the acquiring company (acquirer) has control over the acquired company (target), but the two remain distinct legal entities. A **merger** is similar in that it involves buying shares, except that the acquired company ceases to exist as a distinct legal entity. A **sale of substantially all assets** does not involve shares, but rather the company's assets (including property, equipment and intangible assets such as trade marks of brands). In theory, the seller could survive with no assets, but it is most likely to be **wound up** (liquidated).

The difference between a true merger and a sale of assets (a **de-facto merger**) and the way this affects the **rights of a shareholder** to block the transaction forms the background to Reading D.

The terms *merger* and *consolidation* are likely to cause some problems: in everyday English *merger* is often taken to involve 'a merger of equals' (e.g. http://en.wikipedia.org/wiki/Merger): two companies becoming one new company with a new name. In corporate law / legal English, this is a *consolidation*. Similarly, the legal English term *merger* is often described in everyday English as an 'acquisition' or 'takeover'. Note that this difference is reflected in the choice of prepositions: while in everyday English we talk of *a merger between X and Y*, *a merger of X and Y* or *X has merged with Y*, in legal English we see *a merger of X into Y* or *X has merged into Y*. Obviously lawyers need to use the correct terms, but they should also be aware of potential misunderstandings.

As well as these major fundamental changes, the unit includes an article (Reading B) on another change: **spin-offs**, which occur when a single company becomes two (or more) separate entities.

Lawyers are closely involved in such fundamental changes, working both with the companies undergoing the changes (e.g. advising on legal requirements, drawing up legal documents, dealing with legal obstacles to the changes) and with the other parties who may be affected by the changes (e.g. advising on the legality of the changes and whether they can be prevented or overturned). Listening A features a presentation by a lawyer advising a group of business owners on the legal aspects of the process of acquiring a company. The lawyer focuses on the important procedure known as **due diligence**: collecting and analysing financial and other information about a company before acquisition. This is a common and time-consuming task for many lawyers, and is an attempt to ensure that the **acquiring company** is buying what they think they are buying, and that there are no hidden secrets about the **target company**.

The unit also presents and practises several major communication skills which lawyers regularly need: they will learn some useful language and techniques for **beginning a presentation**, for **writing a formal letter** (in this case, a **letter of advice**) and for **explaining a procedure** (in this case, how to use a **checklist** of actions to be taken and documents to be filed in the process of increasing a company's share capital). They will also work with the **minutes of a meeting** (an official record of the proceedings).

### Further information

○ A good starting point for information on **mergers and acquisitions** is http://en.wikipedia.org/wiki/Merger, which has links to articles on many of the key terms from this unit.

○ For a very informative article on the **relative power and rights of majority and minority shareholders in the UK**, see http://www.law-office.demon.co.uk/art%20minority-1.htm.

○ There are many **legal checklists** for mergers and acquisitions, as well as hundreds of other documents and resources for lawyers and law students, at http://www.practicallaw.com/ 8-103-0969. This is a subscription service.

○ An invaluable source for **useful phrases for presentations** is the book *Dynamic Presentations* (Mark Powell, Cambridge University Press, 2010).

# Discussion

Use these questions to generate a discussion.

a   What types of changes in companies involve lawyers? (Try to steer the discussion towards some of the seven structural changes listed in Exercise 1 below.)

b   Can you think of some well-known companies which have changed in these ways? (Obviously this will depend on the types of change generated in question 1, but you might expect some well-known examples such as: BP (merger with Amoco, then renamed, so BP no longer stands for British Petroleum); Daimler Chrysler (Daimler Benz bought Chrysler); Philip Morris Companies (renamed Altria Group); TWA (acquired by American Airlines and then disappeared in 2001); AOL Time Warner (merger); Gillette (bought by Procter & Gamble); and ABB (consolidation of the Swedish company Asea and the Swiss company BBC).

c   What role do lawyers play in these processes? (Avoid supplying the answers, but if necessary you could suggest some 'obvious answers' including: advising companies before, during and after such changes; drawing up and managing all the legal documentation; and advising shareholders on the impact of such changes on their investments and what steps they can take if they want to resist the changes.)

## 1   Reading A: Introduction to changes in companies

Tell students to work in pairs or small groups to match the key terms with the definitions. Then tell them to read the text to check their answers and to find out more about the seven types of change. When they have finished, tell them to cover the text and discuss with a partner what they remember about each of the changes. Then go through the answers with the class, relating the seven changes to the first two discussion questions above.

**Answers**

**1** d   **2** b   **3** e   **4** c   **5** f   **6** g   **7** a

## Background notes

○ A *petition to the court* (explanation (a)) is a formal written request. It is distinct from a *complaint*, which asks for damages and/or performance.

○ The *objects* of a corporation (explanation (d)) are its stated aims and objectives.

○ A *controlling interest* (explanation (e)) is the ownership of enough shares of stock to control company policy.

○ Paragraph 2 of the text contains a verb in the subjunctive (*a resolution that the name of the company be changed*), i.e. the infinitive form of the verb (here, *be*) instead of the present simple (*is*). This is commonly used in legal English, especially in clauses introduced by *that*. It is a way of referring to an event without asserting that it is true (i.e. if you say *I demand that he go*, you are not claiming that he goes or that he went, but referring to an imaginary/ potential event). In colloquial English (especially British English), the subjunctive is usually replaced by *should* + infinitive (*a resolution that the name of the company should be changed*) or, more commonly, *to* + infinitive (*a resolution to change the name of the company*). There are many more examples of the subjunctive in Reading C.

○ *At common law* (paragraph 4) refers to a historic time before this aspect of the legal system was codified (through statutes) in common-law jurisdictions such as England or the USA. See http:// en.wikipedia.org/wiki/Common_law.

## Pronunciation notes

alter /ˈɔːltəʳ/
unanimous /juːˈnænɪməs/

## 2 Key terms: Opposing concepts in company law

**2.1** This exercise can be done quickly with the whole class. For each concept, elicit its counterpart (NB you may need to check that all students understand the term *counterpart*).

 **Answers**
**1** acquired company  **2** friendly takeover
**3** target  **4** voluntary liquidation
**5** insolvent

**2.2** Tell students to work in pairs. They should take turns to contrast two of the concepts using one of the three prepositions given. Do the first one with the whole group as an example.

 **Suggested answers**
**1** In a merger, the acquiring company survives, unlike the acquired company, which disappears.
**2** In contrast to a hostile takeover, a friendly takeover takes place with the approval of management.
**3** Unlike the acquirer's shareholders, the target's shareholders are invited to sell their stock.
**4** A court may order a compulsory, as opposed to voluntary, winding-up.
**5** In contrast to a solvent company, an insolvent company may be wound up by a court.

## 3 Listening A: Explaining legal aspects of an acquisition

Tell students to read through the introduction (SB page 50) and discuss with the class what they think the lawyer might talk about in his presentation.

**3.1** Ask students to predict the answers to the three questions. Check they understand the vocabulary (e.g. *overview, staffing, prospective*). Then tell them to listen to the recording to check their predictions. After the recording, tell students to compare their answers in pairs. Check the answers with the class.

**Transcript »** STUDENT'S BOOK **page 282**

 **Answers**
1 c  2 c  3 b

**3.2** Tell students to work in the same groups to predict whether they think the six statements are true or false. Check they understand some of the words (but avoid explaining *due diligence* and *warranty*, as these are explained in the recording).

 **Background notes**
- ◯ *Due diligence* literally means 'a fair attempt or reasonable care or attention to a matter'. In legal English, it has come to refer to the process of gathering information before a fundamental change in a company (see Teacher's brief on page 68).
- ◯ *To verify* is to affirm something formally or under oath.
- ◯ *Intellectual property* refers to products of the intellect which have some commercial value, such as patents, business methods or industrial processes.
- ◯ A *warranty* is a written statement of assurance.
- ◯ *To attest to* something is to confirm that it is genuine, typically in writing.
- ◯ *Indemnities* are actions whereby someone is compensated fairly for what they have lost or is protected from (i.e. insured against) any such past or future losses.

Then tell students to listen to the second part of the presentation to check their predictions. (While students are listening, you may write the

additional comprehension questions (see below) on the board.) At the end of the recording, tell students to compare their answers in pairs. Check the answers with the class.

**Transcript »** STUDENT'S BOOK **page 282**

 **Answers**
1 False (They have to be done in the proper order.)
2 True
3 True
4 False (The person conducting due diligence needs to look at contractual obligations with suppliers, but there is no need to terminate them.)
5 True
6 True

**3.3** Tell students to discuss the questions in pairs. After a few minutes, open up the discussion to include the whole class. Try to elicit stories of mistakes made during the due-diligence process, or of problems caused or solved by warranties.

 **Suggested answers**
1 Many lawyers report that due-diligence investigations are one of the least glamorous parts of the job, often requiring the lawyer to spend days, weeks or even longer going through huge amounts of paperwork. In addition to the work being very boring and tiring, there is a lot of pressure on the lawyer to stay alert and not to miss anything.
2 Warranties save time during the negotiation and acquisition, as (to some extent) buyers can base their decisions on the promises made by the sellers, and therefore do not need to check, for example, every asset or employee. If a discrepancy appears after the acquisition, the buyer has solid grounds to sue the seller. Of course, it is better to identify problems beforehand, in order to avoid conflicts later. Furthermore, the seller may be out of business by the time the problems become known. Also, the warranties need to be very carefully worded for them to be of value.

Write these questions on the board.

1   What are the two stages of the acquisition process?
2   What two things need to be scrutinised carefully in preparation for an acquisition?
3   Who is responsible for making sure this process is done properly?
4   What four things does the lawyer say must be done in the course of due diligence?
5   What will provide a level of comfort about the deal?
6   What are some of the warranties that the lawyer mentioned?
7   What sort of indemnity does the lawyer mention?

Ask students to work in small groups to remember / work out the answers. Check the word *scrutinised*, as the word *scrutiny* is used in the recording. Play Part 2 a second time for them to check. Allow them a chance to compare their answers in groups before going through the answers as a class.

**Answers**

1   The due diligence stage and the deal stage.
2   The company's assets and liabilities.
3   Company directors.
4   (a) Obtain proof that the target business owns key assets, (b) get the details of legal cases, (c) look at likely or future contractual obligations with employees, customers and suppliers, and (d) consider the impact that a change in ownership may have on existing contracts.
5   Confirmations and commitments from the seller.
6   Warranties with respect to the business's assets, the order book, debtors and creditors, employees, legal claims and the business's audited accounts.
7   An indemnity for unreported tax liabilities.

## 4   Text analysis: Beginning a presentation

Ask students if they have ever had to give a presentation in English. If they have, ask what their presentations were about and how easy or difficult this was. Ask students to remember what the lawyer did at the beginning of his presentation. Focus on the functions (e.g. introducing himself

and his topic) rather than the actual words he used. Tell them to read the introduction on SB page 51 to compare their list of functions with that in the book.

4.1   Tell students to work in pairs to work out what words or phrases are missing from each fragment of the presentation. Make sure they realise that they may use up to three words per space and that some phrases are incomplete (indicated by ellipses).

Tell students to listen to Part 1 a second time to check their predictions. Play the recording once (or twice if necessary), and allow students to check their answers in groups before going through the answers with the class.

 **Answers**

**1** to introduce myself   **2** I'm with the
**3** be speaking about   **4** going to tell
**5** interrupt me   **6** overview of   **7** few comments on   **8** deal with   **9** discuss
**10** have time for   **11** move on to
**12** conclude with   **13** discussion

 **Language note**

Note that *will* and *going to* are treated interchangeably in this situation. Also, point out the use of *should* in sentence 5 as a formulaic alternative to *if*.

4.2   Tell students to work individually to match the phrases with their functions quickly. Go through the answers with the class.

 **Answers**
**a:** 1, 2
**b:** 3, 4, 6, 7, 8, 9, 11, 12
**c:** 5, 10, 13

This language will be practised in a personalised context after Reading B. For some controlled practice at this stage, write only the missing words from Exercise 4.1 on the board. Tell students to close their books and to work in pairs or small groups to take turns to try to remember the whole introduction, using only the 13 answers as prompts.

## 5   Reading B: Spin-offs

Ask students if they have ever heard of 'spin-offs', and get them to predict what spin-offs might be.

Avoid confirming or rejecting their suggestions. Ask them to read the introduction and discuss the question quickly as a class. (Possible answer: Website articles are better than nothing, but they are no substitute for a face-to-face explanation from a lawyer.)

**5.1** Tell students to read the question quickly, and then to read the text to answer it. Set a time limit (e.g. two minutes) and at the end of the limit, ask them to discuss their answer in pairs. Then discuss the question as a class.

> **Suggested answer**
> A spin-off is *any distribution by a corporation to its shareholders of one of its two or more businesses* (paragraph 1).

**Background notes**

○ It might be worth reminding students of the irregular verb *spin-spun-spun*. The noun is formed from the hyphenated infinitive of the phrasal verb: *a spin-off*. The adjective is formed from the hyphenated past participle: *a spun-off company*.

○ A *gain* refers to an increase in the value of an asset or property. Most gains are subject to capital gains tax. In the example in the text, without Section 355 the company would have to pay capital gains tax on any difference between the original value of the shares and their value at the time of the distribution. The receiving shareholders would also be subject to capital gains tax in that the shares represent new capital for them. In fact, the value of shares in the distributing company should fall by roughly the value of shares in the spun-off company, so neither the distributing company nor the shareholders should be significantly better or worse off, which is why perhaps it is unfair to tax them.

**Pronunciation notes**
accomplish /əˈkɒmplɪʃ/
deferred /dɪˈfɜːd/
entrepreneurial /ˌɒntrəprəˈnɜːrɪəl/
incompatible /ɪnˌkəmˈpætəbl/
separate (*verb*) /ˈsepəreɪt/

**5.2** Answer this question quickly with the whole class.

> **Answers**
> **a** 4 **b** 3 **c** 1 **d** 2

**5.3** Tell students to read the text again quickly to find the answers to the questions. You could also set an additional question: *What are the various types of spin-off?* (Answer: Three types of spin-off are mentioned: pro-rata spin-offs, non-pro-rata spin-offs (= split-offs) and split-ups.) When they have finished reading, tell them to work in small groups to discuss the questions.

> **Answers**
> **1** When two businesses have become incompatible; when investors and lenders only want to provide capital to one business operation, not all; when owner-managers have different philosophies; in the case of publicly held companies, when the stock market would value the separate parts more highly than combined operations; and when the separation of business operations could lead to a greater drive for success.
> **2** Code Section 355 permits a spin-off to be accomplished without tax to either the distributing corporation or the receiving shareholder.

## 6 Speaking: Presenting a spin-off

**6.1** Tell students to read the email to find out what they are expected to do. When they have finished, elicit the points which must be included in their presentations (Answer: What a spin-off is; the rationale behind the planned spin-off; the fact that it will not affect the shareholders negatively). Tell them to spend a few minutes alone planning the beginnings of their presentations, using as many of the useful phrases from Exercise 4.1 as they can. Remind them that they should think about who the presentation is for and what they want to achieve.

**6.2** If you have a small class (up to around six students), you could ask each student to give the beginning of a presentation to the rest of the class. To make it more challenging, tell them that they are not allowed to read, but may only use notes. This will go some way towards simulating the stress (or the thrill) of presenting to a large audience. With larger groups, it may be impractical for all students to give their presentations, although you could still ask several of them to present to the class. The others should present to each other in smaller groups. Give feedback on students' performance (and elicit feedback from the audience).

 **Suggested answer**

Good evening, ladies and gentlemen. It's good to see that so many of you were able to attend my presentation this evening. Some of you may know me already, but allow me to introduce myself. My name is John Daniels. I'm with the Mergers and Acquisitions department of our firm. Right. As you know, I will be speaking about spin-offs this evening, specifically about the spin-off my client is planning, and how it will affect shareholders like yourselves. I'm going to tell you why the spin-off is being done and why you have no reason to be concerned. Please feel free to interrupt me at any time, should you have any questions. OK, at this point, I'd like to give you a short overview of my presentation. I'm going to start out with a few remarks on what spin-offs are and what different types of spin-off exist. Then I'll deal with the issue of how spin-offs affect shareholders, including a look at IRS Section 355, which is much more exciting than it sounds because it means that nobody has to pay tax on capital gains associated with the spin-off. After this, I will discuss the process of spinning-off a subsidiary. I think we'll have time for a short break then. After the break, I'll move on to the spin-off my client is planning, which I will deal with from both a commercial and a legal perspective. At the end, I'll conclude with a look at how the deal itself will affect you personally, and why I think it is in both your interest and the company's. There'll be time for discussion at the end ...

**Optional extension**

There is no need to limit yourselves to the introduction to the presentation. If you think students would enjoy (or benefit from)

continuing, you could ask them to prepare the rest of their presentations as homework. Alternatively, students could work alone or in small groups to prepare an introduction or a full presentation on their own area of expertise. Obviously you will need to think about whether all students should perform their presentations during the following lesson, or whether to save some for a later lesson.

(CD1 T18) **7 Listening B: A checklist**

Use these questions to generate a discussion with the class.
a   What is a checklist?
b   Why are they useful?
c   Have you ever used one?

 **Answers**
   a   See introduction on SB page 53.
   b   They are a good way of making sure all procedures are followed and the necessary documents are drawn up. They show the order of the steps in the process.

**7.1**   Tell students to read through the introduction (SB page 53) and the three questions. Make sure they do not look ahead to Exercise 7.2, as this will give them some of the answers. Tell them not to write the answers down, but simply to listen to the recording and remember the answers. Play the recording once, and then tell students to work in small groups to discuss the three questions, together with any other information they can remember from the dialogue. Check the answers quickly with the class.

**Transcript »** STUDENT'S BOOK **page 282**

 **Answers**
   1   They are discussing an increase in a company's share capital.
   2   A board meeting and an EGM
   3   Three: the ordinary resolution, the notice of increase of nominal capital and the amended memorandum

**7.2** Tell students to look through the checklist in pairs to remember or work out what the missing words might be. Point out that they can use up to three words in each space, and that they can ignore the right-hand column, as this is for the lawyer to tick the steps as he goes through. When they have had a chance to discuss the checklist, tell them to listen again to check their answers and fill in the remaining spaces. Play the recording. Let them compare their answers in groups again before going through them with the class, checking any vocabulary issues that arise.

> **Answers**
> **1** share capital **2** Determine the amount **3** a board meeting **4** directors **5** pass a resolution **6** short notice **7** chairperson **8** a simple majority **9** within 15 **10** nominal capital

> **Background notes**
> ○ A *quorum* /ˈkwɔːrəm/ is the minimum number of people required so that business can be carried out.
> ○ If you *convene* /kənˈviːn/ a meeting, you arrange it formally.
> ○ An *extraordinary general meeting* (EGM) is a special meeting of a company's directors and its shareholders which can be called by company directors or anyone with at least 10% of the voting rights of the company's shares. A resolution must be approved by 75% or more of the shareholders.
> ○ An *ordinary resolution* is a determination of policy by the board of directors of a corporation, which may then be put to the shareholders for approval.
> ○ A *proxy* is written authorisation by a shareholder that someone else can vote for him.
> ○ A *simple majority* means more votes than any of the alternatives. It contrasts with an *overall majority*, which means more votes than all of the alternatives put together, and an *absolute majority*, which means more than 50% of all eligible votes (including abstentions).
> ○ If you *lodge* a document with an organisation, you register it by delivering it to that organisation.

# 8 Language use A: Explaining a procedure

Tell students not to look at their books. Elicit from them (a) the words the experienced lawyer (Rob) used to show the order of the steps (NB you may need to give *firstly* as an example), and (b) the structures he used to indicate necessity (again, you may give *you have to* ... as an example). Then tell students to read the information in the Language use box on SB page 55 to compare it with their suggestions. Finally, check that students all understand the differences between the various expressions indicating necessity.

> **Language notes**
> ○ In this context, *must* and *have to* are broadly equivalent, in that the actions they describe are equally necessary, although *must* carries the suggestion of *don't forget!* or *be careful!*, while *have to* suggests simply *do this*. (The client is unlikely to forget to call a board meeting, but they might forget some of the things which must be stated on the notice.)
> ○ *To be required* and *to be necessary* are also broadly equivalent, suggesting that a law or procedure requires something. Note that *somebody or something is required to do something*, but that *it is necessary that something happens* (or *happen*[1]).
>
> 1 This is another example of the subjunctive. See Background note on page 69.

> **Optional extension**
> Tell students to work in pairs or groups of three. They should re-enact the dialogue from Listening B, using the checklist and the Language use box to help them. If you have an odd number of students, the third student in a group can be another experienced lawyer.

Tell students to work in small groups. They should read the instructions to the exercise and then write their checklist. If they are not experienced lawyers, this may prove difficult for them. You could offer some ideas for their checklists (such as the procedure for setting up a new company or for drafting a contract) and tell them to invent any facts that they do not know. The purpose is to practise the language of checklists, not to test their knowledge of legal procedures. A light-hearted alternative would be to use the useful phrases to make an official-sounding checklist for an everyday procedure such as making breakfast or going shopping.

When they have written their checklists, tell them to work with different partners to present their checklists, and to take notes about their partners' checklists. When one partner has presented a checklist, the other partner(s) should use their notes to report back on the steps in the process.

## 9 Reading C: The minutes of a meeting

**9.1** Tell students to read the introduction on SB page 55 and the two questions. Discuss the questions as a whole class.

**⇒ Answers**
1 The company secretary usually writes the minutes of a meeting.
2 In his or her role as corporate counsel, a lawyer often has to read such texts to make sure everything has been carried out in accordance with the relevant statutes.

You could develop the discussion by using these questions:
a What is the point of keeping minutes at meeting?
b Does the company secretary need to have good knowledge of the law and legal language?

**⇒ Suggested answers**
a In many situations (e.g. directors' meetings), they are a legal requirement. They provide a written record of what decisions were made and what was discussed by whom. They are a valuable source of information for those who did not attend the meeting, and even for those that did, they are much more reliable than memories. They provide focus in that attendees are forced to follow the agenda and to reach concrete decisions, rather than simply discuss. Even if the minutes are not accurate reflections of what was said, if the attendees accept them, they in effect become the truth.

b It certainly helps, but as long as the person is competent and honest, and the minutes accurately describe the proceedings of the meeting, thorough knowledge is not necessary.

**9.2** Tell students to read the minutes to answer the two questions. Set a time limit (e.g. two minutes) and at the end of that limit, tell students to discuss the questions in small groups. Then go through the answers with the class.

**⇒ Answers**
1 The board meeting was called to vote on the allotment of shares (increase authorised share capital).
2 The EGM was convened to authorise the directors to increase the company capital, allot the shares and disapply the requirements of s89 Companies Act 1985.

**Background notes**
○ An *allotment of shares* means 'the distribution or assignment of shares to applicants'.
○ *Respectively* (here) means that Smith applied for 10,000 shares, Bean applied for 20,000, and Sharp applied for 20,000.
○ *Pursuant to* something means 'in accordance with something'.
○ *To disapply* an act means 'to act as if the act did not apply'. For example, Section 89 (= *s89*) of the Companies Act 1985 grants *pre-emption rights* (the right of existing shareholders to buy additional shares in a new issue before it is offered to the general public). In some circumstances, shareholders may agree to disapply their rights. For an interesting analysis of this possibility by a major investor, see http://www.dti.gov.uk/ cld/report_pdfs/barclays.pdf.
○ A *common seal* is a seal used by a corporation to show that a document is validly executed.

**9.3** Tell students to read the minutes again carefully to answer the questions. You may need to check that they understand subsequent to (= after). You could help slightly by telling them how many resolutions (three) and steps (five) they need to find, although they could argue that some of the steps listed below contain several parts. When they have finished reading, tell them to compare their answers with a partner. Check the answers as a class.

**Answers**

**1** a) That the applications for the allotment of shares be approved subject to their approval of the extraordinary general meeting.
  b) That the notice be approved to hold an EGM.
  c) That the application by the members for additional shares be accepted and that the capital of the Company be allotted to the applicants on the terms of the application.
**2** a) Entering the names of the applicants in the register of members of the Company as the holders of the shares allotted.
  b) Preparing share certificates in respect of the shares allotted.
  c) Arranging for the common seal to be affixed to the shares.
  d) Arranging for the share certificates to be delivered to the applicants.
  e) Preparing and filing with the Registrar of Companies Form 88(2) (return of allotments) in respect of the allotment just made; Form 123 (increase of capital); and the special and ordinary resolutions in connection with raising capital for the Company.

**9.4** You could brainstorm this with the whole group, starting with the reporting verbs that were used, and leading into other reporting verbs which might be used in legal documents. Draw a grid on the board with rows for some structures which often follow verbs (see opposite). You will probably need to explain the use and form of the subjunctive (see Background note on page 69), using examples from Reading C to illustrate (paragraph 2: *It was resolved that their applications* **be** *approved*; paragraph 10: *It was resolved that the application ...* **be**

accepted and that the capital of the Company **be** allotted ...). Get one of the students to be the group secretary and to write the suggested verbs in the appropriate rows of the grid. When students have run out of ideas, check whether the verbs are in the correct rows and perhaps elicit some more (see below). Remind students that if the reporting verb is in a past tense (e.g. past simple), the reported speech should also be in a past tense, using so-called back-shifting rules (so that *will* becomes *would*, *has* becomes *had*, *did* becomes *had done*, etc.). However, this is probably not a good time for an in-depth analysis of the rules of reported speech.

**Answers**

| | Reporting verbs from the text | Other common legal English reporting verbs |
|---|---|---|
| Verb + 'something' | to propose (s7) to declare (s3) | to acknowledge to assert to clarify to deny to explain to pledge to state |
| Verb + *that*-clause | to confirm (s1) to note (s3) to report (s4, s5, s9) | to acknowledge to agree to allege to assert to claim to declare to explain to state to submit |
| Verb + 'somebody' + *that*-clause | to inform (s6) | |
| Verb + subjunctive *that*-clause | to resolve (s2, s7, s10) | to propose to suggest |
| Verb + *to*-infinitive | to propose (s4) to agree (s7) | to pledge to resolve to undertake |
| Verb + 'somebody' + *to*-infinitive | to instruct (s7, s11, s12, s13) | |
| Verb + other structures | | to inform sb of sth |

# 10 Language use B: Collocations

**10.1** Tell students to work alone to underline the collocations of *meeting* and *resolution* in the text. Do the first as a group as an example. Make sure students notice passive verbs using *meeting* and *resolution* as the grammatical subjects. When they have finished, check that all students have found the same number of collocations for *meeting* (seven) and *resolution* (five) before collecting these as a class.

 **Answers**

- ○ to give notice of a meeting (*notice of the meeting had been given*) (s1)
- ○ to be present at a meeting (*was present at the meeting*) (s1)
- ○ to present something to a meeting (*Applications were presented to the meeting / There was presented to the meeting*) (ss2, 7)
- ○ to propose a resolution (*resolutions would be proposed*) (s7)
- ○ to hold a meeting (*the meeting be held immediately / to enable the extraordinary general meeting to be held*) (ss7, 8)
- ○ to adjourn a meeting (*The meeting was adjourned*) (s8)
- ○ to resume (*meeting* = subject) (*The meeting resumed at 8 p.m.*) (s9)
- ○ to set out a resolution (*the resolutions [which had been] set out*) (s9)
- ○ to pass a resolution (*the resolutions ... had been duly passed*) (s9)
- ○ to prepare a resolution (*The Secretary was instructed to prepare ... the special and ordinary resolutions*) (s13)
- ○ to file a resolution (*The Secretary was instructed to ... file ... the special and ordinary resolutions*) (s13)
- ○ to close a meeting (*the meeting was closed*) (s14)

**10.2** Tell students to work in pairs to decide which verbs can collocate with which of the two nouns. Point out that several can be used with both nouns. When most groups have finished, go through the answers as a class, checking the meaning of the verbs as you go through.

 **Answers**

meeting: arrange, attend, call, cancel, convene, preside at, schedule, summon
resolution: adopt, authorise, draft, endorse, introduce, oppose, pass, table

💬 **Pronunciation note**

schedule /'ʃedjuːl/ (UK), /'skedʒuːl/ (US)

---

**Optional extension**
**Photocopiable worksheet 4.3**

The text contains several examples of grammar which is sophisticated and/or typical of legal documents. For example, there are many examples of the subjunctive (see Background note on page 69).

Tell students to close their books. Hand out Photocopiable worksheet 4.3, which contains simpler versions of some of the sentences from the text. The changes all relate to grammar structures and some legal constructions such as *subject to* and *pursuant to*. Students have to transform these back into the original 'sophisticated' version, using the framework provided for each question.

The exercise may be too difficult for weaker classes, as it assumes existing knowledge of grammar structures such as passive voice and reported speech. Divide the class into small teams. For each sentence, go round the class eliciting from each team one word from the transformed sentence. If the word is correct (and in the correct form), tell the class where it should go in the sentence. If the word is wrong, that team gets a penalty point. At the end of the game, the team with the fewest penalty points is the winner. Finally, discuss a) what is strange or sophisticated about each sentence, and b) why the writer has chosen this structure over a simpler version.

**Answers**

1. The Chairperson confirmed that **notice of the meeting had been given to** all the Directors of the Company.
   a Passive voice and reported speech.
   b Passive voice avoids the need to identify who did what, only that something was done. Reported speech is much more formal than direct

speech, which would not normally be found in legal writing.

2 It **was resolved** that **the applications be approved**, subject **to the approval** of the extraordinary general meeting.

   a Passive voice. Note that the dummy subject *it* is used to avoid using a *that*-clause as the subject and that *to resolve* can be followed by either a *to*-infinitive or *that* + something + a verb in the subjunctive (i.e. the same as the infinitive, here *be*). Also note the phrase *subject to*.

   b Passive voice as in question 1. The subjunctive has been chosen to make the structure less personalised: if somebody *resolves to* do something, they will do it themselves. If they *resolve that* something be done, it is not specified who will do it.

3 **It was** noted that Debra Smith and Anna Bean **had declared** their interests in the shares **pursuant** to s317 Companies Act 1985.

   a Passive voice with dummy *it* and reported speech. Also note the phrase *pursuant to*.

   b Passive and reported speech as in question 1; dummy *it* as in question 2.

4 The Chairperson reported that **it was proposed to increase** the authorised share capital of the Company to 50,000.

   a Passive voice with dummy *it*. Reported speech.

   b Passive and reported speech as in question 1; dummy *it* as in question 2.

5 There **was presented to** the meeting **a notice of** an EGM **at which** resolutions **would be proposed** to implement **the above proposals**.

   a Passive voice (*was presented, would be proposed*). Use of the dummy subject *there*. Reported speech (*will* → *would*).

   b Passive voice and reported speech as in question 1.

*There* allows a lengthy subject to be moved away from the beginning of the sentence. Without it, we would have the very clumsy *A notice of an EGM at which resolutions would be proposed to implement the above proposals was presented to the meeting.*

6 **It was resolved that** the notice **be approved**, that the Secretary **be instructed** to send it to all the members and the auditors of the Company, and, subject **to all the members agreeing** to short notice, that the meeting be held immediately.

   a Passive voice (*was resolved, be approved, be instructed, be held*), including with dummy *it*. *To resolve that* + something + subjunctive. *Subject to* + somebody + verb + *–ing*.

   b Passive as in question 1; dummy *it*; subjunctive and *subject to* as in question 2.

7 **It was resolved that** the application by Debra Smith, Anna Bean and Andrea Parker for 10,000, 20,000 and 20,000 shares **respectively be accepted** and that the capital of the Company **be allotted to** the applicants **on the** terms **of** the application.

   a Passive voice (*was resolved, be accepted, be allotted*), including with dummy *it*. *To resolve that* + something + subjunctive. Also note the phrases *respectively* and *on the terms of*.

   b Passive as in question 1; dummy *it* and subjunctive as in question 2.

8 There **being no further** business, the meeting was closed.

   a Use of participle clause to replace *because* (*Because there was ...*). *There + [be] + no/any further* business is a fixed expression, typical of meeting agendas and minutes.

   b *Because* is seen as unsophisticated.

## 11 Reading D: Shareholder rights

**11.1** Tell students to read the introduction and the two questions. Tell them to read the letter quickly to answer the questions. Set a time limit (e.g. two minutes). At the end of the time limit, tell them to discuss the questions in pairs. Then go through the answers with the whole class.

**Answers**

1 It is a letter of advice.
2 The query it responds to is whether it would be possible to set aside the transaction described in the letter on the basis of the shareholder's rights.

**Pronunciation notes**
determine /ˌdɪ'tɜːmɪn/
doctrine /'dɒktrɪn/
mere /mɪə<sup>r</sup>/
query /'kwɪəri/

**11.2** Tell students to read the letter again to decide whether the four statements are true or false. When they have finished, tell them to discuss their answers in small groups. Then go through the answers as a class. Check all students have understood the term *appraisal rights*, which is explained in the fourth paragraph.

**Answers**

1 False (He did not vote, but there is no mention of his not being allowed to vote. He argues that the transaction should be set aside because he was not afforded any appraisal rights.)
2 False (In a true merger, the statutes do provide these rights, but in a de facto merger such as this one, no such rights are provided.)
3 True
4 True

**Optional extension**
Tell students to read through the letter again slowly a) to identify and underline typical expressions which are used in legal English but rarely in everyday English, and b) to circle any useful formulas for letters to clients, especially letters of advice. Then go through the letter with the whole group to collect all the answers. Point out that this is a very effective way of building their legal English vocabulary, as long as they take steps to learn the useful language. You may also want to point out that the letter is written in American English (indications are the full stop

after *Mr* in the greeting (*Dear Mr. Fitzwilliam*), the use of double quote marks (*the "Target Corporation"*), putting the month first in dates (*October 1*), use of *–ize* spelling (*Reorganization*)).

**Suggested answer**
Some important legal English expressions are in **bold**. Students may find many more. Some phrases are paraphrased into everyday English in *italics*. Formulas for writing are boxed.
Dear Mr. Fitzwilliam
You have requested advice regarding your rights as stockholder in Alca Corporation (the "Target Corporation") which **entered into** a stock for assets **agreement with** Losal Corporation (the "Purchasing Corporation"). The advice and statements **set forth** below are based on the facts you presented to me in our telephone conference of January 27. This advice should be viewed **in light thereof** [= *in the light of that*] and remains **subject to** future discovery and research.
The facts are as follows: you are a stockholder in the Target Corporation. **On or about** October 1 last year, the Target Corporation and the Purchasing Corporation **entered into** a Reorganization Agreement **by which** the Target Corporation agreed to sell all its assets to the Purchasing Corporation **in consideration for** 350,000 shares of the Purchasing Corporation's stock. The Target Corporation called a stockholders meeting to approve the Reorganization Agreement and the voluntary dissolution of the Target Corporation **upon** distribution of the shares to the Target Corporation's stockholders. As I understand it, the stockholders meeting approved the plan, 70% **of all stockholders voting** [= *and 70% of all stockholders voted*]. You did not vote at the meeting. Your query to me is whether it is possible **to set aside** the transaction based on your rights as a stockholder.
Generally, a stockholder's rights in a merger situation are **twofold**. First, the stockholder has the right to approve or disapprove the agreement. Second, the stockholder **holds an appraisal right**, which means that he is entitled to **have an independent appraiser determine** what his shares are worth [= *to have the value of his shares determined by an independent appraiser*]. **The aforesaid provides** the stockholder **with** assurance that

the Purchasing Corporation is not getting a discount on the shares. As I understand it, you were not **afforded** any appraisal rights. The difficulty **in the instant case** is that the transaction is not a "true" merger **but rather** a sale of assets in exchange for shares. In the latter case, strictly speaking, the statutes do not provide the shareholder appraisal rights. However, it might be argued that due to the fact that the transaction **at issue** achieved the same results as a merger, the court should look at **the substance of the transaction rather than its form** in order to protect your rights as a shareholder. In essence, the argument is that a "**de facto**" merger has taken place and that you should be entitled to the same rights **as if** a "true" merger had taken place. If the court **finds in your favour**, the transaction could then **be set aside as being in violation of the applicable statutes**. Although I consider the argument above to be **persuasive**, I doubt whether the courts of this jurisdiction will **accept** it. The **doctrine of** de-facto merger is widely accepted in many other **jurisdictions** for the reasons I have set forth above. However, **in this jurisdiction**, the courts have been **hesitant to take a position**. In addition, in one particular case, Heil vs. Star Chemical, the court, **although not addressing** [= *although it did not address*] exactly **the same situation as in this case**, referred to the fact that the **provisions governing** merger and the sale of all the assets in a corporation are separate **and should be treated as such**. The **mere** fact that they overlap does not change the **legislative intent**. In summary, you have an **argument**, but in my opinion your chances are slim. It will most likely take an **appeal** to win, as I suspect the trial court will not **stray from the reasoning established** in the Heil case. Hence, as your **attorney I would suggest that** you take [= *I think you should take*] a look at your options from a financial perspective and **make a determination** as to whether it is worth it. As always, I remain at your disposal **should you wish to** [= *if you want to*] discuss your options. I look forward to hearing from you and answering any further questions you may have.

**11.3** Go through this exercise quickly with the whole class. Elicit from students the context in which each expression was used in the text.

 **Answers**

> 1 e  2 a  3 d  4 c  5 b

**11.4** Tell students to work in small groups to discuss the question. If this generates some interesting differences of opinion, you could open up the discussion to include the whole class. As further discussion, ask students if they have ever written a letter of advice. If they have, ask them how careful they have to be in terms of accuracy, why this is so important in such a letter, and what would happen if they made a mistake.

## 12 Writing: Standard phrases for opening and closing letters and emails

Tell students to read through the phrases in the box and decide which of them were used in the letter of advice (Reading D) (Answer: Only the last, although the writer did also use an expression with *should you ...*).

**12.1** If you have already done the optional extension exercise above, you can go through these questions quickly with the whole class.

 **Answers**

> 1 You have requested advice regarding your rights as stockholder in Alca Corporation (the "Target Corporation") which entered into a stock-for-assets agreement with Losal Corporation (the "Purchasing Corporation").
>
> 2 The advice and statements set forth below are based on the facts you presented to me in our telephone conference of January 27.
>
> 3 As always, I remain at your disposal should you wish to discuss your options. I look forward to hearing from you and answering any further questions you may have.

**12.2** The writing can be set as homework or done in class (see Writing section, page xiv). Encourage students to use some of the formulas and other useful expressions from Reading D.

**Suggested answer**

Dear Mr Louis

I am writing in response to your query of 12 September in which you request information regarding the board meeting and extraordinary general meeting of Longfellow Ltd which were held on 10 September. I will summarise the circumstances under which the meetings were convened, as well as the resolutions passed.

As you may know, a board meeting was held to determine whether new shares could be issued to certain existing shareholders in the company. The proposal, which would raise the share capital of the company by 50,000, was presented to the board. However, as the charter of the company did not grant authority to raise share capital in this manner, a notice of an extraordinary general meeting was presented, containing the details of the proposed increase in share capital. The board approved the notice, and it was forwarded to all of the members, including yourself, for consent to the short notice of the extraordinary general meeting. The board meeting then adjourned to allow for consents to the short notice to be obtained and to hold the extraordinary general meeting.

The extraordinary meeting was then held after consents to the short notice were obtained from all the members, and the meeting approved all of the resolutions in the notice.

Based on the authority provided by the approval of the extraordinary general meeting, the board raised the share capital of the company through the issuance of the 50,000 new shares. The company secretary was then instructed to take care of all the administrative matters related to the increase and the meeting was closed.

I hope that the information I have provided meets your requirements. Should you have any further questions, do not hesitate to contact me.

Yours sincerely

Ann Walsh

 Tell students to do the Internet activity as homework. See Using the Internet for research on page xviii.

# Language focus

## Answers

1 **Vocabulary: distinguishing meaning**

1 *cancel*: The others refer to temporary stops; *cancel* is permanent.

2 *related to*: The others mean 'in accordance with'.

3 *liable*: The others mean 'not liable'.

4 *contend*: The others collocate with *meeting*.

5 *add on*: The others mean 'start again'.

6 *relevant*: The others refer directly to something mentioned earlier in the same document.

2 **Vocabulary: definitions**

2 d  3 a  4 b  5 g  6 e  7 f  8 c

## 3 Word formation

| Verb | Abstract noun |
|------|---------------|
| di<u>str</u>ibute, dis<u>tri</u>bute | distri<u>bu</u>tion |
| merge | <u>merger</u> |
| <u>re</u>gulate | regu<u>la</u>tion |
| sub<u>mit</u> | sub<u>miss</u>ion |
| ap<u>prove</u> | ap<u>prov</u>al |
| con<u>so</u>lidate | consoli<u>da</u>tion |
| ac<u>quire</u> | acqui<u>si</u>tion |
| <u>li</u>quidate | liqui<u>da</u>tion |
| <u>can</u>cel | cancel<u>la</u>tion |
| <u>al</u>ter | alter<u>a</u>tion |

## 4 Language use: verbs plus prepositions

**2** preside at   **3** dispose of   **4** complied with
**5** entered into

## 5 Language use: fixed phrases

(to) reduce share capital

(to) pass (an) ordinary resolution

(to) follow proper procedures

**Note:** This exercise is rather difficult. You may help students by pointing out that each of the four expressions consists of a verb followed by either an adjective + noun or a compound noun (noun + noun).

## 6 Vocabulary: word formation

**2** undertaking   **3** merger   **4** transformations
**5** reconstructions   **6** alteration
**7** amalgamation   **8** union/uniting

## 7 Vocabulary: antonyms

**2** f   **3** h   **4** d   **5** g   **6** b   **7** c   **8** a

---

**Optional extension**
**Photocopiable worksheet 4.4**

As a final exercise, divide the class into four groups of roughly equal size. One group, the company directors, is going to hold a meeting with the second group, their lawyers (corporate counsel). The third group, the shareholders, is going to have a meeting with the fourth group, their lawyers. If you have an odd number of students, add an extra lawyer to one of the groups. Copy Photocopiable worksheet 4.4 and hand out the role cards. Give students time to read their cards, then tell them to work in two groups (directors + corporate counsel, and shareholders + their lawyers) to discuss their options. When they have finished their discussions, set up a major meeting involving all four groups. You will need to decide with students who is going to chair the meeting, and what they are trying to achieve. Allow up to ten minutes for each part of the role-play.

If you have a small group (between one and three students), you will have to run the two lawyer–client meetings separately, and students will have to change roles. If you have one student, you should play the client. With three students, there should be two lawyers and one client in each role-play. The final major meeting will have to be replaced by a group discussion.

Take notes of any interesting language problems, which you can address after the role-play, but make sure you also give feedback on the effectiveness of the meetings in terms of successful and appropriate communication.

# Case study 1: Company law

## The facts of the case

Tell students to read the description carefully to identify the legal issue. When they have finished, discuss the answer with the class.

 **Answer**
The legal issue is whether the two directors acted in breach of their duty of loyalty to the company by taking advantage of a corporate opportunity for their own private gain.

Ask the group these comprehension questions to make sure they have fully understood the facts of the case.

1 What do you know about Greenview?
2 What is the name of the country?
3 Where was the piece of land which was available for sale?
4 Why did the directors and stockholders of Greenview discuss buying the land?
5 Why did Greenview not buy the land?
6 Who bought the land?
7 What happened a few years later?
8 Who profited from the joint sale of the two pieces of land?
9 Why are the stockholders *disgruntled* (= discontented/angry)?

 **Answers**
1 A public company which owned a golf course
2 Westland
3 Next to (= *adjoining*) the company's golf course
4 It would have greatly increased the value of the golf course, perhaps by making it a more suitable size or shape, or by improving access.
5 We do not know. We can speculate that the directors and stockholders were not convinced of the suitability of the investment, or their offer to the seller was not sufficiently attractive. It is possible that the two directors who later

bought the land used their influence to dissuade the company from buying it. See note below.
6 Two Greenview directors acting as private individuals.
7 Greenview sold its golf course, and the two directors sold their land to outside investors.
8 Both the two directors and Greenview. Each piece of land was worth more as part of the package than it would have been alone.
9 Because they feel the two directors stole a corporate opportunity from the company.

 **Note**
The outcome of the case will depend to some extent on whether the two directors somehow 'engineered' Greenview's failure to buy the plot of land. For the sake of simplicity, it may be best to agree with the class that this did not happen (or at least, that there is no evidence that this happened).

## Task 1: Role-play

1 Divide the class into two equal-sized groups, one for shareholders and one for the directors. With large classes, you may decide to have more groups (e.g. four groups of five students rather than two groups of ten). If you have only one or two students, this part of the case study should be done as a discussion, rather than a role-play. If you have one student, you should play one of the roles in step 2.

Tell students to work through the bullet points in their groups. This will involve both speaking (as in a role-play) and reading the relevant legal documents. Encourage them to delegate responsibilities so that, for example, each student reads and reports back on a different text. Monitor closely to help with any vocabulary problems that they cannot resolve within their groups. Set a time limit (e.g. five minutes) so that both groups are ready at the same time.

2 This step can be done in pairs or in small groups. Before the role-plays start, make sure everyone knows that the objective is to negotiate a settlement, rather than to precipitate a costly court case. Again, set a time limit so that all the groups finish at the same time.

3 Discuss the results of the negotiations with the class, and provide feedback on students' strengths and weaknesses in terms of both negotiation skills and language use. Discuss whether similar laws apply in students' own jurisdictions.

## Task 2: Writing

Remind students that Unit 2 contains useful information for writing a letter of advice. The writing can be done at home or in class. (See Writing section, page xiv.)

 **Model answer**

Dear Mr Kim,

**Re. *Greenview minority shareholders v. Kim and Sanders***

In accordance with your instructions, I have reviewed the above-referenced file and can advise as follows. Please note that all the advice stated in this letter is conditional and subject to further investigation.

Based on the available facts, it appears that there is one fundamental issue of law involved in this case. Specifically, the issue involved is whether you and Mr Sanders breached your fiduciary duty of loyalty as directors in Greenview ("Company") by personally taking advantage of a business opportunity of the Company. Based on my review of the law and facts, there is good reason to find that you and Mr Sanders have indeed breached this duty of loyalty. I clarify below.

The relevant law regarding corporate directors' duty of loyalty in Westland is contained in two separate legal provisions. The first is Section 202 of the Westland

Corporations Act, which states in principle that directors must act honestly and in good faith in accordance with the best interests of the company. The second provision, Section 5.05 of the Westland Principles of Corporate Law, is a guideline for interpreting the Corporations Act and states in relevant part that acting in the best interest of the company includes a duty of loyalty to refrain from taking advantage of business opportunities belonging to the company. When applying these two provisions, the court looks first at whether the "opportunity" actually existed. In other words, there is a determination of whether the opportunity was within the area of business of the Company. If the court concludes that there is an actual business opportunity involved, it then moves on to determining whether the relevant director was in some way justified in taking advantage of the opportunity which was in the Company's line of business.

Applying the facts involved to the first part of the stated test logically leads to the conclusion that the purchase of the land adjoining Greenview's golf course was within the line of business of Greenview. In fact, you learned of the availability of the adjoining land through your duties on Greenview's board, and the purchase of the property was discussed at the highest levels within Greenview.

Under the second part of the test, you might be able to justify your actions. In some cases, for example, the courts have found justification based on the fact that the company is incapable of taking advantage of the opportunity. However, there does not appear to be any facts which would support this justification or, for that matter, any other justification. The fact that the Company was aware of your purchase of the land and agreed to sell the property with you as a package is significant. However, in my opinion, it does not justify the purchase in and of itself, particularly in light of the fact that you and Mr Sanders made a considerable profit on the sale. Of course, if you wish we can take this to trial. However, my recommendation at this stage is to approach the shareholders with a settlement offer (with this approach, you and Mr Sanders may be able to salvage part of your profits). Please provide me with instructions at your earliest convenience.

Sincerely

Astrid L. Newton

Attorney-at-Law

## Relevant legal documents

○ **Text 1** is an excerpt from a Corporations Act, which is a piece of legislation governing corporate law. See http://laws.justice.gc.ca/en/C-44 for an authentic version of such an act (in this case, for Canada).

○ **Text 2** is an excerpt from a publication, *The Westland Principles of Corporate Law*, rather than a piece of legislation. The information in the publication is useful as an authoritative – but not legally binding – guideline, and is based on a combination of legislation and case-law precedents.

○ **Text 3** is an excerpt from a textbook. The *doctrine of corporate opportunity*, mentioned in the excerpt, is a genuine doctrine (= a legal principle based on historical precedents). See http://caselaw.lp.findlaw.com/scripts/cases/clcc.html?court=nd&vol=20010313&invol=1 for a definition and notes for an authentic case involving this doctrine.

 **Language notes**

○ Points a–d in Text 2 may cause comprehension problems because they involve complicated relative clauses, including some structures that would be impossible in other languages (and therefore may make no sense to speakers of those languages). A much easier way of understanding these four points is if the preceding sentence becomes *A corporate opportunity is a business opportunity if*, and the phrase *such an opportunity* is inserted in points a–d (i.e. *... becomes aware of such an opportunity ...; ... is offering such an opportunity to the corporation ...; ... be interested in such an opportunity; ... knows such an opportunity is closely related ...*).

○ Text 3 contains the verb *further* (= to promote, to help the progress of). Students may struggle to understand the sentence if they do not realise that *further* can be a verb as well as a comparative adjective.

# 5 Contracts: contract formation

## Teacher's brief

A famous formula, quoted in Reading A, is **offer** + **acceptance** + **consideration** = contract. In other words, if party A offers to do something for party B, and if party B accepts party A's offer, and if party B has given (or promised to give) something valuable in return (**consideration**), they have an **enforceable** (legally valid and binding) contract. A contract is enforceable if the courts can force the parties to abide by it.

The common-law term **consideration** is the least transparent and most controversial of the three essential elements. It is often money, but the term covers everything that is of value to the parties. Both parties provide consideration for the other party. For example, party A may agree to sell a farm (= consideration) in exchange for party B's million dollars (= consideration). Party C may agree to provide clerical work (= consideration) in exchange for food and shelter from party D (= consideration). Consideration may even be something as abstract as a reduction of free choice (for example, a footballer may be paid by a sportswear manufacturer not to wear a rival manufacturer's products). Confusingly, there are two theories of consideration (see http://en. wikipedia.org/wiki/Consideration), both of which may be used in court to argue that a particular contract is or is not valid. There are also nine rules of consideration in English law (see http:// en.wikipedia.org/wiki/Consideration_under_ English_law), each of which has exceptions. An important difference between civil law and common law is that in civil-law jurisdictions, a promise does not need consideration in order to be enforceable. In civil-law jurisdictions such as Mexico (see http://www.mexicolaw.com/LawInfo03.htm), there must be an **object of the contract** (or a **cause of the contract**) i.e. the thing promised to be given or the act promised to be (not) performed. This is not exactly the same as common-law consideration, which requires that both parties give something of value.

It is important to realise that, at least in common-law countries, the term *contract* covers much more than the formal legal documents that are headed by the word 'Contract'. A contract may take the form of any written agreement or a series of letters or even a conversation (an **oral** contract), provided the three essential elements are present (**express** contracts). A contract may even exist where the three elements are implied by the actions of the parties, even if no conversation takes place and no documents change hands (for example, a man who parks his car in a private car park has entered into an **implied contract** with the car park's owners to pay their fees).

As regards other countries, Japanese contracts, for example, do not even require explicit statements of an offer, acceptance and consideration (see http://www.answers.com/topic/ law-of-japan). On the other hand, it is common in other jurisdictions to place much more emphasis on traditional express written contracts. The idea that a contract of employment can be an oral contract (as in the USA: see for example http:// www.timslaw.com/contracts.htm#oral) may surprise lawyers from other jurisdictions.

Contracts are notoriously difficult for non-lawyers to understand. One of the most important things to note about contracts is that they usually contain many 'standard clauses' covering such themes as confidentiality and the circumstances under which the contract may be terminated. Lawyers learn to expect such clauses and can therefore have a good idea of what they will say without even reading them. The Text analysis section of this unit introduces ten **common clause types** and provides examples.

Lawyers often use **templates** to help them draw up new contracts. These are also commonly called 'forms', 'precedents', 'standards' or 'standard form precedents'. In some cases, it may be possible simply to insert a few details such as names, dates and numbers into such a template, rather than creating each contract from scratch. Reading B presents such a template, in this case for a **covenant not to compete**. This covenant (= a specific type of promise in a contract) is part of a transfer of ownership of a business from one corporation to another. According to the covenant, the seller of the company agrees not to use his/

her knowledge and contacts to compete with the business once it has changed hands for a given period of time. All the most important points (what the business is, how much it is being sold for, etc.) are covered in a separate document, the Asset Purchase Agreement.

Reading C presents a more complex and typical use of contract templates, where substantial changes need to be made to the template, in this case part of a **franchise agreement**.

The skill of **negotiating** is an important theme of Unit 5. Listening A introduces some **negotiating techniques**, such as **horse-trading** (trading concessions in exchange for concessions from the other party). The presentation includes a reference to **term sheets**, which include the clauses that each party wants to insert into the contract. Listening B then provides an excerpt from a successful negotiation to illustrate such techniques, as well as some useful **language for negotiations**.

Other skills highlighted in this unit are **giving emphasis** during a presentation, structuring and

writing an **informative memo**, and of course reading and **understanding contracts**.

Note that assignment and third-party rights are covered in more detail in Unit 7.

**Further information**

○ There is a clear **overview of contracts** at http://www.law.cornell.edu/wex/index.php/Contracts.
○ There are thousands of **authentic contracts** at http://contracts.onecle.com/index.shtml. The best way to learn to read them is practice.
○ You can download some **free contract templates** from http://office.microsoft.com/en-gb/templates/CT010117245.aspx and http://www.hooverwebdesign.com/business/menu_legal.php. There are also countless websites offering such templates for sale.
○ The **negotiating skills and phrases** from this unit are further practiced and developed in the worksheet *Improve your negotiation skills*, http://peo.cambridge.org/images/improveyournegotiationskills.pdf.

## Discussion

Use these questions to generate a discussion.

**a** In what situations do people need contracts? (Treat this as a brainstorming activity. Some obvious situations are: company formation, sale or lease of property (real estate), recruitment, agreement to supply a product or service, bank loans, franchising, etc. For a very wide range of contract types, with thousands of real-life examples, see http://contracts.onecle.com/type.)

**b** What are the minimum requirements for a contract to be enforceable? (You could lead this discussion by asking how many pages/clauses/words a contract needs to have. In fact, a contract need not be written, and may not even be a formal oral agreement. The minimum requirements, as described in Reading A, are an offer, acceptance and consideration (i.e. usually money or something valuable). This may be different in students' jurisdictions.)

**Background note**
If a contract is *enforceable*, it meets the minimum requirements for a court to enforce it.

## 1 Reading A: Introduction to contract formation

Tell students to work in small groups to discuss the five questions briefly. You may need to check the difference between elements (e.g. there must be an offer) and terms (e.g. the offer must specify the type and quantity of goods or services being offered). Then tell them to read the text quickly to match the questions with the paragraphs. Allow around two to three minutes for the matching exercise. Then tell students to discuss the questions again in their groups in order to compare the answers in the text to their own opinions. Tell them also to check any words in bold that they are unsure of, first with their partners, and if necessary in the Glossary booklet. When they have finished, go through the answers with the class, and deal with any vocabulary problems that arise.

 **Answers**
**a** 3 **b** 5 **c** 4 **d** 1 **e** 2

**Background notes**

○ *Assignment* involves transferring the rights of the contract to another person.

○ The USA's *Uniform Commercial Code Act* is available online at http://www.law.cornell.edu/ucc/ucc.table.html. For information on the UK's *Sale of Goods Act*, including a link to the Act itself, see http://en.wikipedia.org/wiki/Sale_of_Goods_Act_1979.

○ A *counter offer* is a response to an offer, offering new terms. As such, it is a rejection of the original offer.

○ The *conduct* of the parties is the way they behave. For example, if a customer goes to a hairdresser's and has her hair cut, she can be said to have entered into a contract with the hairdresser to pay the advertised price for that haircut, even though nothing was said or written.

○ An *instrument* is a written legal document, such as a contract or a will.

○ There is a *statute of frauds* in most common-law jurisdictions stating which types of contract must be in writing. This includes not only property, but also marriage, etc. (see http://en.wikipedia.org/wiki/Statute_of_frauds).

**Pronunciation notes**
assignment /əˈsaɪnmənt/
capacity /kəˈpæsɪti/
duress /dʒʊˈres/
fraud /frɔːd/
offeree /ɒfəˈriː/
offeror /ɒfəˈrɔːr/
vague /veɪɡ/

## 2 Key terms: Defences to contract formation

Tell students to work alone or in small groups to match the defences with their definitions. When you go through the answers with the class, discuss briefly whether the same defences exist in students' jurisdictions.

 **Answers**
**1** c  **2** d  **3** b  **4** a

**Background notes**

○ During times of war, an *enemy alien* /ˈenəmi ˈeɪliən/ is a national of an enemy country.

○ If you *induce* /ɪnˈdʒuːs/ somebody to do something, you use your influence to persuade them to do it.

○ *Misled* /mɪsˈled/ is the past participle of the verb *to mislead*.

## 3 Text analysis: Understanding contracts

Ask students if they have been involved in drafting contracts, and what the process involves. Steer the discussion towards the use of templates and forms, and the balance between these tools and the specific nature of each individual contract. Then tell them to read the introduction on SB page 65 to see if it shares their opinions.

**Background note**
In this context, there is no difference between a *template* and a *form*.

**3.1** Tell students to work alone to do the exercise. When they have all matched some of the clauses with their definitions, tell them to discuss any that they are unsure of in small groups. Go through answers carefully with the class, because these definitions are important for the following exercises.

 **Answers**
**1** e  **2** i  **3** d  **4** g  **5** b  **6** h  **7** a  **8** j
**9** c  **10** f

**Background notes**

○ *Damages* refers to the amount of money that a plaintiff may be awarded in a lawsuit. *Liquidated* /ˈlɪkwɪˌdeɪtɪd/ *damages* are one of many types of damages, and are described in a contract. Other types of damages include *special damages* (e.g. money to cover specific costs, such as hospital fees, resulting from the defendant's actions) and *general damages* (e.g. compensation for intangible costs such as pain and suffering or loss of reputation).

○ *Parol* /pəˈrəʊl/ *evidence* is a rule that a contract is a complete document, and that therefore no other documents that contradict it may be used as evidence in a lawsuit. The best way to ensure this is to include an entire agreement clause (or a merger clause).

○ *Consolidated* means 'brought together'.

○ *Severability* means that somebody can sever /ˈsevəʳ/ (cut) something. In other words, if a contract is severable, it means that a breach of one part of the contract does not necessarily entail a breach of the whole contract. The part that was breached can be 'severed', or separated, from the rest of the contract. The remainder of the contract can remain in force despite the breach of one clause.

○ *Ancillary* /ænˈsɪljəri/ *documents* are supporting documents.

**Pronunciation notes**
Force Majeure /ˈfɔːs mæˈʒɜːʳ/
merger /ˈmɜːdʒəʳ/
obligor /ˌɒblɪˈgɔːʳ/
predetermined /ˌpriːdɪˈtɜːmɪnd/
prior /ˈpraɪəʳ/

**3.2** If you have a monolingual class, go through the list with the whole class to discuss the best translation for each of the clause types. If you have a mixed class, ask volunteers from each linguistic background to explain the names of these clauses in their language.

**3.3** Tell students to read through the clauses quickly in order to match them to the clause types. Make sure that they realise that they do not need to analyse the clauses or understand them fully, at least at this stage.

**➡ Answers**
**1** Liquidated Damages **2** Acceleration
**3** Force Majeure **4** Assignment
**5** Termination **6** Entire Agreement /
Merger / Parol Evidence

**Background notes**
○ A person's or company's *credit standing* is their reputation for paying debts, and can be calculated by analysing their history of paying on time or otherwise. It is less official than a *credit rating*, which is provided by an independent company such as Standard & Poors or Moody's.

○ If something is *impaired*, it is damaged. A credit standing might become impaired if a debtor fails to make a payment on time. The precise method of calculation of credit standing and of what would constitute an impairment would usually have to be included in the contract.

○ An *Act of God* is the legal term for natural disasters such as floods, earthquakes, etc.

○ If you *default* on a loan, you fail to make a payment on time.

○ A *covenant* is a legally binding agreement. It typically requires an owner of real property to do (or refrain from doing) something.

○ A *schedule* /ˈʃedjuːl/ (British English), /ˈskedʒuːl/ (American English) is an appendix to a legal document, such as a table of financial data or a list of names and addresses. It will be typed in the same style as the contract. An *exhibit* is also attached to a legal document, and is referred to in the document, but it exists independently of the document, and may well be different in style. For example, a contract might refer to a logo or an architect's plan, and both such documents might be attached as exhibits.

○ If something *supersedes* something else, it replaces it. Note that the alternative spelling, 'supercede', is widely seen as a mistake.

○ In paragraph 6, *respecting* means 'with respect to' or 'regarding'.

○ Below is a plain English guide to the six clauses, which may help students to understand them. The technique of rewriting into plain English is practised, using these clauses as models, in the optional extension activity after Exercise 3.4 on page 91.

1 If the seller breaches the contract, or part of the contract, he/she may have to pay compensation to the purchaser. This clause says that the maximum amount of that compensation is fixed. It can't be more than the value of the delivery that led to the breach of contract (in other words, the price per item times the number of items in that delivery). Of course, the actual compensation might be much less than that, but it can't be more than that.

2 The buyer has a reputation for paying debts on time, which the seller uses to calculate a credit standing for that buyer. If the seller decides that the buyer's credit rating has got worse, for example if the buyer has failed to pay one of the instalments on time, the seller can force the buyer to pay all the remaining instalments within ten days.

3 This clause protects both parties in case something unexpected happens which they can't control. For example, there might be a natural disaster (such as an earthquake), or the government might deny or cancel one of their export licences, or there might be a war. If anything like this happens, the party who is affected doesn't have to pay damages for any failure to pay or deliver on time. The other party isn't allowed to cancel the contract as a result of these unexpected problems. This obviously only applies to deliveries or payments which are directly affected by the unexpected event.

4 The buyer is allowed to assign the agreement to another company if the buyer or the buyer's shareholders own at least 75% of that other company. Apart from this situation, if either party wants to assign the agreement to a third party, they have to get written permission from the other party first.

5 If the operator fails to make the necessary payments, the supplier will give the operator ten days to make the payments. If the operator still fails to make the payments after those ten days have passed, the supplier has the right to cancel the contract. If this happens, the operator loses all the rights he had under the contract, but he doesn't lose his obligations.

6 This agreement is the complete agreement between the parties; no other documents connected with it are valid any more. In other words, all old agreements, promises, representations or documents which are connected with the new agreement have been replaced, and should be ignored from now on.

3.4 Tell students to work in small groups to discuss the words and expressions. Point out that the vocabulary tested here is not the most difficult but perhaps the most essential. This exercise tests students' ability to explain technical language in a non-technical way, as they might have to with a client. When they have finished, discuss the answers with the class, and focus on what makes some explanations clearer than others.

 **Suggested answers**
1 responsibility to pay compensation
2 the party alone can decide
3 carry out later or not at all
4 agreement given before in writing
5 If Operator defaults in performance ...
6 do nothing
7 attachments
8 considered

**Optional extension**
**Photocopiable worksheet 5.1**

Lawyers are often so good at using complicated language that they fail to realise that most non-lawyers do not understand them, and they therefore struggle to explain legal jargon. The exercises in Photocopiable worksheet 5.1 are designed a) to help students understand the six clauses in Exercise 3.3, and b) to introduce some important techniques for making such language less complicated.

Start with a short discussion with the whole class on whether lawyers need to use both very complicated language and very simple language. Discuss which of these is easiest. Ask them if they know any techniques for simplifying complex language, but avoid supplying all the techniques mentioned in Exercise 2 on the worksheet.

1 Hand out Photocopiable worksheet 5.1. Tell students to read the two extracts quickly, and then discuss in small groups any obvious differences between the originals and the paraphrases. Check the answers quickly with the class. Note that question b) is answered fully in Exercise 2, so avoid confirming or rejecting suggestions at this stage.

**Answers**
A is a rewrite of clause 1, and B is a rewrite of clause 4.

2 Tell students to discuss the techniques in pairs or groups of three to find at least one example of each, but point out that one of the techniques is not used. Then discuss the answers with the class.

**Suggested answers**
a   Clause 1's subject was *The seller's liability for damages*. The paraphrase in A starts with *the seller* as subject. In clause 4, the subject *This Agreement* has been replaced in B by *The buyer*.
b   Clause 1's single sentence has been split into two (the second and third sentences of the paraphrase), with three additional sentences to clarify those two sentences.
c   Clause 1 uses two complicated linking structures: *in no case* and *with respect of*. The paraphrase (A) uses *if*, *or*, *that* and *but*.
d   In clause 1, *the original quantity delivered* is an example of a reduced relative clause. It could be expanded into *the original quantity which/that was delivered*. The paraphrase (A) includes a full relative clause: *the delivery that led to the breach of contract*, rather than *the delivery leading to the breach of contract*.
e   In clause 1, *liability for damages* has been replaced in A by *compensation*. In clause 4, *prior written consent* has been replaced in B by *written permission ... first*.
f   Clause 4 has been rearranged. The original started with what *is not* permitted (assignment without consent), followed by the exception. The paraphrase (B) started with what *is* permitted (assignment to a subsidiary,

etc.), followed by the forbiddance of all other cases (*Apart from this situation ...*).
g   Paraphrase A explains the meaning of *the value of the delivery* in the sentence that follows.
h   This technique is not used in these clauses, but some of the other paraphrases below do use it.
i   Paraphrase A begins with background on the concept of *liability for damages*. It ends with further clarification of the *maximum* amount of compensation.
j   Paraphrase A includes the phrases *this clause says that*, *in other words* and *of course*.

3 Tell students to work in small groups to complete the paraphrase. You might decide to do the first as an example. When they have finished, go through the answers with the class.

**Suggested answers**
a   something unexpected happens which they can't control
b   a natural disaster
c   an earthquake
d   the government might deny or cancel one of their export licences
e   there might be a war
f   pay damages for any failure to pay or deliver on time
g   cancel the contract
h   these unexpected problems
i   directly affected by the unexpected event

4 Tell students to work in small groups to arrange the six fragments into a logical order. Note that punctuation has been removed in order to make this more challenging. If students are struggling, point out that there should be three sentences, all starting with the word *if*.

**Suggested answer**
e, a, b, f, d, c
If the operator fails to make the necessary payments, the supplier will give the operator ten days to make the payments. If the operator still fails to make the payments after those ten days have passed, the supplier has the right to cancel the contract. If this happens, the operator loses all the rights he had under

the contract, but he doesn't lose his obligations.

5 Tell students to work in small groups to discuss and rewrite one or both of the remaining clauses (2 and 6). Encourage students to use the techniques suggested. Monitor them as they write, and discuss all the paraphrases with the whole class.

**Suggested answers**
See page 91.

## 4 Reading B: A covenant

**4.1** Tell the class to look at the contract form in order to answer the two questions. Tell them not to read the form at this stage, as this is not necessary to answer the questions. Elicit the answers from the class.

➡ **Answers**
1 A non-competition agreement.
2 Because it is an agreement template.

✏ **Background notes**
○ *Capitalised terms* are those which are consistently written with a capital letter. In this covenant, there are eight: *Covenant, Shareholder, Purchaser, Seller, Purchase Agreement, Business, Closing* and *Agreement*. The capital letter shows that these terms are defined. Some are defined in paragraphs A–F, and we are told (at the end of paragraph A) that the others are defined in the Purchase Agreement. We might imagine the following sentence: *The Shareholder shall not discuss these terms with any other shareholder. Shareholder* refers to the same individual shareholder throughout the agreement who has been defined and named in the agreement. The uncapitalised *shareholder* refers to any shareholder.
○ Paragraph A is potentially ambiguous as to what is actually sold: does "*the Business*" refer to *the ... business owned and operated by Seller* or to *certain assets of the ... business ...*? Fortunately, this will be carefully defined in the Purchase Agreement itself.

○ Paragraphs D and E refer to *time, money and credit. Credit* here refers to borrowing capacity. In other words, the Purchaser has borrowed money and can therefore borrow less for other investments.
○ *Precedent* /ˈpresɪdənt/ is used as an adjective in paragraph F. Here, it simply means 'preceding' or 'before': the Covenant must be completed before the Purchase Agreement can be closed.
○ Paragraph F says that the shareholder must *execute* the Covenant. *Execute* means simply 'sign'.
○ Paragraph 1 mentions *controlling ownership interest (of record or beneficial)*. A shareholder of record is the person named on the share certificate as the owner, but in fact the beneficial owner (= the 'real' owner) may be somebody else. For example, for tax reasons, a shareholder might buy some shares in the name of one of her children, but she has the advantages of being a shareholder. See http://www.investorglossary.com/shareholder-of-record.htm.
○ A *lessee* /leˈsiː/ is a person who *leases* (i.e. rents) something, typically property, from somebody else.
○ Paragraph 2b starts in a very confusing way: it looks as if *the Shareholder shall subject* /sʌbˈdʒekt/ *somebody to something*. In fact *subject* /ˈsʌbdʒekt/ *to* is used as a preposition, here meaning broadly *in accordance with*. In other words, the Shareholder is obliged to keep certain information confidential, as long as he/she isn't going to break any laws by doing so.
○ *Wire transfer* is simply the electronic transfer of funds.
○ A *provision* of an agreement is a clause which states a condition that must be met.
○ *Stricken* is an alternative past participle of the verb *strike*. When *strike* means *hit*, its past participle is *struck*. When *strike* means 'delete', its past participle is *stricken*. In both cases the past simple form is *struck*.

**4.2** Tell students to work alone to read the relevant clauses of the text carefully to identify their type. Make sure they realise that they are looking for the types mentioned in Exercise 3.1. When most of them have finished, check the answers with the class.

➡ **Answers**

Clause 2b: Confidentiality
Clause 3: Consideration
Clause 5: Severability
Clause 6: Payment of Costs

**4.3** Tell students to work in pairs to do the exercise. When they have finished, go through the answers with the class. Point out that the vocabulary tested here is not the most difficult but perhaps the most essential.

➡ **Answers**

**1** to comply with   **2** shall be stricken
**3** ascribed to   **4** commencing
**5** has acquired   **6** contemplated by
**7** shall expend

---

**Optional extension**

**1** Tell students to read the text carefully to decide what information should go in each gap, and to invent some examples to write in the gaps. When they have made some progress working alone, tell them to compare their answers in small groups. When they have finished, discuss the answers with the class.

**Suggested answers**

○ Introduction: gap 1: day and month, e.g. today's date; gap 2: year, e.g. this year; gap 3: somebody's name, e.g. *Cher Holder*; gap 4: a company's name, e.g. *ABC Industries*; gap 5: the relevant jurisdiction of the corporation, e.g. *Delaware*

○ Paragraph A: gap 1: a company's name, e.g. *XYZ*; gap 2: The relevant jurisdiction of the corporation, e.g. *Pennsylvania*; gap 3: day and month, e.g. one month before today's date; gap 4: year, e.g. this year; gap 5: a business's name, e.g. *ABC Chemicals*; gap 6: an address, e.g. *1, Short Street, Littleton*

○ Paragraph C: the name of a branch of industry, e.g. *Chemicals*

○ Paragraph E: same as paragraph C, e.g. *manufacturing chemicals*

○ Paragraph 1, gap 1: a number of years, e.g. *5*; gap 2: a number of miles, e.g. *250*

○ Paragraph 2, gap 1: a type of product or service, e.g. *cleaning chemicals*; gap 2: the name of a place, e.g. *Littleton*

○ Paragraph 3: an amount of money, e.g. *1,000,000*

○ Paragraph 4: a number of months, e.g. *120*

○ Closing paragraph, gaps 1, 2 and 3: date as in introduction paragraph, e.g. today's date; gap 4: Shareholder's signature; gap 5: signature of a representative of the purchasing corporation; gap 6: name of representative of the purchasing corporation, e.g. *Dianne Rector*; gap 7: position of signatory in purchasing corporation, e.g. *Director*

**2** As a further check for students who are unfamiliar with such documents, 'elicit' the following diagram on the board: start by drawing the boxes 'The Seller', 'The Business' and 'The Shareholder', and eliciting the relationships between the three. Gradually add more boxes, and draw arrows for all relationships between them. You may find more relationships than those shown below (e.g. The Shareholder [knows a lot about] the Business, The Shareholder [may not compete with] the Purchaser). Point out that this sort of diagramming technique is a useful way of analysing complex documents.

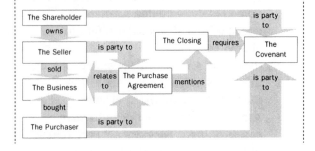

**3** Ask students what the following referring devices refer to.

   **1** ... pursuant /pɜːˈsjuːənt/ *to which* ... (Paragraph A)

   **2** ... capitalized terms used *herein* /hɪəˈrɪn/ ... (Paragraph A)

   **3** ... in consideration of *the foregoing* ... (Before paragraph 1)

   **4** ... the receipt and sufficiency *of which* are *hereby* /ˈhɪəbaɪ/ acknowledged ...

   **5** ... the parties *hereto* /ˈhɪətuː/ agree ...

   **6** ... from the date *hereof* /hɪərˈɒv/ ... (Paragraph 1)

   **7** ... the person entitled *thereto* /ðeəˈtuː/ ... (Paragraph 2b)

   **8** ... on the date *hereof* ... (Paragraph 4)

   **9** ... *such* provision ... (Paragraph 5)

  **10** ... proceedings between the parties *hereto* ... (Paragraph 6)

  **11** ... in connection *therewith* /ðeəˈwɪð/ ... (Paragraph 6)

**Answers**

   **1** ... pursuant *to the Asset Purchase Agreement*.

   **2** ... capitalized terms used *in this Covenant*.

   **3** ... in consideration of *paragraphs A–F*.

   **4** ... the receipt and sufficiency *of the good and valuable consideration* are acknowledged *by stating this sentence* ...

   **5** ... the parties *to this Covenant* agree ...

   **6** ... from the date *of this Covenant* ...

   **7** ... the person entitled *to information* ...

   **8** ... on the date *of this Covenant* ...

   **9** ... *any* provision *which is void or unenforceable* ...

  **10** ... proceedings between the parties *to this Covenant* ...

  **11** ... in connection *with that litigation or those legal proceedings* ...

## 5 Speaking A: Paraphrasing clauses

Ask students to look at the information in the box and the instructions to the exercise, and to decide which of the phrases they would naturally use with such a client. Ask them if they can think of other ways of introducing a paraphrase.

Tell them to work in pairs to take turns to paraphrase the clauses. They should do this orally, as if they were explaining to a client. Tell them to experiment with all six clauses for the exercise, and especially to try to use the phrases they would not normally use. Make sure they realise that they should only paraphrase the second half of the agreement, and that they may use the definitions in Exercise 3.1 to help them explain several of the paragraphs.

When they have finished, discuss some of the best paraphrases with the class.

 (CD1 T19–20)

## 6 Listening A: Negotiating

Use these questions to generate a discussion with the class.

**a** Have you ever taken part in negotiations?

**b** What do you negotiate about?

**c** What makes a successful negotiator?

**d** Do you know any techniques for successful negotiating?

**e** Have you had any formal training in these techniques?

Then tell students to read through the introduction to see if it mentions anything they did not, and if they agree with the comments made.

> ✎ **Background note**
>
> A *contract template* is a contract with gaps, as in Reading B. A *term sheet* is a list of terms (provisions, etc.) which may be added to the contract template during the negotiation.

**6.1** Tell students to read through the exercise, and then to discuss briefly in small groups what the speaker might say about each topic. Then tell them to listen to the recording to tick the topics that she mentions. When you have played the recording, tell students to check their answers in their groups, and then go through them as a class.

**Transcript** » STUDENT'S BOOK **page 283**

 **Answers**

She mentions points 1, 3, 5, 6, 8 and 9.

**6.2** Tell students to discuss what they think the speaker might say about the four questions.

Avoid giving the answers yourself. Tell students to listen in order to answer the questions and also to pay attention to what she says about the topics from Exercise 6.1. After playing the recording, tell students to discuss the questions in their groups. Then go through the answers with the class.

**Transcript »** STUDENT'S BOOK **page 283**

➡️ **Answers**
She discussed two of the topics from Exercise 6.1: *using templates and term sheets* and *general negotiating techniques*.

1 The speaker says it is necessary to review the terms and conditions it contains carefully, as well as to consider what is not in the agreement but should be.

2 The categories she suggests are: things you can't possibly accept, major points, minor points, and things you can easily live without.

3 While bargaining, it means giving up some items in order to get other ones from the other party.

4 The speaker says that negotiators should insist on having such clauses removed. She also says that including a merger clause in an agreement ensures that only what is written in the contract is legally binding.

**Optional extension**
Tell students to listen to the recording again to find all the tips the speaker mentions connected with templates, term sheets, and horse-trading. After you have played the recording, tell students to work in teams to come up with as many tips as possible. Then go through the answers with the class.

This would also be a good opportunity to use the worksheet *Improve your negotiating skills* from Professional English Online: http://peo. cambridge.org/images/ improveyournegotiationskills.pdf.

**Suggested answers**
○ Review existing terms and conditions.
○ Take the time to consider 'what is not in the agreement but should be'.

○ Consult with a senior attorney who has reviewed, negotiated and enforced many variants of the agreements you are negotiating.
○ Keep good notes of all communications when discussing the items on the sheet.
○ Make sure that the information on the sheets is what has been agreed on by all parties.
○ Take care not to include language originally in the template that is not appropriate.
○ Separate the issues at stake into different categories in your mind:
deal-breakers, major points, minor points and 'give-ups'.
○ Make trades with the other side, one item for another.
○ If possible, let the other side throw out the first number.
○ Know the number you want to wind up with and throw out a starting number that will force the other side to return with a number that, when combined with your starting number, will average out to the number you want and suggest meeting halfway by averaging them out.
○ If the other party says 'We're not going to hold you to that, so just leave it in', insist that it be taken out.
○ Be aware that the people involved in making the agreement can all one day be fired or move on to another company, and so their promise not to hold you to something is worthless.

## 7 Language use A: Giving emphasis

Tell students to read the information in the box and to think of further examples of this type of phrase. Collect a few examples from the class. (See below for examples.)

Tell students to work alone to underline the emphasising phrases. You may help a little by telling them to find five such phrases. Tell them to compare their answers with a partner, and then collect the five answers from the class.

○ It's important to realise that negotiating with a contract template means that it's necessary to review the terms and conditions it contains carefully.

○ Please note that you have to consider what is *not* in the agreement but should be, that is, what's missing and should be added.

○ Here, I want to stress that it'd be wise to consult with a senior lawyer, preferably someone who has experience negotiating agreements of the kind that you are negotiating.

○ When using a term sheet as the basis of negotiations, it's imperative to keep good notes of all discussions or emails regarding the items on the sheet.

○ Term sheets are usually used by lawyers to transfer the terms that have been agreed into an official agreement, so it's crucial that the information on these sheets is precisely what has been agreed on by all parties.

Adverbs can be added to:
*It is (particularly) important to realise …*
*Please note (especially) that …*
*Here, I (particularly) want to stress that …*

---

**Optional extension**
Write the five underlined phrases on the board, together with any more you can elicit from the students (e.g. *It's absolutely vital that …, It's essential that …, I'd like to draw your attention to the fact that …, What you need to remember is that …, One thing you mustn't overlook is …*).
Then tell students to work in groups of three or four to make more such emphatic sentences from the rest of the presentation, as outlined in Exercise 6.1. For example, one group should think about 'dealing with objections from the other side', another should look at 'recognising a good deal', etc. When they have prepared their sentences, one student from each group should give a mini-presentation of the group's tips.

## 8 Writing A: An informative memo

Ask students what a memo is, and what two types of purpose it might have. Then tell them to read the introduction on SB page 70 to compare it with their answers.

**Background note**
For lawyers, a *memo* or *memorandum* is a formal paper document. It may, for example, outline some aspect of the law, clarify a point of law or provide a brief opinion of one or two aspects of a client's case. An external memo is often meant for the client, usually for a group of recipients (such as all legal counsel and management board of the client). An internal memo could be from, for example, a lawyer from one department to a lawyer in another department, explaining results of research or how a certain area of law works. There is a set structure for memos (which law students learn in law school) and they are quite formal (even the internal ones, as these are meant to be kept on file). For advice on writing memos, with examples, see http://cherylstephens.com/professional/communication/Organization.pdf and http://sparkcharts.sparknotes.com/legal/legalwriting/section2.php.

**8.1** Tell students to work alone to do the exercise, then go through the answers with the class. You may discuss some of the explanations (e.g. Should you always list points in descending order of importance? Does there have to be a clear call to action? Does the subject have to be less than ten words long?).

**Answers**
1 d  2 e  3 a  4 b  5 c

**8.2** Tell students to work alone to do the exercise, and to identify how many main points there are. Tell them to check with a partner, and then go through the answers with the class.

## Answers

1 The *To*, *From* and *Date* lines
2 *Subject: In-company seminar on contract negotiations*
3 Paragraph 1 (*As part of* ...)
4 Paragraphs 2 (*We would like* ...) and 3 (*The workshop consists* ...). NB There are four main points: the invitation; the time and place; the content; and the need to attend.
5 Paragraph 4 (*Please let me know* ...)

### Optional extension

Tell students to work in small groups to turn the memo into a template for similar memos. To do this, they should first underline all the useful expressions which could be used in other memos. They should then decide what information needs to go between the underlined sections. Point out that the trick to successful writing is to copy useful phrases from similar pieces of writing, in the same way as a contract uses a template. Then go through their answers with the class.

### Suggested answers

<u>As part of</u> [*something*] <u>we have arranged for</u> [*somebody*] <u>to hold a</u> workshop/ meeting/ presentation/seminar <u>on the topic of</u> [*something*].
<u>We would like to invite</u> [*somebody*] <u>to attend this</u> workshop/meeting/ presentation/ seminar<u>, which will take place</u> [*when/where*]. <u>The</u> workshop/meeting/presentation/ seminar <u>consists of</u> [*something*], <u>followed by</u> [*something else*]. <u>Thus it is imperative that you arrange your schedules so that you can be present for the entire</u> workshop/meeting/presentation/seminar. <u>Please let me know by</u> [*time and date*] <u>by email</u> (*address*) <u>whether you can attend</u>.

**8.3** Tell students to read the introduction on SB page 71 to find out who has written the memo, who asked him to write it, what it is about and why he wants you to read it. Students then work in pairs to discuss the task in pairs. When you go through students' ideas with the class, encourage a range of opinions: there is no single correct list of points to include or ideal way of structuring the memo.

**8.4** Students read the memo quickly to see if the writer's ideas were similar to their own in

Exercise 8.3. They then go through the checklist in small groups, discussing each point in turn and suggesting ways of improving the memo. Afterwards, go through the checklist carefully with the class.

## Suggested answer
### Memorandum

| | |
|---|---|
| To: | All non-senior members of the legal staff of the Mergers & Acquisitions department |
| From: | Lydia Brown |
| Date: | 18 February 2011 |
| Subject: | Summary of important points made in the seminar on contract negotiations |

I have been asked to summarise the most important points made in the seminar on Successful Contract Negotiations held last week at the firm by Mr Tom Boland for those who were unable to attend. I would particularly like to call your attention to three suggestions made by the speaker regarding the careful use of contract templates and term sheets in negotiations:

○ It is especially important to review the existing terms and conditions in the contract template carefully; don't leave any language in the agreement which was originally in the template and which is not appropriate. At the same time it is necessary to think about what is missing from the agreement and should be included.

○ It is advisable to ask a senior attorney who has experience with the type of agreement you are negotiating to look at your agreement and offer any advice, if needed.

○ It is particularly important to keep good notes of all communications about the points in the agreement. The only information on the term sheets should be what the parties have all agreed on.

I hope this summary was of interest to you and I would be happy to answer any questions you may have about the seminar.

Best wishes
Lydia Brown

**Language note**

The section of the checklist on Sentence Structure mentions three sentence types:

○ Simple sentences, with only a single main verb, e.g. *This advice* comes *from a highly informative in-company training seminar.*

○ Compound sentences, consisting of two or more simple sentences which are mostly joined with *and, or* and *but*: [*Think carefully about each of these points*] and [*make use of them in your future negotiations*].

○ Complex sentences, where at least one clause could not function independently, and typically functions as part of a larger clause: *It is vital [that you take care {not to include language originally in the template (that is not appropriate)}].*

The distinction between compound sentences and complex sentences may be too subtle to analyse with the class, other than to point out that too many 'and's, 'or's and 'but's make a text feel clumsy.

**Optional extension**

The checklist is, of course, useful for all types of writing, and students should get into the habit of using it with their own writing. You could ask students to look at something they wrote for an earlier unit to see if they made any of the mistakes listed or if there are any other style improvements to be made.

**Optional extension**
**ILEC preparation: Test of Writing Part 2**

If your students are planning to take the ILEC exam, point out that Part 2 of the Test of Writing requires students to write a memo of between 200 and 250 words. You could ask students to rewrite the memo from Exercise 8.4 based on their discussions, either as homework or in class (with a time limit of around 20 minutes). Make sure they stick to the word limit and follow all the advice from the checklist.

NB The time allowed in the exam for both parts of the writing test is 75 minutes, so students should aim to spend no more than 45 minutes on Part 2. In the real exam, of course, they would not have the chance to discuss and plan their writing beforehand, which is why a shorter time limit is suggested here.

 **9 Listening B: Contract negotiation**

**9.1** Tell students to read the introduction (SB page 73) and the questions. Play the recording, then tell students to check their answers with a partner. Check quickly with the class.

**Transcript »** STUDENT'S BOOK **page 283**

 **Answers**

**1** They are talking about a franchise agreement.

**2** The business they are discussing is a sandwich-making restaurant.

**3** The two clauses they mention are the non-competition clause and the arbitration clause.

**4** The franchisee is unwilling to accept a non-competition clause that would prohibit him from operating a similar sandwich-making restaurant in a certain area for the period of three years if the franchise agreement should be terminated.

 **Background notes**

○ The non-competition clause would be along the lines of that presented in Reading B.

○ An arbitration clause is a device which is intended to avoid court trials in case of a dispute. Arbitration involves arbitrators (a person or panel of people who are not judges). The arbitration clause will specify the nature of any arbitration proceedings (e.g. should it follow the rules of the American Arbitration Association?), as well as practical matters such as how to divide the cost of arbitration. See http://www. hg.org/adradd1.html for a comprehensive guide.

**9.2** Tell students to discuss the questions in pairs and to try to remember the answers. You may need to explain that *strike* means *delete*. Then play the recording again for them to check, and discuss the answers with them.

 **Answers**
**1** False (only sandwich restaurants)
**2** True
**3** True
**4** False (he offers only to be more flexible)

**9.3** Discuss this question with the whole class.

 **Answer**
One of the techniques Arthur Johansson used was horse-trading, i.e. trading one item (in this case, offering to be flexible on the arbitration clause) for another (getting the other party to reduce the scope of the non-competition clause). The second technique he used was to suggest a number that he knew the other party would not accept (in this case, he suggested reducing the length of the non-competition clause to one year) in the expectation that the other party would suggest a number that he in turn couldn't accept (the other party suggested two years), with the hope that they would agree to meet halfway at a number Mr Johansson wanted originally.

## 10 Language use B: Negotiating expressions

**10.1** Ask students if anyone knows any useful negotiating expressions, or if they remember any from the recording. Then tell them to read the introduction (SB page 73) and the task, and to see if they remember which of the phrases were used. Then play the recording again for them to check their answers. Afterwards, tell them to discuss in small groups a) which expressions were used, and b) if they can remember which

context each expression was used in. Finally, go through the answers with the class. Note that if you feel students have listened to the recording enough already, you could do this activity using the transcript on SB page 283.

 **Answers**
**a** The lawyers used expressions 1, 2, 3, 4, 5, 6 and 9.
**b** See transcript for contexts.

**10.2** Tell students to work in small groups to discuss the functions of the expressions. Check the answers briefly with the class.

 **Answers**
**a** Our proposal is to ...
We suggest ...
We'd like ...
What we're looking for is ...
**b** That's certainly a step in the right direction.
I think we could live with that.
We'd be happy with that.
**c** I'm afraid we can't go along with ...
That would be difficult for us.
I'm afraid that's out of the question.
We're not entirely happy with that.
The most forceful rejection is *I'm afraid that's out of the question*.

---

**Optional extension**
**Photocopiable worksheet 5.2**

As well as the phrases for making and responding to proposals, the dialogue included many other examples of useful negotiating language. The exercises on Photocopiable worksheet 5.2 are designed to focus attention on this language, especially the signalling devices which refer backwards or forwards to other things mentioned.

**1** Hand out either a complete worksheet for each student and/or a set of cut-up slips for each group. Tell students to work in small groups to put the lines of the dialogue into the correct order. Tell them to look for clues such as *like I said* to help them.

**Answers**
**1** c **2** l **3** o **4** g **5** k **6** e **7** h
**8** j **9** a **10** n **11** f **12** d **13** i
**14** p **15** b **16** m

**2** Tell students to work in the same groups to find as many useful negotiating phrases as possible. Tell them to underline the phrases on the worksheets, rather than slips of paper, as this language will come in useful for the role-plays in Exercise 11. Then go through all the answers with the class, dealing with any vocabulary problems.

**Suggested answers**

**c** If I may, I'd like to address ...

**l** Well, I'll just say upfront that that's standard, that's in all our agreements.

**o** Right. That may be so, but I'm afraid we can't go along with it in its present form.

**g** What do you object to?

**g** It's standard practice, like I said.

**k** Well, the clause in question states, and I quote: ...

**k** What this means is that in the event that the agreement between my client and your corporation should at one time no longer be in effect, my client would ...

**k** I'm afraid that's out of the question.

**e** Well, you must understand that my client has to protect itself – I mean, ...

**h** Yes, I fully understand the reasoning behind that provision, no need to explain. But ...

**h** Let's face it: ...

**h** So I'll say it again: we simply could not accept any clause that would ..., if that should one day become necessary.

**j** What do you suggest? We are not in a position to ..., let me be perfectly clear about that.

**a** Of course. Our proposal is to reduce the scope of the clause.

**a** If you could consider ..., we would be willing to ..., for example.

**n** Well, all right. In that case, I think we could talk about ...

**f** That's certainly a step in the right direction.

**f** How about this: we suggest ...

**d** That would be difficult for us.

**d** We could only ..., and that is already very generous on our part.

**i** Let's agree on ..., shall we? After all, you and I both know that ...

**i** ... let's be honest, ...

**p** I think we could live with that. ... it is.

**b** Very well.

**m** Now, what about ...? You said you would be willing to ...

## 11 Speaking B: Negotiating an agreement

Allocate roles for the role-play. Point out that the negotiation involves two lawyers representing client companies, not the companies themselves. If you have an odd number of students, the third student in one group can be one of the clients (either A or B). Make sure they read their role cards carefully, and remind them that they need to practise the useful language from Exercise 10.1. Allow five to ten minutes for the role-plays and give feedback at the end.

## 12 Reading C and Writing B: Adding a contract template

**12.1** Tell students to read the introduction on SB page 74 to find two ways of adapting a contract template (Answer: fill in the blanks; make additions and rewrite). Students then read the email to try to answer the three questions. Point out that they do not need to read the contract clause at this stage. They discuss their answers in pairs before feeding back to the class.

 **Answers**

**1** He wants Arthur to make the changes he has suggested to the clause and then to send it to the client in a mail in which he also explains what the clause means in a way the client can easily understand.

**2** To 'walk someone through something' means to explain something to somebody step by step (if it is a procedure) or to explain something complicated slowly and carefully.

**3** 'COB' stands for 'close of business' and refers to the end of the working day.

 **Background note**
The *scope* of a clause defines what types of activity, etc. it covers and what it doesn't cover.

**12.2** Students read the clause carefully to identify any sections that are likely to need explaining to the client. They then discuss the clause in pairs or small groups to summarise it in everyday language. Afterwards, elicit a clear summary from the class.

**Suggested answer**
See sample email in 12.3.

**Background note**
In this clause, *covenant* is used as a verb, meaning 'to promise'.

**Optional extension**

Elicit from the class a diagram of the clause (as below), going into as much detail as possible. Point out that this diagramming technique is useful not only as an aid to understanding complex clauses, but also as way of planning such clauses before you write. Once the diagram is on the board, tell students to work in pairs and to take turns to say the whole clause aloud, using only the diagram to help them remember.

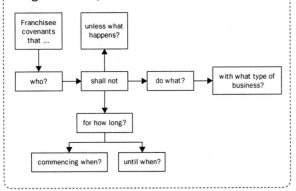

**12.3** Students complete the writing task either in class or at home.

**Suggested answer**

Dear Mr Heslop
I am writing to inform you of the changes that have been negotiated with regard to the non-competition clause of the franchise agreement you wish to enter into. As you will see from the attached document containing the re-worked version of the clause in question, I was able to achieve our primary goals in the negotiation held last week.
If I may, I will briefly explain what the clause means and indicate where changes have been made to the original version. The clause states that you, as the Franchisee, agree that you will not, for the period of one year from the time when the agreement ends, own or operate a business which is similar to the sandwich-making business which is the subject of the contract. Please note that the time period during which this restriction applies has been reduced from two years to one year. According to the clause, you also agree not to be employed by or provide assistance to such a sandwich-making business for this one-year period. However, the clause also expressly states that you have the right to invest in such a business during this time period if you wish. Note that while this was prohibited in the original clause, we have managed to have this restriction removed. Finally, the clause stipulates the size of the geographical area in which you may not own or operate a similar sandwich-making business for this period. The radius around the location of your business has been changed from 25 miles to 10 miles.
I hope that the clause in its present form conforms to your wishes and expectations. Should you require further information, please do not hesitate to contact me.
I await your further instructions in this matter.

Yours sincerely
Arthur Johansson

Tell students to do the Internet activity as homework. See Using the Internet for research on page xviii.

# Language focus

## Answers

1   **Vocabulary: distinguishing meaning**

   **1**   *franchise*: The others are agreements; a *franchise* is permission. It may be set out in a *franchise agreement*, but the franchise itself is not a document.
   **2**   *whereas*: The others can mean 'if', e.g. *Should you need any help, please contact me.*
   **3**   *injunction*: The others are permission; an *injunction* is an obligation.

**4** *breach*: The others involve cancelling a contract; *to rescind* means 'to cancel a contract with the effect that both parties are in the same position as they were before they signed the contract'.

**5** *unwarranted*: The others mean 'taken out', typically a clause from a contract; *unwarranted* means 'unjustified'.

**6** *contention*: The others are suggested by somebody; a *contention* is somebody's argument.

**7** *efficacious*: The others refer to a clause or contract which is valid; *efficacious* /ˌefɪˈkeɪʃəs/ means that something has the ability to achieve a desired effect.

## 2 Collocations

To form or make a contract valid: enter into, execute, sign

To make a contract partly or wholly invalid: cancel, rescind, terminate

To change or add to a contract: amend, modify, supplement

## 3 Verb forms

**2** signed **3** (had) breached **4** is terminated / terminates **5** to be renewed **6** modify

## 4 Word formation

| Verb | Abstract noun |
|------|---------------|
| renew | renewal |
| draft | draft |
| include | inclusion |
| omit | omission |
| terminate | termination |
| encrypt | encryption |
| adopt | adoption |
| negotiate | negotiation |
| propose | proposal |
| transact | transaction |

## 5 Vocabulary: antonyms

**2** express **3** non-binding **4** invalid

## 6 Prepositions

**2** by **3** in **4** for **5** herein **6** hereby **7** by

It is an example of a merger / entire agreement / parol evidence clause.

**Optional extension**
**Photocopiable worksheet 5.3**

Allocate role cards in the following way:
○ If you have one student, you are the franchisee, and your student is your lawyer. As a follow-up, you are the supermarket's lawyer, while your student remains the franchisee's lawyer.
○ If you have two or three students, one should be the franchisee and the other(s) should be the franchisee's lawyer(s). As a follow-up, the student who played the franchisee should change roles and become the supermarket's lawyer. The others should remain the franchisee's lawyer(s).
○ If you have four students, there is one role each.
○ If you have between five and eight students, add second lawyers, a second manager and second franchisee.
○ If you have more than eight students, divide them into groups of between four and eight.

The potential franchisee should meet with his/her lawyer to discuss any potential problems with the deal, and a strategy for the negotiation with the supermarket. At the same time (if you have enough students), the supermarket managers should meet with their lawyers to do the same. Then the two groups should come together to negotiate the terms of the contract.

You may decide to give some pointers for the discussions and negotiations, but it should be possible to borrow a lot of ideas from the Reading and Listening exercises from this unit. Encourage students to use the negotiating techniques and useful phrases they have encountered in this unit.

Take notes of any interesting language problems, which you can address after the role-play, but make sure you also give feedback on the effectiveness of the meetings in terms of successful and appropriate communication.

# 6  Contracts: remedies

Contracts can be thought of as a two-way promise: party A promises to do X in return for party B doing Y. Unlike most promises, however, the promises in contracts are backed up by the threat of legal action if one of the parties fails to fulfil its obligations (i.e. if there is a **breach of contract**). The collective name for the various ways of dealing with a breach of contract is **remedies**. Remedies, which most often take the form of financial compensation (**damages**), have two functions: they deter the parties to a contract from being tempted to breach it in the first place, and they restore some form of justice in the event that a breach does take place.

Remedies most often take the form of damages, but remedies also include **non-monetary relief** (also known as **equitable remedies**; see http://en.wikipedia.org/wiki/Equitable_remedy). For example, a court may order the breaching party to perform some action (**specific performance**). Listening A includes a description of a type of remedy in Denmark: a *foged* is a court official (like a bailiff) who has the power to enforce specific performance.

The many types of remedies may be illustrated by a simplistic example. A supplier agrees to supply a ton of concrete mix to a builder in exchange for €100 so that the builder can use it to build an office for a client. The supplier delivers the concrete mix, but it has become damp and turned to solid concrete. The builder is then unable to start work on building the office for two weeks while he is waiting for new concrete mix. The builder takes the supplier to court, seeking recovery of the €100 for the faulty concrete mix (**general** or **actual damages** = the natural result of the breach), as well as €2,000 for the cost of the two-week delay (**special** or **consequential damages**). The €2,000 is subject to the **foreseeability rule**: the court must ascertain whether the supplier could have foreseen the breach (and therefore made alternative preparations, such as keeping a spare ton of concrete mix in stock for emergencies). In addition to these two types of **expectation damages**

(= attempts to compensate the non-breaching party for the loss of the benefits it would have received if the contract had been performed), the builder might seek punitive damages of €12,000,000 to punish the supplier for its reprehensible actions (e.g. fraud), but this would be unlikely to succeed. He might also seek a court order for **specific performance**: removing the ton of solid concrete from the builder's yard.

Another important issue is **mitigation of damages**, whereby the non-breaching party is obliged to minimise the amount of damage done by the breach. In this case, the builder should have tried to buy concrete from another supplier rather than simply waiting two weeks for the original supplier to deliver a replacement. He could therefore have incurred substantially lower costs (say, €150 for new concrete plus €500 for a delay of a few days). If he is awarded damages, they will probably be based on these lower costs.

Given the messy and unpredictable nature of seeking damages after a breach, companies often try to stipulate in their contracts how damages will be calculated. So the builder from the above example, in his contract with a new supplier of concrete mix, inserts a **liquidated damages** (or **stipulated damages**) **clause**, stipulating that damages will cover all or part of the cost of the concrete mix, plus €200 per working day while awaiting replacement deliveries. However, as Reading B explains, such contractual provisions are not always **enforceable**. The key is that liquidated damages have to be an attempted calculation of fair compensation for the non-breaching party, rather than a penalty for the breaching party. In some jurisdictions, **penalty clauses** are not enforceable. Reading C, which is an example of a liquidated damages clause, even includes the phrase *and not by way of penalty* in a deliberate attempt to prove that it is not a penalty clause.

Reading D is a lawyer's letter to a client. It centres on the issue of an **anticipatory breach of contract**: a breach committed before performance is due. In this case, a customer stated that it would not accept delivery of ordered goods. The case also involves the **reliance principle**: if one party incurs costs in the reasonable expectation that the contract will be honoured by the other party, he is entitled to recover those costs.

Needless to say, with such a complicated area of law, there is plenty of room for disagreement both within jurisdictions and between them. A reasonable claim for damages in one jurisdiction may be considered unreasonable in a second.

The unit also gives useful language techniques and practice for **talking about actions by the court and court rulings**, for **using repetition** when presenting new information, for conducting an **initial interview with a client**, and for writing a **follow-up memo** to a client.

**Further information**

○ There is a clear introduction to remedies, including the differences between **remedies in contract law and tort law**, at http://www.translegal.com/lets/remedies.

○ There is an excellent **background to remedies** at http://www.lawteacher.net/ContractPages/Con16.html – scroll down for the free resources.

○ For an interesting article on liquidated and punitive damages in **common-law and civil-law** jurisdictions, with examples from a wide range of (mainly European) countries, see http://www.reedsmith.com/_db/_documents/0804crit.pdf.

## Discussion

Use these questions to generate a discussion.

a   In what ways can a contract be breached? (Treat this as a brainstorming activity. There are at least as many answers as there are types of contract. For example, a supplier may miss a delivery or deliver unsuitable goods; a contractor may miss a deadline or fail to meet prescribed safety standards; a customer may refuse to accept a delivery or avoid paying an agreed price; or an employee might behave rudely or negligently, or might disclose confidential corporate information.)

b   What can be done to prevent a breach of contract? (You could use this question to mention the question of penalty clauses and liquidated damages, as discussed in Reading B. Obviously you should avoid giving away all the information from Reading B, but instead focus on how breach of contract is avoided in students' jurisdictions. One obvious way to avoid breaching a contract is to make sure the contract is well constructed in the first place: to predict potential breaches and make provision for them.)

c   What can be done if a contract is breached? (Use this to introduce the idea of remedies, especially damages. These terms are properly described in Reading A, so again avoid providing too much information yourself during the discussion. The most obvious thing to do in the event of a breach of contract is to file a complaint against the breaching party. An alternative might be to go to arbitration, to get an independent body to find a reasonable solution.)

## 1   Reading A: Introduction to contract remedies

**1.1**   Ask the class to scan the beginning of the text to find a synonym for *damages*. This should take only a few seconds, as the answer is one of the key terms in bold.

**Answer**
Pecuniary compensation

**Language note**
*Pecuniary* /pɪˈkjuːnɪəri/ comes from Latin (*pecuniarius*). It means 'related to money'.

**1.2**   Tell students to read the three statements to predict whether they are true or false, and to discuss them in small groups. It is important at this stage that students fully understand the statements, so you may decide to discuss them as a group before telling students to read the text.

Tell students to read the text to check their predictions. Allow enough time for them to read the text quite carefully (e.g. four or five minutes), as there is a lot of information to take in. When they have finished, tell them to discuss their answers in pairs or small groups, and then go through the answers with the class.

**Answers**
1   True
2   False (This definition relates to restitution damages.)
3   True

### Background notes

○ Students may struggle with the grammar in the phrase *the loss of the benefits that party would have received had the contract been performed*. If students are familiar with grammar terminology, you could point out that it is a so-called third conditional, which is used to hypothesise about a past event which didn't actually happen. Point out also that *had the contract been performed* is another way of saying *if the contract had been performed*. The concept of hypothesising about the unreal past is central to the field of remedies, which is why such grammar is so common in this unit.

○ You may also point out that the suffix *-able* is added to a verb (X) to make an adjective meaning 'somebody can X it'. For example, if a breach is *foreseeable*, you can foresee (or could have foreseen) it. If damages are *recoverable*, you can recover them.

○ If something *hinges* /'hɪndʒɪz/ *on* something, it depends entirely on it. The expression comes from a door hinge, which holds the door to the wall.

○ The *status quo ante* /ˌsteɪtəs ˌkwəʊ 'ænti/ is the situation which existed before something, in this case before the agreement was made.

○ If you *ascertain* /ˌæsə'teɪn/ something, you calculate it or find it out.

○ The adjective *punitive* /'pjuːnətɪv/ is related to the verb *to punish*. The adjective *exemplary* /ɪg'zempləri/ is related to the noun *example*, and implies that the court awards such damages to set an example to other potential parties who may be tempted to commit the same tort.

○ If behaviour is *reprehensible* /ˌreprɪ'hensəbl/, it deserves severe criticism, either because it is illegal or because it is morally wrong.

○ If you *rescind* /rɪ'sɪnd/ a contract, you cancel it.

### Pronunciation notes

adequate /'ædɪkwət/
consequential /ˌkɒnsɪ'kwenʃəl/
reliance /rə'laɪəns/
remedy /'remədi/

### Optional extension

To check comprehension and reinforce the vocabulary and concepts from the text, use the following questions either as a straightforward comprehension quiz or as a 'Snake game' (see Games and activities section, page xvi). Students should try to answer the questions without looking back at the text, but if they struggle you may allow them to scan the text for the answers.

### Questions

1 What sort of damages does not depend on foreseeability?

2 What is the name for damages for the loss of benefits that would have been received?

3 What four rights are mentioned in the context of sale of goods legislation?

4 What type of damages is likely to be awarded if a party completely fails to perform its obligations?

5 What is the term for damages which are not money?

6 What might a court order if monetary damages would not be an adequate remedy?

7 What sort of damages might be awarded in the event of a reprehensible act?

8 When are liquidated damages agreed?

9 What do special or consequential damages hinge on?

10 What normally accompanies a breach of contract in order for punitive damages to be awarded?

11 What form of damages returns the non-breaching party to the status quo ante?

12 When there is a breach of contract, what terms are used to describe the two parties?

13 What is the general name for damages and other rights resulting from a breach of contract?

**14** What right might a non-breaching party have in the event of default by the other party?

**15** What is another name for *expectation damages*?

**16** What is another name for *liquidated damages*?

**17** What is another name for *punitive damages*?

**18** What is the basic remedy for breach of contract in the Anglo-American system?

**19** What is another name for *special damages*?

**20** What form of damages compels the breaching party to give up any money obtained under the breached contract?

### Answers

1 General damages
2 Expectation damages (or 'benefit of the bargain' damages)
3 Right to reject goods, right to return goods, right to demand repair, and right to demand replacement
4 Restitution damages
5 Non-monetary relief
6 Specific performance
7 Punitive or exemplary damages
8 At the time of entering into the contract
9 Foreseeability
10 Tort
11 Reliance damages
12 The breaching party and the non-breaching party
13 Remedies
14 The right to rescind or cancel the contract
15 Benefit of the bargain damages
16 Stipulated damages
17 Exemplary damages
18 Pecuniary compensation
19 Consequential damages
20 Restitution damages

## 2 Key terms: Types of damages

**2.1** Tell students to work alone or in small groups to match the types of damages with the definitions. When they have finished, go through the answers with the class.

### Answers
1 d  2 e  3 a  4 g  5 b  6 c  7 f

**2.2** This discussion is probably best done with the whole class. If you have a monolingual class, go through the list with the whole class to discuss the best equivalent for each type of damages.

---

**Optional extension**
**Photocopiable worksheet 6.1**

Photocopiable worksheet 6.1 focuses on so-called third conditionals (*what would have happened if something had happened differently*), along with related structures (*what should have / could have happened*). These structures are difficult for many learners of English, but also important for talking about remedies. The three structures all consist of a modal verb (*would*, *should* or *could*) followed by *have* and a past participle. They are all used to hypothesise about the unreal past.

The worksheet does not attempt to teach these structures, so its purpose is only to reinforce known grammar by providing a real-life context for it. If you feel students are too weak to do the worksheet, either avoid sections 2–4 or supplement them from other sources.

**1** Tell students to read through the five case studies alone in order to decide which remedy is most suitable for each client. When they have finished reading, tell them to work in small groups to discuss their answers. Then discuss the answers with the whole class. Of course there may be some disagreement as to which remedy is relevant to which case.

   **Possible answers**
   1   a, b, f, e, g, i
   2   a, b, d, f
   3   i, h
   4   a
   5   c

**2** Discuss these statements as a whole class. Point out that some statements may refer to more than one case study. Make sure students understand that each sentence refers to something in the past which did not actually happen. Elicit the structures used in each sentence (e.g. past perfect, *would have done*, etc.).

   **Suggested answers**
   a 3, 4   b 1, 2, 3, 4, 5   c 1, 4   d 4

---

**3** Tell students to work in small groups to write similar sentences. Each group should focus on a different case study. With stronger groups, you could ask them to do the exercise orally with more than one case study. The groups should aim for around four sentences per case study, one for each of the sentences in Exercise 2. When they have finished, discuss the answers with the class.

**Suggested answers (Case study 1)**

○ If the system had not crashed, the client would never have found out that the software was pirated.

○ The client should claim damages based on the predicted financial benefit of the warehouse tracking system had an authentic version been installed.

○ The client should have stopped using the tracking system as soon as it realised that the software was pirated.

○ The computer system could have been protected had the client made use of an effective firewall to prevent viruses.

**4** Tell students to work in pairs or groups of three to role-play one or more of the meetings with a client. If you have an odd number of students, the third member of one group should be a second lawyer. Encourage them to use the target language, as long as it is used naturally.

## 3 Reading B: Liquidated damages

**3.1** Ask the class for a definition of *liquidated damages clauses*. Write their definition on the board. Then tell students to read the introduction and the beginning of first paragraph to find the definition given and to compare it with their own. Allow a very limited time for this (one minute) before discussing it as a class.

 **Answer**
Liquidated damages clauses are defined as 'provisions in a contract stipulating the amount required to compensate an injured party in the event of a breach'.

**3.2** Tell students to work alone to match the headings with the sections. Allow a limited time (two or three minutes) and then tell them to compare their answers in small groups. Tell them also to discuss what they remember about each paragraph. Then go through the answers briefly with the class.

 **Answers**
**1** d **2** a **3** c **4** b

 **Background note**
Section 4 states that *Customarily, courts look to the time of contract ... . Time* here refers to the date when the contract was agreed, and not to its duration. In other words, they imagine what the parties expected at the time they entered into the contract.

**Pronunciation notes**
deterrent /dɪˈterənt/
incur /ɪnˈkɜːʳ/
sever /ˈsevəʳ/

**3.3** Tell students to discuss the four statements in pairs. When they have finished, check the answers with the class.

 **Answers**
**1** False (This refers to a liquidated damages provision, not a penalty provision.)
**2** False (If they have a liquidated damages clause, they may still recover damages. Several other types of damages, such as expectation damages, may also be recoverable if there was not a liquidated damages clause in the contract.)
**3** True
**4** True

**3.4** Discuss this question with the class. For full information on the Uniform Commercial Code, see http://www.law.cornell.edu/ucc/ucc.table.html.

**3.5** Tell students to work alone or in small groups to complete the legal expressions. Then go through the answers with the class.

**Answers**

1 breach of contract
2 compensate an injured party
3 bargaining power
4 clause at issue

**Optional extension**
**ILEC preparation: Test of Reading Part 3**
**Photocopiable worksheet 6.2**

Photocopiable worksheet 6.2 practises the skill of word-building: transforming a word into a related word, usually by way of a prefix or suffix. This skill is tested explicitly in Part 3 of the ILEC Test of Reading, but is also of course useful in real-life contexts.

Tell students to work in pairs or groups of three to put each word in the appropriate form, obviously without looking back at the text. Point out that one of the words does not need to be changed. Allow a fairly limited time (e.g. five minutes) and then go through the answers with the class. You may use the 'Easy first' procedure or the 'Stake game' (see Games and activities section, page xvi).

**Answers**

**1** contracting; agreement **2** injured; substantial; difficulty **3** reasonably; injuries; enforceable **4** contractual; considerable; non-performance **5** provision; occasioned **6** deterrent; ordinarily; non-breaching **7** unenforceable **8** injured; applicable **9** Consequently; distinction; enforceability **10** quantify; loss **11** stipulated; reasonable; disproportionate; injury **12** apparently; contradictory **13** weight; intent (intention) **14** relative; bargaining; reasonableness **15** Customarily **16** breaching; forecast; unreasonable **17** considering

## 4 Language use A: Talking about court actions and rulings

Ask the class to look at the box (SB page 81). Elicit the meaning of the four phrases, and elicit any similar phrases that students can think of. Note that there are more examples in Exercise 4.2, but do not point these out at this stage.

**4.1** Tell students to work in small groups to find six sentences in the text which refer to court decisions. You might make this easier by telling them that there are no phrases in section 1, two in section 2, two in section 3 and two in section 4. When they have finished, go through the answers with the class.

**Answers**

Section 2: *In many jurisdictions, the courts will sever …*
Section 2: *The result is that the non-breaching party is forced to prove …*
Section 3: *The recent tendency of the courts is to give less or no weight to …*
Section 3: *As such, the court must assess whether …*
Section 4: *The courts generally look to …*
Section 4: *In rare cases, … the courts will not enforce …*

**4.2** Tell students to work in small groups to decide which phrase can be used in place of each underlined phrase from the box. When they have finished, go through the answers with the class.

**Suggested answers**

1 The court overturned/reversed the decision. (opposite meaning to *upheld*)
2 The court rejected the suit on the grounds that … (same meaning)
3 The court agrees/rules that … (same meaning)
4 The court is hesitant to / is unwilling to … (same meaning)

**4.3** This discussion is probably best done as a whole-group exercise. If students have no idea of the situation in their jurisdictions, tell them to find out for the next lesson. This is important information that any corporate lawyer needs to know.

## (CD1 T22–23) 5 Listening A: A Danish remedy

**5.1** Tell students to read the introduction (SB page 82) and the four statements. Then play the first part of the talk for them to decide if the statements are true or false. Tell them also to pay attention to what the remedy is and how it works. After the recording, tell students to compare their answers in pairs, then go through the answers with the whole class.

Transcript » STUDENT'S BOOK **page 284**

 **Answers**
1  True
2  False (There are only a limited number of cases where specific performance will be ordered.)
3  False (The breaching party does not necessarily comply.)
4  True

 **Pronunciation note**
compliance /kəmˈplaɪəns/

**5.2**  Tell students to read the gapped notes and think about what the missing words might be. Then play the recording for them to check their predictions. Go through the answers with the class.

Transcript » STUDENT'S BOOK **page 284**

 **Answers**
1  produced    2  (a) third party
3  signature   4  (the) transfer    5  harmful

**Background note**
A *pledgee* /pleˈdʒiː/ is somebody who makes a pledge. A *pledge* involves depositing property with a lender as security for a loan. If the pledgee defaults on the loan, the lender has the right to seize the *pledged security*.

## 6  Language use B: Using repetition to aid understanding

Elicit from the class whether they found the speaker in Listening A easy to understand. Assuming they did, ask if they noticed any techniques she used to improve communication. Then tell them to read the introduction (SB page 82) to check their answers.

Tell students to do the exercise alone, then compare their answers with a partner. Then go through the answers with the class.

 **Suggested answer**
The whole system works like this: the court must first determine whether an order for specific performance should be granted. Of course, <u>the breaching party can do two things: either comply or not comply with the order. In other words, the defaulting party either takes the action necessary to perform the contract or he doesn't.</u> If he doesn't, the other party can decide to go to the judicial enforcement agent. This <u>judicial enforcement agent</u> is called the *foged* in Denmark. <u>A *foged* is similar to the bailiff in common law. He basically fulfils the functions of a bailiff.</u> The Danish Code of Procedure 17 regulates what the *foged* has to do. This <u>code</u> stipulates that the *foged* can <u>convert the plaintiff's claim into money damages</u>. So, in reality, <u>most claims for which specific performance is granted are converted into money damages</u>.

## 7  Speaking A: Contract remedies

Allow plenty of preparation time for this or consider setting it as homework. Alternatively, ask students to prepare their mini-presentations in pairs or small groups. Make sure they plan which words they are going to repeat.

If you have several students from the same jurisdiction, make sure they are each going to talk about a different remedy, perhaps by organising a quick brainstorm activity.

If you think students will really struggle to find such information, you could allow them to invent the details, or to make funny presentations. For example, they could give their foged-equivalent sweeping powers to punish any breaching parties in humorous ways.

Unless you have a very large class, you should give each student the opportunity to give this mini-presentation, as they will learn a lot from their peers. When you give feedback, ask the other students whether the technique of repetition was successful in making the presentation easy to follow.

## 8 Reading C: Understanding contract clauses

Ask students to think back to the information from Reading B on liquidated damages. Elicit the three essential parts of a liquidated damages clause, plus the important difference between liquidated damages and a penalty clause. Then tell students to read the text to identify whether it meets the three requirements. When they have finished reading, go through the answers with the class.

**Answers**
The standard elements are listed as points a–c in Section 3 of Reading B. Point a) is achieved by the phrase *because it is difficult to definitely ascertain*. Point b) is not dealt with explicitly, but the reference to *expenses for inspection, necessary traveling expenses and other similar expenses* shows that at least the issue has been considered. Point c) is not addressed explicitly, but the phrase *and not by way of penalty* is an attempt to show that this is not a penalty clause but a reasonable means to cover expenses.

**Background notes**
○ The contract is mutually agreed *by and between* the parties. In other words, the parties agree (to) the contract (= *by the*

*parties*) and they agree (to) it with each other (= *between the parties*).
○ *Time is of the essence* means that the times specified in the contract are vital. Any change to the timings constitutes a fundamental change to the contract.
○ A *calendar day* is a 24-hour period from midnight to midnight. It is used to clarify that delivery after midnight on the due date is classed as a day late. A *working day* here means simply a day during the period prescribed in the contract for the job to be done.

**Pronunciation note**
ascertain /ˌæsəˈteɪn/

**8.1** Tell students to discuss the questions in small groups. When they have finished, check the answers with the class.

**Answers**
1 Because on-time performance of the various parts of a construction agreement is crucial. If the foundation of a building is not performed on time, then the next step, and the workers involved, must wait. This may result in workers being paid to wait and, in turn, losses being incurred which must be compensated by the party who has failed to perform on time.
2 *Time is of the essence* means that it is essential to the parties that performance takes place in accordance with the times specified in the agreement. Failure to perform by the time specified is a breach of contract by the non-performing party.
3 $10,000
4 If money is due the Contractor, the amount of damages will be deducted from this, or if no money is due the Contractor, he will pay the amount to the Owner.

**8.2** Tell students to look at the expressions in the same groups and find the equivalents in the text. When they have finished, go through the answers with the class.

**Answers**
1 by way of   2 prescribed   3 in excess of
4 mutually   5 is due   6 inclusive of
7 as aforesaid   8 deducted from

**Answers**

1 the parties *to this contract* 2 the owner will be damaged *by the contractor's failure to complete the contract* 3 *by signing this contract*, the parties agree that ... 4 *by signing this contract*, the Contractor agrees that ... 5 calculated as *$2,000 per day overdue*

**Optional extension**
**Photocopiable worksheet 6.3**
The extract in Reading C is an example of successful legal writing in that it is both sophisticated and easy to understand. Photocopiable worksheet 6.3 focuses on what is good about this extract.

1 Hand out copies of the worksheet. Tell students to work in small groups to put the punctuation back into the extract. When you have finished, go through the answers with the class. For inexperienced lawyers, you may need to point out that the two semi-colons serve to divide the clause into three sections. The commas serve to separate explanatory comments such as *inclusive of expenses for inspection* or *and not by way of penalty*.

**Answers**
See Reading C. Note that there is room for some disagreement over where commas are necessary for grammar and style.

2 Tell students to discuss the statements in groups. Check that they are comfortable with the grammar terms *subject*, *object* and *passive*. When students have finished, discuss the answers with the class. Note that the statements are all tips for clear writing.

**Answers**
1 True (The use of three sections, separated by semi-colons, makes the clause much clearer than it would otherwise be.)

2 True (e.g. *It is / time is / the Owner will be / the amount of such damages shall be / the Contractor hereby agrees / such sum shall be*)

3 Mostly true (e.g. *to complete the contract / ascertain and prove the amount / finishing the Work*), with one exception (*pay to the Owner as liquidated damages and not by way of penalty such total sum*).

4 True (The passive voice is used a lot in the clause, but it always serves a useful purpose. It would be difficult or clumsy to write the opening phrase without the passive.)

5 True (There are three *to*-infinitives in the clause: *to complete, to (definitely) ascertain and prove*, and *to pay*. The split infinitive is necessary because it shows that *definitely* modifies both *ascertain* and *prove*.

3 The clause is deliberately badly written and breaks all of the rules. You could tell students simply to identify the problems, or you could ask them to rewrite the clause to make it clearer. Tell students to work in groups. When they have finished, discuss the answers with the class.

**Possible answer**
CONSEQUENTIAL DAMAGES RESULTING FROM LOSS OF PRODUCTION TIME
The Contractor hereby agrees that, in the event of an interruption or threatened interruption of manufacturing or otherwise processing of raw materials as described in exhibit 14, and if it is shown unquestionably that such interruption was caused solely by the Contractor, its subcontractors, employees, or agents, or employees thereof, while maintaining, repairing, utilising or occupying a facility and/or equipment in the aforesaid Premises, the Contractor will fully and immediately reimburse the Company for all consequential damages resulting from such interruption. The amount of such damages shall be calculated using the costing rates at the time of the incident set forth in exhibit 12. The parties hereto agree that, in the event of a joint investigation by the parties, set up according to principles set forth in exhibit 19, determining that such interruption or threatened interruption occurred as a result of the joint fault or negligence of the parties (the Company and the Contractor), their subcontractors,

employees, or agents, or employees thereof, then the parties shall undertake negotiations to establish a pro-rata formula by which to assess the distribution of such consequential damages incurred by the parties.

 **9 Listening B: Remedies**

**9.1** Tell students to read the introduction (SB page 83) and the questions. Ask them to predict what Mr Anderson's problem might be.

Play the recording. Then tell students to discuss the answers in small groups. Discuss the answers with the class.

**Transcript »** STUDENT'S BOOK **page 284**

 **Answers**
  1  The program written by the software company contained unnecessary code and did not function with Macintosh computers, so the client had to have it rewritten.
  2  The client was forced to find another programmer who could fix the program written by Glaptech.

**9.2** Play the second part of the interview for students to answer the two questions. When they have discussed their answers in pairs, go through them with the class.

**Transcript »** STUDENT'S BOOK **page 285**

 **Answers**
  1  The lawyer says that the client should have mitigated his damages by making a reasonable effort to solve the problem as inexpensively as possible. This would have meant shopping around locally to find the best price for a programmer to do the work.
  2  Read through the contract.

 **Background notes**
  ○ If you *mitigate* your damages, you try to make them less high (see Teacher's brief page 104).
  ○ If you *waive* /weɪv/ your right to something, you give up that right.

You could write the following supplementary questions on the board. These apply to both sections of the interview

**a** What was Glaptech supposed to write for Mr Anderson?
**b** How did Mr Anderson solve the immediate problem?
**c** What does he want to achieve by filing the complaint?
**d** How optimistic does Mrs Hayes feel about Mr Anderson's chances of success?

 **Answers**
  **a** A software program for the website of Mr Anderson's customer, a ferry company, to allow their customers to book online.
  **b** He asked his cousin in New York to rewrite the program.
  **c** He wants to 'make these guys pay'.
  **d** Fairly optimistic: she thinks there is a good chance of recovering the 10% discount, as well as a fair chance of recovering consequential damages if he loses the client, but she sees no chance of recovering damages for emotional injury or punitive damages.

**9.3** Tell students to look through the list of questions and to discuss in their groups which ones Mrs Hayes used, and what Mr Anderson answered to each question. Then play the recording. Tell them to discuss their answers in their groups, and then go through the answers with the class.

 **Answers**
She asked questions 1, 3, 4, 5 and 7.

**9.4** Tell students to discuss the questions in their groups. When they have finished, check the answers with the class.

 **Answers**
  **1** c   **2** c   **3** b

**9.5** Have students work in small groups initially, then discuss this question with the whole class.

**10 Text analysis: Initial interview with a client**

Ask the class whether they thought the interview in the recording (Listening B) was successful, and what made it successful (or not). Elicit the primary aims of a lawyer in such an initial interview. Then tell students to read the introduction (SB page 84) to compare it with their suggestions.

Tell students to work in pairs or groups of three to put the stages into the table. Tell them also to think of variants on each sentence (e.g. *Do please sit down, Would you like a glass of water?*). As you go through the answer, collect a few such alternatives, and point out why some might be inappropriate.

 **Answers**
   **1** e   **2** c   **3** a   **4** d   **5** b

## 11   Speaking B: Interviewing a client

Tell students to read the instructions carefully to find out what they should do. Allocate roles (A and B). If you have an odd number of students, there will have to be a group of three, in which case the third student should be a more senior lawyer in both role-plays.

Tell students to read their role cards for the two role-plays very carefully, and to underline any sections that they find difficult to understand. Point out that the lawyers have a lot of information which will only make complete sense when they have spoken to their clients. Before the role-plays, tell students to check the information for both Case files with other students with the same role, and to ask you to help them with anything they do not understand. Allow plenty of time for this, and monitor carefully, as it is essential that students know all the necessary information before they start their meetings.

When all students know exactly what to do, put them into groups for the first role-play. Make sure they realise that the lawyers should use the useful phrases from Exercise 10, and make notes of the information from their clients. Allow five to ten minutes for each role-play. While students are talking, make notes of appropriate and inappropriate language, and give feedback on this, as well as the overall success of the meetings, at the end. Repeat the procedure for the second Case file. Note that Student A becomes the client and Student B becomes the lawyer, so that everyone gets a chance to practise the new language.

## 12   Writing: Follow-up correspondence to a client

**12.1** Tell students to read the email to answer the first two questions only. When they have had a chance to read it, tell them to discuss the two questions in small groups. Discourage them from reading the whole transcript, but only those sections necessary to identify and check the mistake in the email. When they have finished, tell them to work on the other two questions in the same groups. Finally, go through all the questions with the class.

 **Answers**

**1** The email provides a written record of the meeting. This avoids any confusion or misunderstandings later on and gives the client the opportunity to query any of the points mentioned.

**2** Factual mistake: Client gave a 10% discount.

Additional information: In the initial interview, the lawyer did not know whether the contract with Glaptech waived consequential damages or not. She still had to look at the contract. But in paragraph 3 of the email, she states '... your contract with Glaptech does not waive consequential damages.'

**3** At this stage in the matter, it would be helpful if you could give me any documents or information which relate to the dispute. Naturally we will require a copy of the contract concluded with Glaptech. In addition, it would be extremely useful if you could provide documents indicating the nature and extent of your previous business relationship with the ferry company, as well as anything that would bear witness to the poor quality of the faulty software program provided by Glaptech.

**4** The courts in our jurisdiction tend to strictly construe contracts between commercial parties and are generally hesitant to award consequential damages unless the plaintiff can clearly demonstrate that the loss was foreseeable to the defendant. The court will look at the course of dealings between you and Glaptech, as well as any documentation you can produce which indicates that Glaptech could have reasonably foreseen the loss.

 **Background note**
If you *construe* something strictly, you analyse it and interpret it with as little subjectivity as possible.

**12.2** Tell students to do this quickly in small groups. Then go through the answers with the class.

➠ **Answers**
   **a** 2  **b** 6  **c** 3  **d** 7  **e** 1  **f** 5  **g** 4

**12.3** Tell students to cover the email on page 87. Students then work alone to unscramble the phrases. They discuss their answers, including the function of each phrase, with a partner before feeding back to the class.

➠ **Answers**
   **1** As a follow-up to our meeting on June 24 … (function b)
   **2** According to the facts as I understand them, … (function a)
   **3** At this stage in the matter, it would be helpful if you could give me … (function f)
   **4** While I believe your chances of recovering some damages are good, … (function g)

**12.4** This writing activity can be done in class or at home. See Writing section, page xiv. Make sure students use Mrs Hayes' email as a model and a source of useful expressions.

## 13  Reading D: Types of breach

Tell students to read the introduction (SB page 88) and elicit definitions and examples for the three types of breach.

**13.1** Do this with the whole group. The paragraph is very short, so it is easy to identify the sentence. When you check the answer, make sure students understand that hops are an important ingredient used in brewing beer.

➠ **Answer**
   *I will outline the law in this jurisdiction as it applies to the facts in the instant case.*

**13.2** Tell students to look at the three questions. Then tell them to read the letter of advice to find the relevant sections for each question. Allow three to four minutes for this. When they have finished reading, tell them to work in small groups to discuss their answers, reminding them to use their own words, rather than simply copy words from the email.

**Suggested answers**
   **1** The issue in the instant case is whether a seller may sue a buyer for anticipatory breach of contract when the buyer tells the seller that he will not accept the goods, even though the seller was not yet obligated under the contract to deliver the goods.
   **2** The non-breaching party in this case has two options: firstly, he may trust what the buyer has said and conclude that, legally, he no longer has to do the things he promised to do under the contract. Secondly, he could continue to act as if the contract was still in force, as long as this does not cause any harm to the buyer.
   **3** Under the reliance principle, if one party to a contract tells the other party to the contract that it will not abide by what they agreed to in the contract, then this other party (non-breaching party) can legally rely on this verbal notice of intent to breach and take action accordingly. This principle relates to the case at hand because the seller has attempted to make deliveries under a long-term contract with the buyer, but the buyer refused to accept the goods on the first delivery date. Since the contract was for deliveries over a number of years, the reliance principle can apply if the buyer has informed the seller that it will continue to refuse the goods for the remaining term of the contract.

---

🖋 **Background notes**
   ○ If you *repudiate* /rɪˈpjuːdɪeɪt/ a contract, you refuse to accept its validity.
   ○ If something is *futile* /ˈfjuːtaɪl/, it is pointless.
   ○ If something is *lucrative* /ˈluːkrətɪv/, it can generate a lot of money.

---

**13.3** Do this quickly with the whole class. If students struggle, you could point out that there are four such sentences, one in paragraph 6 and three in paragraph 7. There are other references to proceedings in court, but only these four relate to actions and rulings of the court.

The courts here have reasoned that ...
Admittedly, there is a precedent stating that ...
In a leading case on this point, Judge Hand stated that ...
This seems to be the majority position in this jurisdiction.

**13.4** This writing activity can be done in class or at home. See Writing section, page xiv. Note that this writing activity could be treated as good practice for Part 2 of the ILEC Test of Writing, in which case you could set a word limit (200–250 words) and/or a time limit (45 minutes).

**Suggested answer**

Dear Aidan

I have been informed that you will be taking over the Robillard case from Susan Whiteman during her illness and am therefore writing to fill you in on the nature of the case itself, as well as on its current status.

As you will see from the attached letter from Ms. Whiteman to our client, Dr. Robillard, the case involves a contract for the sale of hops to the Pat Turner Breweries. Our colleague's interpretation of the relevant law with regard to the facts of the case has led her to advise Dr. Robillard to sue the opposing party in order to recover damages for anticipatory breach of contract. Ms. Whiteman is convinced that the prospects for a successful outcome are very good. Ms. Whiteman has asked Dr. Robillard to contact her secretary for an appointment to discuss further steps in the case. I suggest you write to him and inform him that you have been entrusted with the matter in her absence. Should you require any further assistance, please do not hesitate to contact me.

Best wishes
Melanie Tang

 Tell students to do the Internet activity as homework. See Using the Internet for research on page xviii.

# Language focus

## Answers

**1 Vocabulary: distinguishing meaning**
1 *rely*: The others mean 'reject'.
2 *intensify*: The others mean 'make less strong'; *intensify* means 'make stronger'.
3 *injury*: The others are payments for injuries.
4 *occasion*: The others mean 'option'.
5 *curious*: The others mean 'reluctant'.
6 *the Court argued*: The others concern decisions.

**2 Language use**
2 held that / ruled that
3 dismissed/rejected; finding that

**3 Word formation**

| Verb | Noun |
|------|------|
| remedy | remedy |
| breach | breach |
| intend | intent / intention |
| rely | reliance |
| violate | violation |
| enforce | enforcement |
| reverse | reversal |
| anticipate | anticipation |
| compute | computation |
| perform | performance |

**4 Collocations with *damages* and *a clause* 1**
2 a  3 e  4 b  5 d  6 h  7 f  8 i  9 g

**5 Collocations with *damages* and *a clause* 2**
1 award, claim, collect, mitigate, seek, sue for
2 contain, exclude, interpret, perform, strike, violate

**6 Vocabulary: word choice**
2 result from  3 thereof  4 ascertain
5 on  6 herein  7 shall

**7 Vocabulary: adjective plus noun**
2 b  3 f  4 c  5 a  6 d

**8 Word formation**
2 specified  3 expressly  4 breaching
5 repudiating  6 termination

# Case study 2: Environmental law

## The facts of the case

Tell students to read the facts of the case carefully to answer the question. When you discuss the answer with the class, elicit onto the board as much information as possible about the two parties, Newton and Capable. Also try to guess with the class the total cost of the clean-up (e.g. €100 million), and write the figure onto the board. The real-life accuracy of the figure is unimportant, but it will be useful to have a figure in mind during the negotiations.

 **Suggested answer**
The issue is whether Newton Construction Co. is liable in damages to the Capable Company pursuant to Section 320 (a)(3) of the Complete Environmental Reimbursement and Liability Act (CERLA).

 **Background notes**
○ For an analysis of a similar case in the USA, see http://thewaterlaw.blogspot.com/2009/05/arranger-liability-under-cercla.html.
○ *Methyl alcohol*, also known as methanol, is a simple alcohol, often used as anti-freeze or as a raw material for a wide range of chemical substances. It is highly toxic for humans: see http://en.wikipedia.org/wiki/Methyl_alcohol.
○ If something *deteriorates* /dɪ'tɪərɪəreɪts/, its condition worsens.
○ The *Complete Environmental Reimbursement and Liability Act* (CERLA) has been invented for this Case Study, but similar legislation exists in many countries, such as the Comprehensive Environmental Response, Compensation, and Liability Act (CERCLA) in the USA.
○ *Reimbursement* /riːm'bɜːsmənt/ means paying money back, either to a lender or in the form of damages to an injured party.

## Task 1: Role-play

1   Divide the class into two teams and assign a company to each team. Allow at least 15 minutes for the teams to read and analyse the documents and to prepare for the negotiations. Monitor carefully to make sure they have understood the documents properly, but avoid guiding them towards the conclusions presented below (Relevant legal documents).

2   Put students into pairs to negotiate a settlement. If you have an odd number of students, you will need to have one group of three. Encourage students to use the language and techniques from Unit 6 in their negotiations, and make sure they realise that the aim for both parties is to settle this issue without having to go to court. Allow at least ten minutes for the negotiations.

3   Ask each pair to feed back on their negotiation. Focus especially on different conclusions reached by different pairs, and any useful negotiating techniques that students used. Feed back on the effectiveness of students' negotiating language.

## Task 2: Writing

Ask students to do the writing as a homework task.

 **Model answer**
Dear Managing Director,
Re. *Capable v. Newton Construction Co.*
In accordance with your instructions, I have reviewed the above-referenced file and can advise as follows. Please note that all the advice stated in this letter is conditional and subject to further investigation.
Initially, there is one primary issue of law which arises based on the facts which you have supplied me. Specifically, whether Newton Construction can be held liable as an "arranger" under the Complete Environmental Reimbursement and Liability Act (CERLA). If we can convince a court that

Newton Construction qualifies as an arranger under this Act, there is a possibility that Capable could recover all of the costs expended in cleaning up the methyl alcohol. From my review of the relevant CERLA provisions, i.e. Section 320, Sub-section 3, the primary issue above is, in turn, dependent on whether the facts support a conclusion that Newton Construction "otherwise arranged for disposal or treatment" of the methyl alcohol (a hazardous substance). Unfortunately, this issue is not well settled in this jurisdiction. The two most important decisions regarding this issue appear to have two different approaches. One court has focused on both the terms "arranged" and "disposal", leaving room for broad interpretation of both terms. Of course, this decision might permit us to rely on the fact that Newton Construction had an "obligation to control" the methyl alcohol (which it failed to do), thus relieving us from the burden of proving intent to dispose of the hazardous substances. The other decision is, unfortunately, not in our favor, as it narrows the interpretation of both "arrange" and "dispose" by focusing on the requirement of intent by the "arranger." As I understand it from the facts you have provided, proving intent is not likely, since Newton Construction maintains that it was completely unaware of the damage which caused the leak.

I would suggest that the best course at this juncture would be to commence discussions with Newton Construction in order to 'feel them out' regarding settlement. I am uncomfortable with our chances in court due to the conflicting legal decisions regarding the issues at hand. At this stage, I think it would be wiser to play the moral hand, as certainly Newton Construction has caused considerable contamination, with Capable bearing the costs.

I look forward to your instructions on how you wish to proceed. Please contact me if you would like further clarification of any of the points I've raised.

Truly yours
John R. Moore
Attorney-at-Law

## Relevant legal documents

○ **Text 1:** The four persons listed (1–4) are each covered (i.e. liable) for the three types of costs, A, B and C. Note that *person* here could refer to a natural person or a legal person (e.g. a company). For the purposes of this Case Study, Person 1 could apply to Capable, as they owned the pipeline. This depends to some extent on whether a pipeline can be described as a vessel, a term normally reserved for either boats/ships, etc., containers or tubes within a body (e.g. blood vessels). However, it is perhaps more reasonable to describe a pipeline as a facility, in which case Person 1 applies. Persons 2, 3 and 4 may or may not apply to Capable, depending on how disposal is defined (see Text 2). However, this may not be relevant, as Capable is already covered by Person 1. It is hard to argue that Newton is liable according to any of these definitions, although lawyers might try to include Newton as Person 3, as 'a person who otherwise arranged for disposal of hazardous substances owned or possessed by any other party'. This argument depends on the idea that causing a leak is a type of arranging, and a leakage is a type of disposal (see Text 2).

○ **Text 2** is an example of a precedent which may enable the parties to resolve the questions raised in Text 1 above. In the earlier case, a narrow definition of disposal was rejected, leaving open the possibility that the leak caused by Newton was a type of disposal. The issue of arrangement is not resolved in this text, and comes up again in Text 4.

○ **Text 3:** The concept of *joint and several liability* is used in many common-law jurisdictions. Where joint and several liability applies, even if several parties are jointly liable for some costs, a claimant may choose to sue only one of those parties to recover the full amount (= liability for the full harm). It is then up to that party to try to recover some money back from other liable parties. This seems to be what has happened in this Case Study: the Euphorian government has successfully sued Capable, which was unquestionably at least partly liable for the leak, and left it up to Capable to sue Newton, where the liability is much less obvious. Newton could try to argue that joint and several liability does not apply in this case, because there is a reasonable basis for division according to the contribution of each (e.g. Newton is liable for the cost of repairing the pipe but not responsible for the leak itself).

○ **Text 4** returns to the definition of *arrange*, and suggests strongly that Newton was not an arranger, and is therefore not covered under Section 320.

---

**Background notes**

○ *Response costs* are costs incurred when a party responds to a threat (e.g. by closing a shop after a bomb threat), even if the threat is averted.

○ *Remedial* /rɪˈmiːdɪəl/ *action* is action taken to remedy a situation.

○ A *contingency plan* is a plan drawn up to deal with 'what if' situations.

○ *Arranger liability* is an important concept under the CERCLA (see Background notes above), and is defined under Person 3 in Text 1. An Internet search for the term *Arranger liability* will lead to reports of several cases similar to this Case Study.

○ A *bright-line test* is a test to determine points of law (e.g. whether Party A is liable or not). In contrast with fine-line tests, bright-line tests provide clear-cut answers with little room for argument. See http://en.wikipedia.org/wiki/Bright-line_test.

○ A *treatise* /ˈtriːtɪs/ is a scholarly legal publication, which may be treated as the definitive analysis of a particular field of law.

○ *Common parlance* /ˈkɒmən ˈpɑːləns/ refers to everyday language, i.e. the way non-specialists use a particular word or phrase.

# 7 Contracts: assignment and third-party rights

## Teacher's brief

This unit deals with two rather technical and complicated aspects of contract law: **assignment** and **third-party rights**. You can expect some significant differences between your students' jurisdictions and the law of England and Scotland, which are the dominant jurisdictions in this unit. Because there is so much room for variation, the Internet is not especially helpful in providing background information. If you would like to research these areas in your students' jurisdictions, it is recommended that you conduct an Internet search for expressions such as *third-party rights*, *third-party beneficiary contract* and *vesting*, together with the name of the jurisdictions. However, it might be more sensible to assign this research to your students.

The unit begins with an introduction (Reading A) to the two exceptions to the general rule of **privity of contract**, which states that only the parties to a contract have **enforceable rights** under that contract. The first exception concerns **third-party beneficiary contracts**, which give rights to a non-signing party. For example, A agrees to build B's new factory. A then contracts a builder, C, to do the work. When C fails to do the work satisfactorily, the question arises as to whether B can sue C, even though B does not have a contract with C.

Historically, English law held that B could not sue C. However, as a result of the **Contracts (Rights of Third Parties) 1999 Act**, as mentioned in Reading E, such third-party rights have become enforceable, as they are in many other jurisdictions. Reading E is used to introduce the topic of **keeping informed: sources of information** which a lawyer needs to use regularly. The text also raises the issue of 'moving' a contract from one jurisdiction to another, in this case from English law to Scottish law, depending on which jurisdiction is most suited to the needs of the contracting parties.

Within the complicated area of third-party rights, there is the further complication of when such rights **vest** (become legally enforceable): at the time of the contract, or some time later. This is a further area you could ask your students to research.

The second exception concerns **assignation** (or **assignment**): transfer of contractual rights and/or duties from one party to a new party. This most typically happens when one party sells a business or part of a business, and the buyer takes on the rights and duties. As Reading A explains, there is an important distinction between **assignment of rights** and **delegation of duties**.

Reading B is a **Right of First Refusal Clause**, which sets out the procedure for assigning (selling) shares to a third party (i.e. someone other than the parties to the contract). According to such a clause, before the **assigning party** (seller) can assign his/her shares to a third party, the **non-assigning party** (i.e. a party to the contract who is neither the seller nor prospective buyer, but perhaps an existing shareholder) has the right to buy the shares instead. Only if the non-assigning party declines the opportunity to buy the shares can the third party buy them.

An assignment forms the background to a **case study** dominating the middle of the unit (after Listening A): a restaurant owner trying to sell his business to a buyer, but being blocked by the owner of the property in which the restaurant operates, who refuses to consent to the assignment. The case study focuses on the **closing argument** of a lawsuit being prepared by the restaurant owner's lawyer, and is used to exemplify a range of skills and techniques that lawyers need: **emailing a colleague** (Reading C); **constructing a strong closing argument** (Reading D); **persuasive writing and speaking**; and **emphatic stress** (Listening B).

The unit also provides input and practice of several language points, especially words ending in **–ee** and **–or** (e.g. *obligee*/*obligor*) and the use of **verb + –ing** after certain verbs.

### Further information

○ For a **general introduction to contracts**, including many of the issues covered in this unit, see http://contracts.lawyers.com/contracts/.

○ For **more detailed and thorough information**, see http://profj.us/wlac/3rdparty.htm, http://www.lawreform.ns.ca/Downloads/Privity_DIS.

pdf and http://www.lawteacher.net/Contract/Privity/Privity.htm.

○ For the full text of the **1999 Rights of Third Parties Act**, see http://www.legislation.gov.uk/ukpga/1999/31/contents. An excellent article provides both a background to this act and, at the same time, offers clear examples of situations where third-party rights are

important: http://www.cic.org.uk/services/Contracts_%20RightThird%20Parties.pdf.

○ There is a very thorough list of **links to law sites** around the world at http://www.lawguru.com/lawlinks/International_Resources/index.html. The search facility on the same site may also prove useful in finding country-specific information connected with the topics of this unit.

## Discussion

Use these questions to generate a discussion.

a When might a third party have rights under a contract between two other parties?

b What can a third party do if a contract is breached?

c When might a party to a contract assign rights or duties to a third party?

d What conflicts can arise as a result of assignments and third-party rights?

 **Answers**

a The most obvious example is a life assurance policy: the life assurer (party A) doesn't pay the customer (party B) but a member of the customer's family (party C) because party B has died. A similar situation concerns motor insurance: if a driver (party A) crashes into another car, the insurer (party B) pays the owner of the other car (party C) for the damage. Or an employer (party A) might agree with an employee (party B) to pay for medical treatment for the employee's husband or wife (party C).

b This depends on a whole range of issues, as set out in Reading A, and will vary from jurisdiction to jurisdiction. A third party may attempt to sue the breaching party, but is in a much weaker position than the parties to the contract.

c For example, when a business is bought or sold, the former owners will want to assign rights and duties to the new owners as regards things such as property leases, loan agreements and contracts with employees, customers, suppliers, etc.

d An obvious conflict is where one party refuses to acknowledge the rights of the third party, or the right to assign the contract. They may object to the third party becoming involved because they were comfortable with the original two-party contract.

## 1 Reading A: Introduction to contract assignation

Tell students to discuss the four statements briefly in pairs in order to predict whether they are true or false. Then tell them to read the text carefully to check. Allow enough time for them to read slowly (e.g. three to four minutes), as the text is rather difficult. When they have finished reading, tell them to compare their answers with their partners, and then go through the answers with the class.

 **Answers**
1 True
2 True
3 False (It is known as an assignment.)
4 False (The contract is renewed, but one of the contracting parties has been substituted.)

📝 **Background notes**
○ The terms *assignment* /əˈsaɪnmənt/ and *assignation* /ˌæsɪgˈneɪʃən/ are used interchangeably in this unit. Different terms are used in different jurisdictions, e.g. in England and Wales *assignment* is used, while in Scotland it is *assignation*.
○ *Performance* is simply fulfilling the obligations of a contract. The collocation *to render performance*

means 'to perform one's duties according to the obligations of the contract'.

○ Paragraph 2 asks a question: ... *must the intent be from both parties ... or just the recipient ... ?* Although the question is not answered, the suggestion is that if the intent is from both parties, there is no dispute that the third party does have an enforceable right. If the intent is from only one party, however, we get into the grey area discussed in paragraph 3.

○ If something is *inferred* /ɪnˈfɜːd/, it is interpreted in a particular way because somebody or something implies it. For a discussion on the difference between *imply* and *infer*, see, for example, http://www.cjr.org/tools/lc/imply.asp.

○ The exact definition of *assignee* /əsaɪˈniː/ will vary according to the context (e.g. contract formation, third-party rights, etc.). The definition given in the glossary is deliberately general. Students should be encouraged to look at the context to work out a more precise definition in each case.

**Pronunciation notes**

assignor /əˈsaɪnəʳ/
beneficiary /ˌbenəˈfɪʃəri/
confer /kənˈfɜːʳ/
delegate (*noun*) /ˈdeləgət/
delegate (*verb*) /ˈdeləgeɪt/
delegatee /ˌdeləgəˈtiː/
obligee /ɒblɪˈgiː/
obligor /ɒblɪˈgɔːʳ/
privity /ˈprɪvɪti/
promisee /prɒmɪˈsiː/
promisor /prɒmɪˈsɔːʳ/

**Optional extension**
**Photocopiable worksheet 7.1**

Photocopiable worksheet 7.1 contains a visual representation of Reading A, designed to make the rather complicated relationships easier to follow.

Tell students to work alone or in pairs to complete the words in the diagram. Point out that the starting point is the shaded box and

that the answers are numbered mostly in the order they appear in the text. Most, but not all, of the missing words are shown in bold in Reading A, and the first letter of each word has been given. When they have finished, go through the answers with the class.

**Answers**

**1** Privity; contract   **2** confers rights; imposes duties   **3** Third-party beneficiary contracts
**4** promisee; promisor; third-party beneficiary
**5** legally enforceable right   **6** Intent
**7** identified   **8** performance   **9** rights under
**10** inferred; benefit   **11** intended beneficiary
**12** incidental beneficiary   **13** obligee; obligor
**14** obligor; obligee   **15** assignor; assignee
**16** obligee   **17** delegator; delegate(e)
**18** Assignment; contract   **19** assign
**20** delegate   **21** release   **22** Novation

## 2   Key terms: Contracts

**2.1** Tell students to work alone or in pairs to complete the exercise. Make sure they read the text through first before they start filling in the gaps. When they have finished, go through the answers with the class.

**Answers**

**1** Novation   **2** benefits   **3** third party
**4** novation   **5** novation   **6** assignment
**7** Assignment   **8** parties   **9** assignment
**10** novation

**2.2** Tell students to work in pairs to find the collocations and to explain them. If they struggle to come up with their own definitions, when they have found the collocations, read one or two of the sample definitions below for the students to guess which definition relates to which collocation. Encourage students to use similarly straightforward language in their definitions.

**Answers (with suggested definitions)**

**2** impose duties: This means to place obligations on someone in a contract.
**3** enforce contractual provisions: This means to make someone do or not do something as stated in a contract.

**4** render performance: This means to do or not do something as stated in a contract.

**5** delegate duties: This means to give duties to someone else to do on your behalf.

**6** assign rights: This means to transfer the rights to a third party so that they have them.

## 3 Language use A: Nouns ending in –*or* and –*ee*

Ask students to remember which words ending in –*or* and –*ee* were used in the text. Then tell them to read the information in the box to check and complete the exercise.

 **Answers**

**2** delegator; delegate(e)   **3** obligor; obligee   **4** assignor; assignee

Elicit more examples of everyday and legal words with these endings. (See Optional extension below.)

---

**Optional extension**

Put students into teams. Tell them to decide which of the following words are authentic, and which have been invented. This exercise is designed to introduce some of the important vocabulary that will come up in the rest of the unit (*to vest, lessor, lessee, trustor, trustee*). You may need to explain some of the verbs (*to vest, to sue, to lease*) with weaker students. Read through the words slowly, making sure to pronounce the –*or* /ɔːʳ/ and –*ee* /iː/ endings clearly. When you have finished, award points for correct answers to find the winning team.

| | | |
|---|---|---|
| **1** | a contractor | (authentic) |
| **2** | a contractee | (invented, should be *contracted party*) |
| **3** | a payor | (invented, should be *payer*) |
| **4** | a payee | (authentic) |
| **5** | an investor | (authentic) |
| **6** | an investee | (authentic) |
| **7** | a vestor | (invented, should be *vesting party*) |
| **8** | a vestee | (authentic) |
| **9** | a suor | (invented, should be *suing party*) |
| **10** | a suee | (invented, should be *sued party*) |
| **11** | a lessor | (authentic) |
| **12** | a lessee | (authentic) |
| **13** | an employor | (invented, should be *employer*) |
| **14** | an employee | (authentic) |
| **15** | a nominor | (invented, should be *nominator*) |
| **16** | a nominee | (authentic) |
| **17** | an advisor | (authentic) |
| **18** | an advisee | (authentic) |
| **19** | an interviewor | (invented, should be *interviewer*) |
| **20** | an interviewee | (authentic) |
| **21** | a trustee | (authentic) |
| **22** | a trustor | (authentic) |

## 4 Speaking A: Explaining third-party rights

Tell students to read the box to identify three different times when third-party rights can vest. Make sure all the students understand the meaning of the verb *to vest* before they read. When they have finished, elicit the three times. Discuss briefly with the class why this might become important. Elicit examples.

 **Answers**

At the time of the contract; when the third party agrees to accept the benefits; and when the third party takes (or refuses to take) some kind of action in order for his rights to vest

For example: Party A orders a machine from party B, but as a result of a communication breakdown, both parties assume they are responsible for transporting and installing the machine in A's factory. On the Monday that the machine is ready, B contracts C to deliver and install the machine for A, and C sets off on the long journey to A's factory. In some jurisdictions, A already has rights as the third-party beneficiary of the contract between B and C (this is important if the machine is damaged, and A needs to sue C). In other jurisdictions, these rights have not yet vested, as A is not aware of the contract. On the Tuesday, A informs B by telephone that it is planning to send its lorry to pick up the machine the following day (Wednesday), but is pleasantly surprised to find out that the machine is already on its way. In some jurisdictions, A's rights vest on the Tuesday, when it becomes aware of the contract, but in others the rights vest on the Wednesday, when it refrains from taking action it would otherwise have taken (i.e. sending its own lorry), and also takes action it would not otherwise have taken (i.e. receiving the delivery from C and allowing C's engineers to begin installing the machine). In jurisdictions without third-party rights, of course, A's rights will never vest. However, A might still be able to sue C for the damage because it can argue that it made an oral or implied contract with C by inviting C's engineers onto its premises.

**4.1** Tell students to discuss the question in pairs. If they are not sure of the situation in their jurisdiction, they should discuss what they think the law ought to be. If they are struggling, you could write these options on the board and ask which apply to students' jurisdiction(s):

○ Third-party rights arise immediately at the time the contract is made.
○ Third-party rights do not arise until the third party acquires knowledge of the rights and agrees to accept the benefits.
○ Third-party rights do not arise until the third-party beneficiary has changed his position in reliance upon the contract.
○ Third-party rights as described above are not recognised.

When you discuss the answers with the class, if students seem familiar with the concept of vesting of third-party rights, you could ask them to suggest advantages and disadvantages of the four positions.

**4.2** Discuss the question with the whole class.

# 5 Reading B: Understanding contract clauses

**5.1** Tell students to read through the introduction (SB page 96) and the first paragraph of the text (i.e. the section before point 1) (SB page 97) in order to answer the question. Discuss the answer with the class.

 **Answers**
The non-assigning party has the right to elect to refuse and avail himself of or consent to the assignment, transfer or sale of interest in the shares, except for the transfer to the party's heirs, personal representatives or conservators in the case of death or legal incapacity.

 **Background notes**
○ A person's *heirs* /eəz/ are the people who inherit the person's property when that person dies.
○ A *personal representative*, also known as an executor, is the person assigned in a will (or testament) to handle the affairs of a person who has died.
○ A *conservator* is assigned by a court to oversee the financial or personal affairs of a person who has become incapacitated.
○ *Legal incapacity* is the lack of the ability to handle one's own affairs, typically as a result of physical or mental disability. In the USA, the term *mentally incompetent* is used.

**5.2** Tell students to read through the questions. Then tell them to read the text carefully to find the answers. Allow enough time for them to read fairly slowly (three to four minutes). When they have finished, tell them to discuss their answers in pairs, and then check with the whole class.

**Answers**

1 In the case of a transfer of one party's interest in the Agreement to the party's heirs, personal representatives or conservators in the case of death or legal incapacity.

2 The written notice must set forth all of the terms and conditions of the proposed assignment and all available information concerning the proposed assignee, including but not limited to information concerning the proposed assignee's employment history, financial condition, credit history, skill and qualifications, and in the case of a partnership or corporate assignee, of its partners or shareholders.

3 Within ten days after receiving the notice (or, if additional information is requested, within ten days after receiving the additional information), the non-assigning party may either consent or withhold its consent to the assignment, or accept the assignment to itself or to its nominee upon the terms and conditions specified in the notice. The non-assigning party may substitute an equivalent sum of cash for any consideration other than cash specified in the notice.

**Background notes**

○ The *financial condition* of a company or individual is defined by their assets (what they own) minus their liabilities (what they owe) at a given moment.

○ A *credit history* is a record of a company's or individual's past behaviour in terms of borrowing and repaying debts.

**5.3** Tell students to do this exercise in pairs. When you go through the answers with the class, you could make a quick quiz: you read the definition and students have to give the legal expression without looking at their books.

**Answers**

**1** g  **2** c  **3** e  **4** a  **5** f  **6** d  **7** b

**Background notes**

A more accurate synonym of *incapacity* might be *incompetence*. Unfortunately, this term has derogatory connotations in everyday English; in legal English, however, it is purely descriptive.

**Optional extension**

Elicit from the class the function of each of the four paragraphs in the text on SB page 97, and write these on the board.

**Possible answers**

Introductory paragraph: Right of first refusal with exception; §1 what the assigning party must do; §2 the non-assigning party's three options; §3 what happens if the non-assigning party waives the right.

Then tell students to close their books and to discuss in small groups as much as they can remember about one of the paragraphs listed on the board. They should attempt to write the paragraph from memory. Point out that they do not need to copy the original word for word, but that they should include all relevant details and use accurate and appropriate language. When they have finished, they should pass their writing on to another group to check against the original. Give and invite feedback on the strengths and weaknesses of each group's writing.

**CD1**
**T26–27**

## 6 Listening A: Preparing a lawsuit and developing an argument

Elicit from the class a) some time-consuming activities which are involved in preparing a lawsuit, and b) some factors which affect the strength of an argument presented in court. Then tell them to read the introduction (SB page 97) to compare it with their suggestions.

**6.1** Tell students to read through the seven sentences to make sure they understand all the vocabulary. Check that they understand *lessor*, *lease* and *to withdraw an offer*. Then tell them to listen to the recording to tick the facts that the lawyer mentions. After the recording, tell students to compare their answers in pairs, and to discuss what they remember about each of the facts.

**Transcript »** STUDENT'S BOOK **page 285**

**Answers**

He mentions numbers 2, 4 and 6.

**Background notes**

○ If you *defer* /dɪˈfɜːʳ/ making a decision, you avoid making it until a later time.

○ *Personal animosity* is a formal way of saying that somebody got on very badly with somebody else.

**6.2** Tell students to discuss these questions in pairs. With less experienced students, it might be better to do this with the whole class.

**Suggested answers**

Note that three good arguments are mentioned in the second part of the conversation (see answers to Exercise 6.3), so avoid giving away these 'answers'.
A lawyer would have to prove that:

○ the lease permitted assignment, and that Jones Corp. was not permitted to withhold consent unreasonably;

○ Jones Corp. did in fact withhold consent;

○ this withholding was unreasonable.

**6.3** Tell students to listen to the second part to find the three arguments. Allow them a chance to compare and discuss their answers with a partner before checking them with the class.

**Transcript »** STUDENT'S BOOK **page 285**

**Answers**

The three points of evidence Ron will use are:

○ the excellent credit rating of prospective buyer;

○ the expert witness on commercial lease transactions who will testify that Jones Corp. had sufficient information to make a decision;

○ the evidence that suggests the relationship between Keats and Mr Jones was not a good one.

**Background notes**

○ Ron says that Jones Corp. *essentially* withheld consent. *Essentially* here is used in the legal meaning of *of the essence*. In other words, they withheld consent according to the technical definition of *withhold*.

○ If you *keep somebody posted*, it means you keep them informed of any changes.

**Optional extension**
**ILEC preparation: Test of Listening Part 3**
**Photocopiable worksheet 7.2**

If your students are planning to take the ILEC exam, point out that Part 3 of the Test of Listening requires students to insert missing words into sentences. There is usually one word (or a number) for each space. Photocopiable worksheet 7.2 practises this technique, using the recording from Listening A (parts 1 and 2). Of course, in the real exam, students would not have a chance to listen and discuss the recording beforehand, as they will here.

Hand out the worksheet. Tell students to work alone to remember (or work out) which words filled each space. Point out that the sentences are in note form, so words like articles (*a/the*) are not normally used. Then play both parts of the recording again for them to check their answers and fill in the remaining gaps. Allow students to discuss their answers in pairs but not to change their original answers. When you go through the answers with the class, award one point for each correct answer.

**Answers**
**1** commercial  **2** third party  **3** assignment
**4** (written) consent  **5** withhold  **6** personal;
financial  **7** driver's licence  **8** deferred
**9** withdrew  **10** breach  **11** interference
**12** animosity  **13** unreasonably
**14** credit rating  **15** lease  **16** evidence

## 7  Reading C: A follow-up email

Tell students to read the introduction and the questions (SB page 98). Before they read, elicit from the class what they expect the purpose of the email to be. Then tell them to read the email to answer the two questions. Allow a very limited amount of time (30–60 seconds). Tell students to discuss the answers with a partner, and then go through them with the class.

**Answers**

1 The purposes of the email are to inform his colleague about the progress of the case and to get feedback on his closing argument.

2 He would like to get suggestions for improving his argument from his colleague.

---

**Optional extension**

Ask students to work in pairs to underline examples of semi-informal language. Point out that a good way of achieving semi-informality is by adding indefinite language, as this can appear less aggressive. When they have found some examples, collect the ideas from the class.

**Suggested answers**

(semi-informal language underlined, indefinite language boxed )

Hi Sam

Haven't been around for the last couple of days – I've been in court on the Keats case. You asked me to keep you posted on how things are going – I have to say, it's going pretty well. I've finished drafting my closing argument for tomorrow. Would you mind looking at the draft and letting me know what you think of it? I'm basically quite satisfied with it, but I would still appreciate getting some input from you.
It would be great if you could give me some feedback on this. Can I ask you to send it to me by 5 p.m.? That way I'll be able to make any changes that you think are necessary.
I look forward to hearing your suggestions.

---

# 8 Language use B: Verb + –*ing* form

Tell students to read the information in the box to find a common mistake. When they have finished, elicit any rules they know about such verb patterns.

**Language note**

It is often said that there are no rules governing the choice of verb + –*ing* or *to* + verb. In fact there are some rules, but they are not perfect:

**Rule 1**

When a preposition is followed by a verb, the verb is always in the –*ing* form: *I'm afraid **of falling** / worried **about failing** / interested **in going** / fed up **with waiting***, etc. This is a very reliable rule. The problem is that the word *to* is sometimes a preposition (e.g. *I'm looking forward **to** meeting* / *used **to** presenting*) and sometimes simply part of the infinitive (e.g. *I want **to** work*). A second problem is that *about* is sometimes used as an adjective, as in *I'm **about** to go* (cf. *I'm ready to go*).

**Rule 2**

When a verb means 'forward in time', it is followed by *to* + verb (e.g. *I want/need/hope/plan/expect/long **to meet** you*).
When it means 'back in time', it is followed by verb + –*ing* (e.g. *I regret/ remember/ miss/deny/admit/stopped **smoking***).
When it means 'all time', it is also followed by verb + –*ing* (*I like / enjoy / can't stand / spend time **cooking***).
The problem is that there are exceptions, e.g. *I'm dreading **meeting** her* (= forward in time); *I used **to live** here* (= back in time); *I tend **to forget** things* (= all time).

**8.1** Do this as a class.

**Answers**

mind looking ... letting; appreciate getting; look forward to hearing (NB The latter is a phrasal verb (*look forward to*) followed by an –*ing* form.)

**8.2** Tell students to do the exercise in pairs. When they have finished, check the answers with the class.

**Answers**

1 a  2 b  3 a  4 a  5 a  6 b  7 a  8 a

## Language note

Students may ask you to explain why question 7 contains the structure *having had* rather than simply *having*. If the client mentioned *having* an argument, we can imagine that he said *I have an argument* (= a long-running disagreement) *with my landlord*. If the client mentioned *having had* an argument, we can imagine that he said *I had* (or *I have had*) *an argument with my landlord* (= we argued). In everyday English, this distinction is not always made (so *mentioned having an argument* could have both meanings), but in legal English it is useful to be precise. Another example might be *He admitted insulting her* (= he said *I insult her from time to time*) vs. *He admitted having insulted her* (= he said *I insulted her on one occasion*).

**8.3**   Tell students to do the exercise in pairs. Go through the answers with the class.

 **Answers**

**1** suing   **2** giving   **3** breaching   **4** to re-draft
**5** gathering   **6** hearing   **7** to tell   **8** arguing

## Optional extension

Elicit from the class how they can learn such verb patterns.

**Suggested answer**

The first step is to notice the patterns when they encounter them. This is harder than it sounds. The second step is to write the patterns down. In vocabulary notebooks, they could make lists in two columns, e.g.:

| | |
|---|---|
| *to consider* | *doing something* |
| *to mention* | *doing something / having done something* |
| *to refuse* | *to do something* |
| *to urge* /ɜːdʒ/ | *somebody to do something* |

Alternatively, they could make a bank of vocabulary cards (e.g. on one side: *to consider*; on the other side: *doing something*). Point out that all good learners' dictionaries contain such information.

The third step is to learn the patterns. They should either cover the right-hand column in their notebooks and test themselves on the patterns, or they could look at one side of each card to try to remember the pattern on the back. Whichever system they use, they should repeat it regularly until they know the patterns. The advantage of using cards rather than a list is that students can sort cards in order to focus on priority vocabulary (e.g. *to involve doing something*), rather than having to keep studying a mixture of known vocabulary (e.g. *to want to do something*) and more obscure vocabulary (e.g. *to urge somebody to do something*).

Tell students to try one of the two techniques on the verb patterns in the first half of this unit. Conduct the following test twice: once before they have had a chance to try the techniques, and a second time at the end of the unit. Keep a record of their scores. Compare the improvement rates of the two techniques (as well as the improvement rate of any students who do not try either of the techniques).

Read the number and the beginning of the phrase. Tell the students to write either *to* or *–ing*.

**1** to intend for somebody (*to*) (Reading A)
**2** to provide for somebody (*to*) (Reading A)
**3** to fail (*to*) (Reading A)
**4** an intent (*or* to intend) (*to*) (Reading A)
**5** to wish (*to*) (Reading A)
**6** to be entitled (*or* to entitle somebody) (*to*) (Reading A)
**7** to attempt (*to*) (Reading A)
**8** to agree (*to*) (Speaking)
**9** to elect (*to*) (Reading B)
**10** to be permitted (*or* to permit somebody) (*to*) (Listening A)
**11** to decide (*to*) (Listening A)
**12** to be allowed (*or* to allow somebody) (*to*) (Listening A)
**13** to defer (*–ing*) (Listening A)
**14** to keep somebody (*–ing*) (Listening A)
**15** to plan (*to*) (Listening A)
**16** to finish (*–ing*) (Reading C)
**17** to mind (*–ing*) (Reading C)
**18** to appreciate (*–ing*) (Reading C)
**19** to ask somebody (*to*) (Reading C)
**20** to consider (*–ing*) (Language use)
**21** to involve (*–ing*) (Language use)
**22** to risk (*–ing*) (Language use)
**23** to suggest (*–ing*) (Language use)
**24** to refuse (*to*) (Language use)
**25** to mention (*–ing*) (Language use)
**26** to delay (*–ing*) (Language use)

## 9 Reading D: A closing argument

**9.1** Tell students to read the introduction and the list of documents (SB page 100). Point out that this question relates to the discussion in Listening A. Elicit what the lawyers mentioned in Listening A in connection with this question.

 **Answers**
First Jones Corp. requested *personal and financial information about the prospective buyer, followed by things like photocopies of his driver's licence, passport and 15 years of work history.*

Tell students to read through the draft to find the answers, and also to pay attention to Sam's handwritten comments. Tell students to decide whether the comments are all sensible and whether there is anything she missed. When they have finished reading, tell them to compare and discuss their answers in pairs and then go through the answers with the class.

 **Answers**
The lawyer requested numbers 3, 4 and 6. Sam's comments are intended to be both sensible and complete, but students may challenge this assumption. This may lead to some interesting discussion.

**Background notes**
- A *reasonably prudent person* is an imaginary person who uses good judgment or common sense in handling practical matters; such a person's actions are the guide in determining whether an individual's actions were reasonable.
- Note that *criteria* /ˌkraɪˈtɪərɪə/ is plural. The singular, *a criterion*, is very formal and rarely used.
- At the beginning of point 3, Ron uses *Here* to signal a change of focus from a theoretical and general argument to a specific argument about the case in hand.
- A *credit rating* is a score of credit worthiness, often issued by a ratings agency based on a company's history of repaying debts punctually and the likelihood that future debts will be paid punctually.

- Students may misinterpret the phrase *If it was perfect ...* . It looks like the beginning of a so-called second conditional, about an unreal present situation: *If the credit rating was (or were) perfect, we would give consent, but since it is not, we will not*. In fact, the phrase is about the real past: *We can assume that the credit rating was perfect. If this is true, then there is no reasonable reason for withholding.* There is no label (along the lines of first or second conditional) for such a structure.
- An *affirmative act* is an action which deliberately confirms something, such as making an official declaration or participating in a meeting.

 **Pronunciation notes**
arbitrary /ˈɑːbɪtrəri/
inferences /ˈɪnfərənsɪz/
justifiable /ˌdʒʌstɪˈfaɪəbl/
persuasive /pəˈsweɪsɪv/
predicated /ˈpredɪˌkeɪtɪd/
prior /ˈpraɪəʳ/

**9.2** Tell students to discuss the statements in pairs. You may decide to do Exercise 9.3 at the same time. When they have finished, check the answers with the class.

 **Answers**
1 True
2 False (He says *arbitrary considerations ... are not proper criteria*)
3 False (He says *refusing* is not the same as *withholding*.)

**9.3** Students should do this in pairs. When you have checked with the class, tell students to close their books. Read some of the definitions and elicit from the class what the original expression was.

 **Answers**
1 c  2 d  3 e  4 b  5 a

## 10 Text analysis: Persuasive writing and speaking

Elicit from the class some situations when a lawyer needs to use persuasive language. Elicit also the key elements of a strong argument. Then tell students to read the information in the box to compare it with their suggestions.

Tell students to do this exercise in pairs. When they have finished, go through the answers with the class.

 **Answers**
**a** 2  **b** 5  **c** 6  **d** 4  **e** 1  **f** 3

## 11 Writing: A memo giving advice

With the class, elicit language and tips for each of the bullet points. Make sure students are aware of the need for semi-informal language. Make sure they realise that Sam will attach Ron's closing arguments, including her annotations, so there is no need to list them here. Students then write their memos at home or in class. You could treat this as practice for Part 2 of the ILEC Test of Writing, in which case set a word limit (200–250 words) and/or a time limit (45 minutes).

 **Suggested language**
- ○ *Thanks for your memo.*
- ○ *You asked me for some feedback on your draft. Here are some ideas.*
- ○ *I think you need to … / Why don't you … ?/ It's important that you … / I felt that … could be improved / It's imperative that you … / I would recommend mentioning … / I suggest emphasising …*
- ○ *That's all / I hope you find these comments useful / Good luck in court / Let me know if there's anything else I can do.*

**Suggested memo**
Dear Ron
In response to your memo this morning, let me first say that I enjoyed reading your closing argument – well done! You asked me to give you some feedback, which you will find in the margins of the attached document. For the most part, the changes which I think should be made involve giving more emphasis to important points and being more explicit. I suggest emphasising that the delay was clearly unreasonable (due to perfect credit rating and sufficient information being provided). I don't think the importance of this point can be stressed enough. I would even repeat the word 'unreasonable' a few

times! You also need to be more explicit about the evidence showing the delay was based on personal animosity. I also recommend explicitly stating the reason why Mr Jones dislikes your client – that there was a lawsuit is not enough.
It is imperative that you point out that Mr Jones lost the suit and had to pay high damages to your client and therefore dislikes him.
Finally, I suggest emphasising that your client informed the defendants that time was of the essence in the matter of the assignment – this makes the delay appear more like an intentional attempt to harm your client.
Hope that these comments are of use to you. Feel free to contact me again if you have any questions.

Best
Sam
(224 words, not including salutations)

 **12 Listening B: A closing argument**

(CD1 T28)

Elicit a list of the changes that Sam suggested in her notes to Ron's closing argument. Write this list (or key words from each point, given in bold) on the board.

 **Answers**
- ○ If the proposed buyer had a 'perfect credit rating' then there is no reasonable reason for withholding. Jones Corp. had nothing to lose if they approved assignment.
- ○ Ron should stress that the client's expert on commercial lease transactions says enough information was provided. Again, there is no reasonable reason for withholding.
- ○ Sam asks what kind of evidence there was that the defendants' delay in approving the assignment was not related to the buyer's qualifications, but was predicated on a dispute with the client involving a prior lawsuit between the parties.
- ○ The dispute involving a prior lawsuit needs more emphasis. Mr Jones lost a suit to Keats five years ago, which is the reason for the animosity.

○ Did the client expressly inform his landlord that time was of the essence? In writing? If so, then Ron should say so.

Tell students to listen to the recording to answer the three questions. They discuss their answers in pairs before feeding back to the class. Discuss with the class if they think the argument is convincing or not.

**Transcript »** STUDENT'S BOOK **page 286**

 **Answers**
1 Ron says that the defendants' withholding of approval of the proposed buyer was unreasonable because the defendants' lawyer acknowledged that the proposed buyer had a 'perfect credit rating'.
2 Ron suggests that the defendants' real reason for withholding approval was that Mr Jones and his client had been engaged in a previous lawsuit which Mr Jones lost and which led to his having to pay high damages to Ron's client.

**Optional extension**
Students listen again to pay attention to how Ron incorporates Sam's suggestions (from the board) into his argument. At the end of the recording, tell students to work in small groups to try to remember what Ron said for each argument. Encourage them to reconstruct Ron's sentences as accurately as possible when you go through the answers with the class. Focus on the techniques Ron uses: rhetorical questions (*on what grounds?*) and repetition of *unreasonable* (or *not reasonable* or *unreasonably*), which occurs eight times in the argument.

**Suggested answer**
○ If the credit rating was 'perfect', then on what grounds did the defendants withhold approval? Surely not on reasonable grounds.
○ If the amount of information provided was sufficient, then on what grounds did the defendants delay making a decision? Surely not on reasonable grounds.
○ This evidence – a letter in which the defendants threaten to 'ruin' my client – makes it clear on which grounds the

defendants withheld approval: on unreasonable grounds.
○ Mr Jones lost the lawsuit and was required to pay high damages to my client – this is the explanation for the unreasonable withholding of approval.
○ (... my client's indication) in a letter to the defendants (that time was of the essence ...)

 **13 Speaking B: Emphatic stress**

Elicit from the class ways of emphasising key points. Then tell students to read the information in the box to compare it with their suggestions. You may elicit more examples of signalling phrases (e.g. *Let me draw your attention to ...*; *We must not overlook the fact that ...*; *It is essential/ vital/crucial to remember that ...*; *I'd like to underline here the importance of ...*). You could prompt these phrases by writing the key words (*attention, overlook, essential, vital, crucial, underline*) on the board.

**13.1** Elicit the meaning of the first version of the sentence. Elicit a situation when one might expect to hear this version of the sentence (e.g. lawyer A says *Are you ready for Tuesday's meeting with the new client?*, to which lawyer B replies *No, we're meeting the new client on Monday*). Then tell students to work in pairs to discuss the meanings of the other four versions, and to come up with similar contexts when one might expect to hear these versions. When they have finished, check the answers with the class, focusing on good pronunciation.

 **Suggested answers**
1 Monday, not any other day
2 The new client, not the new boss or the new cleaner
3 The new client, not an existing one
4 Meeting, not phoning or emailing
5 We're attending the meeting, not anyone else

 **Language note**
Many other languages employ emphatic stress in exactly the same way (although not always with the same combination of

intensity, duration and pitch that characterises English emphatic stress). This exercise may be second nature to students. However, this exercise aims to turn this subconscious knowledge into an explicit technique. Inexperienced public speakers often forget to use emphasis as they would in a conversation, and simply read their script in a dull, monotonous way. Experienced speakers, on the other hand, plan the *way* they are going to deliver a speech, not just the words. A simple technique such as underlining the words to emphasise can make a significant difference in the effectiveness of a speech.

**13.2** Tell students to look at the transcript (SB page 286). Make sure they understand what is meant by 'emphatic stress'. You may need to read the first sentence aloud to illustrate, first with the correct stress, and then with stress on different words (e.g. *conclude, determination, witheld, assignment*). Discuss briefly why the first version is more effective than the second.

Then play the recording and tell students to underline the words and phrases that Ron stresses. When they have finished, discuss the answers with the class. Expect some disagreement, as stress can be a subjective matter. If necessary, play the section of the recording again to clarify any disputes.

⇒ **Suggested answers**
Based on the evidence presented, the court <u>must</u> conclude that sufficient evidence supports a determination that the defendant <u>unreasonably</u> withheld consent to the assignment.
The defendant nevertheless asserts that it did <u>not</u> refuse consent, but merely <u>delayed</u> giving my client an answer until additional information was obtained. We <u>reject</u> this argument. The terms of the lease provided that the defendant could not <u>unreasonably</u> withhold consent, but this is <u>exactly</u> what it did. As defined in Webster's Third New International Dictionary, '<u>withholding</u>' means '<u>not giving</u>', while '<u>refusing</u>' on the other hand may require some affirmative

act or statement. Jones Corporation did <u>not</u> refuse consent, it is true. But Jones Corporation's decision to <u>delay</u> consent amounted to a <u>withholding</u> of consent, especially given my client's indication in a letter to the defendants that time was of the essence. And, as noted above, the evidence supports the determination that this decision was <u>unreasonable</u>. Therefore, defendants' attempt to distinguish between <u>withholding</u> consent and <u>refusing</u> consent is unavailing under the lease provision here.

**13.3** Tell students to work in pairs and to take turns to practise reading the extract aloud. You might encourage them to gesture with their hands and arms to add extra emphasis to the underlined words. As you listen to students' arguments, choose one or two impressive versions, and ask these students to perform their arguments for the class.

**13.4** Tell students to work in small teams to decide which words to underline. Point out that there are no 'correct' answers. Encourage them to read their versions aloud to practise. When they have finished, ask a student from each team to perform their versions. For each sentence, you (or the other students) could award points (e.g. 1 = terrible, 5 = excellent) to decide which team uses the technique most effectively.

⇒ **Suggested answers**
As we have <u>clearly</u> demonstrated here today, the contract concluded between my client and the defendant, the software design company Glaptech, <u>unambiguously stipulates</u> that the defendant agrees to create a computer program enabling <u>all</u> customers to book a ferry passage online. Specifically, the contract <u>expressly</u> reads that the program must work for "<u>all customers</u> using <u>modern home computers</u>." We heard today, in the testimony of a <u>recognized computer expert</u>, that the concept of "modern home computers" can <u>reasonably</u> be construed to include <u>Apple Macintosh computers</u>. Therefore we <u>must conclude</u> that the creation of a program

which does not function on this very type of computer system constitutes a clear breach of the contract concluded between my client and the defendant.

**Optional extension**
Tell students to work in small groups to take turns to read sentences from the transcript of Listening B on SB page 286. Make sure they understand that they should emphasise the words and phrases that they underlined in Exercise 13.2.

## 14 Language use C: Phrases referring to evidence

**14.1** Do this quickly with the class, and then test students by reading the definitions and eliciting the relevant phrase.

 **Answers**
**1** c **2** a **3** b

🖊 **Background note**
*To give weight to something* is easily confused with *to add weight to something*, which means 'to strengthen': *The threatening letters added weight to the claimant's suggestion that the delay was predicated on personal animosity, so the court gave weight to the suggestion.*

**14.2** Make sure students realise that their sentences should include the three phrases presented in Exercise 14.1. If you prefer, you could allow them to discuss the question and to come up with three oral sentences about the case.

🞕 **Suggested answers**
○ The court's determination that the withholding of consent was unreasonable was supported by the evidence.
○ The court gave weight to the evidence provided by the expert witness.
○ In reaching its decision, the court drew inferences of fact from the evidence submitted.

## 15 Reading E: Keeping informed

Elicit from students why a lawyer might read a blog. Then tell them to read the introduction (SB page 103) to check.

**15.1** Tell students to read the blog quickly to answer the question. Set a very tight time limit (60–90 seconds), at the end of which tell students to discuss the questions briefly in pairs. Finally, discuss the answers as a class.

🞕 **Answers**
**1** The text is about a new law in England, Wales and Northern Ireland which came into force in 1999 and which gives third parties to a contract additional rights.
**2** The intended reader of the text is someone who is interested in third-party rights and contract drafting, who would most likely be a lawyer.
**3** The blogger's primary purpose is to inform, yet he also has a secondary purpose: to persuade readers that the relevant Scots law is in need of reform.

🖊 **Background notes**
○ In paragraph 2, the verb *sign* is in inverted commas because, of course, not all contracts are in written form, so the writer uses *sign* as shorthand for all the ways that a party may enter into a contractual agreement.
○ If you *cover your back*, you take steps to protect yourself in the event of a problem.
○ The writer refers to having his *'cover-your-back' head on*. Speakers sometimes describe their different roles in terms of 'heads' that they wear (*I've got my lawyer head on today, not my friend head*).
○ If somebody is *unwary*, they are unaware of the risks they face.
○ For more on *ius quaestium tertio*, see http://www.biggartbaillie.co.uk/ideas–insights/all-articles/planning–construction/third-party-rights-of-contracts-in-scotland. There is a useful dictionary of Scots law at http://www.govanlc.com/dictionary.

○ If you do something *expressly*, you do it clearly and unambiguously.
○ Note that *mirror* and *better* are both used as verbs at the end of the article.

**15.2** Students work alone to answer the questions and then discuss their answers in pairs. Then check with the whole class.

 **Answers**

1 The solution he suggests is that all of the companies in the group are given the right to enforce the contract against the supplier (third-party rights).

2 In English law agreements, it has become easier to give third-party rights to someone who has not signed the contract.

3 He means that he would draft contracts such that Scottish law was agreed to be the law of the contract.

4 Because it requires the laws of two different jurisdictions to be applied to the same contract.

5 He thinks that Scottish law should be updated so that it resembles the English Act with regard to creating third-party rights.

**15.3** Students work in pairs to discuss these questions. If students do not know the answers, allow them to discuss what they think the law should be. Tell them to justify their opinions using real or invented examples to illustrate the advantages and disadvantages of the various possibilities. Go through the answers to all three questions with the class.

**15.4** Do this quickly with the whole class.

**Answer**
loss

# 16 Language use D: Informal style

**16.1** Tell students to work in small groups to identify features of informal style. You may want to guide their discussion by suggesting that they find informal punctuation, vocabulary, conversational devices, sentence structure and imagery.

 **Suggested answers**
Examples of spoken language style in the text:
○ The reader is addressed as *you*: 'Imagine you are …'
○ The writer uses *I* to refer to himself: 'I say "easy" …'
○ Some colourful and slangy words and expressions are used instead of more neutral ones: 'Scots law stuck in the 17th century', 'so each of them can "kick" the supplier', 'with my "cover-your-back" head on'
○ Contractions: 'isn't liable', 'didn't "sign"'
○ Subjective, personal statements of opinion: 'You can tell it's really old because it has a Latin name!', 'Very ugly'
○ Use of emotionally coloured adverbs as modifiers of adjectives: 'fairly valid', 'fairly easy to do'
○ Use of question and answer words that simulate dialogue: 'Why? Well, …'
○ Informal punctuation: inverted commas ('sign'); brackets for comments ('I say "easy" …'); exclamation marks ('… a Latin name!')
○ Informal vocabulary/idioms: 'gone wrong', 'ugly'
○ Conversational devices: vague language ('quite a bit longer'); conversational discourse markers ('Well, …'); personal opinions ('So I think …')
○ Informal sentence structure: short sentences ('So you sue the supplier'); sentence fragments ('Well, because the IQT is massively inflexible …'; 'very ugly'); active voice with generic subject instead of passive ('Once you create a third-party right …'); simple conjunctions to link sentences ('but')
○ Imagery: 'Imagine you are a bank …'; '"kick" the supplier'; 'with my "cover your back" head on'; 'I find myself doing …'; 'kill (a third-party right)'.

**16.2** Students discuss the questions in small groups and then feed back to the class.

## 17 Speaking C: Discussing and evaluating sources of information

**17.1** Tell students to discuss these questions in small groups. If they generate some interesting discussion, open them up to involve the whole class. Elicit the names of any useful legal blogs that students know / have used.

> **Background note**
> It is very easy to find law blogs online (e.g. search for *law blogs*). Many blogs contain links to other similar blogs that the writer recommends (often as part of a 'blog roll'). A good starting point is http://www.ringsurf.com/ring/lawblogs/, which contains a large list of law-related blogs. TransLegal's Legal English blog (http://www.translegal.com/blog) is an excellent resource for both teachers and learners of legal English.

**17.2** Students discuss the three questions in small groups and then feed back to the class.

**17.3** Set this as a homework task, and use it to generate some discussion in the next lesson. Encourage students to follow blogs in English as a way of keeping up to date and also of improving their English.

> **Optional extension**
> You could ask students to write their own blog posts, for example on the topics they discussed in Exercises 15.3 to 15.5, using some informal English. You could even start your own class blog, which is extremely easy using tools such as Blogger (www.blogger.com).

Tell students to do the Internet activity as homework. See Using the Internet for research on page xviii.

# Language focus

## Answers

1 **Vocabulary: distinguishing meaning**
  1 *right*: The others are obligations.
  2 *intensity*: The others are intentions.
  3 *enlist*: The others are verbs connected with writing contracts.
  4 *propose*: The others mean 'persuade'.
  5 *appeal*: The others mean 'choose'.

2 **Vocabulary: word choice**
  1 contrary; shall; to
  2 withhold; thereof; conditions
  3 have; approval
  4 to; entity

> **Language note**
> *Demised* here means 'transferred'.

3 **Prepositions with *contract* 1**
  2 to   3 under   4 from   5 to   6 against
  7 to   8 upon

4 **Prepositions with *contract* 2**
  1 to; under; to   2 to; to; under   3 to; on
  4 of; against

5 **Vocabulary: nouns ending with –or and –ee**
  2 lessor/lessee, a   3 mortgagor/mortgagee, c   4 transferor/transferee, b

6 **Word formation**

| Verb | Abstract noun | Person |
|---|---|---|
| delegate | delegation | delegator, delegate, delegate |
| assign | assignment | assignor, assignee |
| oblige | obligation | obligor, obligee |
| imply | implication | |
| intend | intention/intent | |
| consult | consultation | |
| enact | enactment | |
| rebut | rebuttal | |
| construe | construction | |
| determine | determination | |
| draft | draft | |
| transfer (UK) | transfer | |
| transfer (US) | | |

This role-play is a continuation of the dispute between Jones and Keats from this unit. Divide students into groups of four to seven and distribute role cards.

Around half should be Jones's lawyers and the others should be divided between Keats's lawyers and those for Ketchup's.

First there should be two short meetings as set out on the role cards: a strategy meeting between all the Jones lawyers, and a progress update between the Keats lawyers and those for Ketchup's. You will need to set a time limit to ensure that both meetings finish at the same time. At the end of these meetings, the lawyers for Ketchup's change roles and become additional lawyers for Keats. Either set up a meeting between the two sides to try to solve their dispute without going to court, or go straight to a court case. Tell the groups to prepare for the court case by writing a closing argument. Make sure they think about emphatic stress. Finally, tell each side to present their closing arguments in order that you, the judge, can make a decision.

If you have one, two or three students, the first stages will be impossible, so you will need to go straight to the Jones–Keats meeting (if you have one student, you are Keats's lawyer; if you have three students, there should be two lawyers for Jones). If the meeting fails, each side should prepare (as homework) a closing argument to use in court. Later, both sides should read their closing arguments, paying attention to emphatic stress.

# 8 ) Employment law

Employment law is a wide and complex area. It covers the rights and obligations of employers and employees before employment (during the **recruitment** process), during **employment** and at the end of employment (**termination**). It is related to, but not the same as, **labour law** (US **labor law**) which deals with relations between employers and trade unions. Labour law is not a focus of this unit.

In many countries (e.g. civil-law jurisdictions such as France), employment law is tightly regulated by an employment code. In other countries (e.g. common-law jurisdictions such as the UK), there is much more freedom for both parties to decide their own conditions of employment (e.g. how many hours the employee is expected to work).

A theme running through much of the unit is **discrimination** (treating certain employees differently from others on the basis of sex, age, disability, etc.). Discrimination is a highly controversial and delicate area, about which many people have deeply held views. One problem is that even the most passionate opponents of discrimination disagree with each other about which types of discrimination are fair or justified and which are not. An example is affirmative action in the USA (also called positive discrimination), which is an attempt to redress past discrimination against certain groups by discriminating against different groups. Another example is discrimination based on nationality, which is practised by every government (e.g. countries almost always prefer their own nationals when recruiting their civil servants, their army and their president). A second problem is that discrimination can be extremely difficult to prove.

Listening A deals with a claim for **unfair dismissal**. A lawyer advises a client (an employer) what to expect from an **employment tribunal**. Such tribunals are judicial bodies in the UK which deal specifically with employment disputes. They can involve several stages: a **case management discussion**, a **pre-hearing assessment** to decide if

the case has merit, and a **final hearing** to decide whether the case succeeds or fails. The lawyer in this case believes that his client's case is so strong that the pre-hearing assessment will throw out the claim, thus saving the employer a lot of time and money.

Reading D describes a new alternative to employment tribunals in the UK: a **voluntary arbitration scheme** for unfair dismissal cases. Under the new scheme, administered by ACAS (the Advisory, Conciliation and Arbitration Service, an independent but publicly funded organisation), disputes can be resolved in a few hours (rather than weeks or months), and are intended to be 'non-legalistic'. Decisions are based on *general principles of fairness and good conduct in employment relations*, rather than strict legal tests and case law. This is a good illustration of the informal nature of employment law in the UK, compared with many other countries. The article argues that both the traditional tribunals and the new arbitration hearings have their advantages and disadvantages for both employers and employees.

A similar system exists in Canada, where an **arbitration board** hears **grievances** (= claims) of unfair dismissal. In the case presented in Reading C, the arbitration board finds that a dismissal was justified, and raised important questions concerning the limitations of **freedom of speech** with respect to employer–employee relations.

Listening B focuses on the restrictions imposed by employment law (and human rights law) on employers. In this case, some employers are frustrated that they cannot force their employees to take drugs tests, even though they believe their employees' drug abuse is damaging their business. In the listening, their lawyer explains the **liability risks** involved in various courses of action and suggests a compromise solution.

In addition, Unit 8 provides guidance on the differences between **formal and informal language** in an email. There is practice of useful phrases for **expressing an opinion, agreeing** and **disagreeing**. Finally, two ways of **structuring an explanatory email** are presented and practised.

## Discussion

Use these questions to generate a discussion on employment law. The first three are controversial, and if you are concerned that students might upset each other (or you) with their views, you should ask questions d–f.

a   On what grounds are people discriminated against in the employment market? Is this discrimination ever justified?

b   Should employment law aim to make all workplaces representative of the general population?

c   Are trade unions an essential protector of employees' rights, or are they an unnecessary irritation to employers?

d   What does employment law involve?

e   How are lawyers involved in a) the recruitment process, b) during an employee's employment, and c) after a dismissal?

f   Have you ever been involved in an employer–employee dispute?

➡ **Suggested answers**

a   People are discriminated against because of their sex, age, race, disability, nationality and many other factors. Some form of discrimination is inevitable: a film production company may specify that it is looking for a middle-aged white woman to play a role in a film, thus discriminating against many other potential actors. Certain types of disability (e.g. blindness) may be simply incompatible with certain types of jobs (e.g. hairdressing). Many language schools have a 'native speakers only' policy, which discriminates against many other teachers on the grounds of nationality.

b   This might be an impossible and unreasonable aim: the reason that there are few women working on oil rigs is apparently not (entirely) discrimination, but (at least partially) due to the fact that few women want such jobs. The same goes for male nursery-school teachers. It might be argued that the aim of the law should be to ensure equal opportunity (within reasonable limits), and to combat discrimination where it occurs, rather than to force people to do jobs that they do not want to do.

c   Both, depending on whether one is speaking to a mistreated employee or an employer struggling to keep his/her business afloat.

d   See Reading A

e   See Reading A

f   This question deliberately leaves open the possibility that students have been involved in such disputes as employees/ employers and as lawyers. Elicit details of the dispute, including its outcome.

## 1 Reading A: Introduction to employment law

Tell students to read the text to match the titles with the paragraphs and to find out as much as they can about each. When they have finished reading, tell students to compare their answers in pairs, and to use the headings to discuss what they understood about each paragraph. Check the answers with the class.

 **Answers**
a 5  b 6  c 4  d 1  e 7  f 3  g 2

 **Background notes**

○ The text uses the term *unlawful* rather than *illegal*. As a general rule, the term *illegal* is often used to refer to something criminal, while something which is *unlawful* is a civil wrong (tort), but not a crime. In fact, there are counter-examples: *unlawful entry* is a crime, while an *illegal contract* is not.

○ If something is *construed* in a particular way, this is how it is interpreted.

○ If you *render a decision*, you officially make a decision.

○ *Loss of prospective earnings* refers to the amount of money that an employee could have earned if he/she had not been dismissed.

**Optional extension**

As a follow-up, write the following phrases on the board (or do this while students are reading):

1 unfair dismissal / discriminatory dismissal / redundancy dismissal
2 collective bargaining / arbitration
3 strike / picketing / injunction / lockout

Tell students to work in small groups to check the phrases in the Glossary booklet. Each student should check different phrases. When they have checked their phrases, they should work out together what the difference is between each set of phrases. When they have finished, go through the answers with the class.

**Answers**

1 *Discriminatory dismissal* is connected with the employee's sex, race, disability, etc. Different jurisdictions will define *discriminatory* in different ways. *Unfair dismissal* is the more general term, and includes discriminatory dismissal as well as many other types of dismissal. *Redundancy dismissal* may or may not be unfair, depending on how the particular employee was selected for redundancy, rather than other employees. See http://www.dti.gov.uk/er/individual/unfair-pl712a.htm#whocan.

2 *Collective bargaining* is a two-way process between an employer and a representative of a group of employees (i.e. a trade union). *Arbitration* is a three-way process, involving these parties and a third, independent arbitrator who will attempt to reconcile the differences between the other parties, particularly during times of conflict.

3 A *strike* is a collective refusal to work, which may or may not be lawful. *Picketing* is a form of protesting and persuading employees to join a strike. See http://www.dti.gov.uk/er/union/picketing-pl928.htm. An *injunction* is a court order to do (or not to do) something. In the context of labour relations, an employer may seek an injunction to prohibit certain types of industrial action such as picketing. A *lockout* is the employer's version of a strike: it refuses to allow employees into its premises.

## 2 Key terms: Employment

**2.1** Tell students to do this exercise quickly alone. Check the answers with the class. You could take this opportunity to elicit more examples for each key term.

 **Answers**
1 c  2 a  3 d  4 b

**2.2** Tell students to work in groups of three or four to discuss these questions. Go through the definitions with the class.

**Suggested answers**

**1** This means 'interpreted or understood to be discriminatory'.

**2** This refers to adjustments which are fitting and appropriate, and not excessively costly.

**3** This refers to damages awarded for feelings of disappointment, frustration, grief, humiliation, etc. arising out of the manner, and possibly the fact, of dismissal.

**2.3** Tell students to work alone or in pairs to do this exercise. Go through the answers with the class.

**Answers**

**1** d **2** c **3** a **4** e **5** b

**2.4** Tell students to discuss these questions in small groups. If they generate some interesting discussion, open them up to include the whole class.

 **3** **Listening A: An employment tribunal claim**

Ask students to read the introduction (SB page 110) to answer these three questions. When they have finished reading, discuss the answers with the class.

**a** What is a tribunal?
**b** What are the stages of a tribunal?
**c** What is an entry of appearance?

**Answers**

**a** A judicial body which resolves disputes between employers and employees

**b** i) Claimant submits claim; ii) If necessary, there is a case-management discussion; iii) Sometimes there is a prehearing assessment or review; and iv) Final hearing.

**c** A written notice of appearance, stating the opposition to the claim and the grounds upon which it is opposed

**Background note**

If a claim has *merit*, it is worth pursuing. At the pre-hearing assessment, claims which do not have merit (i.e. which have no chance of success) are not taken forward to the final hearing. The verb *to merit* is also used in the recording, meaning 'to deserve'.

**3.1** Before students listen, check they know who Jane and Gwen are (see paragraph 3 of the introduction). Play the recording for students to complete the exercise. Then tell them to discuss their answers in pairs, including any other details they remember from the conversation. When they have finished, go through the answers with the class.

**Transcript »** STUDENT'S BOOK **page 286**

**Answers**

1, 3, 4, 6

**Optional extension**

Before the second listening, make sure students have a good understanding of what the case is about. Go through these questions with the whole class.

**1** What is the employee claiming?

**2** Does Jane think the employee has a good chance of winning the case?

**3** What was the employee accused of?

**Answers**

**1** That her dismissal from Gwen's company was unfair.

**2** No. She acknowledges that she has a right to *claim* unfair dismissal, but she thinks her claim will be unsuccessful.

**3** Stealing confidential documents from her employer.

**3.2** Tell students to discuss the questions in pairs to see if they can remember the answers. Then play the recording a second time for them to check. After the recording, tell them to compare their answers with their partners, and then check the answers with the class.

**Answers**

**1** b **2** c **3** a **4** b

## 4  Writing A: Attachments and formality

**4.1**  Tell students to read the question. You may also ask them to find out what three things Gwen requests from Jane. Allow a very limited time for students to read the email to find the answers. Discuss the answers with the class.

 **Answers**
○ Documents attached: revised entry of appearance and document providing complete factual account of circumstances of theft
○ Phrases in the email for referring to attachments:
*I attach the revised entry of appearance form which you requested.*

*... please find attached a document providing ...*
Gwen asks to Jane to let her know a) if anything needs to be changed, b) if she requires further information, and c) whether the case can be handled solely on the basis of a written submission.

**4.2**  Tell students to work in pairs to underline the phrases which contribute to the email's politeness and formality. When they have finished, discuss the answers with the class. Make sure they realise that the email is not extremely formal: it is still friendly and personal.

 **Answers**
See phrases 1–10 in Exercise 4.3.

**4.3**  Tell students to do this exercise in pairs. When they have finished, check the answers with the class.

**Answers**
1 d  2 e  3 i  4 h  5 j  6 b  7 a  8 f
9 c  10 g

**4.4** Tell students to read the task and then work alone or in pairs to write Jane's email. Set a very tight time limit (e.g. four to five minutes) and encourage students to use the more formal expressions from Exercise 4.3. When they have finished, you could ask them to read and comment on each other's emails, both in terms of language (accuracy, appropriacy) and professionalism.

 **Suggested answer**

Dear Gwen,

Further to our phone conversation on Monday, I would like to inform you of the steps I have taken in the Myers case since we spoke.

I have submitted the completed entry of appearance you sent me, along with an application for a pre-hearing assessment of the case. I have also drafted a written submission of the case and forwarded this to the tribunal. These two documents have been attached to this mail for your perusal.

I am now awaiting the response of the tribunal and will naturally inform you as soon as I hear anything. I am quite confident that the tribunal will decide to handle this case solely on the basis of the written submission, and that the outcome will be positive for your firm.

Please do not hesitate to contact me in the meantime if you require any further information or assistance.

Yours sincerely

Jane

(144 words)

## 5 Reading B: A sex discrimination case

Tell students to read the introduction (SB page 112) to find three powers that employment tribunals have in the UK. (Answer: To award compensation (for financial loss or injury to feelings or health); to award aggravated damages; and to order exemplary damages.)

**5.1** Tell students to read the text quickly and decide which of the three headlines is most appropriate.

 **Answer**
Headline 2

 **Background notes**
○ If a discriminatory culture *pervades* a firm, it is present throughout the firm.
○ A *senior equity partner* is one of the partners, in a partnership such as a law firm, who has the largest ownership interests.
○ If somebody's behaviour is *malicious* /məˈlɪʃəs/, it is intended purely to harm somebody.
○ *Aggravated* /ˈægrəˌveɪtɪd/ *damages* are special damages awarded by a court for malicious conduct, such as attempting to humiliate a plaintiff.

**5.2** Ask students to discuss the answers to the seven questions in small groups. When they have finished discussing, go through the answers with the class.

**Answers**

**1** Texts such as these, which summarise the outcome of cases heard by an employment tribunal, are commonly read by employers and lawyers.

**2** The case deals with sex discrimination: two female employees of a law firm (the claimants) claimed they were not promoted to higher positions by their employers (the defendants) on the basis of their sex.

**3** A landmark case generally deals with an important issue and marks a stage in the development of the law in a specific area. Such a case often shows how courts will rule on similar cases in the future.

**4** The women alleged that the firm had an overall 'culture' of discrimination against women.

**5** The court ruled that one of the partners of the law firm had behaved badly during the proceedings and that he had attempted to damage the reputation of one of the claimants.

**6** The high award is expected to lead attorneys to be more cautious about their behaviour when defending cases before the tribunal.

**7** A discriminatory culture is an environment in which certain people or groups are favoured over others, often based on characteristics such as age, religion, sexual orientation, gender or disability.

## 6 Listening B: Liability risks

CD1, T31

Tell students to read the introduction (SB page 113) in order to predict what the conversation on the recording will be about. Discuss their predictions briefly.

**6.1** Tell students to read through the five statements to make sure they understand all the words. You may need to check words such as *unsettled* and *infringement*. Then play the recording. Allow students to compare and discuss their answers with a partner before going through them with the class.

**Transcript »** STUDENT'S BOOK **page 287**

 **Answers**
**1** False (It is Mrs Howard who says this.)
**2** True **3** True **4** True **5** False
(She suggests re-assigning the workers involved to less safety-sensitive jobs.)

 **Background notes**
○ *Facility management* is the management of buildings and services, and covers things such as air conditioning, cleaning, maintenance, repairs, etc.
○ An *infringement* /ɪnˈfrɪndʒmənt/ is a violation of a law, rule or right.
○ *To kick the habit* is an informal expression meaning *to give up*, and typically refers to smoking or use of drugs.
○ A *knee-jerk reaction* is an instinctive and uncontrolled reaction, as when a doctor tests a patient's reactions by hitting a hammer against their knee. In business, a knee-jerk reaction is taken hastily and usually regretted later.

**Optional extension**
Write the following questions on the board (perhaps while students are doing Exercise 6.1).

**1** What is the Howards' line of business?
**2** Why are the Howards concerned about the drugs problem?
**3** Why is this such a tricky area?
**4** In what situations have the courts ruled in favour of employers in such cases?
**5** Why does Ms Brewer recommend against acting hastily?
**6** What is Ms Brewer's suggestion to manage the situation in the short term?

Tell students to discuss in pairs what they remember from the first listening, then to listen again to check and complete their answers. After playing the recording, allow students time to discuss their answers before going through them with the class. You could also take this opportunity to discuss with the class whether they agree with Ms Brewer's advice, and whether employers would face the same dilemma in students' own jurisdictions. Try to avoid discussing students' opinions as to the rights and wrongs of such dilemmas, as there will be a full discussion in Exercise 8.

**Answers**
**1** Cleaning services and facility management
**2** They think it is dangerous and bad for their reputation.
**3** There is no direct legislation, and important legal questions depend on the interpretation of numerous provisions in health and safety, employment, human rights and data-protection law.
**4** In those cases where the dismissed employee has been engaged in safety-sensitive work and where the employer had implemented a long-term workplace safety policy that included not only drug testing, but also the opportunity for the workers to get treatment for their drug problems.
**5** She thinks they risk costly litigation that they would most likely lose.
**6** She recommends re-assigning the workers in question to jobs that are less safety-sensitive, and then launching a new workplace safety initiative, concentrating on drug and alcohol abuse.

## 7 Language use A: Expressing an opinion, agreeing and disagreeing

**7.1** Tell students to work through this exercise in pairs. Then go through the answers quickly with the class, paying attention to the interesting vocabulary (*to kick a drug habit*, *to act on something*, *to act hastily*, *to make a knee-jerk reaction*, *to sit back and do nothing*, *to bear responsibility for something*).

> **Answers**
> **1** A  **2** A+D  **3** O  **4** A  **5** D  **6** O  **7** A+D
> **8** A  **9** A  **10** A  **11** A

**7.2** Do this exercise quickly with the whole class.

> **Answers**
> Expressing disagreement strongly: 1, 8, 10

**7.3** Discuss these phrases with the whole class. There are no absolute answers, but if students disagree with the suggested answers, make sure they justify their arguments. Students may feel that some of the acceptable answers are too tentative, and make the lawyer appear not to know what they think. For this reason, it is important that they are pronounced reasonably firmly and authoritatively. You may wish to practise this pronunciation with students.

> **Suggested answers**
> Phrases 2, 3, 4 and 6 are acceptable.

---

**Optional extension**
Tell students to work alone or in small groups to look through the transcript on SB page 287 to underline useful expressions for managing a meeting with a client. This should include Ms Brewer's expressions from Exercise 7.1 as well as anything else which students might say in a typical meeting with a client. When they have finished, go through the answers with the class.

**Suggested answers (underlined)**
**Ms Brewer:** <u>Good morning,</u> Mrs Howard, Mr Howard. <u>Please come in.</u>
**Ms Brewer:** <u>Please have a seat. Can I get you something to drink</u>?

---

**Ms Brewer:** <u>Right, then. On the phone, you told me that you wanted to speak to me about</u> drug testing at your company. <u>Maybe you could tell me something about</u>
**Ms Brewer:** <u>Right. If I could just jump in here and summarise what you've been telling me. ... is that correct? And you'd like me to inform you about the legality of such a course of action.</u>
**Ms Brewer:** <u>Well, first of all, I should say that</u> ... .
**Ms Brewer:** <u>Well, if you were to ... there's a good chance that</u> ...
**Ms Brewer:** <u>I agree with you,</u> Mr Howard, <u>but we have to look at what the law says. Generally speaking,</u> ...
**Ms Brewer:** <u>I'm afraid I have to disagree with you both. In my opinion,</u> ...
**Ms Brewer:** <u>I see your point, and you're absolutely right ... Let me suggest ...: you could consider ... And then you could</u> ...

## 8 Speaking: Agreeing and disagreeing

Tell students to discuss one, several or all of these opinions in small groups. Point out that they should use as many of the useful phrases from Exercises 7.1 and 7.3 as possible. Point out also that this sort of exercise is more productive and fun if they disagree with each other, so encourage them to argue from standpoints other than their own private opinions.

## 9 Reading C: A justified dismissal

**9.1** Students read the introduction on SB page 114 to find out what the case concerns and where it was heard (**Answers:** It concerns sharing information on the Internet, the limits of free speech and employment relationships. It was heard at an arbitration board in Canada). Then discuss the three questions about the title with the class.

> **Answers**
> **1** *Derogatory* means showing strong disapproval and not showing respect.
> **3** The dismissal is referred to as justified because the arbitration board upheld it.

**9.2** Students read the article carefully to answer
the five questions. They discuss their
answers with a partner before feeding back
to the class.

➡ **Answers**
1 The grievor is an employee who was
dismissed for misconduct.
2 The grievor was dismissed because she
had written derogatory comments about
her co-workers on her blog.
3 The grievor's union challenged the
dismissal because it felt that the
employer had overreacted to the situation,
because the employee had tried to
apologise but the management had made
this attempt unsuccessful, and because
the employee had had a clean record for
six years.
4 The employer believed that the
employment relationship was irreparably
undermined, not only due to the content
of the blog but also because of the
employee's lack of remorse and lack of
understanding as to why the blog had
been so offensive.
5 The reasons the Board gave for
upholding the dismissal included the
view that publicly displaying one's
negative opinions about co-workers can
affect one's employment relationship.
Furthermore, the Board concluded that
the employee had engaged in serious
misconduct that irreparably severed the
employment relationship and justified
the dismissal. The Board also noted
that while a person is free to express
his or her opinion about co-workers,
doing so publicly may have negative
consequence.

✎ **Background notes**
○ A *grievor* is a person with a grievance
(= grounds for a complaint).
○ If something is *irreparably* damaged, it
cannot be repaired.
○ *Remorse* is an emotion experienced
when a person feels guilty and sorry for
their actions. In this context, the
grievor's failure to apologise or accept
that she had done wrong could be
taken as a lack of remorse.
○ If something is *derailed*, it is prevented
from being carried out properly.
○ *Contempt* is an extreme form of lack of
respect.
○ If you *denigrate* /ˈdenɪɡreɪt/ something,
you say that it is not good or important.
○ If you *sever* /ˈsevəʳ/ something, you cut
it off. In this context, the possibility of a
good relationship between the grievor
and her co-workers was cut off by her
actions.
○ If you *invoke* a law or a right, you
request it or use it to improve a
situation.

**9.3** Students work alone to match the words with
their meanings, then compare their answers
with a partner before feeding back to the
class.

 **Answers**
1 unrepentant   2 thereby   3 irreparably
4 discharge   5 unflattering   6 unblemished

**9.4** Students complete the summary in pairs,
then feed back to the class.

 **Answers**
1 engaged in   2 denigrated   3 terminated
4 undermined   5 challenged   6 sought
7 denied   8 upheld   9 invoke

**Optional extension**
As a follow-up, tell students to cover the text
in Exercise 9.4 and to try to remember what it
said, using only the verbs from the box to help
them remember.

**9.5** Have students discuss the three questions in small groups. Encourage them to use the language from Exercises 7.1 and 7.3 in their discussions. Afterwards, open up the discussion to include the whole class.

## 10 Language use B: Participle clauses with –ing

Tell students to close their books. Write these sentences onto the board:

**1** [The employer perceived the Grievor as largely unrepentant] and [it terminated the Grievor's employment].

**2** [The employer perceived the Grievor as largely unrepentant] and [the Grievor's employment was terminated].

Elicit from the class more sophisticated ways of joining the two halves of each sentence. Try to lead the class towards the participle clause from the box on SB page 115, perhaps by providing the first word (*Perceiving ...*). Elicit from the class why this structure is impossible for sentence 2 (Answer: Because the two parts of the sentence have different subjects).

Students then read the information in the box to compare it with their ideas. Elicit some examples of conjunctions and prepositions that can introduce participle clauses (see Language note below).

> **Language note**
>
> All prepositions can be followed by –ing, but a few are especially useful for introducing participle clauses in formal English: *by, on/upon* (= immediately after), *without, instead of, apart from, despite*.
>
> ***Upon hearing*** *of the derogatory posts, the employer decided to take immediate action.*
>
> Only certain conjunctions can be followed by a participle clause, and these are only used in rather formal and official writing: *while, when, if, although, unless*.
>
> ***When*** *(you are)* ***making*** *derogatory statements about co-workers, it is advisable to keep them private.*
>
> Some words can function as both prepositions and conjunctions, and can therefore be used to introduce participle clauses: *since, after, before, until*.
>
> ***Before starting*** *her blog, the employee had had an unblemished employment record.*

**10.1** Discuss the questions with the whole class.

 **Answers**
  **a)** ... the Grievor, in expressing contempt for her managers, ...
  **b)** ... thereby justifying discharge.

The position of the participle clauses in the two sentences is:
  **a)** in the middle of the sentence (after the subject and set off with commas);
  **b)** at the end of the sentence.

**10.2** Students work alone or in pairs to rewrite the sentences. When you go through the answers with the class, elicit a range of possible correct answers.

 **Suggested answers**
  **1** In showing a lack of remorse about the content of her blog, the employee was deemed to have irreparably undermined the employment relationship.
  Showing a lack of remorse about the content of her blog, the employee was deemed to have irreparably undermined the employment relationship.
  **2** Arguing on behalf of the employee, the Grievor's union pointed out that she had had a clean record for six years.
  While arguing on behalf of the employee, the Grievor's union pointed out that she had had a clean record for six years.
  The Grievor's union argued on behalf of the employee, pointing out that she had had a clean record for six years.
  **3** Invoking freedom of speech in defence of her actions, the employee argued that she had the right to express her opinions about her colleagues.
  The employee invoked freedom of speech in defence of her actions, thereby arguing that she had the right to express her opinions about her colleagues.
  The employee, in invoking freedom of speech in defence of her actions, argued that she had the right to express her opinions about her colleagues.
  **4** The Arbitration Board denied the grievance, thereby upholding the termination of employment.

Denying the grievance, the Arbitration Board upheld the termination of employment.

In denying the grievance, the Arbitration Board upheld the termination of employment.

---

**Optional extension**
**ILEC preparation: Test of Reading Part 3**
**Photocopiable worksheet 8.1**

This worksheet provides further practice of word-building, as tested in Part 3 of the ILEC Test of Reading. It also revises the vocabulary from Exercise 9.4 and the grammar from Language use B.

Make sure students close their books. They then work alone to complete the gaps in the text with the correct form of the words on the right. Point out that some of the gaps demand some 'lateral thinking'. Afterwards, go through the answers with the class.

**Answers**

**1** dismissal   **2** Grievor   **3** unflattering
**4** co-workers   **5** referring   **6** Perceiving
**7** unrepentant   **8** employment   **9** contents
**10** understanding   **11** offensive   **12** irreparably
**13** justifying   **14** fairness   **15** challenging
**16** overreacted   **17** apology   **18** derailed
**19** unblemished   **20** service   **21** sought
**22** compensation   **23** reinstated   **24** grievance
**25** upheld   **26** publicly   **27** relationship
**28** expressing   **29** denigrating   **30** misconduct
**31** freedom   **32** derogatory

## 11  Reading D: Unfair dismissal

**11.1** Discuss the question briefly with the whole class.

 **Answer**
The Commentary section.

**11.2** Tell students to read the first paragraph quickly to answer the question. Then check with the whole class and elicit how the new arbitration scheme might work, but avoid explaining the procedure at this stage. Make sure students realise that the new scheme is an alternative to the employment tribunals described in paragraph 1.

 **Answers**
○ Explanation of how employment tribunals work: ... *a public hearing in front of a three-member employment tribunal with a legally qualified chairperson, involving the cross-examination of witnesses and, in the vast majority of cases, the involvement of legal representatives ...*
○ Four adjectives: *speedy, informal, confidential, non-legalistic.*

 **Background notes**
○ *Cross examination* is the process where each party's lawyers ask the other party's witnesses questions. This can be the most dramatic and stressful part of a court case.
○ *Arbitration* and *conciliation* are both types of alternative dispute resolution. *Conciliation* is less formal and is a form of *mediation*: it simply involves bringing the two disputing sides together to try to resolve their differences. The two sides agree a legally binding conciliation agreement. *Arbitration* is more closely associated with claims such as unfair dismissal, and the decision (the *arbitral award*, which is also legally binding) is made by an arbitrator rather than by the parties themselves. For full details, see http://www.acas.org.uk/services/ dispute_individuals_employer.html.
○ The term *non-legalistic* here means 'less formal and more accessible to non-lawyers'.

**11.3** Tell students to work alone to find the answers to the questions. Allow a fairly limited time (three to four minutes) for this. Check with the class.

 **Answers**
○ The opinions of lawyers on the new arbitration scheme.
○ The irony of the new arbitration scheme lies in the fact that employment tribunals were themselves originally intended to be an 'easily accessible, informal, speedy and inexpensive' alternative to the ordinary courts for dealing with individual employment disputes.

**Optional extension**
**Photocopiable worksheet 8.2**

Hand out Photocopiable worksheet 8.2. Tell students to work in pairs. One student in each pair should read the first and third part of the text, and the other should read the second part. (If you have an odd number of students, the extra student in the group of three should read the first part and the first four bullet points of the second part.) Each student should try to complete the middle two columns of the table. Point out that the shaded boxes are not answered directly in the text, but it is still possible to predict what they might contain. Allow time for them to read and make notes on their parts of the text (three to four minutes). When they have finished, tell them to work with their partners to exchange information to complete the whole table. Note that the fourth column of the table, *My jurisdiction*, can be completed later, during Exercise 11.8 below.

**Answers**

Answers in italics are not answered directly in the text.

1 In the mid-1960s (*In fact, they were set up in 1964.*)
2 21st May 2001
3 *Compulsory, as long as one party brings a case*
4 Voluntary
5 Three members with a legally qualified chairperson
6 Experienced arbitrator chosen by ACAS
7 Yes
8 No
9 Yes (in the vast majority of cases)
10 May be used
11 easily accessible, informal, speedy and inexpensive
12 speedy, informal, confidential and non-legalistic
13 *All disputes concerning employment rights*
14 Only unfair dismissal
15 *Public*
16 Private
17 *The hearing itself can be very quick, but the whole process (documentation, decision-making, etc.) may take months – in Listening A, Jane said 'it will be disposed of within, say, six to 12 months'.*
18 Normally half a day
19 Adversarial
20 Inquisitorial or investigative
21 *Each party covers own costs (but compensation may include a sum to cover costs of unfairly dismissed employee)*
22 Each party covers own costs (but compensation may include a sum to cover costs of unfairly dismissed employee)
23 Strict legal tests (statutory tests) and case law
24 EC law, Human Rights Act 1998, general principles of fairness and good conduct in employment relations.
25 Reinstatement, re-engagement and compensation
26 Reinstatement, re-engagement and compensation
27 No
28 Yes
29 Yes
30 Limited
31 ○ more certainty of outcome
   ○ standards less likely to be variable
   ○ wider grounds for appealing
32 confidentiality avoids risk of damaging publicity
33 ○ more certainty of outcome
   ○ standards less likely to be variable
   ○ chance to embarrass employers through damaging publicity of court case
34 *much cheaper, quicker and less stressful than employment tribunals*

**11.4** Tell students to look at Exercises 11.4, 11.5, 11.6 and 11.7 in pairs. Go through the answers to all four exercises with the class, perhaps using the 'Easy first' procedure (see Games and activities section, page xvi).

**11.5** See Exercise 11.4. When you go through the answers, you could test students by reading the synonyms aloud in order to elicit the adjectives.

**11.6** See Exercise 11.4. When you go through the answers, you could test students by reading the definitions aloud in order to elicit the verbs.

**11.7** See Exercise 11.4. If students struggle to come up with more collocations, you could read the additional nouns aloud and elicit which verb each collocates with.

**11.8** Tell students to discuss this question in small groups. They could use column 4 of the table on Photocopiable worksheet 8.2 to guide their discussions.

**Optional extension**
Tell students to find at least two examples of participle clauses in the *Key features* section of Reading D. Elicit from the class another way of expressing each participle clause.

**Suggested answers**
Arbitrators have a general duty to act fairly and impartially between the parties, **giving** each party a reasonable opportunity to plead his or her case and respond to that of the other party. (Or: … which gives each party …). Each party covers their own costs **in attending** the hearing. (Or: … when they attend …)

## 12 Writing B: Advising on advantages and disadvantages in an email

Tell students to read the introduction to find out what the client wants and why. (Answer: He wants information about the new arbitration process because he has to deal with employment rights disputes on a regular basis.)

**12.1** Tell students to read the email carefully to find the three mistakes. Make sure they find factual errors, and not simply errors of opinion. When they have finished reading, tell them to compare their answers in pairs, and then go through them with the class.

employer' are different from those in Reading D, but the exercise focuses on factual errors rather than differences of opinion.

 **Pronunciation note**
advantageous /ˌædvənˈteɪdʒəs/

**12.2** Tell students to work in small groups to discuss the four questions. When they have finished, go through the answers with the class.

 **Answers**
1 B
2 *The following summary presents a selection of key features of both the new arbitration scheme and the existing employment tribunal process.*
3 *Unlike, In contrast to, Both … and …*
4 *This is clearly advantageous, A further advantage of confidentiality is …, this can be regarded as a significant advantage*

**12.3** This writing can be done at home or in class. See Writing section, page xiv.

 **Suggested answer**
Dear Mr Mason

In your email of 9 April, you asked for information concerning the new arbitration procedure. You specifically requested my judgment concerning the advantages and disadvantages of arbitration from the point of view of an employer. I will first explain some of the features of the existing employment tribunal process and then look at the new arbitration scheme.

Employment tribunals hear the full range of employment-related disputes. They are public hearings held in front of a panel of three people. The fact that they are public can be a disadvantage for employers, since well-publicised employee disputes can lead to unwanted bad publicity. As a result, there is also the drawback of a greater tendency to reach out-of-court settlements which are favourable to employees. A further disadvantage of employment tribunals is the fact that they typically take longer than the new arbitration process.

However, employment tribunals have the important advantage that decisions reached by them can be appealed.

In contrast, the new arbitration procedure only deals with unfair dismissal cases. The proceedings are held in a private setting, such as a hotel. Another difference is the relative speed of the proceedings, which typically last only a half a day. This is clearly advantageous for an employer, as it would save a great deal of time and money. However, the new arbitration scheme does have a significant drawback: the decisions reached by the arbitrators are considered binding, and so appealing or challenging a decision is very difficult.

On balance, I would say that the new arbitration scheme is attractive from the point of view of an employer, and I recommend that you consider making use of this new process to deal with unfair dismissal disputes.

Please do not hesitate to contact me if you would like further information. I have attached an article about this topic to this mail which may be of interest to you.

Yours sincerely

Elisabeth Stephens

(313 words)

 Tell students to do the Internet activity as homework. See Using the Internet for research on page xviii.

# Language focus

## Answers

### 1 Vocabulary: distinguishing meaning

**1** *discrimination*: The others remove employees from their jobs.

**2** *reduce*: The others make something illegal.

**3** *primarily*: The others mean 'only'.

**4** *certain*: The others mean 'secret'.

**5** *conventional*: The others mean 'important'.

**6** *vast*: The others mean 'fast'.

### 2 Adjective formation

**2** uncertain **3** non-confidential
**4** unconventional, non-conventional
**5** non-discriminatory **6** unfair **7** unlawful
**8** unnecessary **9** unreasonable
**10** unspecific, non-specific **11** involuntary

### 3 Word choice

(Note that the three sections are all from the same document. Some answers only make sense in the context of the whole document.)

**1** intends; notice **2** complying with; entitled to **3** under

### 4 Writing: formal style

*Suggested answer*

Dear Mr and Ms Howard

Further to our phone conversation this morning, I attach the summary of current workplace safety regulations that you requested. In addition, I attach our firm's brochure on legal issues connected with drug testing.

Kindly let me know if anything is unclear or if you require further information.

Sincerely

Irina Brewer

### 5 Use of prepositions

**2** under **3** to; to; via **4** from; against
**5** of; from **6** in; in **7** for; to

**Language note**

Item 4: *to be immune to* is also possible, but is usually used in a medical context with illnesses or figuratively; *to be immune from* is usually used in a legal sense:

*The doctor confirmed that he was immune to chicken pox.*

*He's very thick-skinned – he seems immune to my insults.*

*He struck a deal with the judge so that he is immune from prosecution.*

### 6 Verbs

**2** file **3** heard **4** resembles **5** goes
**6** includes **7** decide **8** awarded **9** issue
**10** pay **11** incurred

---

**Optional extension**
**Photocopiable worksheet 8.3**

The mini-role-plays on Photocopiable worksheet 8.3 simulate three cases under the ACAS arbitration scheme (see Reading D). It is essential that students are reminded of the structure and format of the scheme before they start. The roles on the cards are for non-lawyers, but in each role-play there is an important role for an arbitrator to manage the hearing and to make a final decision based on 'general principles of fairness and good conduct in employment relations'. There is no role card for these arbitrators.

Students should work in groups of three. They should change roles for the second and third mini-role-plays so that they each have a chance to be an employer, an employee and an arbitrator. If there are more than three students in a group, you could have more than one arbitrator.

If you have only two students, they should argue the case as legal representatives of the two parties, without an arbitrator. If you have only one student, you should play one of the legal representatives yourself.

# 9 Sale of goods

## Teacher's brief

This unit deals with buying and selling **goods**, also known as **movable property** or **tangible chattels**. It does not cover the sale of other types of property such as real property (e.g. land and buildings – see Unit 10), intellectual property (e.g. patents – see Unit 11) or negotiable instruments (e.g. promissory notes – see Unit 12).

Sale of goods law, like many areas of law, is best understood in terms of what happens when things go wrong. If a buyer goes bankrupt between taking possession of goods and paying for them, the seller will need to either reclaim the goods or secure payment for them before other creditors (this relates to secured transactions – see Unit 13). If a buyer purchases goods from a seller and it turns out that there is something wrong with those goods, perhaps because they are incorrectly made, because they have become damaged during delivery or because they did not technically belong to the seller in the first place, it is vital to know who is responsible for putting things right, and what, if anything, is to be done. In the case of damage during delivery, it must be ascertained exactly when and if **transfer** of **title** (legal ownership) took place, and therefore crucially who owned the goods when they were damaged. In the case of faulty goods, there is normally some sort of **warranty** (a promise of **fitness**, good **quality**, etc.), whether **express** (formally stated by the seller) or **implied** (not mentioned by the seller, but imposed by legislation), to protect the buyer. In the USA, a warranty is sometimes called a **promise of fitness for a particular purpose or merchantability**.

This area of law is tightly controlled both by legislation and, usually, in individual contracts. Language use A presents ten common types of clauses (**terms and conditions of sale**) used in sale of goods contracts. These include clauses covering **prices and payment**, **title and risk** (i.e. when is the peril of risk transferred to the new owner), **warranties** and **retention of title** (**ROT**). This last type of clause, an ROT clause, is the topic of Listening A, a legal writing seminar on **drafting clauses**. An ROT clause states that, even after goods have been delivered, they remain the property of the seller until some condition (usually payment) has been met. This is especially important if the buyer is unable to pay for the goods (e.g. if the buyer goes bankrupt) and the seller has to reclaim them (and compete with other creditors for a share of the bankrupt firm's property). ROT clauses are very similar to **charges** (claims on specific items of property to secure payment of a debt), but in the UK there is a crucial difference: charges have to be registered with Companies House to be valid, while ROT clauses do not. It is therefore essential that, when drafting an ROT clause, it is not presented as a charge.

Reading B also deals with ROT clauses. It describes a landmark case in Australia where an ROT clause created a **trust** (the setting aside of the money or property of one person for the benefit of another person or persons). The article outlines the detailed arguments of the various courts as to whether the clause was valid, or whether, as an unregistered charge, the clause was invalid. The issues involved in these cases (e.g. charges and trusts) are more thoroughly explored in Unit 13 (Secured transactions).

Listening B deals with the issue of so-called **shrink-wrap contracts**, which are sale of goods contracts which can only be read after buying the product (typically because they are shrink-wrapped within the packaging of the product).

The cases in Reading B and Listening B are used to illustrate **case briefs**: summaries of the history of a case, including the arguments and rulings of the lower and appeals courts. Lawyers often have to read, prepare or present such case briefs, and the unit provides useful language and practice. In addition, the unit provides practice of **talking about corresponding laws and institutions** between one jurisdiction and another. There is also guidance on **recording and studying vocabulary**, an essential skill for anybody learning a language.

## Discussion

Use these questions to generate a discussion.

a   Have you ever had any legal problems as a result of buying or selling goods?

b   What can go wrong i) before an order is placed, ii) before delivery, iii) before payment and iv) after payment?

c   What can be done to prevent such problems and to resolve them when they arise?

**Suggested answers**

b   i)   There may be problems with the contract between buyer and seller. Perhaps one party may trick the other into signing a highly disadvantageous contract.

     ii)  There may be a hold-up in production leading to delayed delivery. The buyer may refuse to accept the delivery for some reason.

     iii) The buyer may refuse to pay on time, or be unable to pay at all.

     iv)  The goods may be faulty, in which case the buyer may seek damages from the seller.

c   This is where lawyers come in. Careful wording of contracts, orders, warranties, etc. is essential. Court action or the threat of court action is one way to resolve problems.

## 1   Reading A: Introduction to sale of goods legislation

Check that students understand the six words in the box.

**Background notes**

○ As discussed in earlier units, a *contract* need not be a written document signed by both parties (an *express contract*). In fact, many sale of goods contracts are either oral or signed by only one party (e.g. a purchase order, which becomes a contract once it is accepted by the seller) or otherwise simply implied by the conduct of the buyer and seller.

○ A *disclaimer* is a statement of non-responsibility under given circumstances, while an *exclusion* states what is not covered by a contract.

○ *Title* in property is ownership. It is distinct from *possession*, although often the same person holds both title and possession of an item. *Transfer of title* takes place when ownership passes from one party to another, usually at the time of payment. Possession is transferred on delivery to the buyer.

○ A *warranty* /ˈwɒrənti/ is a statement of the good quality (and good title) of merchandise. It can be confused with a *guarantee*, which is a promise to make a product good if it has some defect. In other words, a warranty is about the present and a guarantee is about the future.

Tell students to work in pairs to try to put the words into the sentences without reading the text. Then tell them to read the text to check their predictions. When they have finished, go through the answers with the class.

 **Answers**
1 transfer; title
2 warranties
3 exclusions/disclaimers; disclaimers/exclusions
4 contracts

 **Background notes**
○ If something *fosters* the development of international trade, it supports and promotes it.
○ *Chattels* /'tʃætəlz/ are goods which can be moved, in contrast to real property. Note that *chattel* is countable and may be singular (*a chattel*), unlike *goods* (which in British English is never singular). In civil law jurisdictions, this distinction is often called *movable– immovable*. Note also that the word *chattel* originates from the same source as the word *cattle*.
○ *Tangible* /'tændʒəbl/ means 'touchable'. Tangible chattel covers everything with physical presence. Services (such as teaching, cleaning, consulting or building) are intangible, so they are not chattels. Patents, copyrights and trademarks are also intangible.
○ *Provisions* in paragraph 4 refers to clauses in a contract, while in paragraph 5 it refers to clauses in an Act.

**Optional extension**
The text is a general introduction to the area of sale-of-goods law, and it may raise specific questions, such as the following, among students. They can either research the answers in relation to English law on the Internet, or discuss (either in pairs or as a class) how the questions relate to their own jurisdiction(s).
1 What aspects of the law on the sale of goods might not be governed by legislation? (paragraph 1)

2 In what way might application of the legislation depend upon the type of sale? (paragraph 2)
3 Why might application of the legislation depend on whether the seller is a merchant or non-merchant? (paragraph 2)
4 What other added details might apply to contract formation in the context of sale of goods, but not to contracts in general? (paragraph 4)
5 What might happen if a person who had possession but not title tried to transfer title to a third party? (paragraph 4)
6 How do aspects of good faith and apparent authority come into play in the context of transfer of title? (paragraph 4)

Divide the class into teams of three or four. Tell each team to choose five of the key terms (in bold) from the text to test the other teams on, and to make sure they understand all the other key terms. Then the teams should take turns to read a definition of one of their key terms, either invented or taken from the Glossary booklet. Award a point to students from the other teams if they can identify the key term, or a point to the asking team if nobody can guess correctly. At the end of the game, the team with the most points is the winner.

## 2 Key terms: Sale of goods

**2.1** Tell students to work in pairs to match the key terms with the definitions. When they have finished, go through the answers carefully with the class. Then test students by telling them to cover their books, reading the definitions aloud and asking them to identify the correct warranty.

 **Answers**
1 d  2 g  3 a  4 f  5 b  6 c  7 e

**2.2** Tell students to work alone or in pairs to complete the table. As you go through the answers with the class, elicit differences between the sets of words, as well as additional words (such as those given in brackets below). Avoid giving full explanations, as this will come out in Exercise 2.3.

**Answers**
1  to purchase (+ to procure)
2  to deal in, to offer for sale (+ to peddle, to vend)
3  consumer, purchaser, customer (+ client)
4  merchant, retailer, supplier, vendor (+ wholesaler, trader)
5  commodity, merchandise, wares (+ chattel)

 **Background notes**
The differences between many of the terms concern formality and collocation rather than absolute meaning.

1  *To purchase* means the same as 'to buy', but tends to be used in business contexts. In business, *purchasing* is the process of finding suppliers, placing orders and arranging delivery. *Procurement* typically refers to obtaining supplies for an army or an organisation. Often it is not necessary to *pay for* goods at the time of buying: many shops offer 'buy now, pay later' deals.

2  If a business *deals in* a particular item, it regularly buys and sells that item, without actually producing anything. For example, a shop might deal in antiques. *Offering* something *for sale* refers to a specific item, and naturally takes place before selling. *To vend* has several meanings: it could refer to selling (e.g. soft drinks) in a vending machine, or by a street vendor (e.g. selling hamburgers from a cart). But in legal contexts, it can simply mean selling, typically involving a vendor selling a house or piece of land. *To peddle* means to sell small items by travelling from place to place, or to sell illegal drugs.

3  A *consumer* is the final user of a product, who may not be the same person as the *buyer* (e.g. a mother, the buyer, buys a toy for her son, the consumer). A *purchaser* is typically buying for his/her company. The traditional distinction between a *customer*, who buys goods, and a *client*, who buys a service, is often blurred. *Buyer* is the most neutral of these terms, but generally avoided in preference for one of the more specific terms.

4  In general English, a *merchant* is a person or company that buys or sells in large quantities. In legal and financial English, a *merchant* buys goods at wholesale prices and sells them at retail prices. The everyday term for this is a *retailer*, which typically refers to a shop or other outlet selling goods to members of the public. A *wholesaler* does not sell to the public, but to other businesses. A *supplier* is usually a company that sells goods or services to another company on a regular basis. A *vendor* can be either a seller of a property (in legal English) or a person who sells small items on the street. A *trader* buys and sells goods, without necessarily producing anything.

5  A *commodity* is an article of trade or commerce. It is typically an agricultural product or mining product, traded in commodities markets. *Chattel*, described on page 154, is a very rare and formal word used mainly in legal English. *Merchandise* and *wares* are described on SB page 124. Note that *wares* and *goods* are always plural in British English, *merchandise* is uncountable and *chattel* is countable.

**2.3**  Tell students to discuss the questions in pairs. After a few minutes, open up the discussion to include the whole class. Elicit an example of the techniques which have been used and a possible example of the techniques that haven't been used. When you discuss question 2 with students, encourage them to try new techniques. You could follow this up in a later lesson, to check which techniques they have tried and how successful they have been.

 **Answers (with examples)**
a  Not used. Will depend on students' language.
b  Not used, but would be useful to show stress in *merchandise*.
c  Used, by placing *wares* and *merchandise* together in the word list.

**d** Used in fourth column of table.

**e** Used for *merchandise*.

**f** Not used, although different nouns with *ware* are listed in the fourth column.

**g** Used in third column.

**2.4** This kind of work will only be successful if students have access to good dictionaries. If you have access to the Internet, you could suggest some online dictionaries such as http://dictionary.cambridge.org and http://www.translegal.com/legal-english-dictionary. You may consider that this exercise is best done as homework.

Tell students to work in groups, with each group working on different sets of words to try to find the differences. Encourage them to make notes of the differences they find. When they have finished, ask each group to present their findings to the class. Encourage them to make notes of each other's findings. You should add any important comments regarding the differences.

---

**Optional extension**
**Photocopiable worksheet 9.1**

Photocopiable worksheet 9.1 contains instructions for building a sortable, testable vocabulary bank. Tell students to follow the instructions at home, and encourage them to report back to the class if they have used the method, or if they can think of improvements. Point out that everybody needs to find his/her own preferred method of learning vocabulary, and that they should therefore be prepared to adapt this method to suit their own learning styles. Get further feedback when you reach the end of the unit.

---

## 3 Language use A: Terms and conditions of sale

Elicit from students ways in which lawyers assist suppliers with terms and conditions. Then tell them to read the introduction (SB page 124) to compare it with their answers.

 **Background notes**

○ *Terms* are agreements which have been agreed or stipulated. *Conditions* state the circumstances under which those terms are valid. In practice, the two words are often treated as a single concept.

○ The second sentence makes a distinction between sales based on written contracts (e.g. between businesses) and those without (e.g. to consumers).

○ If something is *relied on* as a legal framework, it forms the basis of a legally binding agreement.

**3.1** Tell students to work in pairs to match the clause types with their descriptions. When they have finished, go through the answers with the class and test students by reading some definitions aloud to elicit the clause types. They could also test each other in this way.

 **Answers**
**1** f  **2** j  **3** e  **4** i  **5** h  **6** d  **7** a
**8** c  **9** b  **10** g

 **Background note**
*Peril of loss* (also *risk of loss*) refers to situations in which goods are damaged or lost (e.g. during transportation or through use). The owner, borrower or transporter of the goods (or their insurer) is responsible for this risk, but obviously the risk is transferred to the new owner during a sale.

**3.2** Tell students to work in pairs to identify the clauses. You may want to check their answers before they go on to plan how to paraphrase each clause, as if they were explaining it to a client. Go through the example together and elicit how the language has been changed. You may need to point out that the most important change is an increase in the number of verbs (*can be changed*, *don't need to give*). The verbs in the paraphrase also contain more meaning than the only verb in the original clause (*are*). When they have finished, elicit some paraphrases for each clause.

 **Suggested answers**

1. **Title and risk clause** When the goods are delivered, title in the goods passes to the buyer.

2. **Orders clause** If the order is a verbal one, rather than a written one, and if the goods are shipped before the vendor receives a written confirmation of the order, the vendor's interpretation of the order is final and binding.

3. **Warranties clause** The vendor states that the goods conform to the specifications which the purchaser supplied. The vendor also states that it will apply all processing in a good workmanlike manner, which means in line with relevant trade practices and standards, or in line with the purchaser's specifications. Apart from these two statements, the vendor is not asserting anything else about the quality of the goods.

4. **Indemnification of vendor clause** The purchaser agrees not to hold the vendor responsible for any loss, damage, expenses, claims (complaints), suits (court cases) and (court) judgments which are caused by the design, installation, maintenance or operation of the goods, whether that cause is direct or indirect.

5. **Changes or cancellation clause** If the purchaser requests that the vendor change the specifications or processing of the goods, the vendor has the right to accept or reject such a request, as well as the right to charge the purchaser for all costs and services involved in those changes.

 **Background note**
A *representation* is a statement of alleged fact.

 CD2 T1–2 **4 Listening A: Legal writing seminar on drafting clauses**

**4.1** Tell students to read the introduction and the questions (SB page 126). Then elicit from the class answers to these questions:
a What is an ROT clause?
b What is a charge?
c Why might it be a problem if the ROT clause is interpreted as a charge?

 **Answers**
a A retention of title clause (see Exercise 3.1).
b See Background note below.
c Avoid confirming or rejecting suggestions at this stage.

 **Background notes**
○ *ROT* is sometimes pronounced as one word /rɒt/ and sometimes as three separate letters. For this reason, it is common to see both *a ROT clause* and *an ROT clause*.
○ A *charge* is similar to a *mortgage*: both are security for the payment of a debt. The difference is that a mortgage passes real property from one party to the other, while a charge passes something else. See http://www.companieshouse.gov.uk/about/gbhtml/gba8.shtml.

Play the first half of the presentation for students to answer the questions. Tell students to discuss the answers in pairs, and then check with the whole class.

**Transcript »** STUDENT'S BOOK **page 287**

 **Answers**
1. If an ROT clause is interpreted as a charge and has not been registered, it is void.
2. In cases in which hundreds of sales of goods are made each day by a seller it is not practically feasible to register each one.

**4.2** Elicit from the class what the five tips might be. Then tell students to listen to the second part of the recording to make notes. At the end of the recording, tell them to compare notes in small groups. Then go through the answers with the class.

**Transcript »** STUDENT'S BOOK **page 288**

 **Answers**
1   A good clause will be clear. It will state that ownership or title in the goods sold will not pass to the buyer until payment is made.
2   The clause should require that the buyer keeps the goods separate from other goods. The goods should be marked as the supplier's property until payment is made. Make sure that a serial number which is on the outstanding invoice is also on the goods.
3   The clause should state that the buyer will not resell the goods until payment is made.
4   Take into consideration what the buyer will do with the goods. If the goods will be used by the buyer, and they lose their form and can't be recovered, the clause may be void.
5   A well-written clause will say that the supplier has a right of entry to recover the goods.

**Background notes**
○ A *serial number* is a number which identifies exactly where and when each batch (or series) of goods was made. Serial numbers enable individual packages and items to be tracked in case of quality control or legal issues.
○ If goods *lose their form*, they are no longer in their original shape/condition.

**4.3** Tell students to work through these questions alone and then discuss them with a partner. If necessary, play both parts of the recording again for them to check their answers. Then go through the answers with the class. You could point out that this exercise is very similar to Part 2 of the ILEC Test of Listening, although in the exam students listen twice to complete the multiple-choice exercise.

**Answers**
**1** b   **2** c   **3** a   **4** c

**Optional extension**
Tell students to look at the transcript on SB page 288 and to underline the phrases which the speaker uses to focus attention and to signal what he is going to say or do. You may need to do the first one or two with the class. Tell students to work alone and then go through the answers with the class.

**Answers**
Now, I'd like to move on to …
As you know, …
Thus …
This means that …
That's why …
Well, now I'd like to …
First of all, …
A second thing to keep in mind is the fact that …
The reason for this is that …
A third point: …
Remember that …
I now come to my fourth point.
Another thing to take into consideration is …
My fifth and final point is the issue of …
Are there any questions?
Well, then I would suggest at this point that we …

**4.4** Tell students to do the exercise alone and then check their answers with a partner. Go through the answers with the class.

 **Answers**
**1** supplied   **2** seller   **3** in full   **4** buyer
**5** value   **6** recover   **7** premises   **8** due
**9** solvency

**Background note**
*Bona fide* /ˈbəʊnə ˈfaɪdi/ literally means 'good faith'. In a bona-fide sale, there is no reason to cast doubt on either party's right to participate in that sale.

**4.5** Discuss this question with the whole class. As a follow-up, you could ask students to correct the clause so that it does include all the necessary characteristics.

The clause does contain a clear statement that titles shall not pass until the buyer has paid in full for the goods. It also contains a provision giving the seller the right to enter the buyer's premises to take advantage of them. Unfortunately, the clause fails to include the other points addressed by the speaker. The clause does not make any mention of requiring the buyer to keep the goods separate from other goods, nor is there mention of serial-number markings on the goods corresponding to invoices. No provisions have been made for a prohibition on further sale until the goods are paid for in full. In fact, the wording appears to state the direct opposite. Finally, no wording exists to deal with the problem of changing or incorporating the goods into other goods.

---

**Optional extension
Photocopiable worksheet 9.2**

The role-play on Photocopiable worksheet 9.2 is based on the ROT clause in Exercise 4.4, and provides a context for the writing in Exercise 7.1.

Tell students that the case took place in an unusual jurisdiction where lawsuits are decided by a panel of judges based on a brief presentation by each party. The trial also includes cross-examination where appropriate. The deliberation of the judges is done in public.

Divide the class into groups of between five and seven. Three students should be the panel of judges, while the others should be counsel for the two companies. With smaller classes, you may have fewer judges, or you may play the judge yourself. If you have only one student, you should each play one of the corporate counsel, and then judge the outcome of the case together (out of role).

Make sure the judges know the procedure (presentation by each party, followed by cross examination of each party, followed by public deliberation and decision by the judges). Point out that the judges should be flexible in their deliberations, and to listen to the other judges' opinions in order to reach a consensus. Then tell one of the judges to manage the role-play. Set a time limit (e.g. around 15 minutes).

---

 **5  Listening B: A case brief**

This case is described fully at http://laws.lp.findlaw.com/7th/961139.html. Elicit from the class a) what a case brief is, b) who prepares case briefs and c) why they do it. Then tell students to read the introduction (SB page 127) to compare it with their ideas. When they have read the introduction, elicit what students think 'shrink-wrap' contracts might be.

**5.1** Tell students to listen to the presentation to answer the questions. At the end of the recording, tell them to discuss the questions in small groups, as well as anything else they remember from the presentation. Then discuss the answers with the class.

**Transcript »**  STUDENT'S BOOK **page 288**

---

**Answers**

1   The product is a software program containing millions of telephone numbers and addresses, as well as a retrieval program.
2   The central legal issue is whether a shrink-wrap licence constitutes an enforceable contract.
3   According to the Court of Appeals, buying shrink-wrapped software is like buying an airline ticket as both involve payment before the terms of sale are fully known to the consumer.

---

**Background notes**

○ A *shrink-wrap contract* is one which can only be read when the wrapping has been removed from a purchase. There is no way to read the contract before buying the product. See http://en.wikipedia.org/wiki/Shrink_wrap_contract.

○ If a Court of Appeals *remands* a case back to the District Court, it instructs the District Court to reconsider the case.

○ The *Uniform Commercial Code* (UCC) is an Act which aims to regulate and harmonise trade within the USA. See http://en.wikipedia.org/wiki/Uniform_Commercial_Code.

**5.2** Tell students to discuss the statements in pairs. If necessary, play the recording a second time before going through the answers with the class. Discuss with students whether they agree with the courts' decisions in this case.

 **Answers**
1 False (The court decided in favour of the defendant.)
2 True
3 False (The UCC states that the vendor may put limitations on the kind of conduct that constitutes acceptance.)
4 True

 **Background note**
In this context, an *instance* is a legal proceeding or lawsuit.

# 6 Text analysis: A case brief

**6.1** Do this with the whole class. It can probably be done quickly using the transcript (SB page 288).

 **Answer**
In the second paragraph, the speaker mentions: the facts of the case, the stages of litigation, the holdings of the courts, the reasoning of the courts.

**Optional extension**

Tell students to look through the rest of the transcript to underline more useful phrases for case briefs. You may need to do the first one or two with the class. Tell them to work in pairs. When they have finished, go through the answers with the class.

**Suggested answers**

First, I'll tell you the <u>facts of the case</u> and then something about <u>the stages of litigation</u> and the <u>holdings of the courts</u>. Finally, I'll explain <u>the reasoning of the courts</u>.
<u>Here are the facts: the plaintiff</u>, ProCD, produced the CD-ROM product Select Phone. <u>The defendant</u>, Mr Zeidenberg, purchased copies of Select Phone, but decided to ignore the licence.
ProCD <u>sued, alleging breach of the express terms of the</u> shrink-wrap licence <u>agreement,</u>

<u>among other things.</u> <u>The main issue raised by the case is whether</u> a shrink-wrap licence constitutes an enforceable sales contract.
<u>The first instance, the District Court, decided in favour of the defendant.</u> <u>It held that</u> because the terms of the licence agreement were inside the box instead of printed on the outside, Zeidenberg had no opportunity to disagree with or negotiate them when he paid for the product at a store.
<u>Then the case went to appeal.</u> <u>The Court of Appeals reversed the District Court decision in favour of the vendor, ProCD.</u> <u>It remanded the case back to the District Court</u> to determine damages and other legal relief. <u>In its decision, the Appeals Court noted that</u> the Select Phone box contained a clear statement that use of the product was subject to the licence terms contained inside.
What was <u>the reasoning of the court?</u> <u>The Appeals Court made comparisons to</u> other types of transactions where money is also exchanged before the detailed terms and conditions are communicated to the consumer. <u>One example the court gave was</u> buying airline tickets.
<u>The Court also noted that</u> the Uniform Commercial Code provides that a vendor may invite acceptance of an offer by conduct. A buyer may accept that offer by performing the acts the vendor will treat as acceptance. <u>And that, concluded the Court, is what happened.</u> ProCD proposed a contract that a buyer would accept by using the software after having an opportunity to read the licence at leisure.
So, <u>the court reasoned</u>, he was bound by its terms.

**6.2** Tell students to scan the transcript again to find the device and the two examples.

 **Answers**
The technique used by the speaker is to pose rhetorical questions to signal a move to a new topic.
The examples are *So, what is the procedural history of the case?* and *What was the reasoning of the court?*

**6.3** Tell students to work through the exercise in pairs. When they have finished, go through the answers with the class.

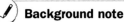

**Answers**
**1/2** b; h   **3/4** c; g   **5/6/7** d; f; i
**8/9** a; e

**Pronunciation notes**
appellant /əˈpelənt/
appellee /ˌæpəˈliː/

## 7 Writing and Speaking: Presenting a case brief

**7.1** This can be done in class or at home. (See Writing section, page xiv.) You may need to suggest sources of information, such as http://www.lawreports.co.uk or http://caselaw.lp.findlaw.com/casesummary/browse.html, which both contain thousands of summaries which can be turned into case notes. For ready-made case notes, see http://www.4lawschool.com/casebrief.htm. You could also instruct students to write a case note on the role-play (Photocopiable worksheet 9.2).

**7.2** This will need to wait until students have completed the research in Exercise 7.1. If you would prefer not to wait, choose one of the case notes available online (e.g. http://www.4lawschool.com/casebrief.htm). Make sure you give students time to prepare, including deciding which of the useful phrases from the transcript to use. If you have a large group, it may be better to tell students to work in groups, rather than giving individual presentations to the class.

## 8 Reading B: Retention of title

Tell students to read the introduction (SB page 129) to find out what a trust is. When they have finished, discuss with the class the difference between a trust and a charge.

**Background note**
It is easiest to think of the difference in terms of the everyday meaning of trust and distrust. A *charge* is based on distrust: party A holds something which belongs to party B in order to guarantee that party B will repay a loan to party A. A (legal) *trust* appears to be based on (moral) trust: party A holds something which belongs to party B. Party A is morally and legally obliged to return that thing at some point to party B. In practice, there is little or no moral or emotional difference between the two devices: the only question is which is more likely to secure a vendor's rights in the event of the buyer's bankruptcy.

**8.1** Tell students to read the text carefully to match the phrases with the paragraphs. When they have had a chance to read the text, allow them to work in pairs to work out or check the answers. The text is rather difficult, so allow time for them to help each other. When they have finished, go through the answers with the class, and help with any language problems. You could also discuss why the issue is important. (Answer: Because it gives priority to certain creditors of an insolvent company to recover money and/or goods ahead of other creditors.)

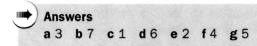

**Answers**
**a** 3   **b** 7   **c** 1   **d** 6   **e** 2   **f** 4   **g** 5

**Background notes**
○ *Insofar as* means 'to the extent that'.
○ *Book debts* are money owed to a company by its customers. A *charge over books debts* (or *on book debts* – see http://www.companieshouse.gov.uk/about/gbhtml/gba8.shtml) is a type of charge which uses book debts as security.
○ *Secured creditors* are those creditors who have a *charge* over the assets of a debtor.

### Pronunciation notes

adduced /əˈdʒuːst/
ascertainable /ˌæsəˈteɪnəbl/
confer /kənˈfɜːʳ/
indebtedness /ɪnˈdetɪdnəs/
proprietary /prəˈpraɪətri/

**8.2**  Tell students to discuss the four questions in small groups. Then go through the answers with the class.

**Suggested answers**

1  The clause involved had an effect such that the income in question was held by the buyer for the benefit of the seller rather than having the effect of causing the buyer to have some type of security in the goods.

2  It means that the Court could not ignore the legal relationship actually created (a trust) by the wording of the ROT clause.

3  On an evidential ground for not having shown a connection between the goods it supplied and what was eventually paid for the finished product.

4  Sellers may use this decision to draft similar clauses in their contracts in order to ensure payment, even where the buyer is in insolvent liquidation.

**8.3**  Exercises 8.3, 8.4 and 8.5 can be done together. Tell students to work in pairs to work through the three exercises. When they have finished, go through the answers with the class.

**Answers**

  **1** into  **2** to  **3** of  **4** in  **5** over  **6** in
  **7** for  **8** between  **9** in  **10** into

**8.4**  See Exercise 8.3. Point out that there may be several phrases for some components. When you check the answers with the class, point out that these introductory phrases will be useful in students' own writing.

**Answers**

  **a**  *the Court has upheld ... (paragraph 1)*
      *The Judge at first instance, and the Court of Appeal, had held that ...; The majority*

*in the High Court rejected that reasoning. In the majority's view, ... (paragraph 4)*
*... the Court dismissed ... (paragraph 6)*

  **b**  *The critical provision in the clause stated ... (paragraph 2)*

  **c**  *The question for the Court to consider was whether ... (paragraph 3)*

  **d**  *In the case of ... (paragraph 2)*

  **e**  *In drawing the distinction in relation to the particular clause in question, the Court noted that ...; On that basis, the Court held that ... (paragraph 5)*

**8.5**  See Exercise 8.3. When you check the answers, you could test students by reading a definition and eliciting the phrase from the text.

**Answers**

  **1**  void for non-registration
  **2**  the proceeds of such manufacturing or construction process
  **3**  adduced evidence
  **4**  held in trust
  **5**  proprietary interest
  **6**  on an evidential ground
  **7**  by virtue of

---

**Optional extension**
**Photocopiable worksheet 9.3**

Reading B includes some rather long and complex sentences. Photocopiable worksheet 9.3 draws attention to the techniques used in these sentences with the aim of a) increasing awareness and comprehension when students encounter such sentences again, and b) increasing the probability that they will use such structures themselves where appropriate. Tell students to work in small groups to put the words back into the correct order. Make sure they do not have their books open as they do this and that they help each other as much as possible. Allow a very limited time (around five minutes) for groups to think about the sentences and fill in some of the easier gaps. Then elicit the answers one word at a time following the 'Easy first' procedure (see Games and activities section, page xvi). When giving an answer, students should say the question number and the preceding and following word (e.g. *question 1: proceeds of sale*).

## Answers

1 By **a** four **to** one **majority**, the **Court** has **upheld** the **effectiveness** of **an** agreement **providing** for **the** proceeds **of** sale **of** manufactured **goods** to **be** held **in** trust, **thereby** securing **the** manufacturer's **indebtedness** to **the** seller.

2 It **was** agreed **that** the **Seller** had **not** retained **title** to **the** steel **products** since **the** steel **it** had **supplied** was **no** longer **ascertainable** in **the** products; **the** steel **products** were **physically** different **property**.

3 **The** Judge **at** first **instance**, and **the** Court of Appeal, **had** held **that** the **clause** insofar **as** it **operated** to **confer** on **the** Seller **a** proprietary **interest** in **the** proceeds, **was a charge** over **book** debts **and** was **void** for **non-registration**.

4 **In** drawing **the** distinction **in** relation **to** the **particular** clause **in** question, **the** Court **noted** that **effect** had **to** be **given** to **the** legal **relationship** the **parties** had **entered** into.

5 In **the** end, **and** despite **substantially** upholding **the** Seller's **arguments** as **to** the **effect** of **the** clause, **the** Court **dismissed** the **Seller's** appeal **on** an **evidential** ground.

6 However, **despite** the **Seller's** ultimate **failure**, the **majority's** decision **strengthens** a **seller's** position **and** consequently **could** alter **the** balance **where** sellers **and** secured **creditors** compete **for** priority.

## 9 Language use B: Talking about corresponding laws and institutions

Tell students to read through the box and to work in small groups to describe the equivalents to the three items given. Make sure they use the phrases given. When they have finished, ask a few students to report back on what they learnt from their partners.

 Tell students to do the Internet activity as homework. See Using the Internet for research, page xviii.

# Language focus

## Answers

1 **Vocabulary: distinguishing meaning**

1 *vendor*: The others are buyers.

2 *distinct*: The others mean 'the same'.

3 *defendant*: The others bring a case.

4 *decide*: The others involve putting something off until later.

5 *non-arbitrary*: The others mean 'not legally binding'; *non-arbitrary* means supported by evidence or good reason.

6 *material*: The others are adjectives mean 'related to money'; *material* means 'relevant in a lawsuit'.

7 *lead to*: The others mean 'result from'.

2 **Word formation**

| Verb | Noun |
|------|------|
| disclaim | disclaimer |
| exclude | exclusion |
| indemnify | indemnification |
| tolerate | tolerance |
| specify | specifications |
| retain | retention |
| postpone | postponement |

| Verb | Adjective |
|------|-----------|
| suit | suitable |
| accept | acceptable |
| imply | implied |
| bind | binding |
| ascertain | ascertainable |

3 **Prepositions**

**2** of **3** in **4** with **5** by **6** under

4 **Word choice**

**2** in respect of **3** fit **4** vendor **5** merchandise **6** entitled **7** reasonable **8** deemed **9** claim

5 **Contract expressions**

**2** c **3** a **4** f **5** g **6** d **7** b

6 **Disclaimer expressions**

**a** 7 **b** 8 **c** 4 **d** 5 **e** 2 **f** 3 **g** 9 **h** 6 **i** 1

# Case study 3: Contract law

## The facts of the case

Ask the class if they know (or can guess) what a *battle of forms* is. Then tell students to read the description of the case carefully to find out. When they have finished, discuss the answer with the class.

 **Answers**
A battle of forms is a legal dispute where the legal documents of the two parties (their forms) state different things. In this case, the purchaser, Colonial, sends a purchase order containing certain terms, and the supplier sends an acknowledgement containing different terms. The issue is: which form takes precedence?

Ask the group these comprehension questions to make sure they have fully understood the facts of the case.
1    What do you know about the three companies?
2    What sort of contract exists between Colonial and Lehigh?
3    Which two forms are in conflict?
4    Who is suing whom?
5    What are *consequential damages*?

 **Answers**
1    Colonial makes cooling units. Lehigh makes steel tubing, which it supplies to Colonial. Best Produce uses (or has bought) a faulty cooling unit from Colonial.
2    Colonial's annual purchase order, accepted by Lehigh, constitutes a contract. The release orders are based on the terms agreed in the purchase order.
3    Lehigh's *acknowledgement* disclaims liability for defects, while Colonial's *purchase order* makes no mention of this. Colonial's *release orders* are also forms, but they presumably agree with the annual purchase order.

4    Best Produce is suing Colonial for damages, including consequential damages. Colonial is suing Lehigh for recovery of those damages.
5    Although not mentioned in this section, students should remember from Unit 6 (Reading A) that consequential damages arise from the special circumstances related to the transaction in question. Consequential (or special) damages apply when it can be established that the damage was foreseeable at the time the contract was entered into.

## Task 1: Role-plays

1    Allocate roles for Role-play a. If you have an odd number of students, one group should have two lawyers for each role-play. If you have only one student, you should play the role of the client in both role-plays.

Tell students to read the instructions and then to study the relevant legal documents carefully in order to prepare for *both* role-plays, especially the one in which they will play the lawyer. Allow plenty of time for them to read the documents, and help with any vocabulary/comprehension problems.

With weaker classes, it would be useful for students to work with partners with the same role in order to make sure they have fully understood and to prepare for the role-play.

2    Put students in pairs for the first role-play and set a time limit so that they all finish at the same time.

3    At the end of the time limit, collect feedback from the 'lawyers' on the results of the conference and add your own comments on the effectiveness of the role-plays in terms of language. Then tell them to go on to Role-play b. There should be no need for additional preparation time, as they should have prepared for both parts before the first role-play.

## Task 2: Writing

Elicit from students where they have studied the structure of memos (Unit 5) and what they can remember about them. The writing can be done alone or in groups, in class or at home. (See Writing section, page xiv.)

➡ **Model answer**
**Memorandum**

To:         Samuel Clemmens, Senior Legal Counsel Colonial Incorporated
From:       John D. Rockway, Associate Counsel Conway & Conway
Date:       September 15
Subject:    Legal argument regarding the Best Produce Corporation v. Colonial Incorporated v. Lehigh Steel Incorporated case

Pursuant to your request, please find below my proposal for our legal argument regarding the above referenced matter.

As I understand the facts of the case, Colonial's potential liability to Best Produce hinges on whether Lehigh's disclaimer of liability for consequential damages is valid. This is a classic battle of forms situation. In this jurisdiction, Section 2–207 of the Uniform Commercial Code applies to this case. As you are aware, this section provides rules of contract formation when, as in this case, the forms involved do not correspond. Section 2–207 (1) converts a counteroffer (i.e. Lehigh's acknowledgement form) into acceptance unless expressly made conditional on its full acceptance. Since Lehigh has done exactly this, 2–207 (1) does not apply.

In cases where acceptance is made conditional on assent to additional terms, the original offeror can rely on Section 2–207 (3). This section provides for contract formation based on the conduct of the parties. The terms of such contract are those terms which correspond in the writings between the parties. Hence, our argument should be that the parties acted as if there was a contract and, as a result, the terms of such contract are those on which the parties' forms agree. In addition, the disclaimer provisions of Lehigh's acknowledgment cannot form part of the contract because no assent whatsoever to limit liability was expressed by Colonial in its conduct. This conclusion is supported by the provisions of Section 2–207 (1), which require a "definite and seasonable expression of acceptance."

That's really it in a nutshell. I imagine Lehigh will argue that our client accepted the liability waiver by virtue of the fact that it continued to pay for and accept Lehigh's tubing. However, in my opinion, this argument is bound to fail because it would in essence require the court to accept the old common-law "last shot" rule. This rule is inherently unfair and the very reason that Section 2–207 (3) was enacted. Certainly, you should have no difficult in convincing the court of this fact.

Please get back to me if you have any questions. I'll be very happy to meet or telephone conference with you to iron out the details of the argument. I am very positive regarding our chances of recovery against Lehigh.

## Relevant legal documents

○ **Text 1** is an extract from Lehigh's acknowledgement form. This form is sent in response to a release order from Colonial. The question is whether Colonial is deemed to have accepted the new terms on the acknowledgement. Colonial does not have to sign acceptance on the acknowledgement form, but it can be argued that Colonial's failure to reject the new terms, and its continuing with the transaction after it has received them, constitutes acceptance of them.

○ **Text 2** is a genuine extract from the US's UCC, legislation which governs commercial transactions. According to paragraph 1 (... *unless acceptance is made conditional on ...*),

Lehigh's acknowledgement does not constitute acceptance of the original offer to buy.

According to paragraph 2, the new terms in the acknowledgement *might* become part of the contract, subject to the three exceptions (a–c). Exception (a) relates to the original offer, in this case Colonial's purchase order and release order. We do not know if these forms expressly limit acceptance, but for the sake of simplicity, we can assume they do not. Exception (b) relates to the new terms included in the acknowledgement. It can be argued that the new terms do materially alter the original offer (as they disclaim liability for defects). Exception (c) applies only if Colonial has formally objected to the new terms. Again, for the sake of simplicity, we may assume that this has not happened. Therefore the key to paragraph 2 in this case appears to be the word *materially* in exception (b).

According to paragraph 3, if Colonial's conduct implies that it recognises Lehigh's acknowledgement to be a contract, then that is enough to make it a contract. However, Colonial could easily argue that it was unaware that the acknowledgement contained new terms in its small print. This would leave only those 'writings' on which the two parties agreed (i.e. the purchase order and release order) as setting out the terms of the contract, with any remaining details (such as liability for damages) coming from the UCC itself. Of course, the question remains whether Lehigh really has agreed to the terms of the purchase order and release order (see paragraph 1). If this is the case, the UCC will supply all the terms of the contract. In this case, the UCC's sections on *implied warranty* (sections 2-314 and 2-315 of http://www.law.cornell.edu/ucc/2) suggest that Lehigh is under obligation to supply goods which are merchantable and fit for the particular purpose intended.

○ **Text 3** is an extract from a court decision. It highlights the importance of paragraph 3 in Text 2 (above).

**Background notes**

○ In Text 2, sections 2a–c, *they/them* refers to proposed additional terms, while *it* refers to the original offer.

○ In Text 3, the phrasal verb *do away with* (= eliminate) may cause some problems.

# 10 Real property law

The term **real property** (or **real estate** or **realty** in the USA) is not connected with the concept of reality, but rather derives from the Latin word *res*, meaning 'thing', and contrasts with the concept of personal property. The laws governing personal property, such as those concerned with sale of goods (see Unit 9), do not apply to real property.

Real property is defined as land and improvements on that land (e.g. buildings, walls, fences, etc.). In most countries, the ultimate owner of all land is the state (e.g. the government or the sovereign); all that can be bought and sold is the **estate** – the rights associated with that land. The state, as ultimate owner, typically retains some important rights over a property, such as the right to tax the property, the right of **compulsory purchase** (also known as **eminent domain**), the right to police the property and the power of **escheat** (/ɪsˈtʃiːt/) – to take possession of the property if the owner dies and leaves no heirs. In the USA, some states have a system of **allodial title**, which in theory means absolute ownership, but in practice the state maintains at least some of the rights listed above.

A further difference between real property and private property relates to the **Statute of Frauds**, a requirement in common-law countries for **sales of land** to be done in writing in order to be enforceable. The document which is used to transfer title to real property is a **deed**. This requirement also applies to some other agreements, such as those involving private property over a certain value ($500 in the USA) and marriage contracts. Also, contracts which cannot be performed within a given period (in England, three years) must be in writing. In real property law, this requirement is relevant for long-term **lease agreements**.

Reading A highlights a key distinction between **freehold estates** (which do not have a determined duration) and **leaseholds** (which are for a limited period). The most important type of freehold is a **fee simple**, which can be bought and sold (although as mentioned above, technically the property itself is not sold, but the estate – the right to use the property). Leaseholds, on the other hand, typically involve a **tenant** paying regular **rent** to a **landlord** for the right to use the property. This key distinction between buying and renting real property is common around the world, although concepts such as freeholds and leaseholds will vary from one jurisdiction to another. For example, in some civil-law jurisdictions, an important right is **usufruct**: the right to use land and the fruits of the land, such as crops.

Listening B contains part of a presentation on **easements** – rights to use another person's real property. For example, a telecommunications operator may have a pylon on private land, and uses an **easement in gross** to guarantee access to that pylon. A house owner may need an **easement by necessity** to allow him/her to use a neighbour's land in order to gain access to a public road. As well as referring to this right, the term *easement* can also refer to the document granting this right or even the part of land where such a right exists.

Reading C presents a section of a lease agreement – a **statutory conditions clause**. This sets out the relevant statutes (laws) which apply to the agreement. These specify the **rights and obligations** of both the landlord and the tenant. One such right, the tenant's right to **quiet enjoyment**, forms the background to Reading D. *Quiet enjoyment* refers to the right not to be disturbed unreasonably by the landlord's activities. The case which is reviewed in the text illustrates the problem of balancing one party's obligation (here, to repair and clean the building) against another party's right (here, to quiet enjoyment).

Listening B and Reading E illustrate some of the complications associated with **buying real property in another country**, in this case an English speaker buying a house in Spain. The client's lawyer finds the client a lawyer in Spain who can deal with the local **procedures and documentation**, and, if he is given **power of attorney**, can even sign the purchase agreement on the client's behalf.

The unit also practises many useful skills for lawyers: **contrasting and classifying information**, **structuring and signalling transitions** in a presentation, **writing a competency statement** of a law firm's practice areas (e.g. for the firm's marketing brochure or website), and **writing emails** to another lawyer. There is also a focus on the use of **present perfect** to talk about a lawyer's or a law firm's experience.

## Discussion

Use these questions to generate a discussion.

**a** Have you ever bought or sold real property? Was it complicated? (If students have no experience of this, you can still discuss the complications of the process of buying and selling real property.)

**b** Why does real property law have to be different from the law on sale of goods? (You could use this question to play devil's advocate, deliberately arguing with students from a naive non-lawyer point of view.)

**c** If you had to lease a room in your home to a complete stranger, what provisions would you put into the lease contract? (Obviously this will depend on students. The discussion may be technical (i.e. covering clauses such as those in Reading C) or more colloquial (e.g. 'I'd make sure I had the right to get rid of the tenant if he broke anything valuable').)

 **Suggested answer**

**b** There seems to be no inherent reason for all the distinctions. It can be argued that real property tends to be more valuable than personal property, and therefore requires more regulation, but the same could be argued with regard to expensive items of personal property, such as specialist equipment, luxury cars and planes or rare minerals. In personal property transactions, the buyer and seller are responsible for taking necessary precautions, and the same could be true in terms of real property. On the other hand, there are, of course, important concepts which are only relevant to real property, such as easements (see Listening A).

## 1 Reading A: Introduction to property law

Tell students to discuss the four statements briefly in pairs to predict whether they are true or false, and then to read the text to check their predictions. Allow enough time for them to read carefully. When they have finished, check the answers with the class.

 **Answers**
**1** True **2** True **3** False (This is granted by a lease.) **4** False (It forbids them.)

 **Background notes**
○ *Easements* are rights to use another party's land for a specified purpose.
○ *Usufructs* are like easements, although they also give rights to the fruits of another person's land. This may be actual fruit, crops, livestock or even rent. The English word *usufruct* /ˈjuːzjəˌfrʊkt/ derives from separate Latin words *usus* (use) and *fructus* (fruit). The holder of such a right is called a *usufructuary* /ˌjuːzjəˈfrʊktʃəri/.

**Pronunciation note**
mortgage /ˈmɔːgɪdʒ/

**Optional extension**
Ask students to describe any similarities and differences between the system in English-speaking jurisdictions and their own. This can be done in small groups or with the whole class.

## 2 Key terms: Parties referred to in real property law

Tell students to work alone to match the terms and definitions. Point out that the word *decedent* (= a person who has died) is not the same as the word *descendant* (= a person's children, grandchildren, great-grandchildren, etc.). When students have done this, check the answers with the class, and test students by reading a definition of one of the six parties to elicit the key term.

 **Answers**
   **1** c   **2** a   **3** b

 **Pronunciation note**
decedent /dəˈsiːdənt/

**Optional extension**

To check comprehension and reinforce the vocabulary and concepts from the text, use the following questions either as a straightforward comprehension quiz or as a 'Snake game' (see Games and activities section, page xvi). Students should try to answer the questions without looking back at the text, but if they struggle you may allow them to scan the text for the answers.

**Questions**

1 In English-speaking jurisdictions, what is real property usually contrasted with?
2 What two synonyms are given in the text for *real property*?
3 Apart from land, what other types of real property are mentioned?
4 What two synonyms are given in the text for *personal property*?
5 What is the general name for estates whose duration is not determined?
6 What is the general name for estates whose duration is fixed or capable of being fixed?
7 What is the name of the transfer of title in a freehold estate?
8 What is another name for a Contract of Sale?
9 How exactly is title transferred in the UK?
10 What is the name of a contract for exclusive possession?
11 Why is the distinction between commercial and residential leases important?
12 What is the difference between a lease and a licence?
13 What two examples are given of licences?
14 What is the name for the requirement that the sale of or interests in land must be in writing?
15 In England, what length of lease contract must be in writing, under the Statute of Frauds?
16 What is the right to use another person's land?
17 What is the right of use and the fruits of another person's land?

**Answers**

**1** Personal property (paragraph 1)
**2** Immovable property, real estate   **3** Anything fixed to the land, and residential and commercial leases (paragraph 1)
**4** Personalty, movable property   **5** Freehold estates (paragraph 2)   **6** Leasehold estates (paragraph 2)   **7** A conveyance (paragraph 2)
**8** Real Estate Contract (notes to paragraph 2)
**9** A transfer of registered title must be filed with the UK Land Registry (paragraph 2)
**10** Lease (paragraph 3)   **11** Because different property laws apply (paragraph 3)   **12** A lease grants exclusive possession; under a licence, the property remains in the control of the grantor. (paragraph 4)   **13** A hotel room and a dormitory (paragraph 4)   **14** Statute of Frauds (paragraph 5)   **15** Three years (paragraph 5)
**16** Easement (paragraph 6)   **17** Usufruct (paragraph 6)

## 3 Language use A: Contrasting ideas

Tell students to read the box to find out how *whereas* and *while* are used.

 **Language note**
These two conjunctions are almost identical in meaning and use when they introduce contrasts. Both, however, have other meanings: *while* also shows time relationships (*I fell over while I was skating / while skating*), and *whereas* is used to introduce recitals (preliminary clauses in a contract stating the factual circumstances leading to its existence – see for example

http://www.wildlaw.org/easements/
sample.html). As conjunctions, they are
followed by finite clauses (i.e. complete
sentences inside bigger sentences).
Contrastive *while* can also be followed by
an *–ing* clause (*While agreeing with your
analysis in principle, I cannot agree with
your conclusion*), although this is might be
less clumsy if it had a finite clause (*While I
agree with your analysis in principle, …*).
They are similar in meaning to the
prepositions studied in Unit 2: *as opposed
to*, *unlike* and *in contrast to*, which are
always followed by noun phrases (or *–ing*
clauses).

Make sure students understand the six key terms.
They will probably have to consult the Glossary
booklet for *easement* and *usufruct*, as these are
not defined in the text. Tell students to work in
pairs to take turns to contrast the expressions.
When they have finished, ask some groups to
present their sentences to the class.

⏩ **Suggested answers**
   **1** Whereas a freehold estate refers to an
   estate in which ownership is for an
   indeterminate length of time, a
   leasehold is the term for the right to
   possession and use of land for a fixed
   period of time.
   **2** A lease is an agreement by which a
   lessor gives the right of possession of
   real property to a lessee for a specified
   term and for a specified consideration,
   whereas a licence is only the right to
   use without having exclusive
   possession.
   **3** An easement is a right to make limited
   use of another's real property, while
   usufruct refers to the right to use and
   derive profit from property belonging to
   someone else, provided that the
   property itself is not harmed in any way.

**Optional extension**
Tell students to make more sentences
contrasting real property law in English-
speaking countries with that in their own
jurisdictions.

⸂170⸃

## 4  Language use B: Classifying and distinguishing types or categories

**4.1** Tell students to read the information in the
box and to work alone to complete the
sentences. Point out that some of the
phrases may fit into more than one of the
sentences. When they have finished, allow
them to check their answers with a partner
before going through the answers with the
class.

⏩ **Answers**
   **1** distinguish   **2** is a general term for
   **3** refers to / includes; fall under the
   heading of   **4** categorised   **5** includes

💬 **Pronunciation note**
   encompass /ɪŋˈkʌmpəs/

**4.2** Do this as a class. Point out that one way
has been given as an example.

⏩ **Suggested answers**
   ◯ Real property *encompasses* land and
   anything affixed to the land, and
   residential and commercial leases.
   ◯ Real property *refers to* land and
   anything affixed to the land, and
   residential and commercial leases.
   ◯ Real property *is a general term for* land
   and anything affixed to the land, and
   residential and commercial leases.
   ◯ Real property *includes* land and anything
   affixed to the land, and residential and
   commercial leases.

⸨CD2 T4⸩ ## 5  Listening A: Easements

Tell students to read the introduction (SB
page 138) to find out what the lawyer is going to
be doing in the recording. When they have read it,
check that they understand what an *easement* is.

**5.1** Discuss this question with the whole class.

**Suggested answers**
Some other legal issues an estate agent might need to be informed about include (among many possibilities):
○ covenants running with land which may be binding against or enforceable by the buyer;
○ zoning restrictions on the property potentially limiting the right of use to the property;
○ historical and environmental preservation issues;
○ environmental law and liability upon discovery of ground or water pollutants;
○ compulsory purchase orders or procedures.

**Background notes**
○ A *covenant* is a promise included in the deed to a property, and may include permanent easements or restrictions on use.
○ *Compulsory purchase* (US *eminent domain*) is the right of a government body to take private real property for public use, with or without permission (e.g. if a road needs to be built through somebody's land).

**5.2** Tell students to discuss the three questions in pairs. Then play the recording for them to check their answers. Go through the answers with the class.

**Transcript »** STUDENT'S BOOK **page 288**

**Answers**
1 The purpose of a temporary easement is to allow access to property so that, for example, work can be carried out.
2 'Open' use means that the use is obvious and not secretive, while 'notorious' means that the use is clearly visible. 'Continuous' means that the use must have occurred for the statutory period.
3 This is a type of easement appurtenant which is created to reach a landlocked property in order to give it access to a public road.

**Background note**
*Appurtenant* /ə'pɜːtənənt/ means 'attached or belonging to something'. It is from the same origin as the verb *to appertain*, despite differences in spelling.

**Pronunciation notes**
gross /grəʊs/
notorious /nə'tɔːrɪəs/
quasi- /'kwɒzi/ (UK), /'kweɪzaɪ/ (US)

**Optional extension**
**Photocopiable worksheet 10.1**

**1** As a second listening task, tell students to discuss in pairs the eight questions on the worksheet. Either play the recording for them to check or go straight to Exercise 2 below. At the end of the recording, go through the answers with the class.

**Answers**
**1** True **2** False (They are permanent easements.) **3** True **4** True **5** True (The statutory period is *at least* 20 years, so a period of 30 years would qualify.)
**6** True **7** False (It is a type of easement appurtenant.) **8** True

**2** Tell students to look at the notes made by one of the estate agents who attended the presentation on easements and to work in pairs to complete the missing information from memory. Play the recording for them to check. Then go through the answers with the class.

**Answers**
**1** right **2** access **3** Permanent
**4** gross **5** quasi **6** records
**7** Prescriptive **8** secretive **9** visible
**10** statutory **11** appurtenant
**12** adjoining **13** subdivision
**14** necessity **15** landlocked

As a follow-up, tell students to work in groups to think of a case study for each type of easement (temporary easement, easement in gross, prescriptive easement, easement appurtenant and easement by necessity). When they have finished, they should describe their case studies in a mixed-up order so the other groups can guess which type of easement is relevant for each.

**5.3** Tell students to do this in pairs. Point out that there are many possible answers. When they have finished, go through the answers with the class. If students' answers are different from the version from the transcript but nonetheless grammatically and logically correct, accept the answers.

**Answers**
1 we distinguish between
2 classified into
3 type includes
4 One important sub-type

## 6 Language use C: Giving a presentation – structuring and signalling transitions

Elicit from the class the difference between structuring and signalling, and any phrases they know for these functions. Then tell them to look at the box to compare the information there with their suggestions.

Tell students to work alone to read the transcript on SB page 288 to identify and underline the signals used by the speaker.

**Answers**
Now, I'd like to move on to another topic.
I'll begin with the first type, ...
Let's move on to the second type.
Finally, I'll come to the third type, ...

**Optional extension**
**ILEC preparation: Test of Speaking Part 2**

Point out that the seven italicised phrases in the box on SB page 139 and the four underlined phrases from Exercise 6 are ideal for Part 2 of the ILEC Test of Speaking, and are therefore well worth learning by heart. Write the phrases onto cards or slips of paper, one word per slip. Give students a pack of slips for them to sort into phrases. Teams then race to put the words into the correct order. Tip: Write a reference number in the corner of each slip, one number per phrase, so you can easily identify which phrase each word came from. Also, if you are planning to use a printer and guillotine (paper cutter) to make the slips, it is easier to start with a

table, with one word in each cell – see examples below.

| I'll 1 | begin 1 | with 1 |
|---|---|---|
| the 1 | first 1 | type, ... 1 |
| Moving 2 | on 2 | to 2 |
| my 2 | second 2 | point, ... 2 |

When the phrases are laid out in the correct order, students take turns to turn over a slip for their partners to remember what the whole phrase was. This will be very easy at first, but it will quickly become a memory challenge. By the end, students should know all the phrases by heart. Encourage them to use the phrases in Exercise 7 below.

## 7 Speaking A: An aspect of real property law

Allow students time to prepare their presentations, either at home or in groups. Make sure they remember to use the structuring and signalling phrases. If they do not know about the topics listed, allow them to invent information for their presentations. Note that this exercise would work well as practice for the ILEC Test of Speaking Part 2, in which case follow the procedure on SB page 275.

When students give their presentations, give (and encourage from the other students) feedback on the content and style of the presentation as well as any language issues.

**Background note**
*Concurrent* /kənˈkʌrənt/ *ownership* refers to ownership by two or more individuals simultaneously, such as a married couple.

## 8 Reading B: A law firm's practice areas

Elicit from the class the sort of document where they might expect to see a description of 'practice areas' and what they would expect it to include. Then tell them to read the introduction (SB page 140) to check.

**8.1** Check students understand the word *explicitly*. Then tell them to work alone to find the answers to the two questions. When they have finished reading, tell them to check in pairs. Then go through the answers with the class.

 **Answers**
1 The firm also handles Natural Resources.
2 The two types of disputes named are property boundary disputes and ownership disputes.

🖊 **Background notes**
○ *Grazing* refers to allowing grazing animals (sheep, cows, etc.) to graze (eat grass) on a piece of land.
○ *Communication sites* are constructions (e.g. towers) which house radio equipment.
○ *Condemnation* is the process when a government exercises its right of eminent domain (see Background note on page 171). In the UK, this is called *compulsory purchase*.
○ *Rights of way* are legal rights of passage (e.g. via a public footpath) over another person's land.
○ A *broad array* /ˌbrɔːd əˈreɪ/ means 'a wide range'.
○ Conservation easements (see http://en.wikipedia.org/wiki/Conservation_easement) are voluntary agreements by a landowner to protect the natural resources and/or wildlife on a piece of land, which will be binding on all future owners of that land.

**8.2** Tell students to discuss the four cases in pairs to decide whether the law firm should be consulted.

 **Answers**
**1** yes **2** no **3** yes **4** no

**Optional extension**
Divide students into at least two groups of between two and six students. (If you have fewer than four students, follow the procedure below, but with only one group.)
1 Each group should take one of the case studies from Exercise 8.2 and decide exactly what the dispute involves. For example, if there is an easement, what exactly does it state? They should try to avoid clear-cut cases, as otherwise there would be no reason for the two sides to be in dispute. They should write down all the necessary details on a sheet of paper.
2 The groups should then hand their notes to a different group, who will use them as the basis for role-plays, in which the client asks his/her lawyer(s) for advice in the dispute. In groups with two or three students, there should be one client meeting one or two lawyers; in groups with four, five or six, both parties should meet their lawyer(s). In the role-plays, the lawyers should build a good relationship with their clients, suggest a course of action, and warn the client of the strengths of the other party's case.

**8.3** Go through these questions with the class.

 **Answers**
1 The phrases are used to express what the firm has experience in doing.
2 The present perfect tense (*have represented, has dealt with*, etc.) is used most frequently. It refers to past actions with present relevance, when the timeframe of the action is understood to continue up to the present (*For the past ten years ... , Since last year ...*). This puts the emphasis on the firm's recent achievements.
3 matter, issue
4 Due to our comprehensive natural resource and property capabilities, our firm can provide experienced counsel for all environmental and natural resource matters affecting property owners.

## 9 Writing A: Describing a firm's practice areas

You could encourage students to look at some authentic descriptions of practice areas on law firms' websites to get a better idea of the style of language that they use. There are many directories of law firms on the Internet (e.g. http://www.scottishlaw.org.uk/lawfirms; http://lawyers.findlaw.com).

Tell students to work alone or in small groups to write their short description. The description may be about a real law firm or it could be invented/humorous. When they have finished, ask them to present their profiles to the class.

## 10 Reading C: Understanding a lease or tenancy agreement

Elicit from the class why a landlord or a tenant might consult a lawyer. Then tell students to read the introduction (SB page 141) to check.

**10.1** Tell students to discuss the sections or clauses in pairs. You may need to check that they understand what all the clauses are. (NB Acceleration clauses and Force Majeure clauses are discussed in Unit 5. Statutory conditions are discussed in Reading C below.) When they have finished, discuss the answers with the class. There are many authentic lease agreements available online at http://contracts.onecle.com/type/16.shtml, which are often conveniently indexed using the titles in this exercise.

**Answers**
- Clauses from the list you would expect to find in a lease: 1 Parties, 2 Term, 4 Statutory conditions, 6 Rent amount and payments, 8 Method of payment, 10 Deposit
- Other clauses you would expect to find in a lease (among many possibilities): Description of the leased premises, Use of premises, Quiet enjoyment, Repairs and maintenance, Alterations or additions, Damage or destruction, Waiver, Defaults and remedies, Entire lease, Amendment and modification, Assignment, Notices, Termination and surrender

**Background notes**
- A *Quiet enjoyment* clause gives a tenant the right to live in peace and without interference from the landlord.
- A *Waiver* clause states the consequences (or non-consequences) of a waiver. For example, if a party waives damages for a breach of covenant, this should not be taken as a waiver of the whole covenant.
- A *Defaults and remedies* clause specifies what constitutes a default (non-payment of money owed), and what remedies are available.
- An *Entire lease* clause, like an Entire agreement clause, states that the lease agreement supersedes all previous written or oral agreements between the parties.
- An *Amendment and modification* clause refers to the amendment and modification of the agreement, not of the leased premises.
- An *Assignment* clause typically refers to the tenant's rights to sublet (rent) the property to a third party.
- A *Notices* clause specifies how notices (e.g. a 24-hour notice that the landlord is going to visit) and other official communications (such as written requests, acceptances or refusals) must be given.
- A *Termination and surrender* clause specifies the arrangements for terminating the contract, leaving the premises and handing back the landlord's property (including keys, etc.).

**10.2** Tell students to discuss the questions in pairs.

**Answers**
1. Statutory conditions are the conditions imposed by law.
2. Things that might come under statutory conditions in a lease agreement are those listed (a–h) in Exercise 10.3.

**10.3** Tell students to work alone to complete the exercise, then to compare their answers with a partner. When they have finished, go through the answers with the class.

➡️ **Answers**
1 e  2(a) f  2(b) g  3 h  4 b  5 a
6 c  7 d

💬 **Pronunciation notes**
arbitrarily /ˌɑːbɪ'trerəli/
cleanliness /'klenlɪˌnəs/
sewers /'suːəz/

**10.4** Exercises 10.4, 10.5, 10.6 and 10.7 can be done in pairs, and checked together at the end.

➡️ **Answers**
1 2b  2 2a  3 5  4 1  5 3  6 7
7 4  8 6a

**10.5** See Exercise 10.4. You can test students (or they can test each other) by reading one of the definitions to elicit the words and expressions.

➡️ **Answers**
1 h  2 g  3 i  4 b  5 e  6 c  7 d  8 k
9 f  10 a  11 j

**10.6** See Exercise 10.4.

➡️ **Answers**
1 c  2 a  3 d  4 b

**10.7** See Exercise 10.4.

➡️ **Answers**
1 iii  2 iv  3 ii  4 i

**Optional extension**
**Photocopiable worksheet 10.2**

The lease agreement in Reading C contains many ideas linked together to make complicated sentences. The structures used are typical of good legal writing. The exercise on Photocopiable worksheet 10.2 aims to draw attention to these devices so that students might use them in their own writing.

Tell students to work in pairs to put the linking devices back into the lease agreement. Make sure they do not look at the original document. When they have finished, allow them to check their answers in their books, and then discuss any problems they had.

**Answers**
1 The following  2 during  3 Where  4 that is
5 such as  6 but not as to restrict the generality of  7 the foregoing  8 in such a manner as not to  9 caused by  10 whom
11 subject to  12 which  13 unless  14 in respect of  15 If  16 otherwise than in the manner  17 that may be caused by  18 to the extent that  19 Except in the case of
20 without  21 unless  22 for the purposes of
23 Except by  24 during  25 under  26 cause to be  27 that

## 11 Reading D: A case review

Ask students what they understand by the term *case review*, and who might find one useful. Then tell them to read the introduction (SB page 143) to check their answers.

**11.1** Tell students to read the text and then discuss the questions in pairs. When they have finished, go through the answers with the class.

➡️ **Answers**
1 The business sector is the restaurant business. The case could be relevant for any type of business that requires uninterrupted use of easily accessible, well-lit and clean premises for its customers.
2 *Quiet enjoyment* refers to the right of an owner or tenant to use property without interference.

✏️ **Background note**
If you take steps *in deference* /'defərəns/ *to* a covenant, you *defer* /dɪ'fɜːʳ/ to (i.e. act in accordance with) the rules in the covenant.

**11.2** Tell students to work alone to find the answers, then go through them with the class.

**Answers**
**1** covenant of quiet enjoyment   **2** precaution
**3** contractor   **4** estimate   **5** postpone

## 12  Speaking B: A case discussion

Tell students to discuss the questions in small groups. If appropriate, open up the discussion to include the whole class.

**Suggested answers**
**1** Reasonable precautions might include the steps he actually took (postponing the work, meeting the tenant's requirements, etc.), as well as additional steps such as placing a 'business-as-usual' sign outside the restaurant so that it did not appear closed. Possible precautions might involve limiting the work to mornings (when the restaurant was closed) and removing the scaffolding and sheeting before the restaurant opened every day.
**2** The statement means that the court should try to find a fair balance between the two provisions. It should take them both into consideration.

---

**Optional extension**
**Photocopiable worksheet 10.3**

Exercise 8.3 above drew attention to the use of present perfect in a statement of practice areas. Understanding a tense means knowing not only when to use it, but also when not to use it. The exercise on Photocopiable worksheet 10.3 highlights the absence of present perfect from Reading D, and also draws attention to authentic uses of other problematic areas connected with tenses: past perfect, third conditionals and reported speech.

Tell students to work in pairs to put the verbs from the text into an appropriate form. Point out that sometimes there is a choice between several correct answers. Point out also that although some sentences from the text are not included in the exercise, these missing sentences make no difference to the choice of tense in the sentences given. When they

---

have finished, go through the answers with the class, perhaps following the 'Stake game' procedure (see Games and activities section, page xvi). Discuss any other possible correct answers and the differences between them.

**Answers**
**1** take; complying   **2** Is; to take / to have taken; is the landlord required; disturbing
**3** brought; to repair; was let / had been let
**4** erected; fixed   **5** became; appeared
**6** said; come/came; to be interpreted; to give
**7** to keep; had/has   **8** take / have taken
**9** have been; to have restricted / to restrict; was closed; have been   **10** had sent; (had) agreed   **11** had also postponed; interfering; (had) arranged; could   **12** to take; to avoid; had done

**Language notes**
○ Present perfect is not used in the text because all the events took place at determined times in the past: the time of the repairs or the time of the trial.
○ Sentence 2 could refer to the time of the repairs (*is it enough to take all reasonable precautions*), or it could be looking back from the time of the trial (*is it enough to have taken …*).
○ In sentences 3, 4 and 5, all the events are recounted in chronological order, which is why they are in all past simple. The third gap in sentence 3 could be interpreted in two ways: the building *was let* (i.e. at the time of the repairs, a lease agreement existed) or *had been let* (i.e. at the time of the repairs, a lease agreement *had been signed* earlier).
○ Sentences 6 and 7 both report the speech of the appeal court judges, but in sentence 6 they were talking about general truths (which is why there is no backshift in verb tenses), while in sentence 7 they were talking about the (earlier) facts of this particular case, which is why past simple is used. Sentence 6 includes a passive infinitive (*to be interpreted*). The infinitive here is used to show the way things should be in the future, rather than the way they are at present.
○ Sentence 8 can be interpreted in two ways: it could be a decision about such cases in general (*should take*) or it could

be a comment on what went wrong in this particular case (*should have taken*).

○ Sentence 9 is an example of a third conditional, which describes a hypothetical past situation. In fact, the work was not restricted to the days the restaurant was closed. In the second gap there is no difference in meaning between *to restrict* and *to have restricted*, as it is already clear that the sentence refers to the hypothetical past. It can be argued that the simpler version would have been preferable here.

○ Sentences 10, 11 and 12 all make use of past perfect, as they refer to the time of the repairs as interpreted at the time of the trial. Where a sentence contains a list of past perfect verbs (linked with commas or *and*), there is no need to repeat the word *had* after the first verb in the sentence, which is why sentences 10 and 11 allow both options. However, the tense is still past perfect even if *had* is omitted.

 **Background notes**
○ *Señor* /senˈjɔːr/ (often abbreviated in writing to *Sr*) is the Spanish version of *Mr.*
○ *Power of attorney* is a document authorising one person to act in legal matters (e.g. signing contracts) on behalf of another person.
○ A *fiscal number* is a personal identification number issued by a tax office.
○ An *agent's commission* is the percentage of the value of a sale which he/she receives in payment.

**13.3** Tell students to discuss the five statements in pairs. If necessary, play the recording again for them to check their answers before checking with the whole class.

 **Answers**
1 False (Sr Martínez will translate it.)
2 True
3 True
4 False (Mr Watson asks her to review the contract, which she agrees to do.)
5 False (Sr Martínez will represent him, so he does not have to attend.)

 **13 Listening B: Buying a house in Spain**
CD2 T5

Elicit from students the stages in a lawyer's involvement in a real property sale. Then tell students to read the introduction (SB page 145) to compare it with their suggestions.

**13.1** Discuss this with the whole class.
**13.2** Tell students to read the questions and to predict the steps that must be followed. Then play the recording for them to check. After the recording, tell students to compare their answers in pairs, and to discuss what else they remember from the conversation. Then go through the answers with the class.

**Transcript »** STUDENT'S BOOK **page 289**

 **Answers**
1 Señor Martínez is the Spanish solicitor contacted by Ms Blackwell on behalf of her client.
2 a, c, e, f, h, i, j, k

**Optional extension**
Tell students to work in pairs to read the transcript of the conversation on SB page 289 to find phrasal verbs and their collocations. When you go through the answers with the class, you may also point out some other useful expressions (*by the way, if I might ask, everything is in order*, etc.).
You could test students on the collocations by reading the first half of one of these sentences aloud (e.g. *Why don't we get down …*) and eliciting the rest.

**Possible answers**
Well, why don't we get down to business, then?
Why don't I walk you through the process?
I've printed out an email from him.
Señor Martínez will draw up a power of attorney.
Your solicitor can carry out any necessary steps when you are back in England.

Unit 10 Real property law **177**

The next step is to <u>set up a bank account</u> for transferring all funds.
Your lawyer will <u>draw up a contract</u> for you in both English and Spanish.
It will also <u>set forth the timeframe</u> of the house purchase.
At this point, you will <u>hand over the 1%</u> to the Seller.
Señor Martínez will be <u>taking care of further paperwork</u>.
He will withdraw the money from your account and <u>hand it over</u> to the Seller.

## 14 Reading E: A reference email

Elicit from the class which email was referred to in the listening exercise (Answer: an email from Sr Martínez making contact and offering his services). Then tell students to read the email quickly to answer the two questions. When they have finished, allow them to discuss their answers in pairs, and then check with the class.

 **Answers**

1 Sr Martínez's specific area of expertise is negotiating terms of sale of a property.
2 His credentials include:
   ○ 15 years' experience in assisting buyers from the UK in purchasing homes;
   ○ successful completion of hundreds of transactions;
   ○ expertise in negotiating the terms of sale;
   ○ studied law in both Spain and England;
   ○ speaks English fluently.

 **Language note**
Many students are taught never to use *if* with *would*, so they may be surprised at Sr Martínez's final paragraph. In fact, there is nothing wrong with the structure (which is used here for delicacy), as long as it is not used in the wrong contexts.

**Optional extension**
Tell students to close their books. Then elicit the two main tenses that are used in Sr Martínez's email. Tell students to check by looking at the email again, and to find other tense structures used by Sr Martínez.

**Answers**
The two main tenses are present simple (*you request, I have 15 years' experience, (I) possess knowledge, I also speak*) and present perfect (*I have provided, I have … accompanied, (I) have also gained particular expertise, I have studied*).
Sr Martínez also uses an imperative (*Allow me*) and several structures with modal verbs (*May I also add, I would appreciate, if you would inform, I would be happy, please could you forward*).

## 15 Writing B: Summarising and requesting

**15.1** Ask the class to find and underline the requesting phrases from Sr Martínez's email, and to add them to the list.

 **Answers**
<u>I would appreciate it very much if you would</u> inform Mr Watson that I would be happy to assist him in purchasing a home.
<u>Please could you</u> forward this email to him and ask him to contact me at his convenience.

**15.2** The writing can be done as homework or in class – see Writing section, page xiv. Exercises 15.2 and 15.3 would work well as an email role-play (see notes below Exercise 15.3), with students working either individually or in small groups.

 **Suggested answer**
Dear Sr Martínez

Thank you very much for your email of 17 May, in which you offer to provide your services in assisting my client, Mr Edward Watson, in purchasing a house in the Costa del Sol region of Spain. I had a meeting with Mr Watson this morning, and I would like to inform you of the matters we discussed in connection with the sale.

First of all, Mr Watson stated that he would gladly make use of your services for the transaction, and has agreed to the flat fee of 1,000 euros you have requested. I also informed Mr Watson about the steps involved in the process, from the initial drawing up of a power of attorney, to setting up a bank account and arranging financing, through to the final signing of documents. Mr Watson now knows what to expect.

I have one request: could you please provide me with copies of all documents you draw up in connection with the house purchase?

Please do not hesitate to contact me if I can be of any assistance.

Thank you for your efforts on Mr Watson's behalf.

Yours sincerely

Teresa Blackwell

(185 words)

---

**15.3** Again, this can be done at home or in class.

 **Suggested answer**

Dear Ms Armstrong

Thank you for your email of 11 June in which you requested information about my experience and areas of expertise as a real-estate lawyer.

As a sole practitioner specialising in the sale of real estate, my work involves helping individuals and businesses negotiate fair deals in both the residential and the commercial real-estate markets. I have ten years' experience in drafting landlord–tenant agreements and other documents related to the purchase of multiple-family dwellings or single-family homes. During this time, I have also negotiated the terms of leases, sales and purchases of commercial properties. Furthermore, I have extensive experience in real-property litigation, having successfully represented clients in a number of court cases involving easements and property boundaries.

I hope this information was of interest to you. I would welcome the opportunity to provide any legal assistance you may require.

Yours sincerely

Matthew Wright

(139 words)

---

**Optional extension**

This can be used as an alternative to Exercise 15.3. After Exercise 15.2, tell students to pass their emails on to a different student (or group of students), who will then have to write a reply, explaining that Sr Martínez is no longer available to assist Ms Blackwell. They should offer their own services instead, following the instructions to Exercise 15.3. This could be followed up with a reply from Ms Blackwell.

---

 Tell students to do the Internet activity as homework. See Using the Internet for research on page xviii.

# Language focus

## Answers

1   **Vocabulary: distinguishing meaning**
   1   *to license*: The others grant exclusive possession.
   2   *heir*: The others have permission to live in somebody else's real property.
   3   *to set forth*: The others mean 'to act in accordance with'.
   4   *opportunity*: The others describe permanent states; *opportunity* is short-term.

2   **Word formation**

| Noun | Adjective |
|------|-----------|
| statute | statutory |
| reason | reasonable |
| negligence | negligent |
| capability | capable |
| inheritance | inheritable |
| prospect | prospective |
| necessity | necessary |
| safety | safe |

**3 Vocabulary: completing clauses**

　1　reasonable; Premises; thereon; deemed
　2　liable; Lessee; harmless
　3　herein; rules; quietly

**4 Verb tenses: past simple or present perfect**

　**2** won　**3** have handled　**4** has advised
　**5** was involved

**5 Collocations**

　1　abandon: premises, site
　2　comply with: contract, lease, regulation,
　　　requirement, statute
　3　terminate: contract, lease, tenancy

**6 Sentence completion**

　**2** comply with　**3** terminate　**4** terminate
　**5** comply with

**7 Adjective or adverb?**

　**2** well-　**3** actually　**4** specific　**5** continually
　**6** persistently　**7** temporary　**8** essential

**Optional extension**
**Photocopiable worksheet 10.4**

Exercise 3 in the Language focus section contained the words *thereon*, *hereby*, *herein* and *hereof*. These words, and similar ones with *here–*, *there–* and *where–* + preposition are often the least understandable parts of legalese for non-lawyers and non-natives alike. Photocopiable worksheet 10.4 is intended to present the meaning of many of these words in a systematic way, and to provide examples of their use, mainly in the context of real property law.

Tell students to work in groups to do the matching exercises first, and only then to attempt the gap-fill exercises. When they have finished, go through the answers as a class, perhaps following the 'Easy first' procedure (see Games and activities section, page xvi). You may point out that the key to using and understanding these words correctly is knowing about dependent prepositions (e.g. *to be accused of something*, *a party to an agreement*, etc.).

**Answers**

**1** c, G　**2** d, F　**3** e, H　**4** a, E　**5** g, C　**6** b, B
**7** h, A　**8** f, D　**9** o, N　**10** k, P　**11** n, K
**12** p, O　**13** i, I　**14** l, M　**15** m, J　**16** j, L
**17** t, V　**18** w, Q　**19** q, R　**20** x, U　**21** v, T
**22** r, S　**23** s, X　**24** u, W

# 11 ) Intellectual property

## Teacher's brief

The term **intellectual property** (**IP**) covers a wide range of diverse issues. It contrasts with real property (see Unit 10) and chattels (see Unit 9), and covers the ownership of **rights** connected with the **intangible** products of the intellect. It is important to realise that the word *property* refers to the rights and not to the intellectual product itself. Like other forms of property, IP can be bought and sold, and the rights of IP owners can be protected by law.

Historically, different jurisdictions have varied in the way they treated IP rights, but globalisation is rapidly leading to the **harmonisation** of regulations around the world. This has been led by the UK and USA, the only two countries which are consistently net beneficiaries of IP payments. Many other countries, such as India and China, have traditionally been less keen on enforcing IP rights. Harmonisation of IP rights has been an important element of **world trade negotiations** (for example, the World Trade Organisation's (**WTO**) Agreement on Trade-Related Aspects of Intellectual Property Rights (**TRIPS**) and treaties such as the Paris and Berne Conventions, which are administered by the World Intellectual Property Organisation (**WIPO**)).

Reading A identifies the three main areas of IP: copyright, trade marks and patents. **Copyright** is concerned with the rights of authors, artists, musicians, film-makers and other creators of artistic works. Copyright may be obtained from a government, but in many countries (such as the USA), it is considered automatic: if somebody creates original material (i.e. in material form, rather than simply an idea), the author automatically has protection as long as the material meets minimum standards of originality. There are advantages to having **registered copyright** (in the same way that there are advantages to having written contracts rather than oral ones), but registration is not essential. Copyright holders typically have the **exclusive right** to produce and sell copies of the material. However, there are important **exceptions** to this monopoly, such as those granted by the **fair use doctrine** in the USA and the **fair dealing doctrine** in the UK and many other common-law countries. The **tests** for whether a particular use

of copyrighted materials is fair (and therefore legal) are discussed in Listening B, in the context of distance education.

**Trade marks** also do not need to be registered to be protected. Any **sign** which identifies a particular brand or product (e.g. a word, phrase or **logo**) is a trade mark, whether registered or not. As with copyright, **registered trade marks** have the advantage that there is no doubt as to whether they really constitute a trade mark. Trade marks give exclusive rights to use a particular sign within a particular range of products or services – they generally do not prevent others from using the same sign in unrelated industries, and they do not prevent members of the public from using trade marks. (For example, the toy company Fisher Price has a trade mark for the name Michael, but this does not prevent members of the public from using this name.) Reading D is an extract from a European Council Regulation dealing with the Community Trade Mark (**CTM**). The extract sets out the process and conditions for renewing a CTM.

**Patents** are rather different from copyright and trade marks in that they have to be registered to be enforceable. They give rights to prevent others from making or using an **invention**. To be **patentable**, an invention has to pass a series of **tests**, such as **novelty**, **originality**, **usefulness** and **non-obviousness**. These are more fully described in Reading A and Listening A. Traditionally, **business methods** have been considered unpatentable, but Reading B and Reading C illustrate an area where the concept of patentability has expanded in recent years: **business method-related software**.

The unit also practises a range of useful language skills (such as **defining technical terms**, using **discourse markers** to make writing more cohesive, and **paraphrasing in plain language**) and professional skills (such as writing a **case brief**, writing an **email** and taking part in a **discussion**).

### Further information

○ All aspects of **IP** are covered comprehensively and in simple terms at http://en.wikipedia.org/wiki/Intellectual_property. This site also has many links to further sources of good information on all aspects of IP, including extremely useful articles on each of the three main areas covered in this unit.

○ For a very thorough guide to the WTO's **TRIPS treaty**, see http://en.wikipedia.org/wiki/ Agreement_on_Trade-Related_Aspects_of_ Intellectual_Property_Rights. The TRIPS site itself (http://www.wto.org/english/tratop_e/ trips_e/trips_e.htm) is also an excellent source of information, especially the FAQs section.

○ The **World Intellectual Property Organisation's** website is at http://www.wipo.int/portal/index. html.en.

○ The EU's **Office for the Harmonization of the Internal Market** (OHIM) Trade Marks and Designs section contains a good deal of useful information, including plenty of background on the **Community Trade Mark** (CTM): http:// oami.europa.eu/ows/rw/pages/index.en.do.

○ The website of the **European Patent Office** (EPO), http://www.epo.org/index.html, is an invaluable resource for anyone interested in patents. Its e-learning section is especially useful.

○ Two very good websites offering a wealth of **IP-related information** and links are http:// www.ip-links.de and http://www.ip-watch.org.

## Discussion

Use these questions to generate a discussion.

**a** What do you understand by the term *intellectual property*? (You could try to avoid answering the questions to Exercise 1 at this stage, but it may prove impossible to discuss IP without mentioning copyright, patents and trade marks.)

**b** What is the smallest thing that can be protected by intellectual property rights? What is the largest?

**c** What would happen if there were no IP rights? In the short term? In the long term?

➠ **Suggested answers**

**b** Small things: the design of a microchip (or a sub-component), a modified gene, a virus, nanotechnology, a short name (e.g. 3M), but probably not a single letter, although the design of a single letter may constitute a trade mark (e.g. McDonald's 'golden arches' 'M' logo), a tune (three notes? See http://www. brandrepublic.com/news/197359/ European-ruling-protects-ad-jingles for some thoughts on protecting Intel's famous five-note sonic logo). Big things: the design of a building (although it can be argued that the design itself is just a document, not the building itself) or a plane, an encyclopaedia.

**c** In the short term, third parties would have rights to use protected materials, designs, etc., and the world would unquestionably be better off. However, there would be less incentive for businesses, inventors, designers, artists, etc. to create new 'intellectual property', so the world might be worse off in the long run. However, the rise of free, voluntary projects, such as Linux, most weblogs and Wikipedia, demonstrates that people do not always need financial incentives to create something new and useful. Some critics of IP rights believe that the feared long-term effects have been exaggerated by interested parties, such as 'big business'. Chris Anderson, in his book *Free* (see http://www. thelongtail.com/), argues convincingly that many people and businesses have profited from giving away their intellectual property (e.g. musicians allowing their music to be pirated widely and then making money from concert tickets, which are more expensive because their music is more popular).

## 1 Reading A: Introduction to intellectual property

Tell students to read the text quickly to answer the questions. If they have already answered some of the questions during the discussion stage, tell them to find two interesting facts about each of the three main types of IP rights. When they have finished reading, ask them to close their books and to discuss their answers with a partner. Then elicit an interesting fact from each group about one type of IP. Keep going round the groups collecting facts until they run out of ideas.

**Answers**

1 copyright (suggested interesting facts: only provides a partial monopoly; US right of fair use provides exceptions by which a work can be copied; include the typography of published editions)

2 patent (suggested interesting facts: statutory period of 20 years in the UK; typically needs to be novel, inventive, useful and non-obvious; things can be excluded for moral reasons)

3 trade mark (suggested interesting facts: must be distinctive; trade-mark deception includes cybersquatting)

4 injunction

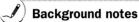 **Background notes**

○ *To afford* here means 'to provide' / 'to give'.

○ In the USA, *trademark* is spelled as one word. In the UK and EU, it is spelled as two words – *trade mark* – but can be hyphenated when used as an attributive adjective (e.g. *a trade-mark statute*). In Canada, it is always hyphenated (*trade-mark*).

○ Unlike patents or copyrights, *trade secrets* do not have to be disclosed. They are typically enforced through non-disclosure agreements (NDAs) in employees' contracts. See http://en. wikipedia.org/wiki/Trade_secret. A famous example is the recipe for Coca-Cola, which has never been patented, but remains officially a secret.

○ *Typography* /ˌtaɪˈpɒɡrəfi/ refers to the appearance of printed matter (e.g. the choice of font, the layout, etc.).

○ An *account of profits* is a remedy available for infringement of IP rights. It requires a breaching party to pay damages based on unfairly obtained gains. See http://ojls.oxfordjournals. org/cgi/reprint/24/3/471.pdf for a discussion on this remedy.

 **Pronunciation notes**

cybersquatting /ˈsaɪbəˌskwɒtɪŋ/
infringing /ɪnˈfrɪndʒɪŋ/
intangible /ɪnˈtændʒəbl/
patent /ˈpeɪtənt/
pursuant /pəˈsjuːənt/
statutory /ˈstætjətri/

---

**Optional extension**
**Photocopiable worksheet 11.1**

Photocopiable worksheet 11.1 tests students on some useful or unusual collocations and prepositions from Reading A.
Tell students to work in pairs to match the two halves of each phrase. When they have finished, go through the answers with the class. Then tell them to fold their handouts and test each other on the second halves of each phrase.

**Answers**
1 l  2 p  3 a  4 k  5 b  6 d  7 h  8 c
9 m  10 g  11 i  12 o  13 j  14 f
15 n  16 e

---

2 **Key terms: Intellectual property**

**2.1** Tell students to do this exercise alone. Tell them that they may check in the Glossary booklet if necessary. When they have finished, go through the answers with the class.

 **Answers**
1 c  2 a  3 e  4 b  5 d

**2.2** Elicit from the class the structure of the definitions in Exercise 2.1: *The term X refers to a/the Y which ...* or *The term X refers to the practice of (somebody) Y-ing ...* Then tell students to work in pairs to make similar sentences about the three terms. Point out that they do not have to follow the formulas. When you go through the answers with the class, accept any good definitions.

**Suggested answers**
1 The term *intangible rights* refers to intellectual property rights or rights to assets which lack physical existence.
2 The term *right of fair use* refers to a privilege which is afforded to third parties to use a copyrighted work without the consent of the copyright holder.
3 The term *infringement of rights* refers to the use of an intellectual property right without authorisation from the holder of the right.

**Optional extension**
Ask students what they know about the following issues which were raised in the text. They should think of examples of each, and whether they think that such things are good or bad.
○ passing off
○ design rights
○ trade secrets
○ gene patenting
○ genetically modified food
○ peer-to-peer networking
○ cybersquatting
○ copyright in typography of published editions
You could also elicit the practical difference between the concept of *fair dealing* (in the UK) and the doctrine of *fair use* (in the USA), mentioned in footnote 2 to Reading A. For more information, see http://en.wikipedia.org/wiki/Fair_dealing.

**CD2 T6** 3 Listening A: Training of junior lawyers

Elicit from the class ways in which junior lawyers learn from more experienced lawyers, and what they understand by the term *shadowing*. Then tell students to read the introduction (SB page 152) to compare it with their ideas.

**3.1** Note that the questions, especially question 3, require students to take notes. Tell students to read the three questions, then play the recording for them to check. Allow them to compare their answers in pairs and then go through the answers with the class. You may also elicit what students understand by the terms 'business-method patents' and 'one-click ordering solution', but avoid confirming or rejecting their answers at this stage.

Transcript »  STUDENT'S BOOK **page 289**

**Answers**
1 Business-method patents.
2 It involves an Internet sales application featuring a one-click ordering solution.
3 The examiners at a patent office base their decision to award a patent to an inventor on the following four requirements: utility, novelty, non-obviousness, and patentability.

**Background notes**
○ If a company *lands* a new client, they 'catch' the client, like a fisherman lands a fish (brings it to land).
○ *Proprietary rights* /prə'praɪətəri 'raɪts/ are ownership rights.
○ If something is *in the public domain*, it is known by enough people that it cannot reasonably be described as a secret.
○ A *person having ordinary skill in the art* is a legal fiction, sometimes abbreviated to *PHOSITA* /fə'ziːtə/, used in patent law. Such a person has normal technical knowledge and skills in a particular technical field, but is not a genius.

**3.2** Tell students to work in pairs to predict which words will go in each space. When they have finished, play the recording for them to check. Allow them to discuss their answers in pairs and then check with the class.

**Answers**
1 landmark cases   2 utility
3 tangible benefit
4 non-obviousness requirement
5 subject matter
6 barred from

**3.3** Tell students to answer these questions in pairs. When they have finished, go through the answers with the class.

**Answers**
1 False (It is decided by examiners at the patent office.)
2 True
3 False (Abstract ideas cannot be patented, but the idea for a machine can.)
4 True

**Optional extension**

Tell students to work in pairs to look at the transcript on SB pages 289–290 to underline useful language for presentations. When they have finished, go through their answers.

**Suggested answers**

Well, good morning, ladies and gentlemen.

I'm going to be talking to you today about …

It's the topic of …

I'm told …

I understand that …

And so I will be covering the topic with you in detail.

I'll begin with the basics, and then we will move on to look at …

Finally, I'll discuss …

Feel free to interrupt me at any time if you have any questions.

Right. Well, allow me to start by going over what happens when …

Let's have a look at …

The first/second … is that …

This is also known as …

The third … is called …

This word refers to the quality of something being …

OK, so much for …

There is a fourth … as well, and this is the one that is particularly relevant for the issue of …

But here's where it gets interesting.

That's right: …

We can assume that the thinking behind this was that …

I'd like us to have a look at some landmark cases …

# 4 Reading B: The State Street case

**4.1** Tell students to read the introduction, the questions and the title of the article (SB pages 152–153). Then tell students to read the first three paragraphs to answer the two questions. Allow a limited time (one or two minutes) and then tell students to discuss the answers in pairs. Then check the answers with the class.

**Answers**
1 It has extended patent protection to a large number of previously unpatentable areas.
2 It involves a data-processing system for managing mutual funds.

**Background notes**
○ A *hub* is the centre part of a bicycle wheel, from which the *spokes* radiate to the rim. The metaphor of a hub and spokes is used for any arrangement of a central part with many links coming from it, such as a major airport which has connecting flights to many local airports.
○ A *mutual fund* is a form of collective investment, where several people pool their money to invest in, for example, property or shares. An *investment portfolio* is the set of investments held by one party. The Hub and Spokes system therefore involved two levels of pooling: individuals pooled their money to create mutual funds, which in turn pooled their money in the partnership.

**4.2** Tell students to read the rest of the text and then to discuss the three questions in pairs. When they have finished, go through the answers with the class.

**Answers**
1 On the grounds that it was unpatentable subject matter.
2 The court reasoned that the software used in a machine constituted a useful, concrete and tangible result, warranting patentability.

**3** Because it establishes, in contrast to cases preceding it, that business methods are not per se unpatentable due to their subject matter.

**Background note**
In each of these words, *patent* may be pronounced either with an /eɪ/ or an /æ/ sound. The former pronunciation is more widespread, but the latter pronunciation is preferred by many IP professionals.

---

**Optional extension**
**ILEC Preparation: Test of Reading Part 1**
**Photocopiable worksheet 11.2**

Photocopiable worksheet 11.2 draws attention to some useful vocabulary used in the text, and also provides practice for Part 1 of the ILEC Test of Reading. Tell students to work in pairs or small groups to complete the exercise. Make sure their books are closed. When they have finished, go through the answers with the class, perhaps following the 'Easy first' procedure (see Games and activities section, page xvi). Make sure students understand all of the words. Draw attention to collocations (e.g. *to allow for something to happen*, *to rely upon something*).

**Answers**
**1** D  **2** A  **3** D  **4** C  **5** B  **6** A  **7** C
**8** C  **9** B  **10** A  **11** D  **12** B  **13** B
**14** A  **15** C

---

**4.3** Do this with the whole class. Point out that *patent* can be a noun and a verb. Elicit more members of this word-family, including compound nouns.

**Answers**
**1** patentability  **2** patent  **3** unpatentable
**4** patent  **5** patentable  **6** patented

○ Word-family also includes: *unpatented, unpatentability, patently* (as in *patently obvious*)
○ Compound nouns include: *patent office, patent statutes, patent examiner, patent-at-issue, patent pending*[1]

---

[1] The term *patent pending* tends to be used as a noun referring to a statement by a patent office that a patent has been applied for but not yet granted. It is usually abbreviated to *pat. pending* or *pat. pend.*

---

## 5 Writing: Notes for a case brief

Elicit from the class the function and format of a case brief. Then refer them back to Unit 9 to check. Tell them to work in small groups to plan a case brief for the State Street case. They could write the case brief in their groups, or you may decide that it is enough for them to discuss its structure. When they have finished, discuss the structure with the class, particularly with regard to the four bullet points.

**Suggested answer**

○ **Facts of the case** State Street Bank & Trust Co. vs. Signature Financial Group (1998) (known as the 'State Street' case) involved the patentability of a data-processing system for managing mutual funds.

○ **Legal issue in question** The legal issue was whether a patented data-processing system fell within two exceptions to patentability – mathematical algorithms and methods of doing business – and the issued patent was thus invalid.

○ **Holdings and reasoning of the courts** The lower court held that the software patent involved was invalid on the grounds that it entailed two exceptions to patentability. However, the United States Court of Appeals for the Federal Circuit affirmed the patentability of business method-related software and rejected both exceptions to patentability. The court held that since the claims of the patent-at-issue were directed to a machine programmed with software, and such a machine produced a useful, concrete and tangible result, the software constituted patentable subject matter.

○ **General legal significance of the case** As a result of the ruling, business-method software may now be patented.

## 6 Reading C: Business method patents

**6.1** Tell students to read the text to find the answers to these general questions:
  a What does the letter of advice concern?
  b Who is it addressed to?
  c What does it recommend?

When they have finished reading, tell them to discuss their answers with a partner, and then go through them with the class.

 **Answers**
  a It concerns the general question of whether business methods can be patented and the specific question of whether Ms Costa's Express Lane is a patentable business method.
  b It is addressed to Ms Costa, whose company, Libris, has developed the Express Lane Internet ordering solution.
  c It recommends a more detailed investigation of whether Express Lane meets the patentability requirements of novelty and non-obviousness.

Then tell students to read the text again to answer the two more specific questions.

**Answers**
  **1** paragraph C  **2** paragraph G

 **Background notes**
  ○ *Streamlined* literally means 'aerodynamic' (as in a car whose shape minimises wind resistance), but here is used metaphorically to mean quicker and more efficient.
  ○ If something is stated *unequivocally* /ˌʌnɪˈkwɪvəkli/, it is stated in such a way that nobody could be in any doubt about the speaker's opinion. *In my reserved opinion you might be mistaken* is equivocal; *You are wrong* is unequivocal.

 **Pronunciation notes**
  confer /kənˈfɜːʳ/
  eligible /ˈelɪdʒəbl/
  misappropriation /mɪsəˌprəʊpriˈeɪʃən/

**6.2** Tell students to do this exercise alone, then to check their answers with a partner. When you go through the answers with the class, focus on the links between these sentences and the rest of the text, as this will lead into the concept of discourse markers in Exercise 7.1.

 **Answers**
  **1** d  **2** e  **3** a  **4** c  **5** b

**6.3** Do this quickly with the whole class. Then test students by reading some of the definitions to elicit the phrases.

 **Answers**
  **1** c  **2** a  **3** d  **4** b

## 7 Text analysis: Discourse markers as sentence openers

Elicit what students understand by the term *discourse markers*, and whether they know which functions they can fulfil. Then tell them to read the information in the box to compare it with their ideas.

**Language note**
These discourse markers are also known as *conjuncts* (because they join sentences in the same way that *conjunctions* join clauses within sentences). A common mistake is to use a conjunct (such as *however*) instead of a conjunction (such as *but* or *although*): *She denied the allegation, however she was lying.* This should be split into two sentences (or separated with a semi-colon between the clauses) and there must be a comma after the conjunct: *She denied the allegation; however, she was lying.*

Conjuncts can always be removed from sentences without destroying their grammaticality, but they play a central role in creating cohesion – a sense of flow that indicates writing of good quality.

They do not always occur at the beginning of sentences, although this is the most common position, and also the least complicated. For example, the word *however* is possible in each of the positions marked in this sentence: *She denied the accusation. (However) it is (however) clear (however) that she was lying (however).* In each case, the discourse marker is set apart from the rest of the sentence by commas. The focus of this exercise, however, is on sentence-initial discourse markers.

**7.1** This exercise can be combined with Exercise 7.2. Tell students to work in pairs to complete the table. Point out that some expressions may go in more than one box. It might be worth eliciting an example for each function before students work in pairs. When they have finished, go through the answers with the class. You could try to elicit more discourse markers for some functions.

 **Answers**
Answers to Exercise 7.1 are followed by answers to Exercise 7.2 (in *italics*) and suggested additional discourse markers (in **bold**).

| Function | Examples |
|---|---|
| Establishing a sequence | As a next step, Finally, First of all, Secondly, To begin with, To conclude |
| Expanding on a point | Besides, In addition, *Furthermore, Moreover* |
| Contrasting | In contrast, On the other hand, *However, Alternatively* |
| Referring to the past | Formerly, Previously, *Traditionally, Historically,* **Initially** |
| Drawing a conclusion or inference through reasoning | As a consequence, Therefore, Thus, *Accordingly, Consequently, As a result* |
| Emphasising | In fact, In particular, *Of course, Clearly, Notably, Ultimately,* **Indeed** |
| Giving an example | For example, For instance, Specifically |
| Summarising | In short, Summing up, *In other words, Briefly,* **Overall, Basically** |

 **Language note**
Students might argue that *To conclude* is used for summarising. However, it is much more natural to use it to introduce a final point in a sequence, and should not be confused with *In conclusion.*

**7.2** See Exercise 7.1.

## 8 Reading D: Trade-mark statutes

Elicit from the class which matters relating to trade marks lawyers assist their clients with. Elicit also what *CTM* might stand for. Then tell students to read the introduction (SB pages 156–157) to check their predictions.

**8.1** Tell students to read the article to answer the question. Tell them also to underline the three key words in each sentence which could serve as a summary of the sentence. (These will be useful in the optional extension after Exercise 8.2.) When they have finished, tell them to discuss their answers with a partner, and then go through the answers with the class. There will be disagreement over the key words, so encourage students to justify their choices.

**Answer**
The Trade Mark Office informs the owner of the trade mark when that trade mark is about to expire.

**Suggested key words**
1 Registration, renewed, fees
2 Office, inform, expiry; Failure, not, responsibility
3 request, submitted, six; fees, paid, period; further, additional, fee
4 some, goods, those

**Background note**
The *Office* referred to is the *Office for Harmonization in the Internal Market (OHIM)* (http://oami.europa.eu). The full text of the Council Regulation on the Community Trade Mark is available at http://oami.europa.eu/en/mark/aspects/reg/reg4094.htm.

**8.2** Tell students to do this matching exercise quickly alone, and then check their answers in pairs if necessary. Then go through the answers with the class.

**Answers**
**1** e   **2** d   **3** f   **4** g   **5** b   **6** a   **7** c

**Optional extension**
This exercise is a way of drawing attention to the structure of sentences in legal English. Write on the board the three key words from one of the sentences (see Exercise 8.1), marking the other words in the sentence with lines, as well as any punctuation, as in this example:
Registration ...... ...... ...... ...... ...... ...... ......
renewed ...... ...... ...... ...... ...... ...... ...... ......
...... ...... ...... ...... ...... ...... ...... ...... ...... , ......
...... ...... fees ...... ...... ...... .
Divide the class into teams of three or four students and tell students to close their books. Elicit the rest of the sentence by asking for one word at a time from each team. If the suggested word is in the sentence, write it in the appropriate space (or spaces if it is used more than once). If the word is wrong, give that team a penalty point. Keep going until the whole sentence is on the board. The team with the fewest points at the end is the winner.
A quicker (and non-competitive) version of this game would be to elicit the missing words from the whole class. Repeat the activity with several of the sentences from the article.

**8.3** This can be done with Exercise 8.2, following the same procedure.

**Answers**
**1** expiry   **2** request; renewal   **3** fees
**4** trade mark

## 9 Writing and speaking: Paraphrasing in plain language

Elicit from the class reasons and techniques for paraphrasing legal English into plain language. Then tell them to read the information in the box (SB page 158) to compare it with their ideas.

**Background notes**

○ These techniques have to be used with common sense: they may change the meaning of a sentence. For example, *the request may be submitted* allows the possibility that either the client or his/her lawyer can submit the request, whereas *you can submit the request* does away with this choice. The key to successful plain language is to find a balance between comprehensibility and accuracy.

○ A further technique which is not mentioned in the box is to change abstract nouns into verbs. For example, in the first sentence from Reading D, the nouns *registration*, *request* and *proprietor* may be rewritten as verbs: *The office will register the trade mark again if the person who owns the trade mark requests it*. Of course, like all techniques, it should not be overused.

**9.1** Discuss the task with the class. Comment on any changes of meaning (see Background note above), and whether all the changes are for the better.

**Answer**

The long sentence has been broken down into shorter sentences; passive sentences have been made into active ones; *shall* constructions have been replaced with other verbs; formal vocabulary has been replaced with more common, everyday words.

**Language note**

The paraphrased paragraph highlights one of the problems with English which is especially apparent when plain language is used: the lack of a non-sexist personal pronoun. The use of *he/his/him/himself* to refer to a party of non-specified gender is still fairly common in legal English, but is increasingly seen as unacceptable. The alternatives *he/she* and *(s)he* are clumsy, and the use of *they* to refer to a single person is often seen as too colloquial. Legal documents often avoid the problem by using *it* (= the party, the company, etc.), but

this is unacceptable in other varieties of English. This is one reason why impersonal constructions (e.g. *registration shall be renewed*) are so useful, despite their disadvantages. A good solution in everyday English is to use *you*, but in legal English, it is best to use defined terms. In other words, a person might be referred to as 'the Owner' throughout a document.

**9.2** Tell students to work on the task in small groups. You may decide to give them only one paragraph per group to write, or to tell them to do the exercise orally for all the paragraphs. When they have finished, go through the answers with the class, paying particular attention to the changes based on the techniques.

**Suggested answers**

○ Paragraph 2: The Office will tell the owner of the Community trade mark, and anyone who has a registered right in it, when the registration will run out, in good time before it runs out. If the Office doesn't give this information, it will not be the fault of the Office.

○ Paragraph 3: The owner has to send in the request for renewal within a period of six months ending on the last day of the month in which protection ends. He also has to pay the fees within this period. If this has not been done, he can submit the request and pay the fees within a further period of six months following the day referred to in the first sentence, as long as he pays additional fees within this further period.

○ Paragraph 4: If the owner submits the request or pays the fees in respect of only some of the goods or services for which the Community trade mark is registered, the Office will only renew registration for those goods or services.

**9.3** Tell students to read the client's email to answer the question and then to discuss with a partner what the reply should include.

 **Answer**
She is asking for information about renewing a Community Trade Mark.

 **Background note**
If something *jeopardises* /ˈdʒepəˌdaɪzɪz/ your rights, it puts them in jeopardy (= at risk).

**9.4** You could set the writing as homework or ask students to write it alone or in groups in class. (See Writing section, page xiv.) Remind them to use some interesting discourse markers in their writing.

 **Suggested answer**
Dear Ms Fox

In response to your request of 18 December for information concerning the renewal of registration of a Community trade mark, allow me to answer the three questions you posed.

○ First of all, the Office for Harmonization in the Internal Market (OHIM) informs the owner of the Community trade mark (as well as any person having a registered right in it) when the registration will expire in good time before it expires. However, even if you don't get notice of expiry, you still have to renew your registration, so you should be aware of the date of expiry.

○ Secondly, as the owner of the trade mark, you can renew the registration of the trade mark yourself. Alternatively, another person can renew the registration if you, the owner, have authorised this person to do so. Naturally, this means that I can do it for you if you wish.

○ Finally, in response to your third question, you must submit the request for renewal six months before the last day of the month in which protection ends. Furthermore, you must pay the renewal fees within this six-month period. If you don't pay the fees within

this period, you can submit the request and pay the fees within a further period of six months, but you would then have to pay additional fees.

I hope that the information I have provided is of use to you. If you would like further assistance in this matter, please do not hesitate to contact me.

Yours sincerely
Estella Walters
(250 words)

 **10 Listening B: Discussing issues – copyright and fair use**

Tell students to read the introduction to find out the answers to these questions:

a Who are Thomas, Patrick and Rebecca?
b What are they going to be talking about?
c What does the lawyers' case involve?

 **Answers**
a Thomas is a junior lawyer, Patrick is a senior lawyer and Rebecca is Patrick's associate.
b They are going to be talking about the use of copyrighted material for educational purposes.
c The case involves the 'fair use' doctrine in connection with distance learning.

 **Pronunciation note**
doctrine /ˈdɒktrɪn/

**10.1** Remind students of the difference between the question of fair use in the USA and the British concept of fair dealing (see Reading A). Tell students to listen to the recording to answer the questions. Go through the answers with the class.

**Transcript »** STUDENT'S BOOK **page 290**

**Answers**
1 They say that fair use is when you're allowed to make limited use of copyright material without permission. The Copyright Act allows teachers to display and perform the works of others in the classroom for educational purposes.
2 It is to strike a balance between the rights of copyright owners and society's interest in ensuring the free flow of information.
3 Copyright holders
4 The four factors which need to be taken into account when assessing the fair use of copyrighted materials online include the purpose and character of the use, the nature of the copyrighted work, the amount of the work used in relation to the whole, and the effect of the use of the material on the market for the work.

---

💬 **Pronunciation note**
naive /naɪˈiːv/

---

**10.2** Tell students to work in pairs to answer the questions from memory. If necessary, play the recording again for them to check their answers. Then check quickly with the class.

**Answers**
1 False (It also applies to distance learning, but is much more limited.)
2 True
3 True
4 True
5 True

---

**Optional extension**
While students are listening to the recording, write the following 12 words and phrases from the conversation on the board. For weaker classes, you may prefer to list them in the order they are heard, rather than alphabetical order, as given here.
*battles   educational purposes*
*fair-use analysis   find a balance*
*foundation of education   Internet*

*millions   normal and customary*
*photocopies   poem   shadowing   uploaded*
After Exercise 10.2, tell students to discuss in small groups what the context was for each of the expressions. Then tell them to listen to the recording again to check their answers. Go through the answers with the class, perhaps following the 'Easy first' procedure (see Games and activities section, page xvi).

**Answers**
1 Thomas will be **shadowing** Pat and Rebecca on the case.
2 The teaching is done via technology, such as the **Internet**.
3 You can use copyrighted material for **educational purposes**.
4 A teacher can read a **poem** aloud in class without permission.
5 A teacher can make **photocopies** of a text for classroom use.
6 Distance learning usually involves materials being **uploaded** to websites.
7 The materials can be transmitted all over the world, potentially to **millions** of people.
8 Freedom of information is something like the **foundation of education**.
9 The aim of copyright law has always been to **find a balance** between the rights of copyright owners and society's interest in ensuring the free flow of information.
10 Important **battles** are being fought over digital copyright issues.
11 Copyright owners will soon be arguing that activities which we all have always considered **normal and customary** fair use are copyright infringements.
12 There's a **fair-use analysis**, a way of analysing the use of copyrighted material.

## 11  Speaking: Phrases for discussions

Tell students to read the introduction (SB page 159), and to remember any useful expressions for expressing opinions and for reacting to statements. Tell them to look back at the relevant units (3 and 8) to remind themselves of phrases they would like to use more often.

**11.1** Tell students to work alone or in pairs to complete the table. Note that it is much quicker to write numbers against the phrases, rather than phrases against the numbers, but it is more useful to have a complete table. The act of writing also increases the chance that students will remember the phrases. When they have finished, check the answers with the class. Point out that these phrases are all useful for Part 3 of the ILEC Test of Speaking, where students have to discuss questions together. See the Optional extension below.

 **Answers**
**1** In what way?
**2/3/4** Well, from a legal point of view, the debate is about ...
I think the important issue here is ...
It seems to me that the real issue is ...
**5** So, in other words, ...
**6/7** And what's more, ...
Let me just give you an example.
**8/9/10/11** That may well be true, but you have to see the bigger picture.
Yes, but you can look at it another way, too.
Yes, but that's only one side of the problem.
Yes, you have a point there.
**12** Sorry, can I just finish my point?
**13** As I was saying, ...

---

**Optional extension**
**ILEC preparation: Test of Speaking Part 3**

Remind students that the phrases in Exercise 11.1 are well worth learning as preparation for Part 3 of the ILEC Test of Speaking. Tell students to close their books. Read the first half of one of the expressions (e.g. *I'm not sure I ...*) and elicit the rest of the expression. Do this for a few more expressions, and then tell students to test each other in the same way in small groups.
You could print the 13 phrases on slips of paper for students to sort into categories. You could also add the eight phrases from Exercise 11.2. Students could then use these slips as part of the 'First use' procedure in Exercise 11.3 below.

---

**11.2** Tell students to work alone or in pairs to quickly do this vocabulary exercise.

 **Answers**
**1** point  **2** view  **3** point  **4** view
**5** point  **6** point  **7** point/view  **8** point

**11.3** Tell students to discuss the two questions in small groups. Point out that the purpose of the discussions is to use the useful phrases, so make sure they know they are expected to interrupt each other. You could follow the 'First use' procedure (see Games and activities section, page xvi).

Tell students to do the Internet activity as homework. See Using the Internet for research, page xviii.

# Language focus

## Answers

**1 Vocabulary: distinguishing meaning**
  **1** *dismiss*: The others involve not respecting another person's rights.
  **2** *in addition*: The others introduce examples.
  **3** *review*: The others mean 'confirm'.
  **4** *issuer*: The others own property, including IP.
  **5** *suggestion*: The others are requirements.
  **6** *moreover*: The others are used to draw conclusions.

 **Background notes**
○ If you *encroach on* something, you invade it. For example, a bush on one party's land might encroach on a neighbour's land.
○ A *prerequisite* /ˌpriːˈrekwɪzɪt/ is something which is required, typically before a process can begin.

**2 Vocabulary: phrases with *copyright infringement***

**b** dismissed  **c** would be liable for
**d** filed  **e** settle

Order of the actions: **2** d  **3** e  **4** b  **5** a

**3 Collocations**

1 apply for, enforce, file, grant
2 misappropriate, patent, register
3 apply for, enforce, file, grant, infringe, register

**4 Legal expressions: prepositions**

2 to  3 on  4 to  5 for  6 against

**5 Adjective formation**

2 non-obvious  3 dissimilar
4 unauthorised  5 invalid
6 non-patentable, unpatentable
7 unsuitable  8 non-commonplace
9 non-exclusive

**6 Vocabulary: court holdings**

2 has been registered  3 enforce
4 had ruled  5 to be determined
6 be infringed  7 to issue; allege

**7 Paraphrasing**

*Suggested answers*

1 If you only want to transfer the registration of some of the things protected by the trade mark, you have to say which ones these are on the application.

2 You have to divide up the things that are protected by the remaining registration and the new registration and make sure they don't overlap.

3 The Office will set up a separate file for the new registration which will include the original registration as well as the application for partial transfer. They will put a copy of the partial transfer application in the file of the remaining registration. They will also give the new registration a new number.

**Optional extension**
**Photocopiable worksheet 11.3**

Photocopiable worksheet 11.3 contains an agenda for a meeting. Divide the class into lawyers and managers of the company, and tell them to read the instructions and the agenda to find out what sort of company they work for. The managers could be from key departments such as Sales, Marketing, Production, Corporate Affairs, Finance and Human Resources. Allow them to decide whether they are as unscrupulous as their bosses at headquarters.

Make sure you decide before the meeting begins who will be chairing the meeting, and how long it should take. Make sure also that students know to use the useful phrases from Exercises 11.1 and 11.2 during the meeting. At the end of the role-play, give feedback on the language used and the overall success of the meeting.

# Case study 4: Intellectual property law

## The facts of the case

Tell students to read the facts of the case to identify the legal issues. When they have finished, discuss the answer with the class.

 **Answer**

The question concerns copyright rights in software developed by Linxus. Fleming claims that it bought rights when it bought the software from Linxus, and that this was implied in their contract. The legal issue is whether such an implied term exists.

Ask the group the following comprehension questions to make sure they have fully understood the facts of the case.

1   What do you know about the two companies?
2   When did Linxus design the codes it used in Fleming's software?
3   What led to the dispute?

 **Answers**

1   Fleming helps immigrants with bureaucratic procedures. Linxus is a software developer.
2   Before its co-operation with Fleming, *it had previously designed* the codes and used them with other companies.
3   Fleming attempted to sub-license the software to a third company.

## Task 1: Role-play

**Optional lead-in**
Part 91 (1) of Text 2 is a classic example of legalese: non-lawyers (as well as many lawyers) would find it extremely difficult to understand. Therefore, it is a good idea to do some work on this section with the whole class before they think about the role-play. Elicit from the class a) the main clause of the sentence, and b) where all the extra sections begin and end. They should mark these by underlining the main clause and using ([{brackets}]) for extra sections (as in the answer below).

**Suggested answer**
Where [by an agreement (made in relation to future copyright, and signed by {or on behalf of} the prospective owner of the copyright),] the prospective owner purports to assign the future copyright (wholly or partially) to another person, then [if, (on the copyright coming into existence), the assignee {or another person claiming under him} would be entitled {as against all other persons} to require the copyright vested in him,] <u>the copyright shall vest in the assignee</u> (or his successor in title) (by virtue of this subsection).

In other words: Where the prospective (= *future*) owner of the copyright purports (= *claims/intends*) to assign the future copyright to another person, then the copyright shall vest in the assignee (= *the assignee shall hold the copyright*).

1   Divide the class into two groups, one representing each party in the dispute. If you have only one student, you should play one of the roles yourself.

Tell students to read the instructions and then to study the relevant legal documents carefully in order to prepare for the role-plays. Allow plenty of time for them to read the documents and to discuss them with others in their groups, and help with any vocabulary/comprehension problems.

2   Elicit from students which unit dealt with negotiating skills (Unit 5) and what they can remember about them. Put students in pairs for the first role-play and set a time limit so that they all finish around the same time. If you have an odd number of students, one group will have to contain two representatives from one of the companies. Remind them that the objective is to reach a settlement in order to avoid a costly court case.

3   Collect feedback on the results of the
    negotiations, and comment on students' use
    of negotiating skills and language.

## Task 2: Writing

Part 1 should be done in the same pairs as the
role-plays, and should be done in character. Part 2
can be done at home or in class. (See Writing
section, page xiv.)

➠ **Model answers**
1   **3  Development of software**
        Linxus hereby agrees to develop
        computer software for Fleming with
        respect to an Internet-based
        database to be used in conjunction
        with Fleming's business (the
        'Developed Software').
    **5  Licensing**
        Linxus hereby grants a perpetual
        license to Fleming for the Developed
        Software for the purposes of its
        business, which includes the right to
        prepare, maintain and upgrade it for
        the purposes of Fleming's business,
        as well as to sub-license the
        Developed Software to contractors
        retained by Fleming for purposes
        connected to the Immigrant
        Assistance Project.
2   Dear Ms Fleming,
    We have now reviewed the contract with
    Linxus, as well as the relevant case law
    and sections of the Copyrights Act. As we
    discuss in detail below, we do not believe
    that Fleming Co. would prevail in a
    copyright claim against Linxus.
    The primary issue presented is whether
    Fleming Co. is entitled to sub-license the
    software which Linxus developed for the
    Immigrant Assistance Project. This raises
    several subsidiary issues: (1) who owns
    the copyright in the software; (2) if Linxus
    owns the copyright, whether that would
    change as a result of any upgrades
    made by Fleming Co.; and (3) if Linxus
    originally owned the copyright, whether,
    by virtue of the contract, the copyright
    has been assigned to Fleming Co.
    Section 11 of the Copyrights Act of
    Bloomland provides that the author of a

work is the first owner of any copyright in
it, unless it is a literary, dramatic, musical
or artistic work made by an employee in
the course of employment, in which case
the employer owns the copyright. This
section does not confer ownership in
Fleming Co., firstly because software is
not a literary, dramatic, musical or artistic
work and, secondly, because Linxus
developed the software in its capacity as
a contractor and not as an employee.
Section 91 of the Copyrights Act provides
that the prospective owner of a future
copyright may assign that copyright by
way of a written, signed agreement. To
the extent that Fleming Co. makes any
upgrades of the software, it will not be
deemed an 'author of the work', since
any upgrade (under Section 5 of the
agreement) is made by Fleming Co. as
licensee and not Fleming Co. as copyright
owner. Accordingly, Section 91 of the Act
would not entitle Fleming Co. to assign
the copyright to a third party. Moreover,
there was no written, signed agreement
assigning copyright in this case.
The contract is clearly a licensing
agreement. By its nature, a licensing
agreement is an agreement whereby a
party holding an exclusive right allows
another party to utilise the benefits of
that right. By framing the agreement as a
licensing agreement, it is clear that
Linxus did not intend to assign copyright
to Fleming Co. and, pursuant to the case
of *Bangarth Management v. Business
Linx plc* (discussed in detail below), the
court would probably not read the
contract as an implied assignment of
copyright on the grounds that it would be
unreasonable to do so.
The Bangarth case involved facts
somewhat similar to those involved here.
A software designer was commissioned to
design software for the plaintiff. After the
job was completed, he was contacted by
the plaintiff's key competitor and sold
them software, using much of the same
code, which performed most of the same
functions as the original software. The
issue before the court was whether the

contract governing the design and delivery of the software contained an implied term that copyright would be transferred to the plaintiff upon completion of the job. The court found that a term can be implied into the contract where the term: (1) is reasonable and fair; (2) is necessary to give the contract business efficacy; (3) is completely obvious; (4) can be expressed clearly; and (5) does not contradict any express term of the contract. The court focused on the question of business efficacy. Since the plaintiff was engaged in a highly competitive business, the sale of the software sold to its competitor destroyed any advantage that the plaintiff had gained in commissioning the (rather expensive) software, rendering the contract useless. Accordingly, the agreement had no business efficacy unless it was deemed to include assignment of copyright.

Unfortunately, the Bangarth case is likely to be inapplicable here. First, this agreement is clearly a licensing agreement and to interpret it as an assignment of copyright would contradict an express term of the agreement. Second, Fleming Co. suffers no disadvantage by virtue of the agreement being a licensing agreement and not an assignment of copyright. Finally, it does not 'go without saying' that a licensing agreement assigns copyright; in fact, the opposite is true.

Please do not hesitate to contact me if you have any questions.

Yours sincerely,

Prudence Beresford

## Relevant legal documents

○ **Text 1** is a series of extracts from the contract between Fleming and Linxus. Paragraph 3 refers to specific software being developed by Linxus. If Linxus argues that it has rights over its software by virtue of having used it with other companies, Fleming could point to this clause and argue that Linxus agreed to produce *new* software.

Paragraph 3 grants a *perpetual* (= never-ending) licence to Fleming, but does not clarify whether this includes the right to sub-license the software to other companies.

Paragraph 8 prohibits Linxus from disclosing confidential information, including the Developed Software. Fleming could argue that this implies that Linxus has no rights over the software (as this would breach confidentiality) and that therefore all such rights remain with Fleming.

○ **Text 2** consists of extracts from a piece of legislation, the Copyrights Act. Part 11 relates to the normal ownership of copyright: by the author or the author's employer. Part 91 relates to documents concerned with future copyright. In this case, the contract between Fleming and Linxus was signed before the software was supposedly written, and therefore the question of future copyright is relevant. As explained above (Optional lead-in activity), the paragraph simply states that assignment of future copyright is possible. The key word is *purports*, and the key question is whether the extracts in Text 1 prove that Linxus really purported to assign copyright to Fleming.

○ **Text 3** is an extract from a case brief, which is a summary of court decisions for a particular case (see Unit 9). Note that in order for an implied term to be included in a contract (as Fleming wants to do with the ownership of rights to sublicense the software), it must fulfil all five criteria listed. With this in mind, point 2 seems to cause the most problems: the contract still seems to be effective even though it does not mention sub-licensing. Point 3 is also problematic: the fact that Linxus is disputing the case strongly suggests that it is far from obvious.

---

✒ **Background notes**
○ If a term is *equitable,* it is fair and just.
○ *Efficacy* means 'effectiveness, or the power to produce effective results'.

## Teacher's brief

The easiest way to think of **negotiable instruments** is as a kind of substitute for money. Andy borrows €100 from his friend Beth and writes an IOU[1] (a statement that 'I, Andy, owe you, Beth, €100'), which he signs and gives to Beth. Beth then uses the IOU to pay a third party, Charlie, for a television worth €100. She does this by writing and signing a message to Andy on the back of the IOU, instructing him to pay the outstanding €100 to Charlie, and not to Beth. Andy then owes Charlie €100, and Beth neither owes nor is owed anything. Charlie then writes and signs a new message on the back – 'Pay Diane' – and sells the IOU to Diane for €90. Diane is happy with the deal, because she has a chance of a €10 profit when she claims the money back from Andy.

This is a very simplified version of the theory behind negotiable instruments, which are very official documents containing very specific legal language. They are **negotiable** in the sense that they can be easily transferred from party to party. In the above example, the IOU was made out **to the order of** Beth, which meant that she was the intended beneficiary. Such an instrument may still be transferred to a new beneficiary by **endorsement** (writing and signing an instruction, such as 'Pay Charlie', on the back of the document). Some negotiable instruments are made out **to the holder of** the document, which means they do not need endorsement, but simply **delivery** (handing over) to the new holder.

An interesting aspect of negotiable instruments is that they are not subject to a general principle of law: the *nemo dat* rule. This rule states that only holders of **good title** (i.e. legal owners) can transfer ownership. If Charlie had previously stolen the television from Ed, he had no right to sell it to Beth, so even though Beth bought the television **in good faith**, she does not have good title to the television and must give it back to Ed. She is then left with the problem of recovering some money from Charlie. Diane, on the other hand, can keep the IOU, which she obtained in good faith, because negotiable instruments are not subject to the *nemo dat* rule. Diane is referred to as the **holder in due course** (**HDC**).

Negotiable instruments are most relevant for businesses which lend money, most obviously **banks**. Banks and other big lenders obviously do not accept IOUs written by their clients, but they do accept **promissory notes**, which fulfil broadly the same function. For obvious reasons, they tend to prepare the promissory notes themselves, specifying very precisely the terms and conditions of repayment, so that all the client has to do is sign the note and give it back to the bank. A similar function is played by **debentures**, which are usually **secured** by the assets of the borrower[2]. For example, if a company uses a debenture to borrow €1,000 from a bank to buy a machine, but then fails to make the necessary repayments, the bank can seize the company's assets, in this case the machine (or whichever assets were specified in the debenture).

As well as lending, banks also borrow money from their clients every time a client makes a deposit. **Certificates of deposit** (**CDs**) can be thought of as IOUs from banks (and similar institutions). They are issued for fixed-term deposits of money, typically with no option of early withdrawal by the client, and typically with higher interest rates than normal savings accounts. In practice, there may not actually be a written certificate, but merely an item on customers' periodic bank statements.

As Reading A describes, negotiable instruments have two functions. Promissory notes, debentures and certificates of deposit all fulfil the **credit function**; the second function, **payment**, is served by **bills of exchange** and **cheques**. The principal difference between these two and other negotiable instruments is that they do not include interest charges. These instruments are often considered safer or more convenient than cash. For example, if Fred wants to buy a car from Grace for €10,000, he

---

[1] IOU (= I owe you) is not a legal term, but is used here merely to illustrate the rather complicated area of negotiable instruments in everyday terms. A handwritten IOU would almost certainly not be so easily transferable as illustrated, although it is still a legally binding agreement.

[2] The US definition of *debenture* is slightly different (see footnote on SB page 167).

may prefer not to carry the cash with him to Grace's house, but to keep the money in the bank, so he writes Grace a **cheque**. The cheque is an instruction for a third party (Fred's bank) to pay Grace €10,000. Grace may simply take the cheque to Fred's bank to exchange it for money, or she may transfer it by endorsement to a fourth party (such as her own bank), who is then faced with the same choice. **Bills of exchange** are broadly the same as cheques, but they do not have to involve banks as the third party. They are very commonly used in international trade.

Most of the exercises in the unit focus on promissory notes: Reading B is an extract from a well-drafted promissory note, including an **acceleration clause** (i.e. outlining the circumstances under which the **outstanding principal** (= money borrowed) and **accrued interest** have to be repaid earlier than the date specified). Listening A and one of the speaking exercises highlight the problems associated with badly drafted promissory notes and the six requirements that ensure that a note is negotiable. Listening B focuses on another problem with promissory notes: what happens if some of the **principals** (= parties to the transaction) are unavailable to sign the note.

There is a Speaking activity on **usury** (charging exorbitant interest on loans), which is commonly known as loan-sharking and can be accompanied by threats of violence in the event of default. Historically, it used to be a crime to charge any interest on loans (as it still is under Islamic law), but the rules were relaxed in many jurisdictions in the early modern age. In the USA, there is a trend for usury limits to be relaxed in many jurisdictions, and in the UK there are no limits.

Reading C introduces a new type of negotiable instrument: a **transferable record**, which is used for electronic transactions. As this is new, there may be no equivalent in some jurisdictions.

The unit also practises many language skills for lawyers: **explaining difficult ideas** to a client, **writing letters and emails**, and **giving advice** and **making recommendations**, both in formal and informal contexts.

**Further information**

○ There is some very useful information on **negotiable instruments** at the following sites: http://en.wikipedia.org/wiki/Commercial_paper and http://www.answers.com/topic/negotiable-instrument. http://dictionary.law.com also has some useful definitions of the terminology used in this unit.

○ There are hundreds of authentic **promissory notes and debentures** at http://contracts.onecle.com. For a sample bill of exchange, see http://www.export911.com/e911/export/bill.htm.

○ Article 3 of the US Uniform Commercial Code http://www.law.cornell.edu/ucc/3 provides **technical definitions and rules for negotiable instruments**.

○ In connection with usury, http://www.lectlaw.com/files/ban02.htm lists the maximum permitted interest rates in each US state. There is an interesting article on **usury** in other countries at http://www.microfinancegateway.org/gm/document-1.9.26998/25620_file_The_effect_of_interest_rate_controls.pdf.

## Discussion

Use these questions to generate a discussion, introducing as many of the key words and concepts as possible. This will make Reading A much easier.

**a** If you wanted to lend your teacher a lot of money, what document would you ask him/her to sign?

(If you feel uncomfortable in the role of lender, you may, of course, change the question. However, it is much easier to understand negotiable instruments with a specific person in mind (and perhaps a specific sum of money). Non-lawyers might think of writing an IOU, but if students are familiar with negotiable instruments they might suggest a promissory note.)

**b** What terms and conditions would you specify? (At the very least they should specify the repayment date(s) and what happens if a repayment is late. If students want to charge you interest on the loan, the interest rate must also be specified. Listening A contains full requirements for properly drafted promissory notes, so it is not necessary to go into too much detail at this stage.)

**c** Could you sell the signed document from your teacher to somebody else? (This is the test of whether an instrument is negotiable or not. Discuss what terms and conditions would convince a third party that the loan is worth taking on, and what instructions would convince the borrower (you) to repay the third party.)

# 1   Reading A: Introduction to negotiable instruments

Tell students to read the statements in small groups to predict whether they are true or false. If students are unfamiliar with negotiable instruments, you may discuss the questions with the whole group (although obviously you should avoid giving answers).

Then tell them to read the text to check their predictions. When they have finished, tell them to compare their answers in pairs and then go through the answers with the class.

 **Answers**

1 True
2 True
3 False (Negotiable instruments are not subject to the *nemo dat* rule.)
4 False (The named person is entitled to payment, not the bearer.)
5 True

---

 **Background notes**

○ The terms *negotiable*, *transferable* and *alienable* /ˈeɪljənəbl/ can be considered near synonyms, although there are important differences. In legal English, *negotiable* (in this context) means 'transferable through delivery and/or endorsement' (i.e. transfer through the proper methods and with the proper documentation), which is not the same as simple *transferability* (which may not require any specific methods or documentation) or *alienability* (ability of ownership of a right or property to be transferred to another, especially through the act of the owner).

○ The phrase *nemo dat* /ˌneməʊ ˈdæt/ comes from a longer Latin expression: *nemo dat quod non habet*. The translation is 'no one gives what he does not have'. Apart from negotiable instruments, there are many other exceptions to the *nemo dat* rule (for example, some real property transactions).

○ The *bearer* is the person who holds a document, from *to bear* meaning 'to carry'.

○ *Bona fide* /ˌbəʊnə ˈfaɪdi/ is a Latin expression meaning 'good faith'. A purchaser *for value* is one who makes some sort of payment (money or some other form of *consideration*) to the seller. The terms *bona-fide purchaser for value* (BFP) and *holder in due course* (HDC) can be treated as synonyms. *In due course* means 'at the proper or reasonable time'.

○ The *underlying transaction* refers to the reason the promissory note was created in the first place: typically, it is the sale of something expensive (such as a company), which is paid for partly at the time of sale and partly at some later date.

○ *Defences to payment* are legal justifications for avoiding payment. For example, if party A agrees to buy a car from party B without knowing that the car is stolen, and the car is reclaimed by its rightful owner before party B has finished paying for it, party B can reasonably claim that she does not have to pay party A the outstanding instalments.

○ *In lieu of* /ɪn ˈluː əv/ means 'in place of' or 'instead of'. *Lieu* is French for 'place'.

○ Many of the key terms have British and American versions. In practice, both *endorsement* and *indorsement* are used in American English (with no difference in meaning): see, for example, the American website http://dictionary.law.com. The term *negotiable instrument* is also not exclusively British: see for example http://www.answers.com/topic/negotiable-instrument, and the Uniform Commercial Code (http://www.law.cornell.edu/ucc/3), which governs trade rules in the USA.

○ A debt is *secured* if it is tied to some asset of the borrower. For example, party A borrows €100 from party B to buy a sofa and secures the debt by that sofa. If she then fails to make the regular €10-per-month instalments on the debt, party B can repossess the security (the sofa). An *unsecured debt* has no such security, and is therefore more like a *gentlemen's agreement*. Such an unsecured debt works if the borrower wants to build a reputation for reliability with the lender, perhaps in order to borrow again in the future. Note the difference in the meaning of *debenture* between Britain (where it usually means a secured debt) and America (where it may be either secured or unsecured).

**Pronunciation notes**
debenture /də'bentʃə'/
drawee /drɔː'iː/
drawer /'drɔːə'/
promissory /'prɪsəri/
realm /relm/
transferee /ˌtrɑːnsfə'riː/

**Optional extension**
Tell students to work in small groups to test each other on the key terms (in bold) in the text. They should take turns to read a definition (from the Glossary booklet), and their partners should guess which key term is being defined.

## 2 Key terms: Negotiable instruments

**2.1** Tell students to work alone to find the five negotiable instruments. When they have finished, go through the answers with the class. Discuss with the class whether the same instruments exist in students' jurisdictions, and whether there are any differences.

 **Answers**
1 certificate of deposit   2 debenture
3 cheque/check   4 promissory note
5 bill of exchange; draft

**2.2** Tell students to work in pairs to match the parties with their definitions. When they have finished, go through the answers with the class. Test students by telling them to close their books and reading a definition to elicit the name of the party.

 **Answers**
1 c   2 d   3 f   4 g   5 b   6 a   7 e

 **Background note**
If a negotiable instrument is *endorsed in blank*, it has been endorsed (signed on the back) but without stating, for example, 'Pay Diane'. This has the effect of making it payable to the bearer.

## 3 Reading B: A promissory note

Elicit from students why there might be an *acceleration clause* in a promissory note. Then tell them to read the introduction (SB page 168) to check their predictions. You may refer them to Unit 5 (Exercise 3.1) to remind themselves what an acceleration clause is.

**3.1** Tell students to read the questions. Avoid explaining vocabulary (e.g. *principal*, *default*, *instalment*) at this stage, as they are partly explained in the text, and then defined in Exercise 3.3. Then tell students to read the promissory note to find the answers. When they have finished, tell them to compare their answers with a partner, and then go through them with the class.

 **Answers**
1 When the bank demands payment or on April 1st 2013.
2 The maker is obliged to make interest payments to the payee on or before the 1st day of each month.
3 The whole sum of principal and interest will become immediately due and payable at the option of the holder of the note.

 **Background notes**
○ *Per annum* is Latin for 'each year'.
○ The term *breach* is more general than *default*. In the context of loans, *default* is failure to make a necessary repayment, while a *breach* is any action which breaks the terms of the agreement.
○ The words *due* and *payable* can be treated as synonyms in this context.

**3.2** Tell students to discuss the phrases in pairs, as if they were explaining to a client. Then discuss their suggestions with the whole class.

**Suggested answers**

1 for money or other performance received
2 the party who has signed the promissory note and has thus agreed to repay the debt under the terms laid out in the promissory note
3 to be paid when requested
4 to fail to fulfil the obligations or abide by what was agreed; to breach the agreement

**3.3** Tell students to work alone or in pairs to complete the exercise. When they have finished, go through the answers with the class. Test students by asking them to define the expressions from the box without referring to their books.

 **Answers**

1 interest  2 principal  3 outstanding
4 due  5 accrue  6 Maturity
7 instalment

---

**Optional extension**
**Photocopiable worksheet 12.1**

Photocopiable worksheet 12.1 focuses on some of the legal terminology and collocations from Reading B. It also provides practice of the skills needed for Part 1 of the ILEC Test of Reading.

Tell students to close their books and to work alone or in small groups to choose one option for each space. When they have finished, go through the answers with the class, perhaps using the 'Easy first' procedure (see Games and activities section, page xvi). You may elicit why the alternatives are wrong, but try to avoid getting into too much detail. For most answers, it is simply a question of collocation/register (e.g. one word is used in legal documents while the others are not).

**Answers**

1 c   2 d   3 d   4 a   5 a   6 b   7 a   8 c
9 b   10 d   11 c   12 a   13 c   14 b   15 b
16 d   17 b   18 d   19 a   20 c   21 b   22 c
23 d   24 a

---

## 4 Speaking A: Describing the legal situation: usury

Elicit from students what they understand by the term *usury* /ˈjuːʒəri/. Then tell them to read the introduction (SB page 169) to check.

Discuss the questions with the whole class. If students do not know, discuss how they could find out (the Internet, reference books, etc.). Also discuss whether high-interest loans are always a bad thing, or whether they provide a valuable source of credit for less-privileged members of society. See http://www.microfinancegateway.org/gm/document-1.9.26998/25620_file_The_effect_of_interest_rate_controls.pdf for a good analysis of four approaches to usury limits (in the UK, the USA, France and Germany).

 ## 5 Listening A: Drafting a promissory note

**5.1** Tell students to work in pairs to predict which of the eight statements are genuine requirements for negotiability. Then play the recording for them to check their predictions. After the recording, tell them to discuss their answers and what the speakers said about each requirement. When you go through the answers with the class, elicit also who the following people are: Miranda Benton (Answer: the lawyer), Max Carter (Answer: the client; the endorsee of the promissory note), Wilson Charles (Answer: Mr Carter's long-time business customer; the transferor of the note) and John Ellis (Answer: the maker of the note).

**Transcript »** STUDENT'S BOOK **page 290**

 **Answers**

She mentions the following: 1, 2, 3, 4, 7 and 8.

**5.2** You could do this quickly with the whole class or tell students to discuss the answers in pairs first. When you discuss the answers, discuss also what, if anything, Mr Carter can do to recover his money. (Suggested answer: He could try to recover cash from John Ellis even though the note is faulty. Ellis is described as 'a decent guy' with 'some experience with this kind of thing'. Ellis might make the payment in order to preserve his reputation so that he can continue to make promissory notes in future. If necessary, Carter could threaten to expose Ellis as a cheat. If all else fails, Carter could try to recover money from his customer, Charles, who has effectively failed to pay for the services provided by Carter's company.)

 **Answers**

1 Max Carter was given the promissory note by a customer of his, Wilson Charles, who owed him approximately $2,500. The note, which had a value of $5,000 had been made by another person Max Carter knew, John Ellis.

2 Requirements 7 and 8 (the requirement that the note makes an unconditional order or promise and the requirement that the note states that the outstanding sum is payable either on demand or at a definite time).

3 The borrower made the condition that as soon as he is paid out his inheritance, he will start paying the debt back.

## 6  Speaking B: Explaining ideas to a client

Elicit from the class phrases for rephrasing difficult ideas. Then tell students to compare their suggestions with those in the box.

Tell students to read the instructions. When you allocate roles, check that students know who is the lawyer and who is the client, and what each has to do. If there are an odd number of students, one group should have two lawyers who should take turns to explain the requirements to Mr West. Encourage the lawyers to use all the useful phrases provided, and the clients to ask lots of questions. Encourage them also to discuss possible next steps for Mr West to recover his money. When most groups have finished, go through the problems with the promissory note with the class.

 **Answers**

Problems with the promissory note which the lawyer should recognise:

○ Unconditional? No, because the language appears to make it conditional upon consideration to be received under a separate agreement.

○ An order? The 'to the order' language is missing, so this would be non-negotiable under US law.

○ A sum certain? The sum is uncertain. Is the sum 30,000, 3,000 or 30, and is the denomination US dollars or something else?

○ A sum certain? The interest to be paid must be stated on the note, otherwise any subsequent holder has no idea of what the total amount due is.

○ Signed by the drawer? Who is the drawer? Can you tell just from the signature? The drawer must be identified, and the note should preferably be signed by a witness.

## 7  Writing A: Summarising requirements

Tell students to read the letter quickly to find out what Mr West wants. Then go through the two questions with the class.

 **Suggested answers**

○ The information could be arranged using six bullet points, together with an introduction and a friendly closure.

○ Ms Chang can use the same phrases for paraphrasing that she used in Exercise 10 and examples to illustrate difficult ideas.

The writing can be done in class (alone or in groups) or as homework.

 **Suggested answer**

Dear Mr West

I am writing to you in response to your letter of 21 September in which you request a written explanation of the six requirements which a promissory note must meet in order for it to be negotiable. The requirements, which we discussed at our meeting last Thursday, are as follows:

○ The note must be in writing.
○ The note must be signed by the maker.
○ The note must contain an unconditional order or promise to pay what is called a 'sum certain' in money. What this actually means is the amount must be certain, or capable of being made certain by calculation.
○ The note must say that it is either 'payable on demand' (that is, whenever the person for whom the instrument was made wants to be paid) or at a definite time. Put simply, this means that a date or a fixed time after a date must be stated (e.g. '90 days after the date of this instrument').
○ The note must say that it is payable to order or to bearer. In other words, the words 'pay to the order of' or 'payable to bearer' should appear on the note.
○ The note must not contain any other order or promise. This means that no conditions, such as 'if I get my raise' or the like, should be stated in the note.

I hope that the information I have provided meets your expectations.
Please feel free to contact me should you have any questions.

Yours sincerely
Christine Chang
(249 words)

# 8 Reading C: Legislation governing electronic negotiable instruments

Elicit from the class what electronic negotiable instruments might be. Then tell them to read the introduction (SB page 171) to check.

**8.1** As a class, tell students to find the answer to the question as quickly as possible. It should take only a few seconds.

**Answers**
The newly created instrument is called a *transferable* /ˌtrɑːnsˈf ːrəbl/ *record*.

**8.2** Tell students to work alone to match the headings to the paragraphs. When they have finished, tell them to compare their answers

in pairs, and to use only the headings to discuss what they remember about each paragraph.

**Answers**
1 c  2 e  3 b  4 a  5 d

**Background notes**
○ The National Conference of Commissioners on Uniform State Laws (http://www.nccusl.org) is a body which provides ready-made legislation to individual US states, which can then decide whether to adopt all, part or none of the recommended legislation. The aim is to harmonise laws across the whole of the USA in order to avoid discrepancies between states. The best-known Uniform State Law is the UCC (http://www.law.cornell.edu/ucc/index.htm).
○ In paragraph 3, *provision* is used simply as the noun from *to provide*, rather than in the normal legal sense of a clause in a contract.

**8.3** **Collocations with *Act*** Tell students to complete the exercise alone and then to check with a partner. Either go through the answers with the class now or go straight into Exercise 8.4, and check both sets of answers at the end.

**Answers**
1 defines  2 applies to  3 provide
4 contains  5 creates

**8.4** Tell students to work in pairs to find the expressions. Go through the answers with the class.

**Answers**
1 exempt  2 application
3 enforceable contracts

**8.5** Discuss this with the whole class. If students do not know the answer, discuss how they could find out.

Reading C contains several long sentences linked with *and*, *or*, etc. Such sentences can often be ambiguous, and lawyers often need to work out which sections of a sentence are linked to which other sections. Photocopiable worksheet 12.2 provides an analysis of these sentences.

Go through the instructions first, and make sure students understand why the technique might be useful. Point out that it is not necessary to use the same system of brackets – they should experiment to find what feels best. Tell them to work in pairs to discuss how to show the relationships within each sentence. When they have finished, discuss the relationships with the group. There may be some disagreement over some of the more ambiguous sentences. Sentence 3, for example, can be interpreted in numerous ways:

○ the word *electronic* might refer only to *records* or to *records and signatures*;

○ *by government agencies* could belong with *acceptance* or with *signatures*;

○ the whole sentence could be built around *or* (*Other provisions govern [a] or [b and c]*) rather than *and*, as suggested (*Other provisions govern [a or b] and [c]*).

Students may find this sort of analysis a little strange, but it can be very useful in identifying, resolving and avoiding ambiguity.

**Suggested answers**

1 The act [defines the terms ("record," "electronic record," and "electronic signature")] and [provides (as a general rule) that {electronic (records and signatures) satisfy legal requirements that (a record be in writing or signed)}].
*The act [defines the terms a, b, and c] and [provides that ...].*

2 The UETA contains provisions governing [(provision or transmission) of (information in electronic form)], [attribution of electronic (records and signatures)], [distributing risk of (error in electronic transmissions)], and [retention of "original" electronic records].
*The UETA contains provisions governing [a], [b], [c], and [d].*

3 Other provisions govern [(automated electronic transactions) or (the use of so-called electronic "agents")] and [acceptance of electronic (records and signatures) by governmental agencies].
*Other provisions govern [a or b] and [c].*

4 (As long as an entity has "control" of the transferable record,) it [is a holder of the record {as defined by UCC § 1-201(20)}] and [has the same rights and defenses as {a holder of (a negotiable instrument or document) under UCC Articles 3, 7, and 9}].
*(As long as ...,) it [is ...] and [has ...]*

5 A person has "control" (over the record) [if "a system {employed for evidencing the transfer of (interests in the transferable record)} (reliably) established that person as {the person to which the transferable record was (issued or transferred)}."]
*A person has control [if a system established that person as ...]*

6 This requirement can be met by [a system that {(creates, stores, and assigns) the transferable record (in a manner that satisfies six specific conditions listed in the UETA)}].
*This requirement can be met by [a system that {does a, b, and c (in a manner that...)}]*

7 Transactions {(existing or signed) electronically} (that might be unenforceable under traditional principles of law) may become enforceable [when taking into account the UETA's provisions].
*Transactions may become enforceable [when ...]*

 9 **Listening B: Advice from a senior partner**

CD2 T9–10

Elicit from students why junior lawyers request advice from senior partners. Then tell them to read the introduction (SB page 173) to check.

9.1 Check that students remember the meanings of the word *principal* from the box on SB page 169: 'one of the parties to a transaction'. Then tell students to read the questions and to use the introduction to predict what the problem might be. Elicit some suggestions. Then play the first part of the recording. After the recording, tell students to discuss the answers with a partner, as well as anything else they remember from the conversation.

**Transcript »** STUDENT'S BOOK **page 291**

 **Answers**

1 The agent of the buyers group wants to sign the note on behalf of the group because the other three principals are not available to sign it now and they are in a hurry to buy the property.

2 The seller is willing to agree to this because he wants to sell the property quickly.

3 It could be a problem because of recent changes to the law which may result in the position of the client being uncertain in the event that all the principals fail to sign the note.

 **Background note**

A *down payment* is an initial payment at the time of purchase, with the remainder to be paid later.

**9.2** Tell students to discuss the six statements in pairs to predict whether they are true or false. Point out that the answers are not in the same order as the questions in the book. You could also tell students to look at the questions in Exercise 9.3 before listening. Then play the second part of the recording. After the recording, go through the answers with the class.

**Transcript »** STUDENT'S BOOK **page 291**

 **Answers**

1 False (She doesn't want the case to become a test case.)

2 False (She suggests using a courier, a scanned signature or an e-signature.)

3 True

4 True

5 False (She does not mention any timeframe.)

6 True

**9.3** This can be done at the same time as or after Exercise 9.2. Play both parts of the recording again if you do the exercises separately. Tell students to discuss the questions in pairs, and then check with the whole class. You could point out that this

exercise is similar in form to Part 2 of the ILEC Test of Listening, although there are five questions in that part of the test.

 **Answers**

**1** c  **2** b  **3** b

## 10 Language use: Making suggestions and recommendations

Elicit from the class some ways of making suggestions and recommendations. Then tell them to look at the information in the box to compare it with their ideas. You could elicit further useful expressions such as *If I were you I'd ...*, *You could always ...*, *Have you thought about ... ?* and *I think you'd better ...*

 **Language note**

Note that *advise* is much more natural with *would*: *I would advise you to ...* .

*Recommend* is often more formal and assertive than *suggest*. *I recommend* would be most natural coming from an expert, while *I suggest* could come from anyone with a good idea. Note the patterns that follow the three verbs: *to advise somebody to do*, *to recommend doing* and *to suggest doing*.

The suggesting verbs can be negated in two ways each: for example, *I would advise you not to deal with the principal in jail* is much more assertive than *I would not advise you to deal with this man.*

**10.1** Elicit from the class some situations which require a formal style and some which require a less formal style. Then tell them to read the explanation and do the exercise quickly in pairs. When they have finished, check the answers with the class. Elicit which two of the eight expressions are followed by an *–ing* form (Answers: *Try ...* and *How about ... ?*), and which is followed by a person and a verb (Answer: *I recommend that ...*).

 **Answers**

**1** F, I  **2** I, F  **3** F, I

**10.2** Tell students to work in pairs and to treat this as a mini-role-play: one student should be Ms Wadman, the junior lawyer, and the second should be Mr Lawson, her client. If you have an odd number of students, there can be two lawyers in one group. The lawyer(s) should make recommendations for getting signatures from the three missing principals. The client should think of reasons why those recommendations will not work. Encourage them to use as many of the useful phrases as possible in their discussions, as long as they maintain an appropriate style (either formal or informal, but not mixed).

**10.3** Tell students to close their books. Elicit from the class onto the board some ways of giving negative advice or suggestions, i.e. saying what not to do. Students then look at the box (SB page 175) to compare it with their ideas. Discuss the two questions with the class.

 **Answer**

The sentences are listed in order from least emphatic to most emphatic.
They are formal.

**10.4** Students work alone to make sentences, then compare their ideas in pairs. Make sure students know to use a range of structures in their sentences. Finally, check with the class.

 **Suggested answers**

1 I strongly advise you against signing the promissory note for all of the principals. / I suggest not signing the promissory note for all of the principals.
2 I would advise against making a business deal with a man serving a prison sentence for tax evasion. / I strongly suggest you not to make a business deal with a man serving a prison sentence for tax evasion.
3 I would advise you against putting our clients in the position of being a test case for this issue. / I would strongly suggest you not to put our clients in the position of being a test case for this issue.
4 I advise you not to risk being sued by the drawee. / I strongly suggest not risking being sued by the drawee.

 ## 11 Writing B: Providing advice and making suggestions

This can be done in class or at home. It might be a good idea for students to plan the letter in groups before writing it alone (see Writing section, page xiv).

 **Suggested answer**

Dear Mr. Lawson

I am writing to you in respect of the promissory note which the prospective buyers of your property intend to give you for a down payment. I would like to advise you not to accept this note in its present form for the following reasons:

○ The safest way to bind all the principals is to have all of them sign the note as makers.
○ As you know, one of the principals is currently serving a jail sentence on a financial charge. I do not recommend entering into a business transaction with a person whose financial trustworthiness is questionable.

I propose that you refuse to accept the note unless it has been signed by all of the principals. I also suggest that I contact the agent on your behalf and inform him of this fact. I can recommend ways for him to obtain the signatures of the other principals quickly (fax, e-signature, courier), as all of the parties involved are interested in concluding the deal as soon as possible. I look forward to receiving further instructions from you in this matter.
Yours truly
J.P. Wadman
(182 words)

Tell students to do the Internet activity as homework. See Using the Internet for research, page xviii.

# Language focus

## Answers

**1 Vocabulary: distinguishing meaning**

1 *with consent*: The others mean 'on demand'.

**2** *monetary*: The others mean 'overdue'.

**3** *principle*: The others are adjectives meaning 'main'; *principle* is a noun.

**4** *incur*: The others suggest that something grows in quantity.

**5** *make a requirement*: The others mean 'fulfil'.

**6** *impose*: The others are suggestions.

**2 Vocabulary: legal Latin**

**1** e.g.; e.g.   **2** i.e.   **3** per annum
**4** inter alia

**Background notes**

○ *Inter alia* means 'among other things'.

○ A *bearer check* (or *cheque*) is one made out 'to the bearer', while an *order check* (or *cheque*) is one made out to the order of a specific person.

**3 Word formation**

| Adjective | Adverb |
|---|---|
| basic | basically |
| electronic | electronically |
| principal | principally |
| reliable | reliably |
| specific | specifically |
| strict | strictly |
| uniform | uniformly, uniformly |

**4 Prepositions**

**2** in   **3** of   **4** for   **5** to   **6** in   **7** of   **8** in

**5 Vocabulary: word choice**

**2** due   **3** maturity   **4** principal
**5** per annum   **6** Maker   **7** lawful

---

**Optional extension**
**Photocopiable worksheet 12.3**

Two types of negotiable instrument, bills of exchange and certificates of deposit, are mentioned fairly briefly in Unit 12. Photocopiable worksheet 12.3 is intended to raise awareness of these instruments by providing samples of each document.

---

Before handing out the worksheet, elicit what students remember about the two instruments (e.g. from Reading A). Then hand out the worksheet and tell students to work in pairs to put words from the box in the numbered spaces. Tell them also to think about how they would fill in the documents for a client.

When they have finished, discuss the answers with the class. Discuss also with the class whether it would be possible to create a legally binding document by signing the worksheet.

**Answers**

**1** order   **2** sum   **3** received   **4** behalf
**5** Certificate   **6** Depositor   **7** deposited
**8** Account   **9** maturity   **10** interest
**11** annum   **12** completion   **13** withdraw
**14** substantial   **15** penalty   **16** evidenced
**17** transferable   **18** accordance

**Background notes**

○ The amount of the bill of exchange should be stated in numbers after *For* and in words after *The sum of*.

○ The word *At* may be followed by *sight*, meaning that payment can be immediate, or a delay (e.g. 60 days) may be stated.

○ *Sole* means that there is only one copy of the bill of exchange. Sometimes two (or more) copies are issued, in which case the word *first* or *second* would be inserted.

○ The payee is named after *Pay to the order of*, and the full name and address is given after *To*. Alternatively, *Pay to the order of* can be followed by *Ourselves*.

○ *For and on behalf of* is followed by the name of the organisation making the payment and the signature, name and title of its authorised representative.

○ In the certificate of deposit, the depositor is named at the beginning, with his/her address given after *of*.

○ According to the small print, the date of maturity should be 12 months and one day after the date of deposit.

# 13 ) Secured transactions

Everyone is familiar with buy-now-pay-later deals, for example for consumer goods such as washing machines. The seller hands over the washing machine before receiving full payment, so needs some form of **security** arrangement to ensure that the **debt** gets paid. This could mean arranging the deal so that the seller retains **title** to the washing machine (the **collateral**) until payment, or it could mean transferring title but giving the seller the right to reclaim the washing machine if the loan is not repaid according to the agreed terms. The former arrangement uses the washing machine as **quasi-security** on the debt. The latter uses it as **security**, so the sale of the washing machine is a **secured transaction**. The seller does not own the washing machine, but instead has a **security interest** (= property rights) in it. The concepts of security and quasi-security are functionally very similar: they provide a way to pay for something after taking possession of it. There is however, a major legal difference. With security, the debtor both **possesses** (holds) and **owns** (has legal title to) the property. With quasi-security, the debtor merely has possession; the creditor is still the owner until the debt is paid off. Quasi-security relates closely to the **ROT** (retention of title) **clauses** examined in Unit 9. The focus of Unit 13, however, is security.

A well-known example of a security interest is a **mortgage**, which gives a lender rights over real property (e.g. a house). If a homeowner fails to keep up with mortgage **repayments** on a house, the lender has the right to repossess the house. Outside the field of real property, another well-known form of security is **pawning**: borrowing money from a **pawnbroker** by leaving something valuable (a **pledge**), such as a television, in the possession of the pawnbroker as a guarantee of payment. This is an example of a **possessory security interest**, in contrast to the example above, where the washing machine seller has a **non-possessory security interest**. This unit focuses on such non-possessory security interests, especially the concept of **charges**. **Fixed charges** give rights to a **creditor** (= lender) over a specific

piece of the **debtor**'s (= borrower's) property (such as the washing machine mentioned earlier). **Floating charges**, on the other hand, give rights in a non-specified part of the debtor's property. This gives the debtor greater freedom, for example, to trade with third parties.

As with Unit 9 (Sale of goods), secured transactions can best be understood in terms of when things go wrong, in particular when the debtor goes bankrupt and various creditors compete to recover their money or property. In this situation, those creditors with security interests have a greater chance of recovering their property than other creditors. Those with fixed charges will have a stronger claim on particular property than those with floating charges. **Debtor–creditor law** is dealt with more fully in Unit 14, along with the concept of **liens** (= a creditor's claim on a debtor's property).

A theme throughout the unit is the **creation of a security interest**, using the procedure in the USA as an example. Listening A sets out the seven steps in this process. One of these steps involves drafting a **security agreement**, which grants a security interest to secure a loan. Reading B includes two fragments of such a security agreement, which set out the nature of the security interest and the consequences of a **default** (= if the debtor fails to keep to the terms of the agreement). The final step in the creation of a security interest is **perfection**. After perfection, third parties (e.g. other creditors) cannot have rival claims on the same piece of property. Perfection can be done in three ways: the security interest may be registered with the appropriate authority for that jurisdiction; the creditor may take possession of the collateral; or an **attachment** of the security interest may be granted by a court to a particular creditor.

Reading E analyses the technical question of whether it is possible for party A to have a fixed charge on party B's **book debts** (= the money that is owed to party B by third parties). In one of the cases discussed in the article, a bank in the UK (party A) secured a loan to a company (party B) by making the company set up a bank account, into which the company's own debtors (e.g. customers who paid in arrears for goods) had to pay off their debts. This account was used as security for the company's loan from the bank. Because the company was not allowed to withdraw money from its account, the arrangement was treated as a fixed charge. A court decision in 1979 confirmed this reasoning. As a fixed charge, the bank had a greater chance of recovering its loan than other creditors who had only floating charges. However, in a later case in 2004, a court ruled that the 1979 case had been wrongly decided, and that the bank merely had a floating charge on the company's book debts. The 2004 case was then overturned by the Court of Appeals, but that overruling was itself overruled by the House of Lords in 2005 (after Reading E was written). These cases are presented as an unsettled area of law.

Another area of law which is unsettled in many countries concerns whether **intellectual property** (IP, see Unit 11) can be used as collateral in a secured transaction. Listening B deals with the situation in various countries: in the UK, for example, charges against IP have to be registered with Companies House, but it is unclear whether this applies to foreign companies. In China and Hong Kong, a security interest cannot be created in a trade mark. In the USA, different types of IP have to be perfected in different (and often unexpected and complicated) ways.

The unit also contains input and practice of some important language areas, such as **contrasting information**, **anticipating events and planning contingencies** (how to plan for various possible situations), and **requesting and presenting information**. There is also the theme of a seminar on **revised legislation** (Article 9 of the USA's Uniform Commercial Code, **UCC**, which deals with secured transactions). There is an **advert** for this seminar in Reading C, an **internal email** concerning the seminar in Reading D, and an extract from the seminar in Listening A. The internal email is used to present **levels of formality** and **adverb–verb** collocations, both of which are practised in the writing task: a **polite refusal**.

### Further information

○ The concept of **quasi-security** and other related concepts are explained at http://www. proeconomics.com/Law/Banking/Quasi-Security.html.

○ For the **revised Article 9 of the UCC**, see http://www.law.cornell.edu/ucc/9.

○ http://en.wikipedia.org/wiki/National_ Westminster_Bank_plc_v_Spectrum_Plus_Ltd contains background information on the **two cases discussed in Reading 5**, and the **2005 House of Lords judgment** on the most recent case makes surprisingly interesting reading (http://www.parliament.the-stationery-office. co.uk/pa/ld200506/ldjudgmt/jd050630/ nat-1.htm).

## Discussion

Use these questions to generate a discussion.
a How many ways to pay for something without cash can you think of? (Treat this as a brainstorming activity.)
b If you are the buyer, which of these ways is the best way of buying? What about if you are the seller?
c How can a lender make sure he/she is paid?

▥➡ **Suggested answers**
a Hire purchase (where the seller retains title and the buyer only has possession until the goods are paid for), buy-now-pay-later deals (using the goods as security), mortgages on real property (where the lender can repossess a property if the borrower fails to keep up with repayments), credit cards (where you pay interest on any money you borrow), debit cards (where the money is debited immediately or almost immediately from your bank account), payment terms (e.g. in business-to-business transactions, a customer may have negotiated 60-day or 90-day payment terms), cheques, promissory notes, a tab/slate (an informal late-payment arrangement between a regular customer and a shop/pub, etc.).

b The obvious answer is that it depends. Sometimes cash is best, but it depends how cheap credit is. The same goes for the seller: cash in hand is safe, but a secure high-interest credit arrangement can also be very attractive. Use this discussion to lead into the idea of different types of security, and their relative attractiveness for both parties.

c This may be partially covered under the previous questions, but note that this question includes not only sellers giving credit but also other lenders, especially banks. Some examples are: threatening violence (or blackmail); holding the borrower's property (e.g. pawn-broking); signing a contract to give the lender rights to the borrower's property (or other assets, including intangible assets, future assets, specific or general assets); retaining title to goods and effectively hiring them out to the borrower until they are paid for (hire purchase); and using the borrower's conscience / honesty / fear of damage to reputation / hope of future co-operation to persuade the borrower to repay the loan.

# 1 Reading A: Introduction to secured transactions

Tell students to read the four sentences and to discuss with a partner what they think the correct word is for each definition. Then tell them to read the text slowly to check. Note that question 4 is not answered explicitly in the text, but it can be worked out by a process of elimination after answering the other questions. When students have finished, check the answers with the class. Use this opportunity to check that they understand all the key terms.

 **Answers**
**1** loan  **2** mortgage  **3** pledge  **4** lien

 **Background notes**
○ For most of this unit, *interest* is a countable noun referring to *rights in property*, whether total or partial rights (such as a right to prevent sale to a third party). However, question 2 refers to repaying a loan *usually with interest*. This is the more familiar meaning of *interest* (= a percentage which is added to the loan amount every month/year, etc.), where it is uncountable.
○ In the sentence *The most obvious example of this is a loan*, note that *a loan* is an example of *credit*, not of a *secured transaction*. Another form of

credit is *delayed payment*, whereby a seller allows a buyer a period after delivery to pay for goods received (typically a multiple of 30 days). Both loans and other forms of credit may be secured or unsecured.
○ The terms *creditor* and *lender* are effectively synonyms. The difference is that a *lender* lends money willingly, while a *creditor* is owed money, but may not have lent the money willingly. The same can be said about a *borrower* (who has borrowed) and a *debtor* (who owes).
○ *Pawning* involves depositing one's possessions (e.g. jewellery) with a *pawnbroker* in exchange for a cash loan. If the *pledgor* fails to keep to the terms of the loan, the pawnbroker has the right to sell the *pledge* to a third party.
○ Note that a *charge* is like a *mortgage*: a *mortgage* is a loan on real property, using the property as security, while a *charge* is a loan on a chattel (movable property). In fact, prior to the UCC, the term *chattel mortgage* was used in American English to refer to a charge.
○ A fixed charge *affords* (grants) the creditor control over the *alienation* (ability to transfer title) of a property.
○ *To invoke consensual security interests against third parties* means 'to rely on the interests to prevent third parties from buying or seizing the collateral'. For example, if a borrower goes bankrupt, there may be several creditors seeking to recover assets, so it is important to prove who has rights to which assets.
○ A *vested interest* is an absolute right to possess something, either now or at some time in the future.
○ *Sanctioned by statute* means 'authorised by law'.
○ *Attachment* sometimes means the seizing of goods (see http://dictionary.law.com), but in this text it simply refers to the formal creation of an enforceable right. See Reading B for an example of the former meaning.

**Optional extension**

**Photocopiable worksheet 13.1**

Photocopiable worksheet 13.1 is a graphic illustration of the key terms from Reading A and their relationships. It can be used to make sure that students have fully understood the text.

Tell students to work in pairs to write a word from the text in each space. Note that the first letter of each word has been given. Most of the missing words are key terms (in bold in the text). The diagram also includes some information concerning quasi-security which is not mentioned in the text (in shaded boxes). When students have finished the worksheet, go through the answers with the class. Discuss the meanings of the difficult words and concepts, and find out if the concepts are the same in students' jurisdictions.

**Answers**

**1** Secured transactions   **2** Credit   **3** Security
**4** loan   **5** mortgage   **6** right; rem   **7** Quasi-security   **8** Non-consensual   **9** Consensual
**10** unpaid sellers' liens   **11** Possessory;
pawning   **12** Non-possessory   **13** pledgee
**14** pledge   **15** pledgor   **16** Fixed charge
**17** specific property   **18** alienation; property
**19** Floating charge   **20** assets; debtor; given
time   **21** ordinary course; business
**22** default; crystallises   **23** Security
agreement   **24** Perfection   **25** interest;
collateral   **26** Registration; security
agreement **27** Possession; collateral
**28** Attachment; security interest

**Optional extension**

One reason the text may be difficult is that some of the key words have several radically different meanings. This exercise highlights this problem and is an attempt to reduce confusion.

Elicit from the class what the word *security* refers to in the first sentence (secured transactions provide *security for the lender*). (Answer: Here, it means 'a promise of security', which the lender receives.) Then ask the same question about the fourth sentence (*buying the security*). (Answer: This time, it refers to the assets used as a guarantee (= *collateral*), which the borrower possesses.) Tell students to work in small teams to find more words from the text with several meanings, and to think of a sentence for each word to illustrate each additional meaning. The sentences should have some connection, however tenuous, to law.

When students have finished, go round the teams eliciting sentences. Award points for good sentences, but only if no other team has already given a sentence illustrating that meaning of the word. The team with the most good sentences is the winner.

**Suggested answers**

*Paragraph 1*

| | |
|---|---|
| provision | 'Credit' refers to the provision (= act of providing) *of a benefit …* Alternative meaning: *The contract contains a provision* (= clause) *stipulating that …* |
| interest | *… the security interest* (= rights in property) *…* Alternative meaning: *According to the promissory note, interest* (= percentage added to loan) *on the loan accrues at an annual rate of …* |

*Paragraph 2*

| | |
|---|---|
| form | *… mortgages are a form* (= type) *of security …* Alternative meaning: *When drawing up a contract, it is useful to use a form* (= like a template). |

*Paragraph 3*

| | |
|---|---|
| charge | *… the fixed charge and the floating charge* (= non-possessory security interests) *…* |

| | |
|---|---|
| | Alternative meaning: *Lawyers tend to charge* (= request as a fee) *a lot for their services.* |
| *alienation* | *... affords the creditor control over its alienation* (= transfer of title). Alternative meaning: *If a lawyer spends too much time at work, it can lead to a sense of alienation* (= feeling isolated) *from her family.* |
| *deal* | *... the debtor cannot deal in* (= buy and sell) *the property ...* Alternative meaning: *The parties finally reached a deal* (= an agreement) *at midnight.* |

## 2 Key terms: Comparing and contrasting concepts

**2.1** Tell students to work alone to complete the texts, and then to compare their answers with a partner. Then go through the answers with the class.

 **Answers**
> **1** seize  **2** sell  **3** defaults  **4** owns
> **5** has  **6** attaches  **7** attaches
> **8** crystallises  **9** make

**2.2** This can be done with the whole class. You could also elicit other ways of contrasting ideas (e.g. *whereas*, *on the other hand*, *unlike*, *in contrast to*) and how the sentences would have to be changed in order to use these expressions.

 **Answers**
> However, in the case of quasi-security, ...
> ... while the debtor only ...
> While a fixed charge ...

**2.3** Tell students to work in pairs to come up with as many collocations as they can. Point out that the text will help a little, but they will also have to use their own ideas. When they have finished, go through the answers with the class.

 **Answers**
> **1** to attach payment, a security interest, collateral
> **2** to perfect a security interest
> **3** to pledge collateral
> **4** to secure credit, indebtedness, a loan, payment, performance
> **5** to provide collateral, credit, a loan, payment, performance
> **6** to enforce a loan, payment, performance, a security interest

 **Background note**
Only one of the verbs is actually used in the text (*to secure payment or performance* and *the indebtedness secured by the property*); the others are included as nouns (*attachment of the security interest, perfection of the security interest* and *the pledge*).

## 3 Reading B: A security agreement

Elicit from the class what a *security agreement* is, and in what ways lawyers deal with them. Then tell students to read the introduction (SB page 180) to compare it with their suggestions.

**3.1** Tell students to read through the security agreement to find the answers to the two questions. When they have finished, tell them to compare their answers with a partner, and then check the answers with the class. Discuss what each of the terms included in the collateral might cover.

 **Answers**
> **1** The debtor's tangible possessions (... *all inventory, equipment, appliances, furnishings, and fixtures now or hereafter placed upon the premises [...] or used in connection therewith and in which Debtor now has or hereafter acquires any right and the proceeds therefrom*) as well as intangible assets (... *right, title and interest to any trade marks, trade names and contract rights in which Debtor now has or hereafter acquires*).
> **2** All obligations become immediately payable.

**Background notes**

○ The collateral includes *inventory* (a company's stock of goods), *equipment* (such as tools), *appliances* (such as photocopiers), *furnishings* (such as chairs) and *fixtures* (items which are fixed to the ground, such as machines). The *proceeds therefrom* means 'the money from selling any of these items'. The term *right* is more general than *title* (= legal ownership) and *interest* (= present or future entitlement to possess or use property).

○ A *contingent* /kən'tɪndʒənt/ *liability* is a liability which may or may not arise, depending on the outcome of another event (such as a court decision).

○ Three types of evidence that the debtor is in financial difficulty are listed: (i) an *assignment for the benefit of creditors* is a form of liquidation of a company (see http://www.thehamergroup.com/genassign.htm); (ii) an *attachment of assets* means their seizure by a law enforcer in expectation of a court judgment. *Receivership of assets* means their seizure by a receiver when the owner is insolvent. As both attachment and receivership are temporary measures, after which a company may either recover or be declared bankrupt, the security agreement specifies that they only count as evidence of financial difficulties if they are not dissolved within 30 days; (iii) *institution of bankruptcy proceedings* takes place after a company is already *insolvent* (unable to pay its debts). If an insolvent company is declared *bankrupt*, its assets are distributed among its creditors, and a fresh start is declared, even if not all creditors receive all that is owed to them.

**3.2** Tell students to discuss the questions in pairs. You may also tell them to complete Exercise 3.3 before you go through the answers with the class. When you check the answers to question 2, discuss what each type of evidence involves (see Background note above).

**1** The inventory is located upon the 'Premises' (at 99 Appleby Road, Baltimore, MD) and anywhere else used in connection with it.

**2** Financial difficulty would be given in any of the following circumstances:

○ an assignment for the benefit of creditors

○ an attachment or receivership of assets not dissolved within 30 days

○ the institution of bankruptcy proceedings, whether voluntary or involuntary, which is not dismissed within 30 days from the date on which it is filed.

**3** The remedies of a Secured Party under the Uniform Commercial Code are available.

**3.3** This can be done with Exercise 3.2. Tell students to work in pairs to match the words and definitions. When you check the answers with the class, you can test students by reading a definition and eliciting the relevant word.

**1** e  **2** d  **3** b  **4** a  **5** c

**Optional extension**
**Photocopiable worksheet 13.2**

The text contains many words formed from other words. For example *the institution of bankruptcy proceedings* does not refer to an institution in the normal sense, but the situation in which bankruptcy proceedings are instituted. It is important for lawyers to be able to transform, for example, verbs into nouns, as this is a very effective way of making writing more formal. (The reverse process is also important, as this makes language easier to understand and friendlier.) Photocopiable worksheet 13.2 focuses on this skill.

Tell students to close their books and to work in pairs to transform the words in brackets so that they fit the context of the security agreement. When they have finished, go through the answers with the class.

## Answers

**1** Debtor  **2** appliances  **3** fixtures  **4** located
**5** connection  **6** therewith  **7** proceeds
**8** therefrom  **9** additional  **10** security
**11** hereafter  **12** payment  **13** promissory
**14** herewith  **15** performance  **16** liabilities
**17** obligations  **18** description  **19** indirect
**20** arising  **21** Agreement  **22** happening
**23** misrepresentation  **24** connection
**25** non-compliance  **26** non-performance
**27** difficulty/difficulties  **28** evidenced
**29** receivership  **30** institution  **31** bankruptcy
**32** involuntary  **33** default  **34** thereafter
**35** payable  **36** Commercial

---

## 4 Language use A: Anticipating events and planning contingencies

### Background note
A *contingency* /kən'tɪndʒənsi/ is an event which may or may not happen, depending on the outcome of another event. A secondary meaning of *contingency* is the provisions made (e.g. setting aside funds, establishing procedures) in anticipation of such an event. This is the meaning used in this section.

Elicit from the class what they understand by the phrases *anticipating events* and *planning contingencies*. Using the context of the security agreement in Reading B, elicit what sort of events are anticipated and what sort of contingency plans the agreement makes. Then tell students to read the information in the box (SB page 181) to compare it with their ideas.

**4.1** Tell students to do this in pairs, and then go through the answers with the class.

### Suggested answers
Note that only liabilities are discussed below. Similar distinctions may be made for obligations.

○ *Direct liability* is liability for one's own actions; *indirect liability* is liability for someone else's actions (e.g. a parent may be liable for the actions of a child;

an employer may be liable for the actions of an employee; an website owner for the actions of a user).
○ An *absolute liability* is one which exists; a *contingent liability* may or may not exist, depending on other factors.
○ If a liability is *due*, it must be paid immediately; if it is *to become due*, it must be paid at a later date.
○ If a liability is *now existing*, it has already been agreed; if it is *hereafter arising*, it will be agreed at some point in the future.

### Background note
A *liability* is a legal responsibility, which becomes important when something goes wrong. It is also an accounting term meaning *money owed*. The security agreement covers both meanings of *liability*. An *obligation* is something that a party must do, not only when things go wrong.

**4.2** This can be done with the whole class.

### Answers
... now or hereafter placed upon the premises ...
... in which Debtor now has or hereafter acquires any right ...
... contract rights in which Debtor now has or hereafter acquires.
... bankruptcy proceedings, whether voluntary or involuntary, ...
Upon default and at any time thereafter ...

### Optional extension
Tell students to work in groups of between two and four to role-play a negotiation over the security agreement from Reading B. In each group, there should be one or two lawyers for the borrower (Richard Cross) and for the lender (Appleby Designs).
Cross's lawyers should argue that the security agreement does not have to be as inclusive as the one drawn up by Appleby's lawyers. Both parties should be prepared to give some ground, as their clients have a good relationship, and both are keen for the loan to be agreed.

## 5 Reading C: Seminar on revised legislation

Elicit from the class why lawyers attend seminars on revised legislation and what exactly the UCC is. Then tell them to read the introduction (SB page 181) to compare it with their ideas.

**5.1** Tell students to work alone to answer the questions. When they have found the answers, they should compare their answers with a partner. Then check with the class.

**Answers**
1 An advertisement like this would probably appear in a law journal or other publication read by practising lawyers.
2 Understanding Revised Article 9 of the UCC

---

**Background note**
According to the advertisement, the target audience includes *attorneys* (US English term for 'lawyers'), *paralegals* (who have no complete legal training but assist lawyers with legal matters), *vice presidents* (one of several second-in-command executives in a company, typically responsible for a section of the company such as finance or law), *commercial loan officers* (an official of a commercial lender who is empowered to authorise loans), *credit and collection managers* (an official of a business who oversees the granting of credit to customers and the recovery of debts) and *branch managers* (of e.g. a bank or other lending institution).

---

**5.2** Tell students to discuss the statements in pairs. When they have finished, check the answers with the class.

**Answers**
1 True
2 False (It is suitable for junior personnel such as paralegals as well as non-lawyers.)
3 False (By registering they automatically give their consent.)
4 False (The money may be transferred to pay for a later seminar, but not repaid.)

5 False (... *including drafting security agreements*)
6 True

**5.3** Discuss this with the whole class.

## 6 Reading D: An internal email

**6.1** Tell students to read the email carefully to answer the questions. Point out that question 1 requires information on who 'All' and 'Jennifer Sampson' might be. When students have finished, discuss the answers with the class.

**Answers**
1 It was sent by a superior to the secured transactions team which reports to her.
2 Because they will soon be dealing with several new cases in the area.

**6.2** Tell students to discuss the three questions with a partner. When they have finished, go through the answers with the class. Don't spend too much time on question 2, as this is covered in depth in Exercise 7.1.

**Answers**
1 It is respectful, distanced and formal.
2 See the table in Exercise 7.1.
3 When addressing someone you don't know, or don't know well; when addressing someone in a senior position to you; when addressing someone in a junior position, with whom you wish to preserve a sense of professional authority.

## 7 Text analysis: Formality / Adverb–verb collocations

**7.1** Tell students to read the box, and to work in pairs to complete the table. Point out that the italicised text in the right-hand column provides paraphrases of the nine formal phrases. Tell students also to find examples of the first three features listed in the table (absence of potential contractions, sentence length and sentence structure). When they have finished, discuss the answers with the class.

**Answers**

1  The seminar will be held ...
2  ... there are two young newcomers ...
3  it may be necessary ...
4  I ... would strongly advise that ...
5  I firmly believe that ...
6  Sincerely
7  I look forward to your response in this matter.
8  ... and participate in the seminar ...
9  ... which commences on Thursday morning.

**Language notes**

There are several important differences between subordination (using conjunctions like *although*) and co-ordination (using conjunctions like *but*):

1  Identical elements can be omitted from co-ordinated clauses, but not subordinate clauses:
   *I can play the piano, but I can't sing* → *I can play the piano, but ~~I can~~ not sing.* ✓
   *I can play the piano, although I can't sing.* → *I can play the piano, although I can not sing.* ✗

2  Subordinators can be moved with their clauses, while co-ordinators always stay in the middle:
   *I went to the party although I hadn't been invited.* → *Although I hadn't been invited, I went to the party.* ✓
   *I went to the party, but I hadn't been invited.* → *I hadn't been invited to the party, but I went.* ✓

3  Tenses often behave differently in subordinate clauses than in co-ordinated (or independent) clauses:
   *I will finish and then I will go home.* → *When I have finished, I will go home.*
   *She finished and then she went home.* → *When she had finished, she went home.*

There are three main co-ordinators in English: *and*, *or* and *but* (plus *nor*). There are hundreds of subordinators, many of which are made up of several words (e.g. *in case, as long as, pursuant to*).

**7.2**  Do this quickly as a group. Note that *highly respected* is an adverb–adjective combination.

**Answers**

strongly advise, firmly believe, sincerely hope

**7.3**  Tell students to do this in pairs. When they have finished, discuss the answers with the class. There may be some disagreement over what constitutes a collocation and what does not.

**Suggested answers**

1  deeply: believe, hope, regret
2  firmly: believe, object to, support
3  fully: agree, recommend, support, understand
4  sincerely: believe, hope, regret
5  strongly: advise, agree, object to, recommend, suggest, support
6  wholeheartedly: agree, believe, recommend, support

**Language note**

It is easy to check collocations on a search engine such as www.google.com by typing the two words surrounded by quotation marks (e.g. "deeply advise"). The number of hits is a rough indication of the popularity of any given combination. For example, the results for *deeply* are as follows: "deeply advise" (1,570), "deeply agree" (13,100), "deeply believe" (457,000), "deeply hope" (103,000), "deeply object to" (9,060), "deeply recommend" (21,300), "deeply regret" (1,030,000), "deeply suggest" (4,360), "deeply support" (17,600) and "deeply understand" (443,000). This shows that *deeply* collocates most strongly with *regret*, followed by *believe* and *understand* and, rather less strongly, by *hope*.

# 8  Writing: A polite refusal

**8.1**  Tell students to read the task and then elicit from the class polite ways of refusing (e.g. *I am afraid I will be unable to attend / Unfortunately the seminar is on the same day as ..., which I am obliged to attend / Owing to* *the sensitive nature of the meeting scheduled for the same day, I feel it would be unwise to attend the seminar*). Elicit also possible alternative ways of acquiring the necessary knowledge without attending the seminar (e.g. formal or informal training from colleagues who can attend, private research of subject matter, attending a later seminar, in-house training from Shuttleworth). The writing may be done at home or in class (see Writing section, page xiv). Remind students to use at least two of the collocations from Exercise 7.3 and the same level of formality as Jennifer Sampson's email.

 **Suggested answer**

Dear Ms Sampson

In response to your email concerning the upcoming seminar on Revised Article 9, I am writing to inform you that I will unfortunately be unable to attend. The Balboni case is going to trial, and I am scheduled to appear in court on the days the seminar takes place. I am sure you will agree that this court appearance takes precedence over the seminar.

I would like to add that I fully support the initiative you have taken to provide more training opportunities for the secured transactions team. I firmly believe that both my experienced colleagues and the junior members of the team will profit from the chance to learn more about the changes in the law that directly affect our work. However, I am afraid that a few of my colleagues will also be unable to attend. Therefore, I strongly recommend that we arrange for the seminar to be held on another date. To my knowledge, the Shuttleworth Institute also carries out in-company training courses upon request. Might that be a solution for our team as well? If you would like me to make arrangements for such a seminar I would be happy to do so.

Best regards

Chiara Lawson

(197 words)

**Optional extension**

This can be done as an alternative to Exercise 8.1. Divide the class into groups of two or three, and give each group a sheet of paper. Tell half the groups to start writing a polite refusal to Jennifer in formal English, and the other half to start writing in informal English. Each group should write one or two lines of their letter and then pass it on to the group to their right, who should read the beginning of the letter and write the next couple of lines in the same style. They should continue like this for several more turns. If some groups reach the end of their refusals, they could start writing Jennifer's response to the refusal, following the same level of formality as the refusal. After about ten turns, tell the groups to draw their letters to a close. When the letters are finished, ask students to read their letters aloud to the class.

**8.2** This can be done as a writing exercise at home or in class. Alternatively, it may be done as a speaking exercise, either in groups or with the whole class: students should take turns to transform one line of Jennifer's letter into less formal English. Point out that the less formal English should not be completely informal: it still needs to be polite and should not be too direct, aggressive or over-friendly.

 **Suggested answer**

Dear All

I know this comes at really short notice, but there's going to be an interesting seminar at the Shuttleworth Institute in Boston next Thursday and Friday. I really think that all the members of the secured transactions team should attend. Have a look at the attached flyer – John Kellogg will be holding the seminar and he's a real expert on Revised Article 9. Since two of you are newcomers and also since you've got some big cases coming up, I think this is just what we need right now.

You may need to rearrange your schedules to be able to take part. It's probably a good idea to fly to Boston on Wednesday, since the seminar starts on Thursday morning.

I think this is a good opportunity for us. Let me know what you are going to do.

Best wishes

Jennifer Sampson

(138 words)

## 9  Listening A: Creating a security interest

**9.1**  Discuss the seven steps quickly with the class (but obviously avoid confirming or rejecting students' suggestions). Make sure they remember what *perfection* and *collateral* mean (see Reading A), and that they know who the *secured party* is.

**Answers**
5, 1, 7, 4, 2, 3, 6

**Background notes**
- If the *secured party* (the lender) has *given value*, it has provided some form of consideration, typically money, to the borrower.
- A *bill of sale* is a legal document that states that ownership has been transferred.

**9.2**  Play the recording for students to check their predictions. After the recording, tell them to compare their answers with a partner, and to discuss what the speaker said about each step. Then go through the answers with the class. Elicit also what students understand/ remember from the recording about the terms *holding company*, *blanket lien*, *roadblock* and *constructive notice* (see Background notes below).

**Transcript »** STUDENT'S BOOK **page 292**

**Answers**
See Exercise 9.1

**Background notes**
- A *holding company* is a company which owns other companies (or owns enough shares in them to influence their management). The term usually refers to companies that do not manufacture or offer services themselves, but which exist only in order to own other companies.
- A *blanket lien* effectively uses the borrower's entire assets as collateral. It creates a *roadblock* (impassable obstacle) because there are no other assets to offer to other lenders as collateral.
- Step 6 (authentification) binds the parties to the agreement: the debtor and the creditor. Step 7 (perfection) binds third parties (usually other creditors). In other words, in the event that the debtor cannot repay several creditors, other creditors cannot make claims on the collateral.
- *Constructive notice* is a device used to give a legal notice to somebody who might be difficult to deliver to in person (e.g. because they are in hiding or because the notice is addressed to many non-specific people such as potential creditors). For example, the notice may be posted on a courthouse's notice board or published in an approved newspaper. In the context of security interests, constructive notice is given by filing a financing statement with the relevant jurisdiction's filing office.

**Optional extension**
The recording contains many useful expressions for presentations and for talking about secured transactions. Many of these use very common verbs (such as *have*, *make* and *put*), which tend to be overlooked when students learn vocabulary. This exercise is designed to remind students to pay attention to such words. Note that collocations like these are well worth learning in preparation for the ILEC exam, especially for Parts 1 and 2 of the Test of Reading.

While students are listening to the recording for Exercise 9.2, write the following on the board.

| | | | |
|---|---|---|---|
| **1** | to turn | **a** | a deal |
| **2** | to feel | **b** | a financing statement |
| **3** | to grant | **c** | a loan |
| **4** | to conduct | **d** | a question |

| | | | |
|---|---|---|---|
| **5** | to serve | **e** | a security interest |
| **6** | to strike | **f** | as collateral |
| **7** | to have | **g** | documentation |
| **8** | to provide | **h** | free to interrupt at any time |
| **9** | to subject | | |
| **10** | to give | **i** | funds |
| **11** | to make | **j** | into more detail later |
| **12** | to advance | **k** | one's business |
| **13** | to go | **l** | pen to paper |
| **14** | to put | **m** | property to the security interest |
| **15** | to file | | |
| **16** | to bind | **n** | the debtor and the secured party |
| | | **o** | to the topic of creating security interests |
| | | **p** | value |

After Exercise 9.2, ask students to match the verbs with the phrases that followed in the recording. This can be done in pairs or with the whole class. Point out that several answers are possible for some verbs. When you go through the answers, elicit the context in which each expression was used in the recording (which may be checked during the second listening for Exercise 9.3). As additional practice, erase the verbs from the board and ask students to work in teams to try to remember as many as they can.

**Answers**
**1** o   **2** h   **3** e   **4** k   **5** f   **6** a   **7** d
**8** g   **9** m   **10** p   **11** c   **12** i   **13** j   **14** l
**15** b   **16** n

**9.3** Tell students to discuss the questions in pairs and then listen again to check their answers. After the recording, go through the answers with the class.

**Answers**
**1** Since a borrower may conduct its business through several entities, it is necessary to make sure that the property in which the security interest is granted is owned by the borrower.
**2** A blanket lien refers to a situation in which 'all of the personal property of the debtor' is named as the collateral for a debt. The speaker says that this is problematic because the debtor would

not be able to acquire any more secured borrowing.
**3** This would happen when the debtor agrees to subject its after-acquired property to the security interest.
**4** According to the speaker, the requirement of value is easily met in the typical lending relationship because the lender either agrees to make a loan or actually advances funds to the debtor.
**5** This means signing the agreement, either by hand or electronically.

**9.4** Tell students to discuss this in small groups, and then open up the discussion to include the whole class.

## 10 Reading E: An unsettled area of the law

Elicit what is meant by *an unsettled area of the law*, and which areas of law are likely to be unsettled. (Suggested answers: Anything connected with new technology (especially the Internet, other IT issues, biotechnology, etc.), as well as rapidly changing areas such as international (e.g. EU) law, intellectual property, etc.) Then tell students to read the introduction (SB page 186) to compare it with their suggestions.

**10.1** Do this quickly with the whole class. Allow a short time for students to read (10–20 seconds), and then make sure they understand what *fixed* and *floating charges* are (see Reading A). Discuss what *book debts* are, and whether students think they can be classified as *fixed* or *floating charges*. Discuss also why this distinction might be important. Avoid confirming or rejecting their suggestions at this stage. (*Book debts* are defined in Exercise 10.3; the importance of the distinction between *fixed* and *floating charge* is addressed in paragraph 5 of the text.)

**Answers**
**1** The issue involved is whether it is possible to have a fixed charge on the book debts of a company.
**2** The issue affects company directors, bankers, other lenders and creditors.

**10.2** Tell students to read the rest of the text carefully in order to check their suggestions (from Exercise 10.1) and to complete the summaries. When they have finished, tell them to discuss the answers in pairs, and then go through them with the class. Discuss with the class whether they agree with the reasoning of the court in each case, and the importance of the distinction, as discussed in paragraph 5.

 **Answers**

1 c  2 e  3 a  4 d  5 b

**Background notes**

○ In the cases described in this text, the *fixed charge on book debts* involved the borrower setting up a special account into which book debts were paid. In effect, the fixed charge was on the present and future contents of that account. This meant that other creditors (such as the Inland Revenue) could not claim the money in that account if and when the borrower went bankrupt. See http://en.wikipedia.org/wiki/National_Westminster_Bank_plc_v_Spectrum_Plus_Ltd or http://www.parliament.the-stationery-office.co.uk/pa/ld200506/ldjudgmt/jd050630/nat-1.htm for an accessible overview of the cases.

○ In paragraph 2, the judge said that *the critical feature distinguishing a floating charge from a fixed charge was the company's power to deal with assets in the ordinary course of business*. In other words, if the company was unable to deal with assets in the ordinary course of business (as was the case with Siebe Gorman), the charge was fixed.

○ *To draw an account* means 'to withdraw money from it'.

○ *Debenture* is used in the British English sense of a secured debt instrument, rather than the American definition, whereby debentures may be secured or unsecured. See footnote 1 on SB page 167.

○ A *bank guarantee* (see definition in Exercise 10.3) is a kind of indirect secured transaction. For example, party A

buys some goods from party B, to be paid for at a later date. Party A could enter into a security agreement with party B, or may simply provide a bank guarantee (of payment from the bank, in case party A fails to repay). In order to persuade the bank to provide the guarantee, party A is likely to have provided some form of security to the bank.

○ The Court of Appeal's decision (paragraph 4) looks like a third conditional (for unreal past events), but in fact it refers to the real past, and uses past perfect because it is reported speech. There is no name for this type of conditional. The judge's actual words might have been 'Even if it is true that the interpretation in the Siebe Gorman case appeared erroneous, I would hold that the wording [...] has acquired the meaning [...] attributed to it.'

○ *Inland Revenue,* the UK's tax office, and *Customs and Excise*, the UK's agency for collecting excise duties on imported goods and preventing illegal imports, have since merged to form *HM Revenue and Customs*.

○ *Unsecured creditors* are among the last to receive their money when a company goes bankrupt. According to the text, the first in line are employees and secured creditors with fixed charges, followed by creditors with floating charges. Unsecured creditors (including debenture holders, Inland Revenue and Customs and Excise) are next, followed by shareholders.

○ A *personal guarantee* is a promise made by an individual to repay a creditor if that individual's company is unable to pay.

**10.3** Tell students to do this quickly by themselves, and then go through the answers with the class.

 **Answers**

1 Book debts  2 floating charge
3 bank guarantee  4 preferential

**10.4** Discuss this with the whole class.

## 11 Listening B: Intellectual property in secured transactions

Elicit from the class the relationship between IP and secured transactions. Then tell them to read the introduction (SB page 188) to compare it with their suggestions.

**11.1** Tell students to read through the questions and then to listen to the recording to find the answers. Ask them also to pay attention to which countries were mentioned in the seminar. After the recording, tell students to compare their answers with a partner, and to try to remember what the speakers said about each country.

**Transcript »** STUDENT'S BOOK **page 292**

 **Answers**
**1** b  **2** c  **3** c  **4** a
○ US: revised UCC / Article 9 has new provisions about IP as collateral / not all general intangibles are perfected in the same way.
○ UK: charges against IP have to be registered at Companies House, but unclear whether this applies to foreign companies.
○ China and Hong Kong: not allowed to create a security interest in a trade mark.

**11.2** Tell students to read the statements and then listen again to check the answers. After the recording, allow them to check with a partner, and then go through the answers with the class.

 **Answers**
**1** True
**2** False (It is unsettled everywhere.)
**3** True
**4** False (He offers to lend her their seminar materials.)

---

**Optional extension**
**Photocopiable worksheet 13.3**

A common misconception is that informal sentences are never complex. In fact, there are many complex structures which are especially common in informal English, such as unmarked relative clauses (i.e. with the relative pronoun omitted), *what*-clefting (e.g. *what he said was ...*), indirect questions (e.g. *he told us what she wanted*) and phrasal verbs (often with prepositions separated from their nouns in relative clauses, etc.). Photocopiable worksheet 13.3 highlights the many examples of complex informal English used in Listening B. Tell students to work in small groups to find which sentences are right and to correct the mistakes in the incorrect sentences. You could simply go through the answers at the end, or you could follow the 'Stake game' procedure (see Games and activities section, page xvi).

**Answers**
**1** Old Kellogg knows **what he's talking about**.
**2** He had some good stories to tell about cases ~~what~~ (**that**) he worked on.
**3** *correct*
**4** That's where things are going, if you ~~will~~ ask me.
**5** *correct*
**6** *correct*
**7** Then he talked about how **specific types of IP collateral are perfected** here in the US under the revised UCC.
**8** He started off by talking ~~us~~ (**to us**) about the importance of intellectual property as an asset.
**9** *correct*
**10** *correct*
**11** The main point he made was that the law is still anything but ~~not~~ settled.
**12** *correct*
**13** The law is still unclear about **whether/ how this applies** to a foreign company that has no presence in the UK.
**14** *correct*
**15** *correct*
**16** What **did he have** to say about perfecting security interests in the US?
**17** *correct*
**18** *correct*
**19** Where **could I** get more information on what **was covered in the seminar**?
**20** Everything (**that**) you want to know is in there.

## 12 Language use B: Requesting information

With the class, elicit how Jack and Peter answered Matsuko's questions (SB page 189). Elicit whether the questions are formal or informal, and general techniques for making questions more formal. Then tell students to read the rest of information in box to compare it with their suggestions. Elicit rules for making indirect questions.

> **Language note**
> Indirect questions are questions inside sentences (e.g. *I don't know what she said*) or other questions (e.g. *Can you tell me what she said?*). The word order is the same as for sentences (e.g. *She said something*) and not direct questions (e.g. *What did she say?*). Yes/no questions are introduced by *if* or *whether*.

Tell students to do this in pairs. Then elicit a wide range of answers with the class.

 **Suggested answers**
- ○ Could you fill me in on what he said?
  I wonder / was wondering if you could fill me in ... Would you mind filling me in ...?
- ○ Could you tell me what he said about the situation internationally?
  I wonder / was wondering if you could tell me ...
  Would you mind telling me ...?
- ○ Could you give me an example?
  I wonder / was wondering if you could give me ...
  Would you mind giving me ...?
- ○ Could you tell me what he had to say about perfecting security interests in the US?
  I wonder / was wondering if you could tell me ...
  Would you mind telling me ...?
- ○ What could you tell me about copyrights?
  I wonder / was wondering if you could tell me something about copyrights.
  Would you mind telling me something about copyrights?
- ○ I wonder / was wondering if you could tell me where I could get more information on what was covered in the seminar ...
  Would you mind telling me where ...?

## 13 Speaking: Requesting and presenting information

Tell the class to read the instructions. Elicit what sort of information they could research, and where they could find information. Lawyers should be able to find this sort of information very easily, but inexperienced law students may struggle. If necessary, you could allow them to invent facts for a fictitious jurisdiction.

The research and presentations can be done individually or in groups. Ideally, you should ask students to present their findings to the whole class, as a formal training seminar, but if you have a lot of students (who all do their homework), this may be impossible. Encourage the audience to ask questions. Give feedback on both the presentations and the politeness of the audience's questions.

> **Optional extension**
> **ILEC preparation: Test of Speaking Part 2**
>
> Note that Exercise 13 could be conducted following the procedure for Part 2 of the ILEC Test of Speaking (there is a sample script on SB page 275). Even though this may seem like a daunting topic to talk about with no preparation, it is quite possible that students could be asked to give a presentation about secured transactions in their exam, although of course they always have a choice of two topics. Therefore it is good to prepare a range of strategies for 'difficult topics' such as this one. Discuss these strategies below, together with your students' own strategies, with the class:
>
> **1** Remember that the examiner is checking your English, not your knowledge of law. So you can invent details.
> **2** If you don't know what the situation in your jurisdiction is, talk about what you think it could be, or what it should be.
> **3** Turn the question round so that it addresses something you do know about.
>
> **Suggested answers**
> **1** This is a good strategy if you can get away with it, but inventing details can be mentally very taxing. It is always better if you know at least something about the topic you are presenting. For this reason, it is well worth studying the 16 topics of

this book carefully, paying particular attention to the Glossary booklet. The trick is to sound confident and fluent and not to worry about the legal accuracy of your presentation.

2 This is a very sensible strategy, because it involves no deception. Again, it is important to sound confident and fluent, but nobody is expected to know every detail about every subject (at least not in the ILEC exam). Again, the knowledge and vocabulary from this book will enable you to sound intelligent and informed, even if you don't know much else about the topic. Note that using modal verbs (e.g. *might*, *should*) will make you sound a little more sophisticated (grammatically) than if you simply state facts.

3 This is a dangerous strategy, as examiners are trained to listen out for pre-rehearsed answers which are clearly off-topic. However, a small change (e.g. from your own jurisdiction to a jurisdiction you know better) might be acceptable.

 Tell students to do the Internet activity as homework. See Using the Internet for research, page xviii.

# Language focus

## Answers

1 **Vocabulary: distinguishing meaning**

  1 *loan*: The others are secured transactions; a *loan* is not necessarily secured.

  2 *instalment*: The others mean 'debt'.

  3 *to attach*: The others mean 'give as security'.

  4 *unconditional*: The others introduce conditions.

  5 *hereby*: The others mean 'from now on'.

2 **Prepositions used with expressions of time**

  **1** on; of   **2** of   **3** upon   **4** within   **5** from; on   **6** upon; at

3 **Collocations**

  **2** d   **3** e   **4** b   **5** a

 **Background note**
*Categorical description* (mentioned in Exercise 9.1) means simply a description of a category (e.g. all equipment and inventory), as opposed to an identification of a specific item.

4 **Expressions with *take***

  **2** place   **3** charge   **4** part   **5** precedence   **6** care

5 **Formal verbs**

  **2** g   **3** o   **4** j   **5** b   **6** l   **7** c   **8** n   **9** d
  **10** e   **11** i   **12** f   **13** h   **14** a   **15** k

 **Pronunciation notes**
evince /ɪˈvɪns/
intimate /ˈɪntɪˌmeɪt/
peruse /pəˈruːz/

6 **Writing: formal style**

*Suggested answer*

Dear colleagues

Several of our corporate clients possess the rights to valuable intellectual property assets, and they have enquired if we could assist them with matters concerning secured transactions and these assets. For this reason, I firmly believe it is important that we ensure that our knowledge in this area is up-to-date.

Therefore I am writing to inform you that I have arranged an in-company seminar on perfecting IP assets as security interests. The seminar will be held by a highly respected expert in the field on Monday, October 26 from 9 a.m. to 5 p.m. Please note that the seminar commences at 9 a.m.

I have attached a list of topics to be covered in the seminar which I would ask you to peruse.

I strongly advise you to take part in the seminar. Thus I suggest that you make sure you have no other appointments that day. I sincerely hope you can come. Please inform me whether you will attend by the close of business today.

Yours sincerely

Martin Black

(166 words)

# 14 Debtor–creditor

## Teacher's brief

**Debtor–creditor** is the name for the field of law which deals with interactions between debtors and creditors when their relationship collapses. Typically this occurs when a company goes out of business and many creditors have to fight over a limited pool of **assets**. The popular image of a pack of vultures feeding on a dying animal is a little unfair, as the creditors are simply trying to recover their own money before others claim it for themselves. Much of the work of debtor-creditor lawyers is to protect their clients in anticipation of such a collapse: protecting creditors by **liens** (official claims on property) and protecting debtors' assets by, for example, setting up private limited companies to hold those assets (as in the case study in Listening A).

There is considerable confusion over the terms **bankruptcy**, **insolvency**, **receivership** and **liquidation**. Each term has several meanings, depending on whether one is using British or American English, or general or legal English. In general British English, **bankruptcy** is the most familiar term for 'going bust', but in a strict legal sense, in British English it only applies to individuals and partnerships. British *companies* do not go bankrupt; they are **liquidated**. In American English, on the other hand, companies, like individuals and partnerships, can be declared bankrupt. **Bankruptcy** in American English involves a company or individual handing over control of its financial affairs to a bankruptcy court, which distributes the bankrupt individual's or company's assets between creditors. Bankruptcy is a legal finding, while **insolvency** (in both British and American English) usually refers simply to the state of being unable to pay one's debts – a state which typically leads to liquidation/bankruptcy. Confusingly, in American legal English there is a secondary meaning of **insolvency**: a determination by a court which allows a company's assets to be sold to pay off creditors. **Liquidation**, used only in British English, is the process of turning a company's assets into cash to be distributed among creditors. Finally, **receivership** is more like intensive care than a vultures' feast: it involves placing the affairs of an insolvent company under the control of an official receiver, who manages that company pending a court decision on liquidation/bankruptcy.

Reading A highlights the concept of **favoured status**: the ability of some creditors to recover their money ahead of other creditors. This is important, as there is usually not enough money available to pay all the creditors. Those who are not favoured are more likely to lose their money. Unit 13 dealt with one such mechanism for achieving favoured status: **consensual liens**, which must be **perfected** through registration. Other types of lien are those which can be imposed by court action (**judicial liens**) and those which apply automatically as a result of the relationship between the creditor and the debtor (**statutory liens**). Apart from liens, creditors may have some sort of **priority** status (e.g. unpaid employees and tax offices).

One important type of judicial lien is an **attachment lien**, which involves the seizure of a debtor's assets in advance of a court decision. Such liens are imposed when there is a high risk that the debtor will attempt to evade the court's decision. Reading B provides an extract from a US Civil Practice and Remedies code setting out the circumstances under which such a lien can be imposed. Listening A then presents the differences between these pre-judgment attachments liens and **judgment liens**, which are imposed after a case is decided. The speaker in Listening A is a lawyer advising clients how to protect their assets from such liens.

Reading C is an excerpt from a guide for lawyers considering a career as an **insolvency practitioner** (IP). This is a very specialised profession within the UK, and as well as providing essential advice during delicate restructurings and liquidations, IPs can find themselves running insolvent companies themselves.

Most of the rest of the unit focuses on the **recruitment** process, and uses the field of insolvency law as a context for **job adverts**, a **covering letter** (to accompany a CV in a job application), a **job interview** and a post-interview **thank-you letter**). All of these are important skills, both for new lawyers who may be looking for a job and for existing lawyers who may have to recruit other lawyers.

Reading E is an article arguing for the EU's insolvency laws to make use of **court-supervised restructurings**, as in the US's Chapter 11 Bankruptcy process. The EU does have a common insolvency regulation, but there is no middle ground between **out-of-court restructurings** (which are often messy attempts to keep a company alive) and **liquidations** (which are the end of a company's existence). Chapter 11 Bankruptcy, on the other hand, allows a court to take control of a company's debts and to protect the company from collapse while it solves its problems. This process is hailed as a (qualified) success in Reading E, but others might argue that it offers too much protection to insolvent companies (such as, recently, two of the biggest car makers, General Motors and Chrysler), which they use to compete unfairly with more successful companies.

**Further information**

○ The UK's Insolvency Service, part of the Department of Trade and Industry, offers very thorough information on all aspects of **insolvency**, including a useful glossary, on its website (http://www.insolvency.gov.uk).

○ Reading B is an extract from a **Civil Practice and Remedies code**. Each US state has its own code. See, for example, section 61 of Texas's code at http://law.justia.com/texas/codes/2005/cp.html.

○ For an excellent guide to **asset protection**, see http://law.freeadvice.com/estate_planning/asset_protection. For a guide to the shady side of the asset protection industry, see http://www.quatloos.com/asset_protection_scams.htm.

○ There are countless websites devoted to **job adverts for lawyers** (such as those in Reading D), for example http://www.simplylawjobs.com and http://www.lawjobs.com.

○ There are many online articles on **insolvency in the EU**, as a search for 'European insolvency regulation' will demonstrate. See, for example, www.insol-europe.org/download/file/575, which provides some background to Reading E.

○ **Chapter 11 bankruptcy** is explained succinctly at http://en.wikipedia.org/wiki/Chapter_11. For the complete US Bankruptcy Code, see http://www4.law.cornell.edu/uscode/html/uscode11/usc_sup_01_11.html.

## Discussion

Use these questions to generate a discussion.

a   What is the difference between insolvency, bankruptcy and liquidation? Can you think of famous cases?

b   Is liquidation always a bad thing? Think about its positive and negative effects on the following groups: owners, employees, customers, creditors, debtors, competitors, the market.

c   How can creditors minimise their risks? (This question leads directly into Reading A, so avoid giving any answers. Try to get students thinking in terms of liens.)

**⇒ Suggested answers**

a   See Teacher's brief above. Most famous cases of insolvency also involve bankruptcy/liquidation (e.g. BCCI, Barings Bank and Railtrack in the UK, Lehman Brothers, Enron and TWA in the US, Sabena in Belgium, etc.), but in the US, insolvent companies may file for

Chapter 11 bankruptcy, which prevents liquidation (e.g. most of the major US airlines, General Motors, Chrysler). Famous individuals who have been declared bankrupt include Mark Twain, Henry John Heinz (founder of HJ Heinz Company), Oscar Wilde, Henry Ford (founder of The Ford Motor Company), Walt Disney, US President Ulysses S. Grant, and Donald Trump. (Source: http://www.angelfire.com/stars4/lists/bankruptcies.html)

b   Obviously the question is so broad that the answer will be 'It depends', but the question then becomes 'It depends on what?'. The negative effects of liquidation are all too obvious: loss of jobs, financial destitution, destruction of value, inability to recover debts, etc., while the positive effects require a little more thought. As the above list of individuals suggests, bankruptcy for businessmen such as Heinz, Ford and Disney may have been a short-term set-back on the road to greater things, and may well have been what drove them to greatness. The same can be said for employees and customers, or at least some of them. Debtors, if they are well protected (e.g. by liens), may end up losing nothing, and may even profit if they are very clever and lucky. Competitors are the obvious winners, but the effect on the market as a whole is more complicated, as it depends on the interrelationship between all of these groups. In general, the liquidation of a bad company can make room for good companies to take its place, which is arguably better for the economy long term.

## 1 Reading A: Introduction to debtor–creditor

Tell students to read the three types of lien to try to predict which definition matches each one and then to read the text carefully to find out. If the matching is too easy, ask students to find examples of each type of lien. Ask them also to find examples of two classes of creditor.

When they have finished reading, tell them to discuss their answers with a partner, as well as what they understand by the various key terms in bold. Then tell them to close their books before eliciting the answers from the class.

**⇒ Answers**
**1** b   **2** a   **3** c
○ Examples of consensual liens: mortgages and security interests
○ Examples of judicial liens: attachment liens, garnishment, judgment liens and execution liens
○ Examples of statutory liens: tax liens and mechanic's liens
○ Two classes of creditors: priority creditors (e.g. wage earners, landlords and tax collectors) and general creditors (i.e. the majority of creditors)

**Background notes**
○ A *lien* /liːn/ is the general term for any official document which represents a claim against property for payment for a debt. The term includes *mortgages*.
○ In Unit 13, the term *attachment* referred to creation of an enforceable security interest, typically with the consent of both the lender and the borrower. An *attachment lien*, on the other hand, involves the seizure of the borrower's property in anticipation of a *judgment lien*, and is likely to be fiercely resisted by the borrower. Confusingly, the term *attachment* can also be used to mean *attachment lien* (see http://dictionary.law.com).
○ *Garnishment* often refers to the process whereby third parties who owe money to a debtor are ordered to pay that money directly to a creditor. For example, if A borrows money from B to buy a car, and then fails to repay B, B may seek a garnishment forcing A's employers (the *garnishee*) to pay A's salary directly to B until the debt is repaid.
○ *Judgment liens* and *execution liens* are both created by courts. *Judgment liens* are placed on the real property of a debtor, while *execution liens* can be placed on any sort of property. Specifically, *judgment liens* are used as a kind of threat to a debtor: pay what you owe or you'll lose your house. *Execution liens* are more active: they give an officer of the court the right to seize the property of the losing party in a lawsuit (= the judgment debtor) in order to pay for the judgment.
○ *Mechanic's liens* in fact have little in common with (e.g. car) mechanics, as they apply to real estate and not movable items such as cars. They are more likely to benefit builders, architects and other craftsmen who have provided a service on a piece of real estate, and who can use them to guarantee that they receive payment for that service.
○ *First-in-time rules* apply to both priority creditors and general creditors. For example, if there are two claimants for the same asset, the one with the higher

priority should win. But if both claimants have equal priority, the winner is the claimant whose claim was made first in time.

○ A *group action* is simply an *action* (*lawsuit*) made by a group of people (e.g. many creditors).

## 2 Key terms: Types of lien

Tell students to work in pairs to complete the exercise. Encourage them to use the Glossary booklet, as they will probably find it difficult without it. When they have finished, go through the answers carefully, paying attention to differences between similar terms (e.g. *execution lien* and *judgment lien*: see Background notes above). Test students by reading a definition to elicit each of the key terms, and then tell students to test each other in the same way in pairs.

**Answers**
**1** f **2** g **3** e **4** b **5** d **6** c **7** h **8** a

## 3 Reading B: Statutes governing attachment

**3.1** Elicit from the class what an *attachment lien* is, and under what circumstances it might be available to a creditor. Then tell them to read the introduction (SB page 193) and the text to answer the questions. Tell them also to decide which of the specific grounds relates to the most serious risk for a creditor. When they have finished, check the answers with the class.

**Answers**
**1** Writ of attachment
**2** *Grounds* means 'reason' in this context.
**3** Creditor = plaintiff; debtor = defendant
**4** Section 61.001: all four points
Section 61.002: one of the nine

The question of which of the specific grounds relates to the greatest risk is obviously subjective, but they seem to increase in riskiness: there is no automatic reason to assume that a foreign corporation (1) will defraud creditors, while a defendant who has already tricked the creditor (9) seems to represent a high risk.

**Background notes**
○ The text uses American English, where a *writ* /rɪt/ is a written order by a judge requiring a person to fulfil a specific action. In British English, *writ* used to refer to the document that started a claim in court, but this has been replaced by the term 'claim form'.
○ If you *harass* /həˈræs/ somebody, you systematically and deliberately make their life difficult, e.g. by verbal abuse, unwanted telephone calls, following them, etc.

**3.2** Tell students to work in pairs to attempt to define the words, and to use the context of Reading B to help them work out meanings. When they have finished, go through the answers with the class. Check any other vocabulary problems from the text, including *to be about to do something*.

**Suggested answers**
**1** to annoy or upset the defendant through a persistent, unwanted action
**2** to deliver legal documents to someone
**3** to get rid of property so that it is not possible to repay a debt owed to creditors
**4** to acquire property dishonestly, with the intent to defraud

**3.3** Tell students to do this in pairs. When they have finished, check the answers with the class.

**Answers**
**1** 2 **2** 1 **3** 9 **4** 3

## CD2 T13–14 4 Listening A: Protecting assets from judicial liens

Elicit from the class what they understand by the term *asset protection*, and what it involves. Tell them to read the introduction for a brief answer. For a much fuller answer, see http://law. freeadvice.com/estate_planning/asset_protection.

**4.1** Tell students to predict whether each feature is genuine or not. Then play the first part of the presentation for them to check. After the recording, tell them to compare their answers with a partner, and then go through the answers with the class.

**Transcript »** STUDENT'S BOOK **page 293**

 **Answers**
1, 4, 5, 6, 7

**Background notes**
- A *legal adversary* is the opposing party in a lawsuit.
- A *trust deed* (or *deed of trust*) involves handing over title to real property until a loan is repaid. The trustee holds title to the real property on behalf of the lender.
- If a creditor *forecloses* on real estate, he terminates a mortgage and takes title to the real estate.

**Optional extension**
Tell students to work in pairs to try to remember eight things that you cannot do if your assets are frozen, and three things that your adversary can do. Then play the first part of the recording a second time for them to check their answers. Allow them to check again in pairs before you go through the answers with the class.

**Answers**
- You cannot (1) pay bills, (2) run your business, (3) withdraw your money, (4) collect rents, (5) collect incomes, (6) sell your property, (7) refinance your property, or (8) negotiate effectively with your adversary.
- Your adversary can (1) attach your property during or after the lawsuit, (2) foreclose on the real estate, and (3) seize accounts in your name.

**4.2** Tell students to read the questions and to predict the answers in pairs. Then play the second part of the presentation for them to check their predictions. After the recording, tell them to discuss their answers in pairs before going through them with the class.

**Transcript »** STUDENT'S BOOK **page 293**

 **Answers**
1. They set up a plan for him using several limited liability companies to hold the properties.
2. Since the creditor had no security for his judgment and stood to collect nothing, Ed was in a position to negotiate a favourable settlement.
3. The judge in the case ruled that the assets were properly protected and could not be reached by a lien.

**Background note**
*Leverage* /ˈlevərɪdʒ/ is used in business and law to describe a form of financing, whereby money is borrowed to buy certain assets, which are then used as security for additional loans. However, in the context of the listening, *leverage* simply refers to negotiating power. Ed used his strong position to negotiate an extremely favourable deal.

**Optional extension**
Write the following figures on the board:
5   $3 million   $1.5 million   $75,000
$80,000   2   $2,000
Tell students to listen to the recording again to find out what each figure refers to. After the recording, tell them to discuss their answers in pairs before you go through them with the class.

**Answers**
- Ed owned five apartment buildings.
- Ed's buildings were worth $3 million.
- There was a judgment against Ed for $1.5 million.
- He settled the case for $75,000.
- The architect had savings of $80,000.
- The architect was served with a lawsuit two years after setting up the plan.
- He settled the case for under $2,000.

**Optional extension**
The two anecdotes from Listening A provide a good context for practising so-called third-conditional structures.
Write the following fragment from the listening on the board – *Had he not set up the plan, ... –*

and elicit a) another way of phrasing it,
b) how the sentence continued in the
recording, c) what it means (i.e. Did he set
up the plan? Was he in big trouble?), and
d) in what situations such structures are used.

**Answers**

**a**   *If he had not set up the plan, …*

**b**   *… he'd have been in big trouble.*

**c**   He did set up the plan, and as a result
was not in big trouble.

**d**   We use such structures to speculate
about unreal past situations.

Tell students to work in pairs to come up with
between five and ten further continuations of
the sentence *Had he not set up the plan …* for
both Ed and the architect, either directly from
the listening or from students' imaginations.
When they have finished, elicit sentences
from the class, perhaps following the 'Easy
first' procedure (see Games and activities
section, page xvi).

**Suggested answers**

… the plaintiff would have had a lien on all
of Ed's real estate.

… Ed's property would have been frozen and
then seized.

… the plaintiff would not have taken a penny
less than the full amount of the judgment.

… Ed would not have been able to use
leverage to obtain a favourable settlement.

… Ed could have been weak and vulnerable.

… the architect would have lost his savings.

… the plaintiff would not have lost interest in
the case.

**Optional extension**
**Photocopiable worksheet 14.1**

Divide the class into pairs and distribute role
cards (see Photocopiable worksheet 14.1) so
that each pair consists of one lawyer and one
client. If you have an odd number of students,
the group of three should include a pair of
lawyers (with a shared role card). Try to arrange
it so that there are more 'Lawyer 1' roles than
'Lawyer 2' roles, and assign 'Lawyer 2' to the
most experienced lawyers in the class. (Lawyer
2's task is to trick the client. There is no
suggestion that students need to practise this
skill, but they do need to learn to 'think like the
enemy' in order to avoid being tricked
(or having their clients tricked) in this way.)

Tell the groups to role-play a brief meeting (up
to five minutes) between the clients and their
lawyers in order for the lawyers to give some
advice on asset protection. As many students
are unlikely to be familiar with the intricacies
of this field, you may either tell them to do
some research in advance of the role-play, or
you may allow them to invent all the details.
When they have finished, tell the clients to
find a new lawyer in order to get a second
opinion, and to repeat the exercise. It is not
necessary that they meet 'Lawyer 1' once and
'Lawyer 2' once, as each lawyer is likely to
give different advice.
After this second role-play, get some feedback
from the clients on which lawyers gave the
best advice, and which lawyers gave the
worst/ most dangerous advice.

# 5   Reading C: A career as an insolvency practitioner

Elicit from the class what an insolvency
practitioner does, and what they would expect to
read in a guide for lawyers considering a career in
this field. Then tell them to read the introduction
(SB page 195) to check.

**Optional lead-in**
**Photocopiable worksheet 14.2**

Photocopiable worksheet 14.2 contains nine
discussion questions related to the text. Tell
students to discuss the questions briefly in
pairs, and then to read the text to find which
paragraph (1–9) relates to which question.
When they have finished reading, they should
discuss the nine questions again with a
partner, comparing their opinions with those
expressed in the text. Finally, go through the
answers with the class. There may, of course,
be disagreement on the answers to the
questions (e.g. question h), but not on which
paragraph deals with each question. Note that
the skill of matching sentences (or, in this
case, questions) to paragraphs is useful for
Part 4 of the ILEC Test of Reading.

**Answers**

**a** 2   **b** 5   **c** 6   **d** 9   **e** 7   **f** 3   **g** 8
**h** 1   **i** 4

**5.1** Tell students to read the text quickly to find the answers to the two questions. When they have finished, discuss the answers with the class.

➡ **Answers**

1 In the course of insolvency proceedings or the restructuring and rescuing of a business, an insolvency practitioner does not only deal with financial matters. He or she must also be able to work with a wide range of people with conflicting interests – from creditors to directors to employees – many of whom may be in highly emotional states.

2 Recognised professional bodies are responsible for licensing insolvency practitioners.

🖊 **Background notes**

○ The *viability* /ˌvaɪəˈbɪlɪti/ of a business is its ability to continue in business.

○ A *hard-bitten* businessman is tough, experienced and unlikely to be distracted by appeals to the emotions.

○ *Administrations* are arrangements where an insolvency practitioner takes over the running of an insolvent company in an effort to rescue it or at least establish whether it can be rescued. *Administrative receiverships* are similar, although their objective is not to rescue the company but simply to recover money for creditors. *Voluntary arrangements* are arrangements made by company directors to pay creditors over an agreed period of time. See http://www.insolvency.gov.uk for a glossary of such terms.

○ If a licence is *revoked*, it ceases to be valid.

○ A *trustee in bankruptcy* is given ownership and responsibility for supervising the affairs of a bankrupt company.

○ *Sequestration* means 'confiscation'. A *trustee in sequestration* takes over ownership and responsibility for a company which has been confiscated from its previous owners.

○ A *deed of arrangement* is a device for setting up a *voluntary arrangement* (see above). If it is accepted by a majority of creditors (both in number and in value), it applies to all creditors (see http://www.insolvency.gov.uk/guidanceleaflets/deeds/deeds.htm).

**5.2** Tell students to discuss the statements in pairs. You may also ask them to do Exercise 5.3 before you go through the answers with the class. You may speculate with the class as to what an insolvency practitioner would have to do in order for his/her licence to be revoked.

➡ **Answers**

1 False (There are very few insolvency practitioners, and there is no indication that the industry is expanding.)

2 True

3 False (A licence can be revoked if the holder ceases to be a 'fit and proper person'.)

**5.3** This can be done at the same time as Exercise 5.2. When you go through the answers with the class, make sure students know why the alternative answers are wrong (e.g. *to deal in antiques / to deal with a situation*).

➡ **Answers**

1 secured; benefit    2 with; legally
3 proposed    4 up

# 6 Speaking A: Discussing insolvency work

**6.1** Tell students to discuss these phrases in pairs. You may ask them to discuss the questions in Exercise 6.2 as well before going through the answers and opening up the discussion to involve the whole class.

**6.2** This might be best done with the whole class. Elicit what sort of person would make a good insolvency practitioner, what skills and experience they need, and whether anybody in the group would be suitable for such a career.

## 7 Reading D: Job opportunities in insolvency

Tell students to read the introduction (SB page 197) and discuss the two questions as a class. One obvious source of job adverts is the Internet, but try to elicit less obvious sources such as industry journals and newspapers.

**7.1** Discuss this question with the whole class.

**Answers**
PQE = post-qualification experience;
NQ = newly qualified

**7.2** Tell students to work alone to scan the advertisements and answer the questions. Set a tight time limit (two or three minutes), after which tell students to compare their answers with a partner. Then go through the answers with the class.

**Answers**
**1** A  **2** B  **3** B  **4** A  **5** A

**Background notes**
- ○ A *full-service* law firm offers service in a range of specialist areas.
- ○ A company's *core values* are what it sees as the unchangeable philosophies which guide its decisions.
- ○ If you *reconcile* /ˈrekənˌsaɪl/ differing requirements, you find a balance which satisfies both requirements as best as possible.
- ○ The *production of know-how* involves increasing the knowledge, skills and expertise of oneself and one's colleagues.
- ○ A *salaried partner* has limited liability in a law firm, and less influence than a senior or full partner.

**7.3** Tell students to discuss the two questions with a partner. When they have finished, discuss the answers briefly with the class.

**Suggested answer**
**1** The firm behind the first advert is a very large international firm with offices all over the world. The firm behind the second advert is considerably smaller and operates domestically, although it does have some international clients.

---

**Optional extension**

As well as responding to such adverts, students may also need to produce their own adverts in English. It may therefore be useful to analyse the language of the two adverts (and any others you can find, for example at http://www.simplylawjobs.com or http://www.lawjobs.com).
Discuss with the class what they notice about the grammatical subject of each sentence in the adverts.

**Suggested answer**
The subject of almost every sentence involves *we/our* or *you/your*: *Our firm ..., Our vision ..., You will act ..., You will gain ..., You will be working ..., Your general role ..., We are offering ..., Our clients ..., You will be working ..., You will also have ...* .
The *we/our* sentences are at the beginning of the adverts, and the *you/your* sentences are at the end.
You may also elicit/draw attention to the fact that, as is typical of formal written English, the noun phrases tend to be long and to carry most of the meaning, while the verb phrases tend to be used less often and to carry little meaning. For example, all the bullet points in the first advert are noun phrases. There are also many 'hidden verbs' which have been converted into nouns (e.g. *the firms merged → the merger of the firms; we envisage → our vision is; you will restructure corporations → you will act on corporate restructurings; you may co-operate across borders → cross-border co-operation activities*); you could ask students to find more examples.
As a follow-up, put students in small groups to write their own adverts (e.g. for a dream job or a nightmare job), perhaps following the 'Team writing' procedure (see Writing section, page xiv).

---

## 8 Text analysis: A covering letter

Elicit from the class a) what a covering letter is, b) why it is important to write it correctly, and c) what structure it should follow. Then tell students to read the introduction (SB page 199) to compare it with their suggestions.

### Language note
*Résumé* /'rezʊˌmeɪ/ is a French word. It is common in American English to write it without the accents (although this is not advised, as it creates confusion with the verb *resume* /rɪ'zjuːm/).

Tell students to work alone to match the functions with the sentences. When they have finished, tell them to compare their answers with a partner, and then go through the answers with the class.

 **Answers**
**a** 4, 5, 6 **b** 2 **c** 10 **d** 1 **e** 9 **f** 3, 7, 8

### Optional extension
Tell students to underline the phrases from the covering letter which they could use in their own letters. Allow them to compare their answers with a partner before going through them with the class. Note that *Yours sincerely* would also be an acceptable ending to the letter.

### Suggested answer
I would like to apply for the post of a Company Commercial Solicitor in your firm as advertised on the website www.legalpositions. com. As a recent law-school graduate, I was particularly happy to see that the position you are offering is open to newly qualified lawyers. You will see from my enclosed CV that I completed my law studies in Rome with honours, and spent one year studying law in Edinburgh. I am especially interested in the position you are offering, since I have relevant work experience in the field of insolvency. I spent three summers working as a clerk in a mid-si3ed commercial law firm in Manchester. While assisting with the insolvency work carried out there, I developed a keen interest in becoming an insolvency practitioner. In addition, I am a student member of the Insolvency Practitioners Association in the UK, and two articles I wrote in English were published in their newsletter. I may also add that I achieved a high score on the International Legal English Certificate Examination. I would welcome the opportunity to work as part of your successful team, to benefit from

your extensive experience, and to put my training, experience and enthusiasm into practice for your firm.
I look forward to hearing from you.
Sincerely

## 9 Writing A: A covering letter
Encourage students to find their own adverts for jobs in fields that are of interest to them and which they would genuinely have a chance of getting. Encourage them to copy many of the useful phrases from the letter from Exercise 8, but to ensure that their letters are still tailored both to the specific jobs and to their own strengths. The writing can be done in class or at home.

An essential part of this activity is the proofreading stage. Tell students to proofread each other's work and to suggest improvements. They may feel uncomfortable with this idea, but you should point out that the skill of proofreading is extremely important. While they are proofreading you should monitor carefully to deal with any queries and to point them in the right direction.

### Optional extension
**Photocopiable worksheet 14.3**

If students feel uncomfortable proofreading each other's work, or if they need further practice, Photocopiable worksheet 14.3 offers a deliberately poor covering letter which needs some radical proofreading.
Tell students to work in pairs to find and correct mistakes in the letter. Tell them to start with 'local' errors involving spelling, punctuation, grammar and vocabulary. Then they should consider 'global' errors concerning style, content and layout. When they have finished, go through the answers with the class.

### Suggested answers
*Local errors*
Dear Harold [should be *Dear Mr Jackson*]
I'm [too informal: should be *I am*] writting [spelling: should be *writing*] in a response [grammar: should be *in response*] to your advert [too informal: should be *advertisement*] at [vocabulary: should be *on*] the website www.legalpositions.com. You say you are

offering an exciting opportunity for an NQ Company Commercial Solicitor [irrelevant: delete this sentence]. I am a new-qualificated [vocabulary and punctuation: should be *newly qualified*] Company Commercial Solicitor and I want [too direct: should be *I would like*] to join your team. I am enclosing [too casual: should be *I enclose*] my CV.

I am [grammar: add *an*] outgoing and reliable person. I love a challenge, what [grammar: should be *which*] means that working for your firm will [too direct: should be *would*] be a really good [too casual: should be, e.g. *an excellent*] experience for me. I know a lot of about [grammar: delete *of*] IT and e-commerce because I am buying [grammar: should be *I buy*] a lot of computer games on Internet [grammar: should be *the Internet*]. I graduated three months ago. I worked [grammar: should be *I have worked*] in many big law firms. I specialy interested [grammar/spelling: should be *I am especially interested*] in international commercial law, it [grammar: should be *which*] is field [grammar: should be *a field*], [punctuation: no comma] that require [grammar: should be *requires*] much [grammar: should be *a lot of* or *a great deal of*] analitical [spelling: should be *analytical*] thinking and attention to the details [grammar: should be *attention to detail*]. Those [grammar: should be *These*] are my qualities.

Please, [punctuation: delete comma] interview me. I am person [grammar: should be *the person*], [punctuation: delete comma] what [grammar: delete *what*] you look for [grammar: should be *are looking for*]. I'm look [grammar: should be *I look*] forward to hear [grammar: should be *hearing from*] you.

Yours faithfully [style: should be *Yours sincerely*]

Vincent Fott

### Global errors

○ Weak introduction: No clear statement of reason for writing, but too much on the content of the advert. No need to mention CV. There should be something to make the reader interested in Mr Fott as a potential employee.

○ The main part starts badly with subjective character adjectives rather than facts and evidence.

○ The reference to online buying is completely irrelevant (unless it is used as evidence of a real skill which is relevant to the job) and is likely to put off potential employers.

○ The references to education and work experience are too vague; they need to specify succinctly where, when, how long, and what exactly they involved. Mr Fott needs to provide evidence for his qualities, rather than simply claim to have them.

○ The concluding paragraph is weak and makes no reference to any of the points made earlier. The request for an interview sounds desperate, and again there is nothing to suggest that Mr Fott has anything to offer the law firm.

## (CD2 T15) 10 Listening B: A job interview

Elicit from the class what the point of a job interview is, and what interviewers hope to achieve with their questions. Then tell students to read the introduction (SB page 200) to compare it with their suggestions.

**10.1** Do this quickly with the whole class. Do not actually discuss answers to the questions at this stage, as these will be practised later. Tell students to ignore the boxes beside each question, as these will be used for Exercise 10.3.

**10.2** Tell students to listen to answer the two questions, and to underline the sections of the job advert (SB page 198) which are mentioned in the interview. After the recording, tell students to compare their answers in pairs and then check with the class.

**Transcript »** STUDENT'S BOOK **page 293**

➡ **Answers**

**1** He is applying for job A, an associate in the restructuring and insolvency team of the international law firm. Many sections of the job advert were mentioned, including:

○ ... the merger ...
○ ... around the world ...
○ ... corporate restructurings ...
○ ... cross-border ...
○ As our clients' business becomes increasingly global ...

○ ... differing requirements of several domestic law regimes ...

○ Keen interest and relevant experience in restructuring and insolvency work

○ Current membership in a recognised Insolvency Practitioners Association

○ Strong analytical skills

○ Fluency in ... English and preferably another European language

2 Mr Berger says that he likes working on cross-border insolvency cases because the fact that the laws on insolvency aren't unified in Europe means that the work is challenging. He also says that the work is like a puzzle in which people's livelihoods are at stake, and which involves understanding the relevant laws, the personalities involved, and finding the best solution for his clients.

3 When he was a student, he spent a summer working as a clerk at a law firm in the City. He also studied law in London for a semester.

4 Regarding his own English skills, Mr Berger says that he is working on improving his pronunciation.

5 He does corporate restructuring in an Austrian commercial law firm in Vienna and has worked on a few cross-border insolvency cases.

6 He says that he has the background required for the position (experience in insolvency work, an international perspective, knowledge of languages), as well as the required membership in the Insolvency Practitioners Association.

7 He'd like to know how attorneys are trained in the firm.

**10.3** Tell students to discuss with a partner which questions were asked and what Mr Berger said about each. Then play the recording a second time for them to check their ideas. After the recording, tell them to discuss the questions again with a partner. You may also tell them to discuss the questions in Exercise 10.4 before you check all the answers together.

**Answers**

Questions 1, 8, 9 and 11 were asked.

**10.4** Students discuss the questions in pairs and then listen again to check their answers. Then go through the answers with the class.

**Answers**

1 Mr Berger knew of the firm already because it is very well known, and he also heard about the merger in the news. He saw the job advert on the firm's website.

2 He wants to be a part of a large international organisation and to have clients all over the globe. He would like to work in an international context, to make use of his language skills and to work with people from different backgrounds.

## 11  Speaking B: A job interview

Make sure students have a specific job in mind before they go any further with this exercise. Ideally, the job interviews should be based on the covering letters students wrote in Exercise 9. If possible, the interviews should be for jobs that students themselves have chosen (e.g. from Internet adverts).

Allow time (around five minutes) for students to prepare by looking at the questions in Exercise 10.1 and planning their answers.

The role-plays can be done in pairs or, if you want to increase the stress, groups of three or four, with a panel of interviewers. If every student is to have an interview, obviously the larger the groups, the longer the activity will take.

Before you start the role-plays, make sure the interviewers know which job their interviewees have applied for. Set a time limit (around five minutes per interview), and point out that there will probably not be enough time to ask all the questions. After the time limit, tell the interviewers to spend a few minutes giving feedback on their interviewee's performance, and then tell them to swap roles.

At the end of all the interviews, discuss with the group the best answers to each of the questions.

## 12 Writing B: A thank-you note

Elicit from the class what thank-you notes are (in the context of job applications), and whether they are important. Then tell students to read the introduction to compare it with their answers.

**12.1** Tell students to do the exercise alone and then to check their answers with a partner. When you go through the answers with the class, discuss which sections of the letter could be used in any thank-you letter.

 **Answers**
1 d   2 b   3 c   4 a   5 e

Virtually the whole text could be copied into any thank-you letter, other than the following very job-specific references: *Senior Insolvency Practitioner, plans for expansion, corporate insolvency work, supervise a case from commencement of liquidation to closure.* However, there is an obvious danger in copying: other applicants may also copy from the same source. Some degree of originality is still recommended.

---

**Optional extension**

Write the following words on the board: *appreciated background closure compatible confident expansion gathered hearing hospitality members mentioned opportunity position supervise*

Tell students to close their books and to write the numbers 1–14 in their notebooks. Read the thank-you letter aloud slowly, substituting a number for each of the words on the board (e.g. *Thank you again for the one to interview for the two of ...*). Do not repeat any sentences at this stage. Students should choose one of the words from the board for each number. When you reach the end of the letter, ask if any students have all 14 words. If not, allow each student in turn to ask you to repeat the sentence containing one of the numbers. Keep repeating sentences until one student shouts 'Bingo!' to indicate that he/she has all the words. Then go through the answers to see if the winner really has won. If not, keep going until you have a winner.

---

**12.2** Discuss the questions with the whole group.

 **Answers**
1 *I especially enjoyed hearing about your firm's plans for expansion.*
2 *As I mentioned during our conversation, the experience I gathered in my previous employment has prepared me well for corporate insolvency work.*
3 The purpose is to state in concise form what the applicant believes she can offer to the firm; it is also her final opportunity to present a strong reason why the firm should hire her.
4 *I look forward to hearing from you.*

**12.3** It is a good idea to elicit/remind students of what Franz Berger and Ms Hall discussed in their interview (Listening B), as this will provide content for the writing. Alternatively, students could write a thank-you letter for the interviews they role-played in Exercise 11. Remind students that they can copy a lot of useful phrases, as well as the overall structure of the letter, from the sample in Exercise 12.1.

The writing can be done at home or in class. You may decide to do this as a speaking exercise: students dictate their thank-you letters to a partner as if to a secretary (although there is no need for partners to write the letters down). When they have finished, ask some students to dictate their letters to the class. Make sure they have included all of the bullet points.

 **Suggested answer**

Dear Ms Hall

Thank you again for the opportunity to interview for the position of Associate Lawyer in your firm. I appreciated your hospitality and enjoyed meeting you and members of your staff. I especially enjoyed hearing about your firm's mentoring programme.
The interview convinced me that my background as a commercial lawyer, my interest in different legal systems, and my foreign language skills are compatible with the goals of your firm. As I mentioned during our conversation, the experience I gathered in my previous employment has prepared me

well for corporate restructuring work.
I am confident that my ability to deal with complex cross-border insolvency cases will be of value to your firm.
I look forward to hearing from you.
Yours sincerely

Franz Berger

(118 words)

# 13 Reading E: Making a case

Tell students to read the introduction (SB page 202) to find out what the topic of the Reading will be (Answer: insolvencies in Europe).

 **Background note**
*Cross-border insolvencies* are simply insolvencies involving companies from one jurisdiction which have creditors in different jurisdictions. There is a potential for dispute over which jurisdiction's regulations govern the debtor–creditor relationship. The EU's common insolvency regulation (see http://eur-lex.europa.eu/LexUriServ/LexUriServ.do?uri=CELEX:32000R1346:EN:HTML) is intended to resolve any such confusion. The Reading is about European insolvencies in general, rather than cross-border ones.

**13.1** Discuss this question with the whole class.

 **Answer**
In this context, *case* means a set of statements arguing for a standpoint. A synonym would be *argument*.

**13.2** Tell students to read the first two paragraphs to answer the two questions. Set a short time limit (around a minute). When the time is up, discuss the answers with the class. Elicit from students what they know about EU insolvency laws and Chapter 11 bankruptcy.

 **Answers**
1 The weakness they point to is the fact that Europe does not have any legal regime to support court-supervised restructuring, as opposed to bankruptcies or liquidations.

2 The system they propose as a model for reform is the US Bankruptcy Code's Chapter 11.

 **Background note**
*Court-supervised debt restructuring* is an attempt to revive an insolvent company by passing control of the company's debts to a court. The best-known framework for such restructuring is the US Bankruptcy Code's Chapter 11, but some other countries have similar systems. As Reading E notes, however, the EU has no equivalent. Individual jurisdictions have their own methods for restructuring insolvent companies (e.g. the UK's 'administration'), but there is no unified framework for the EU as a whole.

 **Pronunciation note**
regime /reɪˈʒiːm/

**13.3** Tell students to read the rest of the article to decide whether the statements are true or false. When they have finished, they should discuss their answers with a partner. Then go through the answers with the class.

 **Answers**
1 True
2 True
3 False (A company can file for Chapter 11 protection regardless of whether it is insolvent or not.)
4 True
5 False (Provisions provide for the Court to enforce a reorganisation plan, despite objections from some creditors.)

 **Background notes**
○ The article talks of *restructuring their balance sheets*. A company's *balance sheet* is its record of *assets* (what it owns) and *liabilities* (what it owes), so restructuring typically involves selling assets in order to pay for liabilities.
○ The term *destruction of value* refers to the idea that a complete company is worth more than the combined value of its individual assets (just like a new car

is worth more than its component parts if they were to be sold individually). The difference between the value of the complete company and the value of its component parts after liquidation is the destroyed value.

○ A *stay* is a short-term delay, authorised by a court, before a court ruling is enforced. This gives a losing defendant a little time, for example, to find the money to pay damages, or an insolvent company time to pay its debts. The term *automatic stay* has a precise legal meaning, as defined in the text. For more information, see, for example, http://www.moranlaw.net/stay.htm.

○ *Super-priority* is a mechanism to allow a creditor to 'jump the queue' and to be paid before any other creditors. Under Chapter 11, DIP financing places new creditors (i.e. those who lend money while the company is under Chapter 11 protection) in this super-priority position.

○ The phrase *cramdown provisions* derives, according to http://dictionary. msn.com, from the idea of a company's bankruptcy plans being crammed (pushed) down the throats of unwilling creditors.

 **Pronunciation notes**
equity /ˈekwɪti/
onerous /ˈəunərəs/

**13.4** Tell students to do this in pairs, and then check the answers with the class.

**Answers**
**1** d  **2** e  **3** a  **4** b  **5** c

**a** Tell students to look at the first three sentences in paragraph 1, the first sentence in paragraph 2, and the last two sentence-paragraphs to decide which are easy to understand and which are difficult.

**Suggested answers**
The first three are easy, while the other three are difficult.

**b** Elicit why some sentences are easier than others.

**Answer**
The easy sentences have short subjects (underlined below) at or near the beginning of the sentence. All three sentences make use of dummy subjects (*there* or *it*) in order to achieve this. Also, each subject has only one verb (boxed below). The difficult sentences have much longer subjects, and they each have two verbs per subject (co-ordinated by *and*).

**1** Over the last five years, there have been a number of big insolvencies and debt restructurings across Europe.

**2** It must be obvious to all objective commentators that Europe simply does not have an effective, or indeed any, legal regime to support court-supervised restructuring, as opposed to bankruptcies or liquidations.

**3** It is astonishing that there is simply no legal middle ground between out-of-court restructurings, with all of their uncertainties and differences of approach, and liquidations.

**4** The principle that it is preferable for insolvent companies (as well as their creditors and other stakeholders) to be reorganised rather than liquidated has long been recognised in the US and is now accepted in most European jurisdictions.

**5** In addition, two sets of provisions that particularly help insolvent companies to restructure allow the US Bankruptcy Court to reorganise the equity of an insolvent company without a vote of the shareholders and provide for the Court to enforce a reorganisation plan, despite objections from some creditors (known as cramdown provisions).

**6** The absence of provisions equivalent to some or all of the above in Europe both *affects* the economics of restructurings in Europe and *adds* an onerous layer of complexity and transaction risk.

**c** Have students suggest how the easy sentences could be made more difficult, and how the difficult ones could be made easier by using the same techniques. The point of making sentences more difficult is simply to focus attention on the differences between the two styles, and not, of course, to encourage students to make their own writing more difficult to understand.

### Suggested answers
(subjects underlined, verbs boxed, as above)

**1** *Over the last five years, <u>a number of big companies across Europe</u> have become insolvent and had their debts restructured.*

**2** *<u>That Europe simply does not have an effective, or indeed any, legal regime to support court-supervised restructuring, as opposed to bankruptcies or liquidations</u> must be obvious to all objective commentators.*

**3** *<u>That there is simply no legal middle ground between out-of-court restructurings, with all of their uncertainties and differences of approach, and liquidations</u> is astonishing.*

**4** *<u>It</u> has long been recognised in the US that it is preferable for insolvent companies (as well as their creditors and other stakeholders) to be reorganised rather than liquidated. <u>This principle</u> is now accepted in most European jurisdictions.*

**5** *In addition, <u>there</u> are two sets of provisions that particularly help insolvent companies to restructure. <u>One of these</u> allows the US Bankruptcy Court to reorganise the equity of an insolvent company without a vote of the shareholders. <u>The other</u> provides for the Court to enforce a reorganisation plan, despite objections from some creditors (known as cramdown provisions).*

**6** *<u>There</u> are no provisions equivalent to some or all of the above in Europe. <u>This</u> both affects the economics of restructurings in Europe and adds an onerous layer of complexity and transaction risk.*

## 14 Speaking C: Discussion on restructuring

Tell students to discuss these points in small groups. If they generate interesting discussion, open them up to include the whole class.

 Tell students to do the Internet activity as homework. See Using the Internet for research, page xviii.

# Language focus

## Answers

**1 Vocabulary: distinguishing meaning**

  **1** *distinction*: The others mean 'priority'.

  **2** *relinquish*: The others mean 'take by force'; *relinquish* means 'give'.

  **3** *urgent*: The others mean 'difficult'.

  **4** *judicial review*: The others refer to abstract frameworks; a *judicial review* is a legal process.

**2 Word formation**

| Verb | Abstract noun |
|---|---|
| seize | <u>sei</u>zure |
| pro<u>ceed</u> | pro<u>ceed</u>ings, pro<u>ce</u>dure |
| execute | exe<u>cu</u>tion |
| se<u>cure</u> | se<u>cu</u>rity |
| <u>li</u>quidate | liqui<u>da</u>tion |
| re<u>structure</u> | re<u>structuring</u> |

**3 Vocabulary: classes of creditors**

  **2** perfected  **3** paid  **4** pledged  **5** incurred

**4 Asking questions in an interview**

  **2** B  **3** A, B  **4** A  **5** A  **6** A, B  **7** B

  **8** A  **9** A, B

 **Background note**

*Pro bono* work is short for *pro bono publico* (= for the public good), and involves a lawyer helping somebody who is in need of legal support but who cannot afford to pay.

**5 Vocabulary: types of trustees**

  **1** appointed; vests  **2** seizure; ownership

  **3** insolvent; abandon  **4** pledged; trust

**6 Prepositions**

  **1** against; by  **2** in; as  **3** to  **4** on  **5** over

## Optional extension
## Photocopiable worksheet 14.4

Photocopiable worksheet 14.4 revises many of the useful vocabulary structures from the unit. It focuses on prepositions, but requires knowledge of both the surrounding language and debtor–creditor law for completion. Note that knowledge of prepositions and collocations is especially useful for Parts 1 and 2 of the ILEC Test of Reading.

Tell students to work in pairs to complete the exercise. Suggest that they do the easier gaps first, as this will eliminate possibilities for more difficult gaps. Set a time limit (e.g. five minutes) to discourage students from spending too long on difficult questions. When you go through the answers with the class, discuss any alternative answers to those given below (shown in brackets, although these do not fit in with the prepositions in the box). To add a competitive element, follow the 'Easy first' procedure (see Games and activities section, page xvi).

### Answers
**1** to   **2** for; of   **3** for   **4** in; on   **5** of; of; with   **6** about; into; beyond   **7** for; by; under   **8** on   **9** with; for   **10** In; to; through   **11** to   **12** as; from; into; for (with)   **13** with   **14** for; of   **15** out; to   **16** of; to   **17** in   **18** to   **19** without; on; in   **20** against   **21** on; for   **22** from   **23** Within; with   **24** Without; for   **25** at

### Language notes
Prepositions are especially important in legal English as they help lawyers to construct and understand complex sentences. For example, *Insolvency practitioners can find themselves advising creditors, who may be angry at the prospect of losing their investments, directors, who are anxious to protect their livelihoods, and hard-bitten businessmen with an eye for a bargain, on the viability of a business and its restructuring.*

The missing words in sentences 6 (*about*) and 19 (*out*) are not being used as prepositions; *about* is used as an adjective and *out* is an adverbial particle. There is no need to mention this to students.

# Case study 5: Transnational insolvency law

## The facts of the case

Tell students to read the information and to make notes on the two companies and the two countries. As always with complex cases, it is useful to draw a diagram to show the key parties and the relationships between them. After students have read the information, elicit a diagram such as the one below from the class and put it on the board. Note the circles represent the initial challenge from Payme Bank and the interim liquidator of the actions of the City Court and Mr Doright. The later complications (the dismissal of the challenge by the Regional Administrative Tribunal, the rejection by the High Court of the dismissal, the referral to the Supreme Court and the possible referral to the Supreme Court of the UCS) do not need to be added to the diagram, as long as the source of the conflict (circled) is clear.

**Suggested answer**

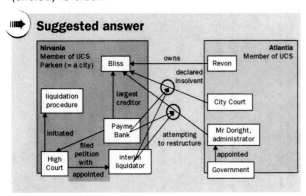

**Background notes**
- ○ A *wholly owned subsidiary* is, as its name suggests, 100% owned by a parent company. Many subsidiaries are only partially owned by one parent company – the standard minimum ownership to define a company as a subsidiary is 50% plus one share.
- ○ An *interim liquidator* is an insolvency practitioner appointed by the courts, who convenes a meeting of creditors to appoint a liquidator. The interim

liquidator may be chosen as the liquidator, or the creditors may make their own choice. See http://www. ensors.co.uk/cms/document/A_guide_ to_Liquidation.pdf for detailed and useful guidance on the roles in liquidation.

## Task 1: Role-play

1. Divide the class into two groups (or, with very large classes, into groups of four or five) and assign each group one side of the negotiation to prepare. Monitor carefully as they discuss the documents and their negotiating strategies, but avoid providing too much guidance. Allow at least ten to 15 minutes' preparation time.

2. Put students into pairs or groups for the negotiations (which could be conducted one to one, or in small groups with two or three students on each side). Remind students that the aim is always to reach an agreement, so some degree of compromise will be necessary. Allow at least ten to 15 minutes for the negotiations.

3. Ask each pair/group to feed back on their negotiation, including what each party conceded. Give and elicit feedback on students' negotiation techniques and the language they used. Finally, discuss any unresolved issues related to the Relevant legal documents.

## Task 2: Writing

Ask students to do the writing task for homework.

 **Model answer**
Dear Managing Director
*Re. Payme Bank v. BlissCosmetics*
You have asked me to provide my opinion as to what will be the main arguments from opposing counsel in respect of negotiations

regarding the above-referenced matter. You have also asked what my strategy will be to meet these arguments. After researching the law and the facts of this case, I provide hereafter my advice in respect to your requests.

In my opinion, the opposing party's position in the underlying legal proceedings is relatively weak. In light of this, it is difficult to foresee all the arguments which might be presented at negotiations. However, I have identified some arguments that opposing counsel must address in order to succeed in the legal proceedings. These arguments are outlined below:

1 The appointment of an interim liquidator and commencement of compulsory liquidation do not rise to the level of a "judgment opening insolvency proceedings" as required by Section 18 of the UCS Regulation on Insolvency. Hence, the City Court in Atlantia should be deemed to have issued the "judgment opening insolvency proceedings"; and

2 Pursuant to Section 5 of the UCS Regulation on Insolvency, Bliss's centre of main interest cannot be located in Nirvania (despite the presumption of such because Bliss's registered office is located there) because the factual elements of the case lead to the determination that Bliss was not an autonomous entity and Revon controlled all of the decisions made by Bliss. The foregoing provides sufficient evidence to rebut the presumption that the location of the registered office is the centre of the main interests of Bliss.

The first argument is, at best, weak. It has already been rejected by the High Court of Parken and has no support in case law or statute. It relies on semantic distinctions rather than legal precedent or sound reasoning. I find it unlikely that Mr. Doright will attempt to maintain this argument if made. It simply does not hold water.

The second argument has more merit. It relies on the UCS Supreme Court finding that the presumption contained in Section 5 is rebutted based on the fact that Bliss was not autonomous and

was completely controlled by the parent company, Revon. My argument in response will be that there is case law which runs contrary to this interpretation. In the leading case on this issue, it was held that the presumption is difficult to rebut. Specifically, it was held that "Section 5's presumption can be rebutted by factors which are both objective and ascertainable by third parties enable it to be established that an actual situation exists which is different from that which locating it at that registered office is deemed to reflect". In short, the law favors Section 5's presumption because it provides legal certainty to creditors. In this case, whilst arguably there might be objective facts pointing to another company's control, these facts are not readily ascertainable by third parties. And, consequently, the facts on the whole do not rise to a level necessary to rebut Section 5's presumption.

If you require further clarification or would like to make any comments in respect of my advice contained in this letter, please notify me in due time before the scheduled negotiations.

Truly yours
C.S. Kirtley

## Relevant legal documents

### Text 1

○ Although this is a fictional document, it is based on **Council regulation (EC) No 1346/2000 on insolvency proceedings** (http://eur-lex.europa. eu/LexUriServ/LexUriServ.do?uri=CELEX:32000 R1346:EN:HTML).

The parties will use this document to decide whether the proper jurisdiction for insolvency proceedings is Nirvania, where Bliss had its registered office, or Atlantia where, based on the facts, it appears that most of Bliss's actual business was located.

○ **Paragraph 1** states that Nirvania can be assumed to be the 'centre of main interests', but that this can be challenged if it can be proved that another country (e.g. Atlantia) has a better claim. In fact, some arguments can be made to support a claim that Atlantia is Bliss's centre of main interests.

○ If it is determined by the UCS Supreme Court that Atlantia is indeed Bliss's centre of main interests, **paragraph 2** becomes relevant, as it determines whether Nirvania would then have the right to open insolvency proceedings (i.e. a secondary proceeding). This in turn depends on whether Bliss possesses 'an establishment' in Nirvania.

○ **Paragraph 3** highlights the importance of the order in which insolvency proceedings are opened. In this case, the proceedings opened under paragraph 1 (i.e. arguably in Atlantia) happened after those opened under paragraph 2 (i.e. in Nirvania). Therefore, the restrictions under paragraph 3 do not apply.

○ Alternatively, if Nirvania can convince the UCS Supreme Court that in fact it is Bliss's centre of main interests under paragraph 1, Atlantia's proceedings become those covered in paragraph 2 and, because they opened subsequent to (= later than) Nirvania's proceedings, paragraph 3 does in fact apply. In this case, Atlantia's proceedings should have been winding-up proceedings and not the restructuring that Atlantia is actually attempting.

○ In other words, the key issue here is in paragraph 1: where is Bliss's centre of main interests. Assuming that this is deemed to be Atlantia, the scope of Nirvania's proceedings is limited to the actual property owned by Bliss located in Nirvania.

---

> **Background note**
> *Secondary proceedings* are not intended to compete with the main proceedings, but are expected to support and co-operate with them. See http://eur-lex.europa.eu/LexUriServ/LexUriServ.do?uri=CELEX:32000R1346:en:HTML. The EU regulation [recital 20] states that 'Main insolvency proceedings and secondary proceedings can, however, contribute to the effective realisation of the total assets only if all the concurrent proceedings pending are co-ordinated. The main condition here is that the various liquidators must co-operate closely, in particular by exchanging a sufficient amount of information.'

**Text 2**

This section focuses on the issue of recognition, and again depends on paragraph 1 of Text 1. Whatever is decided on the issue of Bliss's centre of main interests must be recognised by other member states.

> **Background notes**
> ○ *Capacity* here refers to the ability of the debtor to have insolvency proceedings brought against him in a particular state. Reasons for incapacity could include inability to travel (e.g. because of illness, imprisonment, visa restrictions, etc.).
> ○ If one action *precludes* another action, it makes that second action impossible.

**Text 3**

This document appears to support Nirvania's claim that it is Bliss's centre of main interests. It refers to the presumption in Article 5 (i.e. the last sentence in paragraph 1 of that text), and suggests that the arguments for rebutting (= disagreeing with) that argument must be based on 'factors which are objective and ascertainable by third parties'. In this particular case, however, there are arguments based on fact which could be used to convince the UCS Supreme Court to rebut the presumption. Specifically, based on the facts, it could be argued with success that Bliss was simply the alter ego of Revon. This would have been objectively obvious to any serious third-party investor, including Payme Bank.

> **Pronunciation notes**
> ascertainable /ˌæsəˈteɪnəbl/
> ascertainment /ˌæsəˈteɪnmənt/

# 15 Competition law

In many countries, it is accepted by governments that **competition** is healthy for an economy. If several companies compete with each other for the same customers, they will fight to find ways of making the customers choose them, either by keeping prices low or by innovating to improve the quality and range of their products. This makes them competitive internationally, enabling them to grow and to create jobs and wealth in their home countries. In contrast, if all the companies in a given market decide to co-operate with each other (i.e. to form a **cartel**), they can decide to raise prices (and therefore their profit margins) and stop bothering to innovate. In the short term, this can be a very attractive prospect for companies. The most famous and successful cartel in history is OPEC, the Organization of the Petroleum Exporting Countries, which together control half of the world's oil exports, and which have become rich by keeping the price of oil high.

When a single firm effectively controls the whole market, it is called a **monopoly**. These monopolies, which are often state-owned, are not subject to competition and have no reason to keep prices low or to innovate. They may employ more people than they need to and may waste money. In the short term, this might be seen as a good thing to those lucky enough to be employed by such a monopoly, and especially to those, perhaps corrupt, individuals who help the company to waste money. In a global market, however, inefficient national monopolies may struggle in the face of competition from more efficient companies from other countries. For customers, the danger of cartels, monopolies and other concentrations of market power is often the same: inflated prices, low quality and lack of choice.

For this reason, governments tend to impose restrictions to prevent companies from forming cartels and from becoming too powerful within a particular market. This unit deals with such **regulations**. A famous example of such regulation is the battle that took place in the USA and the EU to reduce the power of Microsoft, which used its dominance of the market for PC operating systems (Windows) to help sell its software products (such as Internet Explorer and Media Player).

The first thing to realise about **competition law** (**antitrust law** in the USA) is that the biggest companies in the world (and therefore some of the brightest and best-paid lawyers) have a strong incentive to fight any such regulation. It is in their short-term interest to become as big and powerful as possible. But there are also millions of smaller companies and individuals (and their lawyers) who are equally determined that such regulation should succeed, in order to reduce the power of the multinationals. Governments often find themselves arguing on behalf of both sides at different times, depending on which is in their national interests. For example, the EU is usually a fierce defender of open markets and free competition, but its own Common Agricultural Policy is often given as an example of anti-competitive price fixing. In this climate, it is difficult to find an unbiased view, and it is important to keep an open mind when reading about this topic. For example, in economic theory, an important concept is that of a **free market**, but it is not obvious whether free should mean 'unregulated', or whether some form of regulation is needed to ensure that markets remain free.

As Reading A explains, the two major actors in competition law are the USA (where **antitrust** laws date back to the problems created by powerful **trusts**, such as Standard Oil, in the 19th century), and the EU (where the creation of a **single European market** is a key pillar of the EU's mission). Some **antitrust measures** taken in various European countries are outlined in Reading B.

Reading C illustrates an important antitrust case, where the leaders of a cartel of agricultural companies in China were fined for **anti-competitive behaviour**. This has been taken as evidence that Chinese authorities are starting to clamp down on cartels.

Listening A illustrates the importance of antitrust laws, not just for large companies but for small, local businesses. In this case, two taxi operators have discussed co-operating to make life difficult for a new entrant in the market. The suggested co-operation includes **price fixing**, **territorial allocation** (dividing a geographical area into zones where the firms agree not to compete with each other) and **predatory pricing** (co-operating to keep prices artificially low in order to drive third parties out of a market). The lawyer of one of the taxi operators warns his client that even discussing such activities constitutes a **per se violation** (i.e. a violation in itself, even if not followed up by any illegal action), and that he risks fines and even imprisonment if he engages in any of the illegal activities.

Another local antitrust case is illustrated in the Text analysis section, where a lawyer advises a client on **bid-rigging**, which is when firms co-operate during a **call for tender** (a type of auction for a contract to do some work), in order to manipulate the results.

Although media reports can create the impression that **mergers** (see Unit 4) are often blocked by regulators such as the European Commission, the speaker in Listening B points out that most mergers are accepted. He outlines the process of **merger control**, in this case in South Africa, including the **definition of the market** and an analysis of the expected efficiency gains from the merger and its **impact on public interest**.

Reading D also deals with merger control, specifically a change to simplify the process of **notification** of proposed mergers to the relevant regulators, in this case the European Commission or EU member states.

The unit also provides practice of using **passive constructions** in a report to a client, and provides

language for **warning a client of risks**. There is practice of **writing a proposal** and an **informative letter** to a client. Finally, there is some useful language for referring to other people's **opinions** and giving one's own opinion.

**Further information**

○ A good starting point for information on **antitrust** is http://en.wikipedia.org/wiki/Competition_law. Wikipedia also has useful articles on topics such as **monopoly**, **barriers to entry** and **competition policy**.

○ A good source of information on **EU competition law** is http://europa.eu/pol/comp/index_en.htm.

○ There is an interesting article on **China's clampdown on cartels**, as discussed in Reading C, at http://www.mayerbrown.com/antitrust/article.asp?id=9366&nid=112.

○ For more information on **merger control in South Africa**, as discussed in Listening B, see http://www.comptrib.co.za.

○ For an excellent guide to the **EU's single European market**, see http://europa.eu/abc/12lessons/lesson_6/index_en.htm.

○ There are many stories concerning the **Microsoft case** on the Internet, including many which are hostile towards Microsoft. For a balanced and informative introduction to both this case and the history of trusts, see http://news.bbc.co.uk/2/hi/in_depth/business/2000/microsoft/635257.stm.

# Discussion

Use these questions to generate a discussion. Some of the questions (and suggested answers) are rather provocative, and you could play 'devil's advocate' to question conventional wisdom that competition law is essential.

a How can companies restrict competition?

b Is this necessarily a problem?

c How can governments control such restrictions?

d Does such regulation work?

⇒ **Suggested answers**

a The most obvious way is to co-operate in order to fix prices, instead of competing. This is obviously attractive for companies, as they can make more money, but there is the ever-present

danger for them that other companies in the same market will compete by offering lower prices, thereby taking market share. If they are to succeed, the co-operating companies thus need to be sufficiently big or powerful to control the whole market, in order to persuade/force potential competitors either to co-operate, to withdraw from the market, or not to enter the market in the first place.

b There is an obvious risk in allowing companies to fix prices: consumers end up paying more than they otherwise would. Furthermore, the tactics used by companies to maintain control over their markets can often be unsavoury (bullying), but it can be argued that this is a separate issue from companies restricting competition (which may be done between friends). Following this line of thinking, attempts by companies to restrict competition are only a problem if they succeed completely; as long as it is possible for new players to enter a market and to compete in that market, prices will never become too distorted. With these two big exceptions (bullying and total control over a market), it is not obvious that co-operation between companies to restrict competition is a problem. Consumers regularly pay more than they need to (e.g. when they choose branded products over cheaper alternatives), but this is their choice.

c   They may use legislation to restrict anti-competitive behaviour (e.g. price-fixing agreements, predatory pricing), and impose fines on companies that break the rules. They may break up companies that are in too dominant a position within a market, or block mergers that would create such companies (e.g. the European Commission famously blocked a merger between two major US firms, GE and Honeywell).

d   It is impossible to say, as we cannot know what would have happened if a certain restriction hadn't been imposed. The question of whether they work also depends on what is meant by 'work' and who they should work for. The winners from such regulation are obviously competitors or potential competitors, whose position is strengthened against more powerful companies. Consumers also gain in the short term from lower prices. The main argument against such regulation is that it prevents companies from becoming too successful (or striving for such success) and thus discourages excellence/uniqueness. If a single company manages to manoeuvre itself into a dominant position, perhaps through a combination of luck, brilliance and bullying, regulation may force it to wait for weaker competitors to catch up, rather than pushing ahead.

# 1   Reading A: Introduction to competition law

Tell students to read the questions and then to read the text to find the answers. Students may find the questions are rather easy (especially if some of the words are similar in their own languages), in which case you can ask them to find and remember the key terms (in bold) associated with each. You can also ask them to find out who the two major actors in competition law are, and where their competition laws originate from. Allow students time to read the text carefully. When they have finished reading, tell them to discuss their answers with a partner, including what they understand by each of the key terms. Then tell them to close their books, and go through the answers with the class. Elicit the key terms (in bold) and other important words for each of the four words in the exercise, and what each means.

**Answers**

1   oligopoly (key terms: *parallel behaviour*)
2   monopoly (key terms: none)
3   cartel (key terms: *relevant market*, *barriers to entry*, *penetrate the market*, *price fixing*)
4   merger (key terms: *horizontal*, *vertical*)
The two major actors are the EU (origin: the creation of the single European market) and the US (origin: 19th-century trusts and the Sherman Act).

**Background notes**

○ The *single European market* was established by the EEC (the forerunner of the EU) between 1986 and 1993 to remove barriers to trade between member states. See http://europa.eu/abc/12lessons/index6_en.htm.

○ A *trust* holds and manages the assets of an individual or an entity. In 19th-century America, several trusts were created to bring together the shareholders of all companies in a particular industry (such as oil) to create a monopoly. The shareholders passed their shares to the trusts in exchange for regular dividends from the trust. The most famous such trusts were the Sugar Trust, the Tobacco Trust, the Steel Trust and Standard Oil, which was the largest (see http://news.bbc.co.uk/2/hi/in_depth/business/2000/microsoft/635257.stm for a very clear history).

○ An example of *horizontal integration* would be a retailer such as GAP Inc., which sells clothes through different companies, each aimed at a different target group. The best example of *vertical integration* is oil companies, which usually control the whole process of prospecting for, drilling for, refining, distributing and selling oil products. Both types of integration can be dangerous for competition. For example, in terms of horizontal integration, a single parent company may own several 'rival' brands (e.g. Mars Inc. owns the Kitekat, Whiskas and Sheba brands of pet food; most major brands of household cleaning and personal-grooming products are owned by a small number of companies: Unilever, Procter & Gamble and Reckitt Benckiser), thus increasing the risk of excessive power being concentrated in powerful companies. In terms of vertical integration, it can be practically impossible for a new company to enter a highly integrated market. For example, under the old 'studio' system, a small number of Hollywood companies controlled both production and distribution of films, which meant that independent producers struggled to get their films distributed and shown in cinemas, and independent cinemas struggled for the right to show major films. The studio system was broken up after 1948, but the industry is still notoriously difficult to break into (see http://www.guardian.co.uk/uk_news/story/0,,1535332,00.html).

**Pronunciation note**
cartel /kɑːˈtel/

## 2 Key terms: Anti-competitive activity

Tell students to do the exercise alone, and then to compare their answers with a partner. They should also think of real-life examples for each of the key terms. When you check the answers with the class, encourage a class discussion on the rights and wrongs of each form of anti-competitive activity.

➡ **Answers**
**1** c   **2** b   **3** d   **4** a

**Suggested examples**
**1** barriers to entry (see http://en.wikipedia.org/wiki/Barriers_to_entry): e.g. a foreign company might need a local partner in order to get through bureaucratic barriers to investment in e.g. China. A foreign-owned company may struggle to get visas for its managers to physically enter a country (e.g. the USA). A cigarette manufacturer may struggle to launch a brand in a country where advertising is banned and existing brands have already built their images.
**2** price fixing: e.g. OPEC, Sotheby's and Christies (see http://knowledge.wharton.upenn.edu/article.cfm?articleid=1034), the trusts in the 19th-century USA, state-owned (or recently privatised) monopolies in e.g. telecommunications, transport, electricity, etc.
**3** predatory pricing: e.g. supermarket price wars (see for example http://news.bbc.co.uk/2/hi/business/464788.stm).
**4** tie-in arrangement: e.g. Chicken Delight, a fast-food franchise chain, made its franchisees buy supplies from the parent company. This was found to be an illegal tie-in arrangement. See http://www.dynamist.com/articles-speeches/nyt/transaction.html.

## 3 Reading B: Anti-competitive activities and antitrust measures

**3.1** Tell students to read the introduction (SB page 209) to find out where the text in Reading B comes from and who might find it useful. (Answers: It comes from a list of case studies; it might be useful to lawyers who need to keep up to date with anti-competitive measures and actions taken in various countries.) You could discuss the answers to the three questions with the class before they read the text. You could also ask students to find out how many of the cases resulted in a fine. (Answer: At least six.)

**Answers**

1 Competition lawyers; senior management of companies doing business in the EU or affected by EU policy; lawyers at competition authorities in the EU or in countries affected by EU policy
2 To make it easy for the reader to identify at a glance what countries are affected and the measures taken in the particular country.
3 *NCA* stands for National Competition Authority.

**3.2** Tell students to scan the text quickly to find this information. Point out that scanning (= reading a text to get a general idea of its general meaning or its usefulness for a particular purpose) and skimming (= hunting through a text for specific information, as practised in Exercise 3.3) are essential skills for both the ILEC Test of Reading and life as a lawyer.

**Answer**

Yes, as the entries for Bulgaria, Ireland and Germany all relate to the waste-management sector.

**Background notes**

○ If a court *hands down a decision*, it makes an official formulation and delivers it to the proper office of an inferior court.

○ *Der Grüne Punkt* is German for *the Green Dot*, a European system to promote and manage the recycling of packaging. See http://en.wikipedia.org/wiki/Green_Dot_(symbol).

○ The terms *collective waste* and *domestic waste* are broadly equivalent in meaning: both refer to the collection and disposal of household waste (i.e. rubbish).

○ An *export ban* is typically imposed by a government for political, health or strategic reasons. In the case of the Czech mineral-water company, however, the ban was imposed by the company itself on its distributors. See http://www.compet.cz/en/competition/news-competition/the-office-finished-its-fourth-settlement-case for background to this case.

○ A *divestiture* is when a company or person is forced to sell an asset, typically to comply with competition laws. The term *asset/share package* is not widely used. In this text, it seems that the company was forced to sell a package consisting of both assets and shares.

○ *Abusive charges* are charges (= prices charged for a service) which abuse the supplier's dominant position.

○ *Leniency* /'liːnɪənsi/ is the opposite of strictness: if a person is lenient, they allow somebody to get away with less harsh punishment than they might have expected. A *leniency regime* is a system where, for example, the first parties that admit to anti-competitive behaviour are offered lenient punishments (or are exempted from punishment) if their admission helps competition authorities to break a cartel. See http://www.eftasurv.int/competition/cartels-and-the-leniency-programme.

○ An *incumbent* is a company which was once a monopoly (or a dominant player in a formerly restricted market, such as telecommunications), and which still therefore has many advantages when a market is opened up to competition.

**3.3** Tell students to skim the text to find this information. Allow a very short time (e.g. two minutes) or turn this into a race, in order to encourage students to skim, rather than read for detail.

 **Answers**
   **1** Bulgaria
   **2** €17.3m
   **3** In the waste-disposal services sector
   **4** Ten
   **5** They were fined for forming a cartel.

**Optional extension**

Tell students to work in groups of three or four. Each student should read the information on three of the countries in the table carefully in order to imagine what the anti-competitive activities actually involved might be. When they have finished, tell them to explain and discuss their ideas with their partners. Then elicit from the class the best ideas for each country, and any further information that students know about each story.

As a follow-up activity, you could assign one or more story to each student as a research project, to present during the next lesson. Alternatively, they could research and present a more recent story from each of the national competition bodies.

Note that the best way to find further information on each story is to find the website of the relevant national body (e.g. the German Federal Cartel Office, the *Bundeskartellamt*, has an English-language website: http://www.bundeskartellamt.de/wEnglisch/index.php, as does the Polish Office for Protection of Competition and Consumers: http://www.uokik.gov.pl/home.php). See http://ec.europa.eu/competition/ecn/competition_authorities.html for links to all the EU National Competition Authorities.

**3.4** Tell students to work in pairs to complete the table. When they have finished, go through the answers with the class.

 **Answers**
   **1** Bulgarian Competition Authority
   **2** cleared a merger
   **3** formation of cartel

   **4** fined
   **5** telecommunications
   **6** abuse of a dominant position
   **7** Polish Competition Authority
   **8** vertical price collusion

**3.5** Tell students to work alone to do this exercise. When they have finished, tell them to check with a partner and then go through the answers with the class.

 **Answers**
   **1** d  **2** e  **3** b  **4** a  **5** c

## 4 Writing A: Using passive constructions

**4.1** Go through the instructions with the class, making sure students understand the question. Elicit why the client might be interested in such information, and the most useful way of presenting it. (Answer: The client has asked to be informed, so a simple sentence about each case should be enough. There is no need to compare and contrast. The three cases might be presented using bullet points.) Elicit also the form of passive constructions, and reasons for choosing them over similar active voice constructions. You could elicit some examples of passive sentences for the four waste-management cases (e.g. *the cartel was prohibited*) and discuss why sometimes the passive would be unnatural (e.g. *the company's dominant position had been abused* – unnatural because the subject (*the company*) is essential to the meaning). Note that the passive with *it* as the subject is especially useful for reporting the measures taken, without referring to the authority (e.g. *It was decided/found that …*) – see Language notes below.

 **Language notes**
**The passive**
   ○ Passive constructions are formed from the verb *be* (or, in some situations, *get*) in an appropriate tense, followed by the past participle (also known as the third form) of the relevant verb.

- A common feature of all languages is, wherever possible, to place known information (the topic) towards the beginning of a sentence and new information (the news) later. In many languages, it is possible to move elements (such as grammatical subject and object) around in a sentence to achieve this topic–news order. But in English there is the complication that subjects and objects are identified by word order (subject–verb–object). In order to move them around, it is necessary to use constructions such as the passive voice with *by* (e.g. *This picture* [topic] *was painted by my sister* [news]). English therefore uses the passive more often than many other languages (where the same sentence might be something like *This picture* [object] *painted my sister* [subject]).
- In a similar way, there is a universal tendency to place long and complex elements towards the end of a sentence. For example, the subject of the sentence *My sister and her lawyer, who specialises in competition law, painted this picture* might be better as the prepositional object (i.e. after *by*) of a passive construction.
- A second use of passive applies when the agent (the doer of the action) is unknown (e.g. *My car was stolen*), irrelevant (e.g. *Your hotel room is being cleaned*) or secret (e.g. *I'm afraid your vase has been broken*). This use of the passive is also common in other languages.
- English is unusual in that the subjects of passive sentences can be the direct objects, some indirect objects and even certain prepositional objects of active sentences (e.g. *I gave my wife* [indirect object] *this ring* [direct object] → *This ring was given to my wife / My wife was given this ring*; *Everyone made fun of me* [prepositional object] → *I was made fun of*). In many languages, this is not possible, and learners of English often find such structures extremely difficult to understand.

- Verbs with clauses as objects (e.g. *She said that he was a terrible lawyer*) can be used in passive with a dummy subject *it* (*It was said that he was a terrible lawyer*).

**4.2** Tell students to work alone or in pairs to write their emails. Make sure they realise that they should not overuse the passive: it should be just one of the techniques they use to make their email professional and natural. Allow a very short time for the writing (e.g. less than five minutes) in order to encourage students to get straight to the point. When they have finished, tell them to check each other's work for accuracy and appropriate style.

▶ **Suggested answer**

Dear Mr Nazarenko

In your email of 8 November, you enquired about recent anti-competitive activities in the waste-management sector in the EU and the measures taken against them. I would like to provide information about four cases from the past month.

In Bulgaria, the holder of a trade mark was found to have abused its dominant position, while local authorities in Dublin were found by the Irish High Court to have breached competition law. In Germany, a merger in the waste-management market was cleared, although this clearance is subject to remedies which include the divestiture of an asset/share package. Finally, a waste glass joint-purchasing cartel between container-glass manufacturers was prohibited by the German Federal Cartel Office.

I hope that this information is of use to you. Should you require any further assistance please feel free to contact me.

Yours sincerely

Marie Delapre

(135 words)

- - - - - - - - - - - - - - - - - - - - - - -

**Optional extension**
**Photocopiable worksheet 15.1**

Photocopiable worksheet 15.1 provides further practice of forming passive constructions with a much wider range of tense structures. If students already seem comfortable forming the passive, some or all of the questions can be transformed orally. Note that many of the sentences in the exercise are intended to be intrinsically interesting, not simply a means to practise a grammar structure, as they present part of the history and background of trusts.

Tell students to work in pairs to use passive constructions to make the sentences sound more natural. Tell them not to change the tenses. Point out that, in many cases, this will involve deleting the agent (i.e. the subject of the active sentence) and other unnecessary elements. Point out also (or elicit) that many verbs, including all intransitive verbs (those without objects), cannot be used in passive voice. When they have finished, go through the answers with the class. Encourage discussion of alternative answers.

**Suggested answers**

1   In America in the late 19th century, a series of trusts was/were established in industries such as sugar, tobacco, steel and oil to create a monopoly in those industries.

2   Shareholders of other companies in the same sector were often coerced into joining the trusts.

3   Ownership of the shares was transferred (by the shareholders), and dividend-paying certificates were received in exchange.

4   The trusts grew so powerful that it was agreed that something had to be done to bring them under control.

5   Before the Sherman Act was introduced, whole industries had been controlled by so-called barons.

6   The campaign against Standard Oil, which was finally brought before the courts 20 years later, was led by 'muckraking' journalists.

7   It has never been calculated what advances could have been made by the market leader had it been allowed to continue to increase its market share.

8   The firm was being investigated (by regulators) for its alleged abuse of its dominant position.

9   The Single European Market was introduced in 1993. Since then, the free flow of labour and capital within the EU has been protected.

10   It has been argued that more harm than good has been done by antitrust laws. It cannot be calculated how markets would have been affected if antitrust measures had not been enforced.

11   Small companies may be bribed or even threatened in order to persuade them to join cartels.

12   This sort of coercive behaviour needs to be prevented.

13   The accountant was made to conceal evidence of the collusion.

14   It has been pointed out (by critics of regulation) that predatory pricing cannot be defeated by antitrust laws, but that a truly free market can be relied on to undermine such activities.

15   The cartel was agreed upon by the CEOs of the three companies, and an unofficial agreement was entered into a few weeks later. The existence of the cartel was only discovered when the OFT was tipped off by a former director, who had been sacked.

**5   Listening A: Advising on competition law risks**

Elicit from the class what type/size of company might seek legal advice on competition law risks, and what sort of advice lawyers might give them. Then tell them to read the introduction (SB page 212) to compare it with their suggestions.

**5.1**   Go through the terms with the class to make sure they understand them all. Elicit real or imagined examples of each.

**Background notes**

○ *Bid-rigging* is related to *bids* (offers) in an auction or *call for tender* (a procedure whereby various companies make formal bids to carry out work on a project). In an auction, the highest price secures the sale. In a call for tender, the lowest offer usually gets the contract (although other factors will come into play). Bid-rigging involves colluding with other bidders (or with the seller or contracting company) to fix (*rig*) the final price.

○ A *per se* (= by itself) *violation* /ˌpɜː ˌseɪ ˌvaɪəˈleɪʃən/ is an early step in an illegal action (e.g. the planning of a robbery), but even if the later steps do not take place (e.g. the robbery itself), a violation has still been committed. It is a US antitrust concept (not used in the EU). Per se violations in antitrust law are areas which the court will condemn without taking any arguments into account, for example, horizontal price fixing, horizontal territorial or customer division, vertical price fixing and some concerted refusals to deal and tie-in arrangements. This is contrasted with what are called 'rule of reason' violations, in which courts will weigh all the circumstances of a case to come to a conclusion.

○ *Territorial allocation* involves colluding with a competitor to divide a geographical area into 'territories', where each competitor agrees not to compete in another's territory (or to compete less aggressively). Territories are normal for branches (or agents, franchises, etc.) of the same company (e.g. a chain of pizza delivery shops within a single city may divide the city into such territories), but illegal for competitors.

Tell students to listen to the recording and to tick the terms mentioned. After the recording, tell students to discuss with a partner what was said about each term. Then go through the answers with the class.

**Transcript »** STUDENT'S BOOK **page 294**

 **Answers**
Terms 1, 3, 4, 6, 7 and 9 were mentioned.

 **Background notes**
○ A *fleet* is the set of vehicles (in this case, taxis) that a company owns or manages.
○ A *cab* is an informal name for a taxi.

○ The expression *to get a foothold* derives from climbing: if you do not have a foothold (somewhere strong to put your foot), it is almost impossible to climb a cliff. A foothold in a market is a secure base from which to start building a strong market presence.

○ If you *adhere* /ədˈhɪəʳ/ to a limit, you stick to it and do not break it.

○ *It's very hard from an evidentiary* /ˌevɪˈdenʃəri/ *standpoint* means 'it's difficult in terms of obtaining reliable evidence'.

○ If something is *dirt cheap*, it costs very little.

**5.2** Tell students to discuss the statements with a partner to try to remember whether they were true or false. Play the recording a second time for them to check. Go through the answers with the class.

 **Answers**
**1** True
**2** False (The competitor suggested co-operation, not a tie-in arrangement.)
**3** True
**4** False (He mentions the threat of criminal prosecution and serious risks, but does not suggest that prosecution always takes place.)

**Optional extension**
**Photocopiable worksheet 15.2**
The client, Mr Greene, used many examples of semi-informal and idiomatic language, while his lawyer, Mr Langston, used more formal language. Semi-informal language is suitable for a lawyer–client meeting, but would not be suitable for a formal letter. Photocopiable worksheet 15.2 focuses on this type of language.
Tell students to work in pairs to put the words in the gaps, and to decide whether the sentences are semi-informal or more formal. When they have finished, go through the answers with the class.

**Answers**
**1** out; I'd (SI)   **2** used; down; guess; helped (SI)
**3** is; newcomer (SI)   **4** themselves; over (SI)

**5** other; have (SI)   **6** get; over; going (SI)
**7** make; get; in (SI)   **8** off; on (SI)   **9** lower;
to (SI)   **10** in; over (SI)   **11** up; to; into; of (F)
**12** from; for; still (F)   **13** on; dirt; on; left (SI)
The lawyer's two sentences (11 and 12) are
more formal. All of the client's sentences are
semi-informal. The lawyer uses longer
sentences, the passive (*... to be proven*) and
some 'legalese' (*... from an evidential
standpoint ...*). The lawyer is not over-formal,
however; he uses normal conversational
devices such as *of course* and contracted
forms (*it's*).

As a follow-up, you could ask students to work
in small groups to make some of the informal
sentences (1–10 and 13) more formal, as if
they were written in a letter to the lawyer
rather than a face-to-face meeting. You may
suggest that they go over-the-top slightly in
order to achieve the formal effect. Encourage
them to use passive constructions where
appropriate (especially to avoid mentioning
who suggested illegal activities), and to put
most of the meaning/content of the
sentences into the noun phrases (rather than
verbs). Each group should work on different
sentences. When they have finished, discuss
the more formal versions with the class.

**Suggested answers**
1  The new cars have not proved as
   successful as had been initially expected.
2  It appears that use of taxis has declined
   relative to previous periods. This may be
   due to attempts by potential customers to
   reduce their expenditure. The opening of
   the new subway to the airport may also
   have played a part in this decline.
3  It has come to our attention that a
   newcomer is planning to enter the local
   market.
4  The newcomers, known as 'the Orange
   Team', have orange-coloured cars, and
   have been involved in promotional
   activities in a wide range of locations.
5  I received a call recently from Mr Belmont,
   who suggested a meeting to discuss the
   matter and to have a drink together.
6  I was of the opinion that such a meeting
   might be a useful way to discuss the
   current state of the market.

7  At that point, the issue of prices was
   raised. It was mentioned that a way might
   exist to make our market position more
   secure in the face of the competition from
   Orange.
8  It was suggested that the intensity of
   competition between our companies could
   be alleviated and that an agreement over
   territory and prices might be reached.
9  It was suggested that our prices be
   reduced to a level below those of Orange,
   whilst maintaining a lower limit in order to
   minimise losses incurred.
10 It is my opinion that an informal
   discussion in a bar is not harmful per se.
13 A further suggestion was that a significant
   discount on journeys to and from the
   airport would enable us to maintain our
   current level of business activity.

# 6 Language use: Warning a client of risks

Elicit from the class the risks the lawyer warned
the client about in Listening A, and the phrases he
used. Allow them to look at the transcript if
necessary. Elicit other useful phrases for warning
a client. Then tell students to read the information
in the box (SB page 212) to compare it with their
suggestions.

Tell students to work in pairs for the two role-
plays. If you have an odd number of students, you
will need to have a group of three, in which case
there should be two lawyers (one junior, one
senior) in the role-plays for that group.

Before the first role-play, make sure all students
have read and understood the information on their
cards. You may need to check/explain some
vocabulary (especially *a bid / to bid*), but point out
that the key legal terms are defined on the role
cards. Make sure the clients know not to give too
much information at once, but only to answer the
lawyers' questions. Encourage the lawyers to
experiment with the phrases from the box. Set a
time limit (e.g. five minutes) for the first role-play,
after which tell students to swap roles for the
second role-play.

After the role-plays, discuss with the class which
of the two situations is the most serious, and how
they would be treated within students' own
jurisdictions.

# 7 Text analysis: A proposal

**7.1** Tell students to read the letter quickly to answer the questions, and then to discuss the answers with a partner. When you go through the answers, check that students have understood key vocabulary, especially *tendering / calls for tender*.

**Answers**

1. The client's problem is a sharp drop in the number of contracts his construction company has been awarded in the last year.
2. The lawyer proposes that his law firm look into the possibility that anti-competitive agreements have been made by the competition.

**Background notes**

○ A *tender* is a formal offer (bid), typically to do contract work such as a major building project. For example, a city government may launch a *call for tender* (invitation for bids) to build a new bridge (see http://www.publictenders.net for lots of authentic examples). Several construction companies submit their bids in sealed envelopes, and the lowest offer will win the contract (as long as it meets other requirements in terms of quality, safety, etc.). Sometimes the term *tender* is wrongly used to describe the process (the call for tender). The system hinges on the tenders being kept secret, and genuine competition between the bidders. Great care is therefore needed to prevent collusion between bidders. Note that the word *tender* has two other related uses in legal English: if you *tender your resignation*, you make a formal written offer to resign. *Legal tender* is money which cannot be refused within a jurisdiction; the term excludes other forms of payment such as cards and foreign currency.

○ A *marked drop* is a significant or noticeable decline.

○ *Concluding an agreement* is simply a formal way of saying 'making an agreement'.

**7.2** Tell students to work alone to match the functions with the sections of the letter, and then to discuss with a partner, without looking back at the text, what they understood/remembered from each paragraph, by looking only at the functions. Then discuss the answers with the class.

**Answers**

a 4  b 6  c 3  d 1  e 5  f 2

**7.3** Tell students to close their books. Elicit from the class whether they think the letter used more examples of *will* or *would*. Encourage them to think about the function of the letter when working out the answer, and to justify their answers, rather than simply trying to remember. (Answer: There are seven instances of *would* and none of *will*.) Then tell them to read the box on page 213 to check. Students work in pairs to find all the examples of *would* in the letter and to discuss their functions. Afterwards, discuss the answers carefully with the class.

**Answers**

○ (paragraph 1) ... *I would like to make a few recommendations.* (polite expression of inclination)

○ (paragraph 3) ... *I have come to the conclusion that it would be wise ...* (polite expression of opinion)

○ (paragraph 4) *In the event that your competitors are found to have been engaging in activities of this kind, the benefits for your own company would be considerable.* (*would* is used to express a possible outcome; *in the event* is used with the same meaning as *if*.)

○ (paragraph 4) *These benefits would range ...* (*would* is used to express a possible outcome; *if* is understood.)

○ (paragraph 5) *Should you be interested in pursuing this course of action, David Fisher would be happy to assist you.* (*would* is used to express a possible outcome; *should* is used with the same meaning as *if*.)

○ (paragraph 5) *At your request, he could begin an enquiry into this matter, which, in its early stages, would involve information-gathering in the broadest*

*sense ...* (*would* is used to express a possible outcome; *at your request* here means *if you request*.)
○ (paragraph 6) *Please let David Fisher or me know if you would be interested ...* (polite request)

the clauses could be reversed (*If you would be interested ..., please let me know*). In both cases, *would* is used to make the offer more polite; present simple is also possible (*Please let me know if you are interested ...*) but less delicate.

## Language notes

○ The sentence *In the event that your competitors are found to have been engaging in activities of this kind, the benefits for your own company would be considerable* is likely to cause many problems of comprehension, and students may need to deconstruct it before it makes sense. The sentence as a whole is a conditional construction: *If* (= *in the event*) *X happens, Y would happen*. This is highly unusual in that it mixes a real condition (the *if*-clause) with a hypothetical result (with *would*). The *if*-clause itself is highly complicated. The underlying meaning is 'If we find that your competitors have been engaging ...', which can be rewritten (using passive and a dummy subject *it*) as *If it is found that your competitors have been engaging ...* . This can then undergo subject-to-subject raising (a process which is rare in other languages, where the subject of a subordinate clause replaces a dummy subject as the subject of the main clause): *If your competitors are found to have been engaging ...*

○ *Should* + infinitive can be used in a range of conditional structures with a future meaning, where the choice of tense in the main clause is determined more by level of formality than by any significant changes in meaning (e.g. *Should you need any further assistance, we are / will be / would be happy to provide it*).

○ Note that the example from paragraph 6 has two different interpretations. It could be an indirect question, where *if* could be replaced by *whether* (*Please let me know whether you would be interested ...*) or it could be a conditional structure, where the order of

**Optional extension**
Tell students to underline examples of the following tenses in the letter – past simple, present perfect simple and present perfect continuous – and to discuss with a partner why each tense was chosen by the writer, and whether a different tense could have been used in each case. Point out that they should include both active and passive constructions. Then discuss the answers with the class.

**Answers**
○ Past simple: *we **discussed**, you **described**, you **told**, your company **participated**, your bids **were rejected**, the contracts **were awarded*** The first three examples refer to a specific telephone conversation the previous week, so present perfect is not possible. The other examples refer to specific calls for tender which took place before the meeting. Present perfect could have been used, but would suggest that the client has continued participating in such tenders even after the meeting, and his bids are still being rejected. The choice of past simple implies that the client has learnt his lesson and stopped making bids until the legal issue is resolved.
○ Present perfect simple: *the commercial property sector **has** traditionally **been**, I **have come** to the conclusion, agreements **have been concluded**.* The first example refers to a period of time up to and including the present: this sector still is one of the firm's principal areas of activity. *Be* is normally a state verb, so continuous constructions are not possible. The other two examples refer to past events with a concrete result at the moment of writing: the lawyer *now has* an opinion (based on the conclusion) and the competitors *now have* some agreements.

○ Present perfect continuous: *your company* **has been having** *difficulties, you* **have been experiencing** *a decrease, your competitors* **have been engaging** *in activities*[1] All three examples refer to processes (rather than events) which started in the past and are still in progress at the time of writing: the company is still having difficulties and experiencing a decrease; the competitors are still engaging in such activities. The present perfect simple could have been used, but would suggest past events (not processes) with present consequences (e.g. *The company* **has had** *difficulties* = the difficulties occurred in the past, but they are still affecting the company in some way).

[1] Technically, the letter does not use present perfect continuous here, but an infinitive construction (with *to*). However, as described in the Background note, the underlying meaning is present perfect continuous.

## 8   Writing B: A proposal

Tell students to read the task carefully to find out what they have to do. Then check that they have understood, and generate some ideas, by running a quick brainstorming session. Use these questions to generate ideas.

○ Who is your client? What is his name? What exactly does his company do?
○ What cases of cartel formation and price fixing has your client's industry seen in the past?
○ What are the risks for your client?
○ What guidelines should he set up?
○ Which employees might read such guidelines?
○ Which phrases from the letter in the previous exercises could be copied into this letter?

Then tell students to write the letter. (See Writing section, page xiv.)

 **Suggested answer**

Dear Mr Rodríguez

As a follow-up to our telephone conversation yesterday in which we discussed a case of anti-competitive behaviour in your market sector, I would like to propose that your firm establish anti-competitive guidelines as a preventive measure against such behaviour.

As I am sure you are aware, the recent case of price fixing in your industry is not unusual; several cases of cartel formation and price fixing have occurred in recent years. You should also be aware that such behaviour does not always originate at the level of top management, and that employees at all levels are at risk for such activities. Practices such as exclusive dealing arrangements with suppliers or even unintentionally misleading advertising – to name but two examples – can harm competition and may be considered to represent an infringement of antitrust law. Employees at all levels of the firm need to be informed of the wide range of possible anti-competitive activities, as well as of their potential legal consequences. I must warn you that individuals directly involved in serious anti-competitive behaviour face high fines as well as, under certain circumstances, the threat of criminal prosecution.

I propose that we draw up a comprehensive set of guidelines for preventing anti-competitive behaviour by your firm. Initially, these guidelines could be presented to all employees in informative workshop sessions, and later reinforced through regular anti-competitive internal memos.

The benefits for your company are clear: an increased awareness of the risks of anti-competitive behaviour at all levels of your enterprise would greatly lessen your risk of exposure to antitrust lawsuits and actions.

The implementation of this proposal could be carried out in a four-stage process: 1) assessment of anti-competitive behaviour risks; 2) drawing up of guidelines; 3) holding workshops for employees; and 4) follow-up reinforcement. Should you be interested in pursuing this course of action, the Competition Department of our firm could begin work immediately.

If you would like to discuss this proposal and the details of its implementation, please do not hesitate to contact me.

I look forward to hearing from you.

Yours sincerely

Andrew Chase

(338 words)

## 9 Reading C: A cartel case in China

**9.1** Tell students to read the three questions. Allow a very short time (about 30 seconds) for them to skim the first paragraph to find the answers. Discuss the answers with the class.

**Answers**

1  The text is a case summary appearing in a law firm's newsletter providing updates on competition-law news. It was written for lawyers and possibly for clients.
2  The companies involved are agricultural companies who are distributors of mung beans in China. They are in the food sector.
3  The companies were involved in a cartel, which included price fixing, and producing and circulating fraudulent information.

**Background notes**

○ For background to China's *NDRC*, see http://en.ndrc.gov.cn/. For information on the *Anti-Monopoly Law (AML)*, see http://www.insidecounsel.com/

Exclusives/2010/6/Pages/Chinas-AntiMonopoly-LawCause-for-Hope-and-Concern.aspx.

○ *Green mung beans* are a popular food in much of south and east Asia. See http://en.wikipedia.org/wiki/Mung_bean.

○ If a government or authority *clamps down on* something, it starts working much harder to prevent it.

**9.2** Tell students to read the whole text carefully to answer the questions. They could also check their predictions from the Optional lead-in above. Allow plenty of time for students to read and then discuss their answers in pairs before going through the answers with the class.

**Answers**

1  The distributors met to collude on prices and act as a cartel. They fabricated a report stating that mung-bean production had fallen, thus justifying an agreed-on rise in prices. Then they reached a consensus on price.
2  It is the highest amount a company has been fined for anti-competitive activities since the Anti-Monopoly Law was passed in China.
3  It shows that the anti-competition authorities in China are willing to crack down on offenders against the Anti-Monopoly Law.

**Background notes**

○ If you *fabricate* something, you make it up.
○ *RMB* is the currency symbol for *renminbi*, the official currency of China. The primary unit of renminbi is the *yuan*.
○ The *inception* of something is its beginning.
○ If you *step something up*, you increase the energy you put into it.
○ A *dawn raid* is when the police or another law-enforcement agency carries out an unannounced inspection, typically conducted at dawn (= early in the morning), when people least expect it.

## Optional extension

You could draw attention to and discuss with the class some of the sophisticated grammar structures used in the text by asking the questions below after each extract. When you discuss the questions and answers with the class, write the sentences and transformations (see question 5) onto the board.

○ *The Green Mung Bean Cartel is the second cartel case to have been brought ...* (Background, paragraph 2)

**1** What would be a simpler way of saying *the second cartel case to have been brought*?

**2** Does the sentence change in meaning if we say *the second cartel case to be brought*?

○ *The Green Mung Bean Cartel was alleged to have been formed on 17 October ...* (The Green Mung Bean Cartel, paragraph 1)

**3** Who alleged what?

**4** What would be a simpler way of saying this sentence?

**5** What are the rules for transforming the simpler sentence into the sentence from the text?

**6** What other verbs allow this type of transformation?

**7** How many more examples of this type of transformation are in this section of the text?

**8** What grammatical differences do you notice between the examples?

### Suggested answers

**1** ... *the second cartel case which/that has been brought.*

**2** No. The perfect infinitive (*to + have + past participle*) is used to emphasise that the events took place earlier, but in this case the meaning is still clear with a simple infinitive (*to + infinitive*).

**3** We don't know exactly who made the allegation, but it is likely to have been representatives of the NDRC. The allegation was that the cartel had been formed on 17 October.

**4** *The NDRC alleged that the Green Mung Bean Cartel was formed on 17 October.*

**5** The first transformation is that the sentence is made passive, with dummy *it* as subject, in order to avoid specifying who made the allegation. See Language note after Exercise 4.

*It was alleged (by the NDRC) that the Green Mung Bean Cartel was formed on 17 October.*

The second transformation is that the subject of a *that* clause can replace dummy *it* as subject of the main clause, in a process called subject-to-subject raising. See the final Language note after Exercise 7.3. When this happens, the *that* clause without a subject becomes a *to* clause.

*The Green Mung Bean Cartel was alleged to have been formed on 17 October.*

**6** This transformation is possible with many passive reporting verbs (*was thought/ believed/ known/ reported/ found/ rumoured to be ...*) as well as several adjectives of probability (*is likely/ bound/ sure/ certain/ unlikely to be ...*).

**7** There are three more examples, one from each paragraph in this section:

   **(i)** *JCCE is reported to have fabricated a report ...* [= *Somebody reports that JCCE fabricated a report ...*]

   **(ii)** *JCCE, together with ..., is alleged to have fabricated and (to have) spread ... and (to have) reached ...* [= *Somebody alleges that JCCE, together with ..., fabricated and spread ...*]

   **(iii)** *These actions were found by NDRC to be in violation ...* [= *NDRC found that these actions are in violation ...*]

**8** In sentences (i) and (ii), the verb is in the present tense, suggesting that the report/ allegation is still being made at present. In sentence (iii), the infinitive is used (*to be in violation*) rather than the perfect infinitive (*to have been in violation*) because the (past) actions are still in violation of the regulations now.

**9.3** Students work alone to complete the phrases and then explain them to a partner. When you discuss the answers with the class, elicit who did what (e.g. *Who has clamped down on anti-competitive behaviour? What was in high demand?*).

➧ **Answers**
   **1** down  **2** in  **3** on  **4** to
   **5** behind  **6** up; under

**9.4** Discuss the first question with the class. Students then work in pairs to brainstorm as many phrasal verbs as they can. You could turn this into a game: when you collect the answers from the class, write them on the board. Ask each pair in turn to suggest a phrasal verb and to put it into a sentence. Award a point for each new phrasal verb, and two points if the sentence is related to legal English.

**Answers**

The phrasal verbs are *clamp down*, *lag behind*, *step up*.

---

**Language note**
**Phrasal verbs**

Linguists distinguish between true phrasal verbs and prepositional verbs. True phrasal verbs may have no object (e.g. *to wake up*) or, if they have an object, the object may come before the adverbial particle (e.g. *to wake somebody up*). In prepositional verbs, in contrast, the object always follows the preposition (e.g. *to deal with something*). There are also some phrasal prepositional verbs, which have one of each type of particle (e.g. to *clamp down* [adverb] *on* [preposition] something). Many verbs follow more than one pattern (e.g. *lag behind* can be a phrasal verb [*they are lagging behind*] or a prepositional verb [*they are lagging behind their colleagues*]).

In English-language teaching, all of the verbs mentioned above are often described as phrasal verbs, which are defined in terms of their idiomatic meaning or their behaviour as a single semantic unit.

For most learners of English, the distinction between the linguists' definition and the English teachers' definition is probably irrelevant. For them, the key to understanding phrasal verbs is the patterns that follow them. For this reason, it is essential to teach/learn such verbs as part of patterns with objects (e.g. *to lag behind somebody*).

Some examples of important legal English phrasal and prepositional verbs:

○ Phrasal verbs: *to set something aside, to set something forth, to carry something out, to lay something down*
○ Prepositional verbs: *to enter into something, to deal with something, to stem from something*

**9.5** Check students understand the words *severe*, *lenient*, *just* and *deter* from question 1. Students then discuss the three questions in small groups. After a few minutes, open up the discussion to include the whole class.

**9.6** Students work alone to make their summaries. You could set a word limit of 80 or even 50 words for the note-taking task. Then make sure each student knows if he/she is reporting to a lawyer or to a client. Students then take turns to present their summaries.

 **10 Listening B: Merger control**

Elicit from the class what *merger control* is, and how it might involve lawyers. Then tell students to read the introduction (SB page 216) to compare it with their suggestions.

---

**Optional alternative to Exercises 10.1 and 10.2**
**Preparation for Part 2 of the ILEC Test of Listening**

You could treat Exercises 10.1 and 10.2 as a single set of questions in order to make this as similar as possible to Part 2 of the ILEC Test of Listening (i.e. five multiple-choice questions). If so, advise students that the questions in 10.2 are answered before those in 10.1. Play the recording twice. You may allow students to discuss their answers in pairs after the second listening, but not to change their answers.

---

**Background note**
If you *adjudicate* /əˈdʒuːdɪˌkeɪt/, you judge a dispute, often in a less formal context than a courtroom, from a neutral standpoint.

**10.1** Tell students to read the questions and the options, then listen to the recording to choose the best answers. After the recording, tell students to discuss in pairs what they remember from the presentation. Then check the answers with the class.

**Transcript »** STUDENT'S BOOK **page 294**

 **Answers**
  **1** c  **2** b

---

 **Answers**
  **1** b  **2** a  **3** a

**10.3** Tell students to discuss these questions with a partner, then open the discussion to the whole class.

---

**Background notes**
- ○ If you *impute* something, you consider or calculate it.
- ○ *Definition of the market* involves defining its geographical area and the range of products competing for the same target customers within that market.
- ○ If something *impedes* competition, it gets in the way of it.
- ○ If an analysis is described as *sound*, it is conducted properly so that its results may be relied upon.
- ○ If you do something *up front*, you do it in advance of some other step.
- ○ If a merger is *consummated* /ˈkɒnsjʊˌmeɪtɪd/, it is completed.
- ○ *By the same token* means 'in the same way'.
- ○ A *difficult call* is a situation whose outcome is difficult to predict.
- ○ A *public policy presumption* is a presumption (view of the way the world works or should work) which underpins public policies. For example, there might be a public policy presumption that competition is a good thing, and this underpins policies to promote competition.
- ○ If a merger is *susceptible* /səˈsepˌtəbl/ to a negotiated resolution, such a resolution will work for the merger.
- ○ If you *fall foul of* a regulation, you run into legal problems connected with it.
- ○ If you *factor* something *into* your calculations, you include it.
- ○ *Down the line* means 'at a later stage in the process'.

**10.2** Tell students to read through the questions to try to remember the answers, then to listen to the recording a second time to check. After the recording, tell students to compare their answers with a partner and then go through them with the class.

---

 **Suggested answer**
  **2** Efficiency gains arise where the two merging companies both have a team of people doing a particular job which can be done more quickly, cheaply or with fewer people for both merged companies at the same time. Examples include transport, warehousing, accounting, personnel, sales, marketing, IT and legal departments. They also need fewer bosses. Merged companies also need fewer offices and generally smaller premises than the original companies needed, and may also require fewer machines, vehicles, computers, etc.

---

**Optional extension**
**Photocopiable worksheet 15.3**

Listening B contains many examples of the passive voice with a range of tenses. Photocopiable worksheet 15.3 highlights this language and provides further practice, in context, of forming and using passive.

Tell students to read through the extracts from the transcript to find mistakes with the active and passive voice. Point out that some sentences contain several mistakes, but that there are no mistakes with other grammar structures. Then tell them to work with a partner to compare the mistakes they have found, and to correct them.

When they have finished, either go through the answers with the class or play the recording for students to check their answers.

**Answers**
1 do mergers evaluate → are mergers evaluated; to employ → to be employed
2 must be considered → must consider
3 must consider → must be considered
4 may be failed → may fail; have to account for → have to be accounted for

5 does → is done; might approve → might be approved; might reject → might be rejected

6 answers → is answered; finds → is found; may be counter-balanced → may counter-balance

7 be claimed → claim; permit → be/are permitted

8 to evaluate → to be evaluated; has consummated → has been consummated

9 may permit → may be permitted; judges → is judged; may disallow → may be disallowed

10 eases → is eased; may consider → may be considered

11 recognises → is recognised; to easily approve → to be easily approved

12 devise → are devised; will be fallen → will fall

## 11 Reading D: Report on changes in merger regulation

Elicit from the class what recent changes in merger regulation students are aware of, especially in the context of the EU. Then tell them to read the introduction (SB page 217) to compare it with their ideas.

**11.1** Discuss these questions with the class without confirming or rejecting students' suggestions. Then tell students to find the answer to the questions quickly. Note that *turnover threshold* is not explicitly defined, so when you go through the answers with the class, discuss both terms more thoroughly to make sure students understand them.

**Answers**
1 *One-stop shop* is usually used to refer to a store where different kinds of products can be bought: one convenient location where various needs can be met at once. Here, the term is used to indicate that many procedures that formerly were carried out in several different places are now taken care of centrally by the European Commission.
2 *Turnover threshold* refers to the combined turnover of the parties to a merger for purposes of EC merger control. If the combined turnover of the

companies exceeds the amount stated in the EC Merger Regulations, then the merger is said to have a community dimension and the merger is subject to the competence of the European Commission, as opposed to the Member States.

**11.2** Tell students to read the whole text carefully in order to answer the two questions. When they have finished, tell them to compare their answers with a partner. Then discuss the answers with the class.

 **Answers**
1 The first purpose of a pre-notification request is to have the Commission take over the case from the national authorities in cases when the combined turnover of the parties to a merger falls below the existing thresholds, and where notification would otherwise have been required in at least three Member States. The second purpose is to have the case be examined by a national competition authority rather than by the Commission when it can be shown that a distinct market exists in that Member State which would be affected by the proposed merger.
2 Advantages: a single filing (less paperwork and expense); disadvantages: uncertainty of the outcome and a longer clearance process.

**Background note**
The *EEA* is the European Economic Area, an organisation created in order to allow the four members of EFTA (European Free Trade Association) to participate in the EU's single European market. One EFTA member, Switzerland, decided not to join, so current members are the EU states plus Norway, Iceland and Liechtenstein.

**11.3** Go through this quickly with the whole class.

 **Answers**
1 d  2 c  3 a  4 b

## 12 Writing C: An informative email

Tell students to read the instructions to find out what they have to do. Then elicit why a client might want to find out about pre-notification. The writing can be done at home or in class, and individually or in groups. See Writing section, page xiv.

 **Suggested answer**

Dear Mr Easton

I am writing to inform you of a change in the pre-notification procedure for mergers in the EU, as I believe it is relevant for the merger which your company is considering.

According to this new procedure, in cases where the combined turnover of the parties to a merger falls below prescribed thresholds and notification would have previously been required in at least three Member States, a company can now submit a pre-notification request to the Commission, which under certain circumstances would then take over the case from the national authorities. Alternatively, if the merger in question would affect a distinct market in a particular Member State, a company may submit a pre-notification request that the case be examined by that Member State's national competition authority rather than by the Commission.

The clear advantage of these two options is that they result in less paperwork and expense, as only a single filing is required in each case. However, there are disadvantages to the new procedure, including uncertainty concerning the allocation of the case and a likely increase in the length of the clearance process.

I hope that this information was of interest to you. Should you have any questions in this matter I would be happy to provide assistance.

Yours sincerely

Samuel Lee

(209 words)

## 13 Speaking: Giving opinions: a competition-law case

Elicit from the class what they know about the Microsoft case, but try to avoid discussing students' opinions at this stage. Elicit ways of referring to somebody's opinion, and ways of agreeing and disagreeing with their opinions. Then tell students to read the introduction and the information in the box (SB page 219) to compare it with their ideas.

Tell students to read the two opinions to make sure they understand everything. You may need to check some vocabulary (see Background notes below).

The discussion will work best if it is done with the whole class, but if you have a large class, you may divide them into groups of five or six students. Alternatively, you could conduct this as practice for Part 3 of the ILEC Test of Speaking, in which case students should work in pairs. Encourage them to use the language from the box, and to refer to the two opinions quoted. At the end of the discussion, ask if anybody has changed their opinion as a result of what they have discussed.

 **Background notes**

○ A *disincentive* /ˌdɪsɪnˈsentɪv/ discourages somebody from taking a certain action, often unintentionally.

○ If the cost of computing has fallen *ten-million-fold*, it is now 1/10,000,000 as expensive as it was.

○ If two products are *compatible*, they can work together.

 Tell students to do the Internet activity as homework. See Using the Internet for research on page xviii.

# Language focus

## Answers

**1 Vocabulary: distinguishing meaning**

1. *cartel*: The others are companies.
2. *dimension*: The others are levels.
3. *offences*: The others are neutral behaviour.
4. *oligopoly*: The others are illegal arrangements between companies; an *oligopoly* is not in itself illegal, although it can lead to anti-competitive behaviour.
5. *to breach*: The others mean 'to use improperly'.

**2 Word formation**

| Verb | Abstract noun | Adjective |
|------|---------------|-----------|
| monopolise | monopoly | monopolistic |
| collude | collusion | collusive |
| abuse | abuse | abusive |
| compete | competition | competitive |
| discriminate | discrimination | discriminating, discriminatory |
| restrict | restriction | restrictive |
| regulate | regulation | regulatory |
| allocate | allocation | |
| fine | fine | |
| notify | notification | |

**3 Vocabulary: collocations 1**

**2** practices  **3** position  **4** bids  **5** cartel
**6** petition  **7** access  **8** fines  **9** complaint

 **Background note**
If you *lodge* a complaint, you make a formal complaint to the relevant authority.

**4 Vocabulary: collocations 2**

**2** abusive  **3** dominant  **4** imposed
**5** collusion  **6** lodge

**5 Vocabulary: collocations with *merger***

approve, evaluate, investigate, reject

**6 Vocabulary: irregular plural forms**

**2** b  **3** a/b  **4** b  **5** a/b  **6** a  **7** a/b
**8** a/b  **9** a/b  **10** a  **11** b  **12** b

**7 Prepositions**

**2** of  **3** in  **4** by  **5** against  **6** in  **7** to
**8** on  **9** for

## Teacher's brief

**Transnational commercial law** is also known as **private international law**, and deals with the legal relationships between parties involved in **cross-border transactions**, such as import/export and the carriage of goods (transportation). It is becoming increasingly important as the world becomes more integrated and cross-border trade becomes the norm rather than the exception. The Internet has also allowed services to be provided across borders. As Case study 5 (SB pages 206–207) demonstrated, even the issue of a company's **centre of main interest** (COMI) is not always clear-cut: it may be registered in one country but conduct all of its business from another, or from several. The same is true of individual people: they may come from one country (**nationality**), have **citizenship** from a second and live in a third. Further, their country of **domicile** (permanent address) may not be the same as their country of **residence** – where they live at the moment.

As usual, all of these issues become relevant when things go wrong, e.g. if there is a breach of contract or if a tort is committed. In such situations, there may be a **conflict of laws** and the parties need to know which laws apply to their case. As Reading B explains, there are three key questions here: 1) Which country has **jurisdiction** to hear the case? 2) Which country's laws should be used to judge the case (= the **choice of law** question)? 3) Which other countries will recognise and enforce the judgment? (= the **recognition** question). The first question is answered by looking at the defendant, while the second looks at both parties as well as the details of their dispute. Sometimes this may mean that questions 1 and 2 produce different answers, in which case the **forum court** (= the court that hears the case) will apply its own **procedural law** but the **substantive law** of another country.

Obviously, this situation can produce some messy and unpredictable results, which is why contracting parties in cross-border transactions tend to include an **arbitration clause** in their contracts, which states clearly how any disputes will be resolved. **Arbitration** involves a hearing before an **arbitrator** (= similar to a judge), who hears the dispute and issues a binding decision, often ordering the payment of an **arbitral award**. Arbitration is often preferred to litigation (= suing somebody in court) because it tends to be quicker and cheaper for both parties. Listening A focuses on the skill of drafting good arbitration clauses based on rules from the **International Chamber of Commerce** (ICC), a non-governmental body.

As Reading A explains, the ICC has sponsored many sets of **uniform rules** and other instruments which harmonise international trade. Although these are not legally binding, parties to transnational contracts often agree in their contracts to be bound by them. The same is true of **model laws**, which are created by organisations such as UNIDROIT and UNCITRAL, and which countries often choose to adopt. This supports transnational trade because it makes the laws of different countries more similar and therefore predictable.

The second half of the unit is a case study of a **cross-border dispute** involving damage to goods while they were being transported from the Netherlands to France. In this dispute, the defendant, a carrier (= a transport company) is from Germany. The relevant law in such cases comes from the **Convention for the International Carriage of Goods by Road** (CMR), to which all European states are **signatories**. According to this Convention, this case may be heard in any of the three relevant countries. However, the lawyers representing the defendant are keen for the case to be heard in the Netherlands, which is seen as a carrier-friendly jurisdiction. One way for a party to make sure it gets its choice of jurisdiction is by seeking in that jurisdiction a **negative declaration** that the carrier has no liability. Even if this **declaratory action** is unsuccessful, once proceedings have started in this jurisdiction, it becomes the jurisdiction for the whole dispute. In other words, the lawyers have to race to get this declaratory action started in the Dutch courts before the plaintiff can initiate proceedings in a less favourable jurisdiction.

The case study leads in to a substantial writing task, where the lawyers combine a range of information into a letter to a client. For this to work, lawyers need to **plan their writing carefully**. They also need the skills involved in **transforming information** from one source (e.g. an extract from a Convention) or medium (e.g. a conversation with another lawyer) into something new (e.g. a letter to a client). Both of these skills are developed in this unit.

**Further information**

○ As always, Wikipedia is a good starting point for general research on **transnational commercial law**: http://en.wikipedia.org/wiki/International_ commercial_law.

○ The **Transnational Law Portal** (http://www. transnational-law.net) has many links and resources.

○ **Translex** (http://www.trans-lex.org) offers a free research and codification platform for transnational law.

○ The **International Chamber of Commerce**'s website, http://www.iccwbo.org, has plenty of materials and guidance on many of the topics from this unit. Its rules for arbitration are available here: http://www.iccwbo.org/court/ arbitration/id4199/index.html.

○ The full text of the **CMR** (Convention on the Contract for the International Carriage of Goods by Road) is available here: http://www.jus.uio. no/lm/un.cmr.road.carriage.contract. convention.1956/doc.html.

# Discussion

Use these questions to generate a discussion.

a  What are the complications involved in a party from one country buying goods, real property or a business from another country?

b  What would happen if something went wrong with such a transaction?

c  How similar are the laws of different countries?

d  Have you had any experience of dealing with the laws of different countries?

 **Suggested answers**

a  As well as practical complications (e.g. language, currency rates, import/ export restrictions, working through agents/distributors, etc.), there are of course many legal issues, which will vary from situation to situation. As always, the parties to the transaction should plan for what happens if and when things go wrong, by negotiating an arbitration clause as part of the contract, specifying which laws have jurisdiction over the contract, etc.

b  It depends whether the contract contains an arbitration clause. If so, and if the parties agree to abide by the arbitration clause, the dispute could be settled in the normal way. If there is no such clause, however, the parties will first have to settle the issue of conflict of laws, as described in Reading B.

c  This is, of course, impossible to answer, but in general it seems fair to say that the laws of most countries are similar in their relationship to common sense and the concept of fairness. The details, however, are often very different, and cannot be guessed by a lawyer who is unfamiliar with the laws of a particular country. This can easily make the difference between winning and losing a case. For this reason, there is a trend towards harmonisation of laws, as explained in Reading A.

## 1  Reading A: Introduction to transnational commercial law

**1.1**  Students spend a few minutes discussing the six questions in small groups to predict the answers and to share any knowledge they have of these issues. They then read the text quickly to complete the matching exercise, then check with the class.

**Answers**
**A** 2  **B** 4  **C** 5  **D** 1  **E** 6  **F** 3

### Background notes

○ In paragraph C, the use of *some* may cause problems: *It is estimated that some 60 instruments make up ...* In this context, *some* means *approximately*.

○ *Agency and distribution* refers simply to the work done by agents and distributors. An agent is a person who is authorised to enter into agreements with third parties on behalf of a company. An agent often markets and sells products and services on behalf of the company, but is not employed by the company. A distributor, who cannot enter into legal agreements on behalf of the company, is less likely to be involved in sales and marketing, but more in logistical issues such as warehousing and delivery to customers.

○ The *Rome Convention* (Convention on the Law Applicable to Contractual Obligations 1980) aimed to harmonise the choice of law system for contractual obligations in the EU (see Reading B). It was replaced in 2008 by the Rome I Regulation. Choice of law for non-contractual obligations is covered by the Rome II Regulation. See http://en. wikipedia.org/wiki/Rome_I_Regulation for background and a link to the text of the regulation.

○ The *Brussels Convention* (Convention of 27 September 1968 on Jurisdiction and the Enforcement of Judgments in Civil and Commercial Matters) forms part of the Brussels Regime, a set of detailed rules governing the choice of jurisdiction where a dispute can be heard (see Reading B). See http://en.wikipedia.org/wiki/Brussels_Regime.

○ The websites for *UNIDROIT* /ˈjuːnɪdrɔɪt/ (http://www.unidroit.org), *UNCITRAL* (http://www.uncitral.org) and the *International Chamber of Commerce* (http://www.iccwbo.org) all contain a wealth of information, and are well worth exploring.

○ *Incoterms* are an internationally recognised standard and are used worldwide in international and domestic contracts for the sale of goods. See http://www.iccwbo.org/incoterms.

○ *The Uniform Rules for Collections* are standards of collection practices for bills of exchange (US: drafts) for financial institutions. See http://www.iccbooks.com/Product/ProductInfo.aspx?id=178.

○ *The Uniform Rules for Demand Guarantees* are a set of rules specifying uniform practices for securing payment and performance in worldwide commercial contracts. See http://www.investopedia.com/terms/u/urdg.asp.

**1.2** Students discuss the questions in pairs. Encourage them to answer the questions from memory, rather than simply reading the relevant sections aloud. Afterwards, discuss the questions with the class.

 **Suggested answers**

1 UNIDROIT and UNCITRAL. The European Union is supranational, not international. According to the text, the ICC has endorsed rules, rather than introduced them.

2 A set of international conventions, model laws and uniform rules and uniform trade terms which govern international commercial transactions

3 Model laws have the force of law when they are adopted by a state; uniform rules have the force of law when they are invoked through reference in contract or established through previous course of dealing or custom and usage of trade.

4 Public international law relates to relations between sovereign states; private international law relates to the rights and obligations of private citizens.

5 Sales, contract law, electronic commerce, etc. See paragraph C of Reading A.

6 The CISG, etc. See paragraph E of Reading A.

**1.3** Students work in pairs to discuss the four statements, then feed back to the class.

 **Answers**

1 False (It excludes transactions conducted between sovereign states.)

2 True

**3** False (The Rome and Brussels Conventions are related to the EU; UNIDROIT and UNCITRAL are international.)

**4** True

**Optional extension**
**ILEC preparation: Test of Reading Part 5**

Point out that the matching task in Exercise 1.1 is similar to the task in Part 5 of the ILEC Test of Reading, where instead of questions, students have to identify which paragraph a sentence comes from.

Tell students to cover the text, so they can only see the list of six questions in 1.1. Then read some sentences from the text aloud (see below) for students to identify which paragraph they came from, using the questions in 1.1 to remind them of the content of each paragraph. Note that the sentences do not necessarily answer the questions in 1.1. This task will be rather difficult, as it requires some lateral thinking, but this skill will be useful for Part 5 of the Test of Reading.

Sentences to read aloud:

**1** *As such, transnational commercial law encompasses private international law.* (question 4; paragraph B)

**2** *These instruments only provide a model which a State can adopt into law in whole or in part.* (question 3; paragraph F)

**3** *Significant uniform rules and trade terms are endorsed by the ICC, which is a non-governmental organisation.* (question 1; paragraph D)

**4** *Thus, this unit will focus on private law (as opposed to public law) and cross-border transactions (as opposed to domestic transactions).* (question 2; paragraph A)

**5** *Of course, conventions must be incorporated into national law to have the force of law at a national level.* (question 6; paragraph E)

**1.4** Students discuss the questions in pairs. If they don't know the answer to question 1, encourage them to speculate. You could ask them to research this as a homework task. Afterwards, open up the discussion to include the whole class.

**Background note**
It is easy to find online lists of signatories to international conventions. See, for example, http://en.wikipedia.org/wiki/United_Nations_Convention_on_Contracts_for_the_International_Sale_of_Goods.

## 2 Key terms: Transnational commercial law

**2.1** Students work alone to match the terms with the definitions. Suggest that they start with the definitions, and do the easier ones first. After a few minutes, put them in pairs to compare their answers. When you go through the answers with the class, check students fully understand all the terms by asking for examples, etc.

**Answers**

**1** b **2** d **3** f **4** c **5** h **6** a **7** i **8** n
**9** k **10** g **11** m **12** e **13** l **14** j **15** o

**Background notes**

○ *Comity* /ˈkɒmɪti/ is also sometimes referred to as legal reciprocity, i.e. the principle that penalties, favours or benefits that are granted by one state to the citizens or legal entities of another should be returned in kind.

○ *Arbitration* involves a neutral third party hearing a dispute and imposing a legally binding decision on the parties. *Mediation* also involves a third party to facilitate the settlement, but the parties themselves are expected to reach a binding decision between them. *Conciliation* is similar, but the decision is non-binding.

○ The prefix *supra-* (as in *supranational*) has the same meaning as *super-*, i.e. 'above / greater than'.

**Optional extension**
Students test each other in pairs by reading a term from Exercise 2.1 to elicit a definition from their partner. Alternatively, they could ask questions using the definitions to elicit the correct term (e.g. *What term describes binding international treaty provisions?*).

**2.2** Tell students to work alone to complete the sentences, then check with a partner. When you go through the answers with the class, ask volunteers to briefly paraphrase sentence 3, as if to a non-lawyer.

**Answers**
**1** harmonisation; member states
**2** comity; jurisdictions
**3** course of dealing; arbitration clause
**4** forum; lex mercatoria
Possible paraphrase of sentence 3: When the parties agreed orally on the terms of the transaction, they didn't explicitly include a standard arbitration clause. There was also no arbitration clause that could be implied from their previous dealings, for example if they'd always resolved disputes in a particular way before. So the claimant was allowed to take his claim to court, rather than an arbitration tribunal, even though he had referred the claim for arbitration at first.

## 3 Reading B: Conflict of laws in private international law

Tell students to read the introduction (SB page 225) to identify where the text comes from, and why a lawyer might read it. (Answers: It comes from a text assigned to students on an LLM programme. A lawyer would read it to understand the procedural rules which determine which legal system, and the law of which jurisdiction, applies to a dispute involving cross-border transactions.)

**Background note**
LLM stands for *Legum Magister* (Master of Laws). The double *L* simply means that *legum* is plural.

**3.1** Tell students to discuss the questions briefly in pairs, then open up the discussion to include the whole class.

**Answer**
**1** Subjects would depend upon the focus of the programme or student but might include some of the following:
○ Intellectual Property Law
○ International Business Transactions
○ International Law on Foreign Investment
○ International Commercial Arbitration
○ International Trade Law and the Environment
○ World Trade Organisation Law and Practice
○ International Consumer Law
○ Commercial Credit
○ International Competition Law
○ Private International Law
○ Corporate Governance

**3.2** Allow students a very limited time (around one minute) to scan the text and complete the definitions. After the time limit, tell students to close their books and go through the answers with the class. Point out that scanning is an important reading skill, both for the ILEC exam and for life in general.

**Answers**
**1** domicile   **2** choice of law   **3** forum shopping   **4** forum non conveniens   **5** reciprocity

**Background notes**
○ A *constituent element* is an element that constitutes (= forms part of) a bigger item, such as a dispute. The constituent elements of a dispute might include details about the two parties, the contract between them, their business relationship, the circumstances of the event leading to the dispute, the way each party reacted to these events, etc.
○ If an *organ* (e.g. a court, an arbitration tribunal) *adjudicates* a dispute, it hears it and makes a formal decision.
○ *Substantive law* defines the legal relationship of people with other people or between them and the state. It contrasts with *procedural law*, i.e. the rules by which courts hear proceedings.
○ The third paragraph contains the structure *be it*, meaning 'whether it is': *The choice of law question ... seeks to identify the state, be it* (= whether it is) *the forum state or another state, ...*

○ *Concurrent* is used to describe things that happen at the same time as each other. If two courts have concurrent jurisdiction, they both have a fair claim to hear the dispute.

○ Paragraph 5 states that the choice-of-law question may be answered *legislatively*. In other words, by referring to legislation (as opposed to precedents).

○ *Pertinent* means 'relevant, significant'.

○ The *rendering court* is the court which renders (= makes) the judgment.

○ *Reciprocity* /ˌresɪˈprɒsɪti/ is the principle of repaying favours/support to the party who helped you.

○ The *country of rendition* is the country where the judgment was rendered.

○ *Outright* means 'absolutely'.

**3.3** Allow three or four minutes for students to read the text carefully. Afterwards, they discuss their answers in pairs before feeding back to the class.

 **Answers**

1 jurisdiction, choice of law, judgment recognition

2 The jurisdictional question focuses on the relationship between the defendant and the forum state to decide whether the relationship is close enough to justify litigation being carried out there. The choice-of-law question, in contrast, focuses on both parties to the dispute, and looks at the relationship of the dispute to the forum state or another state with regard to the choice of the law that most appropriately applies to the dispute.

3 Procedural law refers to the rules for conducting litigation in a jurisdiction and thus applies to the proceedings in a case, whereas substantive law is the term for the legal principles which apply to the subject matter of the case and which define the rights and obligations of the individual.

4 Recognition of foreign judgments can depend on whether the recognising court would have applied the law that was chosen by the rendering court or whether the recognising court would have reached a comparable result. It can also depend on whether the award of damages in a case is perceived to be excessive, in which case the judgment may not be enforced. Another factor is the question of whether reciprocity exists between the two states, as some countries refuse to recognise judgments when there is no reciprocity agreement.

**3.4** Tell students to complete the task alone and then to compare answers with a partner. When you go through the answers with the class, elicit who or what would do each of the actions (e.g. a court/judge/arbitrator might adjudicate a dispute; a breach of contract might give rise to a dispute, etc.).

**Answers**

1 a dispute (to pass judgment on a disagreement)
2 a dispute (to cause a disagreement)
3 a judgment (to make a party obey a final decision of the court)
4 a judgment (to make a judgment)
5 a dispute (to solve a disagreement)
6 a judgment (to accept a judgment)

**Optional extension**
**Photocopiable worksheet 16.1**

Because the concepts involved in conflict of laws may be rather complicated and confusing, Photocopiable worksheet 16.1 provides a graphical representation of the text in Reading B. This also serves as a comprehension check of the text. Students work in pairs to complete the diagram. If you want to increase the challenge, ask them to try first without referring to the text. Point out that the answers are numbered in the order they first appear in the text, although several occur later as well. Afterwards, go through the answers with the class.

**Answers**

1 disputes  2 Constituent  3 jurisdiction
4 object  5 Nationality  6 Citizenship
7 Domicile  8 Residence  9 Affiliation

10 Jurisdiction   11 adjudicate   12 Choice of law   13 substantive; merits   14 Judgment recognition   15 recognise; enforce
16 Distinct   17 forum; defendant
18 state; dispute   19 concurrent jurisdiction
20 advantageous; forum shopping
21 decline; forum non conveniens
22 procedural law   23 legislatively; judicial precedent   24 pertinent contacts   25 Lex loci delicti   26 Lex loci contractus   27 Lex rei sitae   28 substantive law   29 same; equivalent   30 excessive   31 reciprocity
32 treaty

# 4   Text analysis: Cohesion

Go through the underlined phrases from Reading B to elicit from the class what each phrase refers to and how it holds the text together. Then tell students to read the information in the Text analysis box to compare it with their ideas. Elicit more examples of the four techniques.

Students work in small groups to find and underline more examples of cohesive devices, then share their ideas with the class.

 **Suggested answers**

*These elements* (lexical cohesion, refers back to their constituent elements)
*… that give rise to the dispute* (lexical cohesion, refers back to disputes)
*The jurisdictional question and the choice-of-law question* (lexical cohesion, refers back to these phrases in the preceding paragraph)
*The jurisdictional question focuses on …* (lexical cohesion, refers back to this phrase in the preceding paragraph)
*… the relationship between the defendant and the forum state, and asks whether that relationship* (lexical cohesion, refers back to the relationship in the same sentence)
*… in that state and to justify utilising that state's* (both lexical cohesion, refer back to the forum state in the same sentence)
*The choice-of-law question* (lexical cohesion, refers back to this phrase in the preceding paragraph)
*… focuses on both parties and their dispute and seeks to identify that state, be it the forum state or another state, whose*

*relationship to the dispute is such as to render most appropriate the application of its law to the merits of the dispute* (lexical cohesion, both refer back to *and their dispute* in the same sentence)
*In such a case,* (substitution, refers back to the idea of *the courts of more than one state may have concurrent jurisdiction to adjudicate the same dispute*)
*a technique* (substitution, refers back to the idea *may shop for the most advantageous forum*)
*… to discourage this technique* (lexical cohesion, refers back to *a technique*)
*With regard to the merits of the case* (conjunction and lexical cohesion, refers back to *a case with foreign elements*)
*This* (reference, refers back to the idea *may or may not apply its own substantive law*)
*These rules* (substitution, refers back to *which may be answered legislatively as in most civil-law systems, or through judicial precedent …*)
*Regarding the recognition question* (conjunction and lexical cohesion, refers back to *judgment recognition* in the second paragraph)
*recognition* (lexical cohesion, used several times in the last paragraph to refer back to the main idea of the paragraph)

 **Language note**

It could be said that the feature which best distinguishes good-quality writing from poor writing is the cohesiveness of the text. Poor writers tend to string sentences together in no apparent order, with no clear links between them. A good writer, on the other hand, makes full use of a wide range of cohesive devices to 'glue' the text together. This is one of the key factors that are assessed in the ILEC Test of Writing. A simple way to improve a student's grade in this exam might be to make sure the text contains plenty of such devices. Cohesion is also important in Part 5 of the Test of Reading, where students use cohesive devices to work out which sentence belongs in which part of a text. This is only possible if the text is well written in the first place. A simple way of checking cohesiveness in students' writing, therefore, is to see if sentences could be removed and then put back in the right places by another person using only the cohesive devices as guidance.

---

**Optional extension**

Tell students to close their books. They then use the diagram from Photocopiable worksheet 16.1 to retell part of the text to a partner, inserting plenty of cohesive devices to make their speech flow. They take turns to make one sentence each.

---

## 5 Listening A: Drafting arbitration clauses

Students read the introduction (SB page 227) to find out who is going to be talking to whom about what and why.

**5.1** Students discuss the questions in pairs, then share their ideas with the class. Avoid confirming or rejecting their suggestions at this stage – they can refer to the audio transcript on SB page 295 later if necessary.

**5.2** Tell students to read through the six points to check they understand. Then play the recording for them to tick the points that are mentioned. Afterwards, students discuss their answers in pairs, including as much as they can remember about each point, then feed back to the class.

**Transcript** » STUDENT'S BOOK **page 295**

 **Answers**
1, 3, 4, 5

---

 **Background notes**

○ If a provision is *unequivocal* /ˌʌnɪˈkwɪvəkl/, it has only one possible interpretation.

○ The *exigencies* of a given situation are the difficult or demanding circumstances connected with it.

○ *Scrutiny* /ˈskruːtɪni/ means 'careful and detailed analysis or checking'. When the ICC scrutinises arbitrators appointed by one or both of the parties, it carefully checks their suitability for the job.

---

○ *Fraud in the inducement* occurs when party A enters into a contractual agreement with party B because party B has given false information to A in order to induce (persuade) party A to sign. Party A knows he/she has signed a contract, but did so for the wrong reasons. This contrasts with *fraud in the factum*, where party A may not even know that he/she has signed a contract, or may believe the contents of the contract to be different from what they actually are.

○ If a court *tries* (= hears) a case *de novo*, it hears the same case after it has been settled, perhaps because new evidence has come to light.

○ The latest set of ICC Rules of Arbitration are available from the ICC site: http://www.iccwbo.org/court/ arbitration/id4199/index.html.

○ Note that the speaker uses *better* as a verb, meaning 'to improve': *changes that will better the arbitral process.*

○ At the end of the extract, the speaker says … *ICC rules may be disregarded* (= ignored) *if the ICC will otherwise refuse to administer the arbitration.* Although students often learn that combinations of *if* and *will* are ungrammatical, this sentence is actually correct. *Will* here makes it clear that the refusal is further into the future than the disregarding of the rules. In other words, the rules may be disregarded (tomorrow) if it is clear (tomorrow) that the ICC will refuse (later).

**5.3** Play the recording for students to underline the three key phrases. They then discuss the questions in pairs and feed back to the class.

**Transcript** » STUDENT'S BOOK **page 296**

 **Answers**
The three key expressions the speaker mentions are *All disputes*, *in connection with* and *finally settled*.

**5.4** Tell students to discuss the questions in pairs, then open up the discussion to include the whole class.

**Answers**

1 The speaker advises against relying on an 'all-purpose' arbitration clause for all situations, and believes that parties should always draft a clause to suit the situation at hand, one which takes into account the likely types of dispute, the needs of the parties and the applicable laws.

2 The speaker recommends the ICC because it is the major arbitral institution in the world. Furthermore, it is a brand name and offers certain quality advantages, such as scrutiny of party-appointed arbitrators and arbitral awards.

3 According to the speaker, the advantage of adopting the rules that are in existence at the time of contracting is that these are the rules they know, and future rule changes may have unpredictable effects. The advantage of opting to have the amended or modified rules apply is that the parties can take advantage of future rule amendments, assuming the ICC will only adopt changes that will better the arbitral process.

4 With regard to altering the ICC rules, the speaker advises that parties include a clause providing that any alteration of the ICC rules may be disregarded if the ICC will otherwise refuse to administer the arbitration.

**5.5** Elicit onto the board some possible examples of collocations with *arbitral*. Then play the recording for students to make notes. If you prefer, you could ask students to underline the collocations in the audio transcript as they listen. Finally, go through the answers with the class.

**Answers**
proceeding(s), institution, award, process, clause(s)
Other possible collocations: *arbitral tribunal, arbitral decision*

**Optional extension**
While students are listening for collocations with *arbitral* in Exercise 5.5, they could also listen for other useful collocations, e.g. collocations with *arbitrate*, *arbitration* and

*arbitrator*. Note that *arbitral* and *arbitration* are sometimes used interchangeably before some nouns with no difference in meaning: *arbitral/arbitration proceedings*; *arbitral/arbitration clause.*

**Suggested answers**
international commercial arbitration
an agreement to arbitrate
to administer an arbitration proceeding
to negotiate an arbitration clause
party-appointed arbitrators
sample arbitration clause
Rules of Arbitration / arbitration rules
to govern the arbitration
to conduct the arbitration
a detailed arbitration clause
to administer an arbitration
arbitration proceedings
confirm arbitrators
replace arbitrators

**Optional extension**
**ILEC preparation: Test of Reading Part 3**
**Photocopiable worksheet 16.2**

The first exercise on Photocopiable worksheet 16.2 focuses on the useful vocabulary from Listening A, with a further chance to practise word building, the skill needed for Part 3 of the ILEC Test of Reading. The words are also useful and worth discussing in their own right, as many of them will be new to students. The second exercise focuses on the pronunciation of these new words.

1 Students close their books and work alone to complete the gap-fill exercise. Go through the answers with the class, discussing the meanings of the words in brackets and in the blanks. Make sure students all have the correct answers, as these will be essential for the next part of the activity. You could help a little with pronunciation at this stage, especially with new words (e.g. *exigencies*).

**Answers**
**1** consensual  **2** proceedings  **3** mandatory
**4** unequivocal  **5** supplemented
**6** exigencies; relationship; applicable
**7** inclusion  **8** controversies/controversy; exception  **9** non-contractual; inducement
**10** amendments; substantial  **11** existence;

contracting; unpredictable **12** expressly; absence; commencement **13** alterations **14** determine; scrutinise/scrutinize **15** disregarded; administer

**Notes**

○ In gap 2, *procedures* is also possible but less likely: procedures tend to be carried out rather than conducted.

○ In gap 5, *supplemented* may be followed by either *with* or *by*.

**2** Students work in pairs to complete the table. Point out that several of the words have more than one possible pronunciation (see Notes below). Finally, go through the answers with the class, making sure students pronounce the words correctly when they feed back.

| ●· | ·●· | ●··· | ··●· |
|---|---|---|---|
| ab-sence | con-sen-sual[2] pro-ceed-ings in-clu-sion ex-cep-tion in-duce-ment a-mend-ments sub-stan-tial ex-is-tence con-trac-ting[3] ex-press-ly com-mence-ment de-ter-mine[4] | man-da-to-ry[1] supp-le-men-ted ex-i-gen-cies con-tro-ver-sies[5] | non-con-trac-tual[2] al-ter-a-tions dis-re-gar-ded |
| **●··** | | **·●··** | **··●··** |
| man-da-tory[1] scru-ti-nise/ scru-ti-nize | | (con-sen-su-al[2]) re-la-tion-ship ap-plic-ab-le con-tro-ver-sies[5] ad-min-i-ster | un-e-qui-vo-cal (non-con-trac-tu-al[2]) un-pre-dict-ab-le |

**Notes**

**1** *Mandatory* tends to be pronounced as three syllables in British English (BrE) and four in American English (AmE).

**2** The ending *–ual* is normally pronounced as a single syllable in fluent speech, but may be pronounced as two syllables in careful speech.

**3** Note that although *contract* is stressed on the first syllable as a noun, the second syllable is stressed with all meanings of the verb.

**4** *Determine* is often mispronounced by learners of English.

**5** *Controversy* tends to be stressed on the second syllable in BrE and the first syllable in AmE.

## 6 Speaking: A short presentation

You could set the research as a homework task or, if you prefer, ask students to invent any details they are unsure of. When the presentations are ready, ask students to present their findings to the whole class. Afterwards, give and elicit feedback on the effectiveness of the presentations, and use the topics to generate some class discussion. Note that these topics lend themselves well to Part 2 of the ILEC Test of Speaking, so you could also follow the procedure as set out on SB page 275.

## (CD2 T20) 7 Listening B: A cross-border dispute

Students read the introduction (SB page 228) to find out who is going to be talking to whom about what and why.

**7.1** Go through the questions with the class, making sure students understand the meaning of 'gave rise to' (= caused, led to). Then play the recording for students to answer the three questions. They discuss their answers in pairs before feeding back to the class.

**Transcript »** STUDENT'S BOOK **page 296**

 **Answers**

**1** The parties are TransGerman, a carrier firm, and Lukas Sportswear, a sportswear company.

**2** Goods were transported by trucks from the Netherlands to France. A fire broke out en route in one of the trucks, and the goods were damaged.

**3** The senior lawyer recommends that the client seek a so-called negative declaration, which is a declaration that the carrier has no (or only limited) liability in this case. In this way, they seek to determine in which jurisdiction the dispute is to be resolved and can prevent the plaintiff from initiating further proceedings.

**7.2** Tell students to read the letter carefully to find at least three new facts about the case which were not mentioned in Listening B. Write a list of these facts on the board, as they will be useful for the Writing and Reading tasks that follow. Then play the recording again for students to note the information that the lawyer needs to find out. Students discuss their answers in pairs before feeding back to the class.

*Fax any contractual docs!*

*Where is Lukas incorporated?*

*Police report? Need it immediately!*

*In which country did damage occur?*

▶ **Suggested answers**

We recently contracted with one of our customers, Lukas Sportswear, to transport a consignment of clothing from the Netherlands to France. Unfortunately, some of the goods were damaged in transit, and Lukas Sportswear now wants compensation for the damaged goods and a refund of customs duties.

What actually happened is still not completely clear. However, as I understand it, the goods were picked up in Rotterdam and loaded onto two trucks bound for Lyon, France. During the transport of the goods, the two drivers stopped at a petrol station to refuel and eat dinner. When they left the station restaurant, they discovered that a fire had started in one of the truck trailers. The second truck was damaged by smoke.

I received a letter yesterday from Lukas Sportswear demanding €675,000, representing the loss of

all of the consignment in the fire-destroyed container. They are also claiming loss for smoke damage to the remaining part of the goods plus German duties owed on the goods.

Could you please inform me what our options are and how we should proceed? I have a  meeting scheduled next week with representatives of Lukas Sportswear and would therefore appreciate a quick written response.

*Act qu... to file i... Nether... - expla...*

Sincerely,

Sabina Belling

Assistant Managing Director

TransGerman Forwarding & Shipping, GmbH

**New facts**

○ Lukas Sportswear is seeking damages not only for the damaged goods, but also for customs duties, totalling €675,000.

○ The goods were being transported from Rotterdam to Lyon on two trucks.

○ The fire almost certainly started while the truck was stopped at a petrol station (because the second truck was also damaged, suggesting they were parked together at the time).

## 8 Writing A: Planning the contents and structure of a letter

Tell students to work through the three questions in small groups. Make sure they refer to the appropriate pages mentioned in the tasks. Afterwards, discuss the questions carefully with the class. Note that they will have a chance to write the letter itself in Exercise 10.4, where they will have additional information. However, you may decide to split the writing into two halves, with a short letter-writing task now, based on students' plans (see Optional extension activity below), and a second short letter in Exercise 10.4.

 **Suggested answers**

1  Possible content points
   a  Referring to the subject matter: thanking client for letter
   b  Stating reason for writing
   c  (Briefly) summarising the facts as presented in the client's letter
   d  Requesting further information and documents from the client: police report about the incident, information about TransGerman's client (e.g. where they are incorporated), all contractual documents
   e  Suggesting further course of action: inform about the advantages TransGerman would have from seeking a negative declaration and suggesting that they initiate proceedings in a Dutch court
   f  A suitable closing
2  Possible sentence openers for the content points above:
   a  With reference to your letter of ...
   b  My colleague Ms van Bruggen has asked me to write to you ...
   c  Based on the information provided to us, we understand that ...
   d  Could you please provide me with ... / Could you please inform us ... / I would require information concerning ... / Would you mind sending me ...
   e  In light of the aforesaid, we recommend that ...
   f  I look forward to your reply.
3  The letter could be structured in four parts: the first three content points could be grouped together in an introductory paragraph, while content points d) and e) could each be discussed in separate paragraphs. The letter could end with a final paragraph in which the writer refers to future contact with the client.

**Optional extension**
**ILEC preparation: Test of Writing Parts 1 and 2**

Point out that the detailed planning techniques from Exercise 8 are essential not only for real-life writing tasks but also in the ILEC exam, for both parts of the Test of Writing. Examiners are trained to notice good planning, and will deduct points if it seems that the letter has been written without any preparation. There is, however, a fourth planning technique which can be used during the ILEC exam. During the planning stage, students can plan which vocabulary items and grammar structures they would like to include in order to demonstrate their strong knowledge of legal English, and decide in advance in which paragraph to include them. Tell students to work in the same groups to think of at least five sophisticated items of vocabulary associated with transnational commercial law (e.g. some of the bolded terms from Reading A or the items from the Key terms section). They should also think of at least five examples of impressive-sounding vocabulary for legal writing (e.g. *prior to*, *nevertheless*, ...) and at least five grammar structures (e.g. passive, relative clauses, conditionals, reported speech ...). In their groups, they plan which paragraph would be most suitable for each of these items. Students then write their letter to TransGerman, using the plans they have made. They should aim to use at least half the items or structures they included in their plans. The writing could be done in class (under exam conditions) or as homework. Point out that this technique should not be overused – if it makes the writing unnatural, it could count against the writer. The technique should not be used cynically simply in order to include as much sophisticated language as possible, but rather as a technique to make sure students demonstrate the level of language they genuinely command. Also point out that in real life there is no point in using sophisticated language just to sound impressive, and it may cause additional problems for the reader.

## 9 Reading C: An article from the CMR

Students read the introduction (SB page 230) to find out what the CMR is.

### Background note
The *CMR* was signed in 1956. 'CMR' stands for the French name of the convention, *Convention Marchandise Routière*. All European states are members, along with countries of the former Soviet Union and several others (e.g. Lebanon and Iran). The full text is available here: http://www.jus.uio.no/lm/un.cmr.road.carriage.contract.convention.1956/doc.html.

**9.1** Tell students to read the text quickly to answer the questions. They discuss the answers in pairs, focusing on the relevance of each paragraph to the TransGerman case, then feed back to the class.

### Suggested answers
The article deals primarily with the conflicts-of-laws issues of jurisdiction (paragraph 1) and enforcement of judgments (paragraph 2). This article is particularly relevant to the TransGerman case because it allows for TransGerman to file an action in the Netherlands, since the goods were taken over by them in the Netherlands (paragraph 1(b)). Thus, Lukas will be precluded from filing in Germany, a jurisdiction less friendly to carriers than the Netherlands (paragraph 2).

**9.2** Students discuss the expressions in pairs, then share their ideas with the class. When all students know the meanings of all the expressions, they could explain them again to their partners as they would to a non-specialist client.

### Suggested answers
1. a court or tribunal, which is located in a signatory State of the convention, stated in the contract between the parties
2. location of the head office of a business
3. a suit is presently in the process of being adjudicated by a court

4. new and separate legal process brought in jurisdiction in which the first action is unenforceable
5. the substantive legal issues of the matter

**9.3** Discuss the three questions with the class.

### Answers
1. Assuming the Convention applies, a party may commence legal proceedings in any court or tribunal:
   a. in the state of a contracting country stipulated in the agreement between the parties and;
   *in addition*:
   b. where the defendant is ordinarily a resident, or
   c. where the defendant has his principal place of business, branch or agency, if the contract was made through such entity, or
   d. the place where the goods were taken over by the carrier, or
   e. the place designated for delivery.
2. It is not permissible to bring a new action while a dispute is pending. It is permissible to bring a new action in respect of a dispute for which a judgment has been entered when the judgment of the first action is unenforceable in the country in which the new proceedings are brought.
3. as soon as the formalities required in the country concerned have been complied with

---

**Optional extension**
**ILEC preparation: Test of Reading Part 1**
**Photocopiable worksheet 16.3**

Photocopiable worksheet 16.3 provides further practice of the type of multiple-choice exercise from Part 1 of the ILEC Test of Reading. Tell students to close their books and to work alone to choose the correct answer for each gap. When you go through the answers with the class, discuss why each answer is correct and why the alternatives are incorrect.

**Answers**
**1** A  **2** D  **3** A  **4** C  **5** D  **6** B  **7** B
**8** A  **9** D  **10** C  **11** C  **12** B  **13** D
**14** A  **15** B  **16** C

## 10 Writing B: Textual transformation

Elicit from the class what they understand by the term *textual transformation*, with some examples. Then tell them to read the information in the box to compare it with their ideas. For each of the first five bullet points in the box, elicit one or two example situations where a lawyer might have to make such a transformation. For each of the next six bullet points, discuss how these questions might be answered in the context of Reading C and the TransGerman case.

**⇒ Suggested answers**
- ○ Register: A lawyer receives an informal note on a case from a colleague and then uses the information to write to a client.
- ○ Mode: A lawyer has a meeting with a client and then writes up the notes from the meeting.
- ○ Representation: A lawyer plans a contract clause as a mind-map, then uses this to construct the clause.
- ○ Specialisation: A lawyer transforms a conversation with a client into a carefully constructed closing argument before a court using specialised vocabulary.
- ○ Order and choice of words: Responding to and paraphrasing an offer during a negotiation.
- ○ Technical legal terms: The terms highlighted in Exercise 9.2 may need to be explained.
- ○ Archaic words: Some of the grammar in paragraph 3 (*such action as is referred ...,* *shall*) is rather archaic, but should not present serious problems.
- ○ Shorter sentences: The Article contains three very long and complex sentences, which would need to be shortened and simplified in the letter to the client.
- ○ Personal/impersonal: The lawyer will need to relate the impersonal Article to TransGerman's specific needs, but it should not be made over-personal.
- ○ Formal/informal: The target text should be formal, but less extreme than the Article.
- ○ Cohesive devices: These are needed both to sequence the key points (e.g. *firstly, also, at the same time, in addition*)

and to relate the points to TransGerman's case (*What this means for you is that ...,* *Therefore, So, In other words*).

**10.1** Students work in pairs to select and paraphrase the relevant information. They should work together to write their paraphrases. Afterwards, discuss each pair's choice of relevant sections and their paraphrases with the class.

**10.2** Discuss this question with the class, using the paraphrases from Exercise 10.1 as a starting point.

**⇒ Suggested answers**
The writer of the letter has to carry out the following kinds of textual transformation:
- ○ changing speech into writing (taking notes during discussion with senior lawyer)
- ○ changing informal style (incomplete sentences and individual words of notes) into formal style (written questions in the letter)
- ○ changing highly specialised language into less specialised language, changing the order and the choice of words used (explaining the information in the Article to the client).

**10.3** Students work in pairs to formulate questions and then check with the class.

**10.4** The writing can be done at home or in class – see section on Writing on page xiv.

**⇒ Suggested answer**
Dear Ms Belling
With reference to your letter of 9th May regarding the Lukas Sportswear matter, my colleague Ms Van Bruggen has asked me to write to you.
Based on the information provided to us, we understand the overall nature of the dispute. However, as you mentioned in the letter, what actually happened is not clear, and we will require some additional information in order to take the matter forward.
Initially, could you please inform us of where Lukas is incorporated? In addition, I would require information concerning where and, in detail, how this unfortunate

event took place. Specifically, could you please provide any police reports which have been filed regarding the damage? And, of course, it is of particular importance for us to learn what country the trailers were in when the damage occurred.

Once we have the requested information, we will be better able to advise you regarding all your possible options. At this stage, I can advise that we should bring an action in the Netherlands as soon as possible. This will assist in ensuring that you are in the best possible position to protect your interests. In light of the aforesaid, we recommend that we file suit in the Netherlands.

Could you please confirm at your earliest convenience your authorisation to pursue this course of action?

I look forward to your reply.

Sincerely
Thomas Stormer
(222 words)

 Tell students to do the Internet activity as homework. See Using the Internet for research on page xviii.

# Language focus

## Answers

**1 Vocabulary: distinguishing meaning**

1 *dispute*: The others are official proceedings.
2 *norm*: The others are official documents.
3 *party*: The others are all parties to international treaties and conventions, etc.
4 *litigation*: The others are all examples of alternative dispute resolution (ADR).
5 *render*: This verb needs an object (e.g. *render a judgment*) while the others don't.

**2 Word formation**

| Noun | Verb |
|---|---|
| adjudication | adjudicate |
| designation | designate |
| enforcement | enforce |
| reciprocity, reciprocation | reciprocate |
| recognition | recognise |
| resolution | resolve |

**3 Relative clauses with prepositions**

**2** by which **3** in which **4** under which
**5** to which

 **Background notes**

○ Note that the answers to questions 2 and 4 could be swapped. However, the phrases *the principle by which* and *the agreement under which* are much more common than the alternatives (*the principle under which* and *the agreement by which*).
○ The *European Community* (EC) was the forerunner of the European Union; they co-existed for some years, but the EC officially ceased to exist in 2009 as a result of the Lisbon Treaty.
○ For the *Brussels I Regulation*, see Background note after Exercise 1.1.

**4 Word formation**

**2** settlements **3** wholly **4** proceedings
**5** contracting **6** resident/residing

**5 Vocabulary: Latin terms in transnational commercial law**

**2** e **3** d **4** a **5** c **6** g **7** h **8** j
**9** f **10** i

**6 Vocabulary: collocations with *law***

**2** conflict of laws
**3** domestic law
**4** to incorporate a convention into national law
**5** to have the force of law
**6** choice of law
**7** procedural law

**7 Cohesion**

Being an inexpensive, speedy and amicable method of settling disputes, arbitration – along with mediation, conciliation and negotiation – is encouraged by the Supreme Court. Aside from unclogging judicial dockets, <u>arbitration</u> **[refers back to *arbitration* in preceding sentence]** also hastens the resolution of disputes, especially of the commercial kind. <u>It</u> **[refers back to *arbitration*]** is thus regarded as the 'wave of the future' in international civil and commercial disputes. Brushing aside a contractual agreement calling for arbitration between the parties would be a step backward.

Consistent with <u>the above-mentioned policy</u> **[refers back to *is encouraged by the Supreme Court*]** of encouraging alternative dispute resolution methods, courts should liberally construe arbitration clauses. Provided <u>such clause</u> **[refers back to *arbitration clauses* in previous sentence]** is susceptible of an interpretation that covers the asserted dispute, an order to arbitrate should be granted. Any doubt should be resolved in favour of arbitration.

---

**Background notes**

○ If you *unclog* something, you remove a blockage. In the text, the courts are *clogged up* by the number of *judicial dockets* (= lists of cases waiting to be heard).

○ If something *hastens* an event, it makes that event happen sooner.

○ If you *brush something aside*, you ignore it or get rid of it.

○ A contract clause can often be *construed* (= interpreted, analysed) in several ways (e.g. narrowly, liberally). If an arbitration clause is *construed liberally*, courts should decide that alternative dispute resolution methods are appropriate, unless the clause expressly states otherwise.

○ If a clause is *susceptible* /sə'septəbl/ to a particular interpretation, that interpretation is possible.

# Case study 6: Transnational commercial law

## The facts of the case

Tell students to read the description to identify the legal issue. Tell them to discuss their answers in pairs, including a discussion of why the parties acted as they did at each stage. Afterwards, discuss the answer with the class.

 **Answer**

The legal issue is whether Lynx Distributors Co. is liable to pay Gumlex, Inc. the purchase price of the rubber pursuant to the agreement between the parties and under the provisions of the Convention on the International Sale of Goods (CISG). For possible reasons for actions as well as some background notes, see Optional extension activity below.

> **Optional extension**
>
> Use these questions to ensure students have a thorough understanding of the facts of the case.
> 1 What type of company is Lynx?
> 2 Why exactly did Lynx refuse to pay?
> 3 What do you think a *due notice of defect* is?
> 4 When Gumlex offered to 'take back' the rubber, what do you think it was offering?
> 5 Why do you think Lynx didn't respond to the offer?
> 6 Who is the defendant in this case?
> 7 What does it mean if a contract is *avoided*?
> 8 What is the relevance of the fact that there was no provision in the contract governing which law was applicable?
> 9 What other factors, apart from the strict legal rights and wrongs, may influence the outcome of this case?
>
> **Suggested answers**
> 1 Judging by its name, it is a distribution company.
> 2 The stated reason is that it was because the rubber was of an inferior quality. There

is no indication that the late delivery was a factor.
> 3 A *due notice of defect* is an official statement from one party that something is defective and that the party expects the other party to rectify it. See http://www.docstoc.com/docs/973179/notice-of-defect for an example.
> 4 It was offering to market the rubber. In other words, the rubber would still belong to Lynx (who therefore still needed to pay for it), but Gumlex would help find a buyer for it.
> 5 Perhaps the decision-maker was out of the office or too busy. In such cases, the long-term relationship between the two parties may be worth much more than the value of an individual transaction, so perhaps the managers from Lynx needed to plan their strategy carefully and avoid doing anything they might regret later.
> 6 Lynx, because Gumlex is demanding payment for the rubber.
> 7 If you avoid a contract, you make it void. In other words, you cause it to be inoperative.
> 8 The conflict-of-laws questions may come into play. If so, the fact that the defendant (Lynx) is based in Pennonia may make that the most likely forum state, but this is by no means certain.
> 9 The two companies may have a long-term business relationship, which they might want to preserve. Gumlex also has its reputation as a maker of 'high-quality' rubber to be preserved, and may therefore be keen to avoid a high-profile court case.

## Task 1: Role-play

1 Divide the class into two groups. If you have a very large class, you might prefer to put them into an even number of groups of up to six students. The groups then read through

the documents and discuss the implications for their side of the case and to plan their negotiations. Provide support if students are struggling to understand the relevant legal documents. Allow around ten minutes for this part of the role-play.

2   Put students into pairs. If you have an odd number of students, you could put students into larger groups (e.g. a group of three students versus two). Remind students of the factors mentioned in question 9 of the Optional extension activity above. Allow about ten minutes for the negotiations.

3   Ask each pair or group to feed back on the results of their role-play. Discuss with the class any significant differences between the outcomes of various negotiations, and therefore the most successful negotiating techniques. Give and elicit feedback on the language used during the role-plays, including successful language as well as important mistakes or problems.

## Task 2: Writing

Point out that the letter should be based on the facts of the case, not the results of the negotiation. Students can choose which letter to write, or they could write both if they prefer.

**⇒ Model answer**

Dear Managing Director,

*Re. Gumlex, Inc. v. Lynx Distributors Co.*
In accordance with your instructions, I have reviewed the above-referenced case and can advise as follows. Please note that all the advice stated in this letter is provisional and subject to further investigation.

Initially, there is the issue of what law is applicable to this case. Based on the facts that you have provided, I am of the opinion that the provisions of UN Convention on Contracts for the International Sale of Goods Act (CISG) apply pursuant to Article 1(1)(a) of the CISG. Specifically, both Pennonia and Disperia are Contracting States to the CISG, the subject matter of the contract involved the sale of goods, and there are no provisions regarding choice of law in the contract that would supersede application of the CISG.

The next issue is whether there was an enforceable contract of sale between you and Lynx. Based on the information I have received regarding the oral negotiations and the subsequent purchase order and conduct of Lynx, my opinion is that there was a valid contract of sale based on the provisions of Article 18(1) of the CISG. This provision states that "a statement made by or other conduct of the offeree indicating assent ... is an acceptance".

Naturally, the most important issues are those raised by the defendant's claims that it duly avoided or cancelled the agreement based on either: (1) delay in delivery; or (2) cancellation of the contract of sale by mutual agreement.

In respect of the first issue, in my view the law is on our side. Specifically, although it is clear that delivery was delayed, there is no indication that Lynx, pursuant to Article 47(1) of the CISG, provided Gumlex notice of an additional, reasonable time in which to supply the goods, nor did Gumlex declare that it would not deliver pursuant to Article 47(2) of the CISG. Consequently, in my view, Lynx cannot claim avoidance of the contract of sale under Article 49(1)(b) because it did not first grant Gumlex a reasonable period of time to complete the delivery.

In respect of the second issue, it is my view that, based on the facts provided, Gumlex will be denied the purchase price of the goods. This is essentially a factual issue. As such, it is subject to different interpretations. However, it appears to me that a proper notice of defect was rendered by Lynx and accepted (albeit with some reservation). What is important is what happened after that.

It is clear from the facts that Gumlex offered, without reservation, to take back and remarket the rubber. In return to this offer, Lynx did not object and, more importantly, it failed to demand replacement goods free of defects. An offer to cancel is expressly permitted under Article 29(1) of the CISG. Under Article 18(1) "silence does not in itself amount to acceptance". However, together with other circumstances, silence may be interpreted as an acceptance of an offer. Logically, Gumlex's offer to market was an offer to terminate the agreement, since it would be unreasonable in this circumstance to assume that Gumlex was merely going to assist while leaving primary marketing responsibility to Lynx. Furthermore, it is completely consistent with this reasoning that Lynx would accept this offer by doing nothing, as it believed that the agreement was terminated.

Of course, we can pursue this matter further. The language of Article 18(1) could be used to our advantage. However, I would recommend that Gumlex save time and potential litigation costs and retrieve the goods and resell them.

Sincerely

Renee Byrd
Attorney-at-Law

# Relevant legal documents

○ The *Convention on Contracts for the International Sale of Goods* is an authentic document, ratified by 76 countries. The full text is available here: http://cisgw3.law. pace.edu/cisg/text/treaty.html.

○ **Article 1 (1)(a)** This tells us that the contract in this case study is subject to the Convention, because both parties are from countries which have ratified the Convention.

○ **Article 18 (1)** This is relevant to Lynx's silence in response to Gumlex's offer to take back the rubber. According to this Article, Lynx's lack of response cannot in itself constitute acceptance. However, silence can be important and may be interpreted as acceptance of an offer when read together with Article 29 (1) below.

○ **Article 29 (1)** This tells us that the contract can be ended by mutual consent (i.e. offer and acceptance) which, when read together with Article 18, means that the parties' conduct, together with silence, can result in cancellation of the contract.

○ **Article 47 (1)** This Article relates to Lynx's claim of avoidance due to delay in delivery. When this provision is read together with Article 49 (1)(b), it seems clear that Lynx's 'avoidance through delay' argument must fail because it never granted any extra time for delivery.

○ **Article 47 (2)** This paragraph builds on the issues from paragraph (1). Gumlex did not give notice of non-performance, thus Lynx cannot ask for any breach-of-contract remedy.

○ **Article 49 (1a)** The buyer (Lynx) has declared the contract avoided. The products that were delivered were not in conformity with the agreement. In order to rely on this provision, the buyer must show that the lack of performance by the seller 'amounts to a fundamental breach'. This is a high burden to prove. The only facts provided are that there was a notice of defect and that it was accepted with a reservation – 'the rubber is not in as bad a condition as that claimed'.

○ **Article 49 (1b)** This clause would allow Lynx to avoid the contract due to a delay in delivery if it provided additional time to deliver the goods and Gumlex failed to comply with the new delivery date. However, Lynx did not provide additional time.

○ **Article 49 (2)** This provision, and the provisions which follow – (b) (ii) and (iii) – would appear to be irrelevant, since there is no dispute presented in the facts regarding the actual time of any notice whether related to delay or defects.

> **Background notes**
> ○ *Thereby* in paragraph (2) refers to *by not being allowed to resort to any remedy for breach of contract*.
> ○ *Delay in performance* is less serious (and therefore likely to lead to lower damages) than a breach of contract, unless the delivery date has been stated as a condition of the contract.
> ○ Under generally accepted interpretations of Article 49, there cannot be a fundamental breach if the seller makes a sincere offer to remedy the breach. Hence, a realistic offer to cure the breach prevents immediate avoidance by the buyer. This is perhaps why Lynx did not seek avoidance based on the notice of defect.

# Photocopiable worksheet 1.1

Put a word or phrase from the box into each space.

> ad hoc   de facto   e.g.   et al.   etc.   i.e.   inter alia   ipso facto   per annum
> per se   pro forma   pro rata   quorum   sic   sui juris   ultra vires   v.   viz.

1  Employees may be required to participate in strategy teams, either by assignment or on an ........................ ........................ basis.

2  For tax purposes, taxable individuals who hold their shares as a capital asset should treat each Special Distribution as if the company had purchased, on a ........................ ........................ basis, a percentage of the shares held by each individual.

3  In affirming, the State Court of Appeals held, ........................ ........................ , that the statute was not unconstitutional under the Due Process Clause of the Fourteenth Amendment.

4  It is my recommendation that you obtain affidavits from potential witnesses, ........................ your former colleagues, ........................ .

5  Over the past five years, the value of shares in the corporation has risen by an average of 12% ........................ ........................ .

6  Relying primarily on Harris ........................ Victor Finance ........................ , the Federal District Court concluded that the plaintiff had indeed violated the agreement.

7  She is not a lawyer ........................ ........................ , but she does deal with all legal matters for her company, and is extremely well informed.

8  The following documents shall be considered and interpreted as constituting an integral part of this agreement, ........................ : a) this contract form; b) the Special Conditions; c) ...

9  The forthcoming election is widely seen as a ........................ ........................ referendum on the country's continued membership of the EU.

10  The motion was not passed because a ........................ of members was not present at the meeting.

11  The plaintiff argued that the defendant had already submitted his resignation and thus he was, ........................ ........................ , ineligible to be considered for promotion.

12  The plaintiffs claim that the ordnance (........................) covering all such data is erroneous. Only the data which are in a form in which access or processing is practicable, ........................ print and electronic, are protected.

13  The rules governing conflict of interest do not prevent a lawyer from arbitrating or settling a dispute between two or more clients who are ........................ ........................ and who wish to submit the dispute to the lawyer.

14  The shareholders claimed that the directors had acted ........................ ........................ in obtaining the loan, and that the shareholders were therefore not liable for its repayment.

15  The supplier sent ........................ - ........................ invoices with all consignments on sale or return, and then issued a full invoice at the end of each month to take account of the units actually sold.

# Photocopiable worksheet 1.2

Read the CV (curriculum vitae)[1] below of a young British lawyer and answer these questions.

**1** Where did he work in summer 2007?

**2** What languages does he speak?

**3** Where did he do his first degree?

**4** What was his main duty at the European Commission?

**5** What is he doing now?

---

### Personal information

| | |
|---|---|
| First name(s) / Surname(s) | Linus Walker |
| Address(es) | Frejg 17, SE-118 25, Stockholm, Sweden |
| E-mail | linuswalker@eli.se |
| Nationality | British |
| Date of birth | 12 May 1987 |

### Work experience

| | |
|---|---|
| Dates | **June 2009 – February 2010** |
| Occupation or position held | Legal Assistant within the Legal Department of the Service Commune Relex (SCR) |
| Main activities and responsibilities | Drafting opinions in English and French dealing with contracts awarded for projects |
| Name and address of employer | European Commission, Brussels, Belgium |
| Dates | **Summers 2006–2009** |
| Occupation or position held | Vacation student |
| Main activities and responsibilities | Liaising with clients; conducting research into multiple legal areas, including family law, tort law and contracts; assisting with trial preparation |
| Name and address of employer | G.R. Foster & Co. Solicitors, Cambridge, UK |

### Education and training

| | |
|---|---|
| Dates | **2010 to present** |
| Principal subjects/occupational skills covered | Master's Programme in Law and Information Technology<br>Course covers the legal aspects of Information Technology and the legal implications of the use of the Internet |
| Name and type of organisation providing education and training | University of Stockholm, Sweden |
| Dates | **2005–2009** |
| Title of qualification awarded | LLB (English and French law degree) |
| Principal subjects/occupational skills covered | Course included all the core legal subjects, with a focus on Contract Law, Company Law, Common Law, Property Law and European Law |
| Name and type of organisation providing education and training | University of Essex, Colchester, United Kingdom |
| Dates | **2007–2008** |
| Title of qualification awarded | DEUG (French law degree), Nanterre |
| Principal subjects/occupational skills covered | Part of the degree programme at University of Essex included an intensive course in French. Among subjects studied: European Community Law, Information Law, Civil Law and Penal Law |
| Name and type of organisation providing education and training | Université Paris X, Paris, France |

### Personal skills and competences

| | |
|---|---|
| Mother tongue | English |
| Other languages | French (C2), Swedish (B2) |
| Organisational skills and competences | Member of Law Society, organised two guest lectures |
| Computer skills and competences | Proficient in Word, Windows, Excel, email; Strong Internet researching skills |
| Other skills and competences | Advanced chess player; very good skier |

---

[1] (US) résumé

# Photocopiable worksheet 1.3

Listen to Listening E again and complete the two tasks. You will hear the recording twice.

**TASK ONE**

For questions 1–5, choose from the list A–E what each lawyer says about his/her work.

| | | |
|---|---|---|
| **A** | I advise clients on many types of anti-competitive behaviour. | **1** Speaker 1 _____ |
| **B** | I work as the leader of a team of three people. | **2** Speaker 2 _____ |
| **C** | I've won more court cases than I've lost. | **3** Speaker 3 _____ |
| **D** | I like my current work. | **4** Speaker 4 _____ |
| **E** | I specialise in intellectual property law. | **5** Speaker 5 _____ |

**TASK TWO**

For questions 6–10, choose from the list A–E what each lawyer says about his/her clients.

| | | |
|---|---|---|
| **A** | They tend to be people rather than companies. | **6** Speaker 1 _____ |
| **B** | They come to me to deal with disputes or simply to manage the legal aspects of a sale. | **7** Speaker 2 _____ |
| | | **8** Speaker 3 _____ |
| **C** | They sometimes ask for a service that I can't provide by myself. | **9** Speaker 4 _____ |
| **D** | Some of them need advice on tax issues. | **10** Speaker 5 _____ |
| **E** | Some of them come from other countries. | |

# Photocopiable worksheet 1.4

1  I am a **newly**
2  The firm **offers a wide**
3  Our lawyers **provide advice**
4  **At present, I**
5  **My duties include a good**
6  I am a sole practitioner **in the**
7  **Some of the legal issues I commonly deal**
8  **I also handle**
9  **I counsel**
10  I also **provide**
11  **My clients are primarily**
12  They usually **need advice**
13  **I represent**
14  **I have a good deal of**
15  **I carry**
16  **My work also involves**
17  I also **serve**
18  **I have a good**
19  **My main areas of**
20  **I advise** clients on a regular basis **with**
21  **Some of the industries my clients**
22  I am **head**
23  **I have tried**
24  **I assist**
25  I am **an active member of** several professional organisations, including the state and national bar associations, **to name**

a  **am working in** commercial litigation and am enjoying it.
b  **deal of** client liaison.
c  **range of** commercial law services.
d  **on** many different legal areas.
e  **qualified** lawyer.
f  **clients about** their rights.
g  **area of** employment law in a small city.
h  wage and overtime disputes.
i  **advocacy for** them.
j  **with are** wrongful termination, and discrimination.
k  **out** international trade-mark and service-mark registrations.
l  **in** handling personnel matters and resolving disputes.
m  individuals.
n  both plaintiffs and defendants in trade-mark suits.
o  **experience in** domain-name disputes.
p  **as** an expert witness in IP law.
q  **expertise are** competition law and international trade law.
r  **respect to** restrictive trade practices.
s  providing counselling to photographers.
t  **working relationship with** a large IP firm.
u  **but two**.
v  **clients with** all types of real-estate-related litigation.
w  **of** my firm's Litigation Division.
x  **come from include** transportation and steel.
y  **many cases** (mostly to successful conclusion) in court.

# Photocopiable worksheet 2.1

**1** As a legal person, a company is **distinct** ...

**2** This allows the company to **continue** ...

**3** The court may 'lift the corporate veil' when the company is used to **perpetrate** ...

**4** The court may **subject** the shareholders ...

**5** A partnership is merely ...

**6** The partnership is not precluded ...

**7** Certain rules of partnership law treat a partnership **as if** ...

**8** Partners are not **insulated** ...

**9** The partnership may **cease** ...

**10** A company is formed **upon** ...

**11** The 'constitution' of a company **consists** ...

**12** The memorandum of association **states** ...

**13** The articles of association contain **provisions** ...

**14** The management of a company is **carried** ...

**15** A manager's duties to the company are generally **more** ...

**16** Employees **owe** ...

**17** A secretary cannot be the **sole** ...

**18** This requirement is **not** ...

**19** The auditors' report is **addressed** ...

**20** The directors must **exercise** ...

**21** The fiduciary duty **stems** ...

**22** A director must **act in the best** ...

**23** A director must not act for any **collateral** ...

**24** The courts are generally **reluctant** ...

**25** A company's state of health is **reflected** ...

**26** Healthy profits might **lead** ...

**27** Continuous losses may **result** ...

**a** ... **against** personal liability.

**b** ... an association of owners.

**c** ... **to exist** upon a change in ownership.

**d** ... **fraud**.

**e** ... **from** its officers and shareholders.

**f** ... **from** owning property in its own name.

**g** ... **it were** a legal entity.

**h** ... **perpetually** despite changes in ownership.

**i** ... **to** personal liability.

**j** ... **applicable** if there is more than one director.

**k** ... **a duty of** confidentiality to the company.

**l** ... **burdensome** than those of the employees.

**m** ... **director** of the company.

**n** ... **for** the internal management of the company.

**o** ... **of** two documents.

**p** ... **out** by its officers.

**q** ... **the aims of** the company.

**r** ... **the issuance of** a certificate of incorporation.

**s** ... **from** the position of trust and responsibility.

**t** ... **in** insolvency and the company **going into liquidation**.

**u** ... **in** its accounts.

**v** ... **interests of** the company.

**w** ... **purpose**.

**x** ... **to** interfere.

**y** ... **to** a bonus or capitalisation issue to the shareholders.

**z** ... **to** the shareholders.

**zz** ... **the care of** an ordinarily prudent and diligent person.

# Photocopiable worksheet 2.2

**1**  Listen to the dialogue. Are these statements true (T) or false (F)?

**1**  The lawyer recommends incorporation.                                                                                **T / F**

**2**  Delaware has a highly developed corporate legal system.                                              **T / F**

**3**  The incorporator has to select a name for the corporation.                                        **T / F**

**4**  The lawyer is not permitted to act as the incorporator.                                              **T / F**

**5**  The articles of incorporation include the name and home address of the
       registered agent.                                                                                                              **T / F**

**6**  A corporation may exist indefinitely or for a fixed period of time, which
       may be renewed.                                                                                                              **T / F**

**7**  The articles of incorporation include information about the corporation's
       capital structure.                                                                                                             **T / F**

**8**  A corporation's bylaws are its internal rules and regulations.                               **T / F**

**9**  At the first organisational meeting of a corporation, the organisational
       board resolutions are drawn up.                                                                                        **T / F**

**10** The appointment of directors takes place after the filing of the articles
       of incorporation.                                                                                                              **T / F**

**2**  Look at these extracts from the dialogue. In each extract, delete the one wrong word. Note that the words and phrases in **bold** are all useful expressions for explaining situations to clients.

**1**  So, **based on all the background information you provided to me with, my strongest recommendation is for you to** incorporate …

**2**  Well, **let me to begin by telling you about** how the process works in our State …

**3**  **The first thing what you have to do is** select a name …

**4**  **Of course, that's something I could do it for you**.

**5**  Well, I mentioned the articles of incorporation: **that's** the first main document that needs to be filed in.

**6**  … the registered agent at that office – **that's the person** who to be served if the corporation is sued.

**7**  **Another thing you'd have to provide is** an information about the capital structure.

**8**  Of course, **the other document is necessary** for the company to function as a corporation **is** the bylaws …

**9**  **There's one more thing**: you're also be required to file the organisational board resolutions.

**10** **That's the time** when the first organisational meeting of your corporation will take a place.

# Photocopiable worksheet 2.3

**1** Look at this extract from the text on Wholly Foreign-Owned Entities. Think of the best word to fill each gap.

> One of the most common requests our law firm gets regarding Russia comes from a non-Russian company seeking assistance in setting **1** ............ a Russian joint venture or a representative office. When we tell them **2** ............ response to their queries that only rarely **3** ............ it make sense to go into Russia with a joint venture or a representative office, they commonly respond either **4** ............ surprise that there are other alternatives or by telling us that this is **5** ............ their very well-run competitor had entered the Russian market. When we explain that Russia now allows Wholly Foreign-Owned Entities (WFOE), **6** ............ quickly realise the benefits of not getting enmeshed **7** ............ a Russian joint-venture partner. However, the benefits of a WFOE **8** ............ a representative office are more difficult to explain.

**2** Now read the whole text again (SB page 27) and these questions. For each question, choose one answer (A, B, C or D).

**1** What does the law firm tell its clients about joint ventures?

   **A** They are always dangerous and should be avoided.

   **B** They are less risky than WFOEs, but also more complicated.

   **C** That well-run competitors often set up this type of business entity.

   **D** That they are usually not the best way of going into business in Russia.

**2** Why, according to the text, do many foreign companies use representative offices instead of WFOEs?

   **A** Because they have no other choice.

   **B** Because they are unaware that foreign companies are allowed to own businesses in Russia.

   **C** Because they are ideally suited to buying and selling goods in Russia.

   **D** Because limited liability companies have been forbidden from conducting certain types of business.

**3** Which of these statements is true of representative offices?

   **A** They can generate profits.

   **B** They are subject to tax on their income.

   **C** Employees may be given power of attorney.

   **D** They may request exemption from double taxation.

**4** Which of these statements is presented as an advantage of WFOEs?

   **A** They are considered a legal person.

   **B** They are permitted to conduct marketing activities.

   **C** They pay lower taxes than Russian companies.

   **D** They may be opened and closed quickly and cheaply.

# Photocopiable worksheet 3.1

Put a preposition from the box into each space. You may use each preposition only as many times as it occurs in the box.

| | | | | | | | | | | | | | | | |
|---|---|---|---|---|---|---|---|---|---|---|---|---|---|---|---|
| as | at | by | by | by | for | for | from | from | in | in | in | in | in | into | into |
| of | of | of | of | of | of | of | on | through | to | to | to | to | to | to | upon | with |

1   Initially, company capitalisation takes place ..................... the issuance of shares.

2   The authorised share capital is stated in the memorandum of association, together ..................... the division of the share capital ..................... shares ..................... a certain amount.

3   Issued capital, ..................... opposed ..................... authorised capital, refers ..................... shares actually held ..................... shareholders.

4   A company may authorise capital ..................... excess ..................... the mandatory minimum share capital, but refrain ..................... issuing all of it until a later date – or ..................... all.

5   The payment ..................... dividends is dependent ..................... the performance ..................... the company.

6   Preference shareholders, ..................... the other hand, receive a fixed dividend irrespective ..................... performance.

7   There is also the possibility of share subdivision, whereby, ..................... example, one ten-pound share is split ..................... ten one-pound shares, usually ..................... order to increase marketability.

8   Shares ..................... British companies are subject ..................... pre-emption rights, whereby the company is required to offer newly issued shares first ..................... its existing shareholders.

9   New shares are not always offered ..................... the first instance ..................... the general public, but rather may be sold ..................... a particular group or individuals ..................... a directed placement.

10   Share capital is not, of course, the only means ..................... corporate finance.

11   The grant ..................... security ..................... a loan by giving the creditor the right to recover his capital sum ..................... specific assets is termed a 'fixed charge'.

12   Companies may also borrow money secured ..................... the company's assets, such as stock ..................... trade.

# Photocopiable worksheet 3.2

Match the beginning of each sentence (1–21) with an ending (a–u).

**1** The last two rights clearly apply

**2** Can shareholders exercise

**3** The chairman usually holds enough proxy votes to hold off

**4** Shareholders face

**5** Any one small shareholder will bear

**6** Shareholders accrue

**7** Someone with ownership rights in a company can express

**8** They can either get rid

**9** ... or they may in some way express

**10** All directors must answer

**11** A two-tier board consists

**12** The supervisory board is made

**13** There is reliance

**14** The supervisory boards are legally

**15** In 1998, the power to appoint auditors was vested

**16** The supervisory-board system is designed

**17** The supervisory board may play a role when the corporation comes

**18** Anglo-Saxon boards exert

**19** Anglo-Saxon boards have not been notably successful

**20** The system allows both workers and management to get on

**21** Bad strategic decisions are subjected

**a** any challenge.

**b** to shareholders.

**c** all of the costs.

**d** control if the directors fail to protect their interests?

**e** benefits as a group.

**f** their disappointment.

**g** considerable obstacles in obtaining good information.

**h** of an executive board and a supervisory board.

**i** their concern.

**j** up of outside experts.

**k** bound to incorporate employee representation.

**l** to the annual meeting.

**m** of their shares ...

**n** on the supervisory board for overseeing the management.

**o** under stress.

**p** in preventing crises.

**q** with the supervisory board.

**r** for overseeing and constraining management.

**s** to the public gaze when the 'exit' option is followed.

**t** with the job.

**u** more authority in a crisis.

# Photocopiable worksheet 3.3

## Lawyers

You all work for the same law firm. Your firm has been asked to advise a new but highly successful company on capitalisation. You know very little about the company, other than that it is Internet based and is currently owned by its creators, a group of software engineers and marketing geniuses who know virtually nothing about legal or financial issues. You also know that the company is international in nature, and is considering setting up in either Germany or the UK.

Prepare to meet the client by discussing these issues:

- ○ Bearing in mind the one- and two-tier board systems, would the company be better off setting up in Germany, the UK or in another country?
- ○ What difference would this choice of country have on the marketability of shares?
- ○ Should the company issue shares or should it obtain capital through some other means, such as debentures?
- ○ How many shares should it issue? What would be a suitable price for the shares in order to maximise marketability?
- ○ What proportion of these should be ordinary shares and what proportion preference shares?
- ○ Should the par value of shares be the same as their estimated market price?

You will also need to find out more about the new company. Decide what questions you need to ask.

Note that if you do not know something about the legal system in a particular country, feel free to invent details, as long as you are convincing.

## Clients

You all work for the same Internet-based company. Your company is new but highly successful, and you have asked a law firm to advise you on capitalisation. You are the software engineers and marketing geniuses who both created and now own the company, but you know virtually nothing about legal or financial issues. Your company is international in nature, and you are considering setting up in either Germany or the UK.

Prepare to meet the lawyers by discussing these issues:

- ○ What is the name of your company? What do you do?
- ○ You have vaguely heard something about two-tier board systems, marketability of shares, debentures, par value, ordinary shares and preference shares, but none of you understands what they mean. How will you find out about these things without looking stupid?

Decide what else you need to ask about.

# Photocopiable worksheet 4.1

Complete the chart using words from Reading A. The first letter of each word is given.

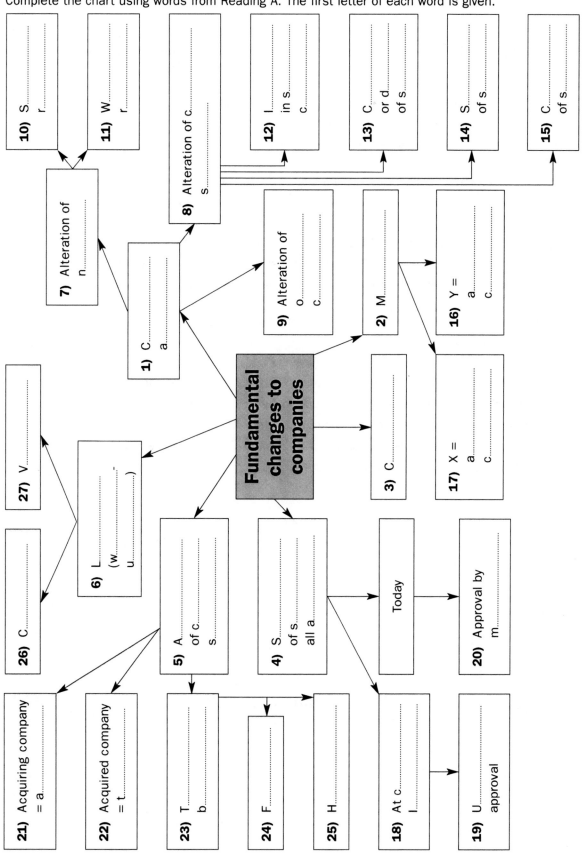

10) S........
    r........

11) W........
    r........

7) Alteration of
   n........

8) Alteration of c........
   s........

12) I........
    in s........
    c........

13) C........
    or d........
    of s........

14) S........
    of s........

15) C........
    of s........

1) C........
   a........

9) Alteration of
   o........
   c........

2) M........

16) Y =
    a........
    c........

3) C........

17) X =
    a........
    c........

**Fundamental changes to companies**

27) V........

26) C........

6) L........
   (w........-
   u........)

5) A........
   of c........
   s........

4) S........
   of s........
   all a........

Today

20) Approval by
    m........

21) Acquiring company
    = a........

22) Acquired company
    = t........

23) T........
    b........

24) F........

25) H........

18) At c........
    l........

19) U........
    approval

# Photocopiable worksheet 4.2

Complete these sentences based on the text in Reading A using the words in the box.

| | | | | | | | | | | | | | | |
|---|---|---|---|---|---|---|---|---|---|---|---|---|---|---|
| apply | aside | at | at | at | be | former | gain | grant | in | into | issue | latter | made |
| members | merely | outstanding | place | provided | some | submitted | substantially | | | | | | |
| such | thus | to | to | unanimous | upon | upon | while | | | | | | |

1  Some of these changes may .................. be basically administrative, .................. as changing the company's name.

2  Other changes .................. the rights of creditors .................. risk and are .................. subject .................. statutory regulation.

3  There are six main types of alterations which fall .................. this group.

4  According .................. British law, a change of name can be .................. by special resolution.

5  The .................. must sign a written resolution that the name of the company .................. changed.

6  A signed copy of the resolution must then be .................. to the Registrar of Companies.

7  If the submission is .................. order, Companies House will .................. a Certificate.

8  A company may alter its capital structure, .................. that the articles of association .................. such power.

9  The court may, .................. its discretion, set .................. such a resolution .................. application by minority shareholders.

10  A company may also .................. control by purchasing .................. all assets.

11  .................. common law, a sale of this kind required .................. shareholder approval.

12  Today, such sales may take place .................. approval by .................. majority of the shareholders.

13  This is achieved by purchasing all or the controlling portion of .................. shares in a company.

14  In the .................. , the takeover is opposed, .................. in the .................. , the action is supported.

15  Various regulations .................. largely to protect the target company shareholders.

# Photocopiable worksheet 4.3

These sentences are based on extracts from Reading C. The original extracts used much more sophisticated grammar, typical of legal English writing. Use the words given to rewrite the sentences to make them more sophisticated.

**1**   The Chairperson said, 'Yes, we gave all the Directors of the Company notice of the meeting.'

The Chairperson confirmed that ............................................................................................................................
........................... all the Directors of the Company.

**2**   The people at the meeting resolved to approve the applications, as long as the EGM approved the applications too.

It ...................... ........................ that ...................... ........................ ...................... ........................ , subject ...................... ........................
........................... of the extraordinary general meeting.

**3**   Somebody at the meeting said, 'Debra Smith and Anna Bean declared their interests in the shares in line with s317.'

...................... ........................ noted that Debra Smith and Anna Bean ...................... ........................ their interests in the shares ........................ to s317 Companies Act 1985.

**4**   The Chairperson reported that somebody proposed to increase the authorised capital of the Company.

The Chairperson reported that ...................... ........................ ...................... ........................ the authorised share capital of the Company to 50,000.

**5**   Somebody presented a notice of an EGM to the meeting. At this meeting, people will propose resolutions to implement the proposals which were mentioned earlier.

There ...................... ........................ ........................ the meeting ...................... ........................ ........................ an EGM ........................
........................... resolutions ...................... ........................ to implement ...................... ........................ ........................ .

**6**   The people at the meeting resolved to approve the notice, to instruct the Secretary to send it to all the members, and, as long as all the members agreed to short notice, to hold the meeting immediately.

...................... ........................ ........................ the notice ...................... ........................, that the Secretary
...................... ........................ to send it to all the members and the auditors of the Company, and,
subject ...................... ........................ ...................... ........................ to short notice, that the meeting be
held immediately.

**7**   The people at the meeting resolved to accept Debra Smith's application for 10,000 shares, Anna Bean's application for 20,000 shares and Andrea Parker's application for 20,000 shares, and to allot the capital of the Company to the applicants in line with the application.

...................... ........................ ........................ the application by Debra Smith, Anna Bean and Andrea Parker
for 10,000, 20,000 and 20,000 shares ...................... ........................ and that the capital of the
Company ...................... ........................ the applicants ...................... ........................ terms ........................ the
application.

**8**   The meeting was closed because nobody had anything else to talk about.

There ...................... ........................ ........................ business, the meeting was closed.

# Photocopiable worksheet 4.4

## Directors

You are all directors of Oldman Tools, a struggling manufacturer of machine tools for industry. Only one division of your company is doing well at the moment, your Laser Cutters division, which is a world leader. You would like to get rid of all your other three divisions (Metal Choppers, Stone Slicers and Plastic Mashers) in order to concentrate on your beloved Laser Cutters. One of your competitors, Shark Tools, might be interested in buying up your unwanted assets, or even the three divisions themselves. If you can get rid of your unwanted businesses, you'd like to rename the company – something like 'Laser Solutions'. But you need to speak to your lawyers about your options with regard to splitting up the company, selling part of it, and renaming the remainder. You know your shareholders aren't going to be impressed, so you need some legal advice on how to keep them quiet.

## Shareholders

You are all shareholders of Oldman Tools. Most of you are also employees or former employees of Oldman, who received shares many years ago as part of a deal to end a strike. Despite your hostile feelings for the directors, you are nevertheless extremely loyal to the Oldman brand and treat the rivalry between Oldman and its main competitor, Shark, as if they were football teams.

You have a strong distrust of the directors, and you suspect that they are trying to break up the company. For some of you, that would be unacceptable, as it would put your jobs at risk. For others, you simply don't know what it would mean for your investments. You have asked some lawyers to advise you as a group on some rumours you have heard concerning a possible merger (or even a takeover). You have no legal background, so you are worried that they might use a lot of jargon.

## Corporate counsel

You represent the directors of Oldman Tools. They have asked you for advice with regard to some fundamental changes in the company, but you don't yet know what they are planning. You are rather concerned that some of their shareholders might be resistant to major changes.

Hold a meeting with the directors to find out what they are planning and to give some initial advice on their options.

## Lawyers representing shareholders

You work for a small law office. You have been approached by a group of shareholders who are worried that their investment is at risk. You know very little about the company they have shares in, but you do know a lot about mergers and acquisitions and their impact on shareholders.

Hold a meeting with the shareholders to find out more about their concerns and to give some initial advice on their options.

# Photocopiable worksheet 5.1

**1** Here are two of the clauses from Exercise 3.3. They have been rewritten so that they make more sense to a non-lawyer, such as a client. Read the extracts and decide a) which paragraphs from Exercise 3.3 have been rewritten, and b) what exactly has changed.

**A**

If the seller breaches the contract, or part of the contract, he may have to pay compensation to the purchaser. This clause says that the maximum amount of that compensation is fixed. It can't be more than the value of the delivery that led to the breach of contract. In other words, the price per item times the number of items in that delivery. Of course, the actual compensation might be much less than that, but it can't be more than that.

**B**

The buyer is allowed to assign the agreement to another company if the buyer or the buyer's shareholders own at least 75% of that other company. Apart from this situation, if either party wants to assign the agreement to a third party, they have to get written permission from the other party first.

**2** Find examples of the following techniques in the paragraphs above. Which technique is not used?

**a** replacing non-human subjects with human subjects

**b** breaking long sentences into shorter ones

**c** using simple conjunctions (*and, but, or, if, because*) to replace more complex constructions

**d** using full forms of relative clauses (e.g. including *that* or *which*)

**e** using everyday vocabulary to replace legal jargon

**f** rearranging sentences to improve flow

**g** adding explanations

**h** adding examples

**i** adding background information

**j** adding conversational devices

**3** Now decide how you would complete the sentences in this version of clause 3.

This clause protects both parties in case **a)** ............................................. . For example, there might be
**b)** ...................................... (such as **c)** ...................................... ) , or **d)** ......................................, or
**e)** ...................................... . If anything like this happens, the party who is affected doesn't have to
**f)** ......................................The other party isn't allowed to **g)** ...................................... as a result of
**h)** ...................................... . This obviously only applies to deliveries or payments which are
**i)** ...................................... .

**4** Look at the following phrases from a rewrite of clause 5. Put the six fragments into three sentences, and put the sentences into a logical order.

**a** the supplier will give the operator ten days to make the payments

**b** if the operator still fails to make the payments after those ten days have passed

**c** the operator loses all the rights he had under the contract, but he doesn't lose his obligations

**d** if this happens

**e** if the operator fails to make the necessary payments

**f** the supplier has the right to cancel the contract

**5** Now rewrite one (or both) of the remaining clauses. Try to use the techniques listed in Exercise 2 above.

# Photocopiable worksheet 5.2

**1** Put the lines from the dialogue in the correct order. Some answers have been given.
(J = Mr Johansson   O = Ms Orvatz)

|   |   |   |   |
|---|---|---|---|
|   | a | **J:** | Of course. Our proposal is to reduce the scope of the clause. If you could consider reducing the time period the non-compete covers, we'd be willing to be more flexible about the arbitration clause, for example. |
|   | b | **J:** | Very well. |
| 1 | c | **J:** | If I may, I'd like to address another one of the clauses in the franchise agreement: the non-competition clause here at the bottom of page three. |
|   | d | **O:** | That would be difficult for us. We could only reduce it to 18 months, and that is already very generous on our part. |
|   | e | **O:** | Well, you must understand that my client has to protect itself – I mean, a former franchisee could just come along and set up a nearly identical sandwich restaurant right near one of our restaurants, and with all the know-how he got from us … |
|   | f | **J:** | That's certainly a step in the right direction. How about this: we suggest reducing the time frame to six months. |
|   | g | **O:** | What do you object to? All our franchisees accept that. It's standard practice, like I said. |
|   | h | **J:** | Yes, I fully understand the reasoning behind that provision, no need to explain. But my client also has skills and abilities of his own, proven skills relevant to the sandwich-making business. That's why your client is interested in concluding a franchise agreement with him in the first place. Let's face it: your client owns a young and upcoming franchise enterprise that may be promising, but it certainly is not well known or well established yet – you need the skills and know-how of experienced franchisees as much as they need you. So I'll say it again: we simply could not accept any clause that would forbid my client from making a living through these skills independently for two whole years, if that should one day become necessary. |
|   | i | **J:** | Let's agree on a year, shall we? After all, you and I both know that your client really wants to enter into this agreement with my client, as he's perfectly suited to run a franchise in that part of town, which, let's be honest, isn't exactly the safest neighbourhood. He knows the area, he has the necessary skills and experience … |
| 8 | j | **O:** | What do you suggest? We're not in a position to remove the non-compete clause from the contract, let me be perfectly clear about that. |
|   | k | **J:** | Well, the clause in question states, and I quote: 'Franchisee shall not, for a continuous uninterrupted period and continuing for two years thereafter own, operate, maintain, or engage in any business that: (a) offers products or services which are the same as or similar to the products and services offered by the Franchised Business under the System and (b) is, or is intended to be, located at or within a 25-mile radius of the Approved Location.' What this means is that in the event that the agreement between my client and your corporation should at one time no longer be in effect, my client wouldn't be able to operate a sandwich restaurant for two full years in his own neighbourhood. I'm afraid that's out of the question. |
|   | l | **O:** | Yes, the non-compete. Well, I'll just say upfront that that's standard, that's in all our agreements. |
| 16 | m | **O:** | Now, what about the arbitration clause? You said you'd be willing to be a bit more flexible … |
|   | n | **O:** | Well, all right. In that case, I think we could talk about a reduction. |
|   | o | **J:** | Right. That may be so, but I'm afraid we can't go along with it in its present form. |
|   | p | **O:** | OK, OK. I think we could live with that. A year it is. |

**2** Underline all the useful negotiating expressions from the conversation.

# Photocopiable worksheet 5.3

## The potential franchisee

You have run a successful independent butcher's shop in a prime location in your city for over ten years, but you have recently started losing business to the large out-of-town supermarkets. You have been approached by some managers from one of the supermarkets, Groceryland, and invited to buy a franchise. The supermarket is keen to re-establish itself in city centres, and wants a chain of branded butcher's shops to spearhead its 'back to our roots' campaign.

You like the idea of the support and marketing you have been offered, and the price – a down-payment of €1,000, plus 5% of profits – seems reasonable. After all, you can always back out of the agreement once you've rebuilt your customer base, if you feel you're paying too much.

You've already told the supermarket that you want to accept, but you need to check with your lawyer(s) before you sign.

## The franchisee's lawyer

Your client is a butcher who has been invited to buy a franchise from a large supermarket, Groceryland. The supermarket has proposed an agreement which would include marketing support and 'branding', and would cost your client €1,000 initially, plus 5% of all profits.

You are concerned that your client is a little too wide-eyed in this transaction, and that the supermarket might take advantage of his/her naivety.

The franchise agreement is apparently non-negotiable, but you think there is room for manoeuvre in the non-competition covenant that the supermarket is demanding. Even though your client seems willing to agree to everything the supermarket is offering, you want to use this covenant to exert some leverage over the rest of the agreement. For example, you are keen to insert an arbitration clause into the agreement: without it, the supermarket might use its huge power to bully your client in the event of a dispute.

## The supermarket

You are a senior manager from Groceryland, one of the country's leading supermarket chains. Your company is losing market share to its main rival, so it has developed a plan to set up franchises in city centres. These are intended primarily to keep the brand visible, but also to reclaim some market share.

You have found a successful butcher in your city centre who seems keen on buying one of your franchises. You have informally agreed the terms of the franchise, subject to approval by the butcher's lawyers. The butcher will pay a start-up fee of €1,000, plus 5% of profits every month. In exchange for this, your supermarket will provide corporate branding materials as well as technical support in marketing and accounting. The butcher will have access to your supplier networks, but will not enjoy the same discounts as the supermarket gets.

Hold a meeting with your lawyer(s) to discuss the terms of the franchise agreement.

## The supermarket's lawyers

You are in-company lawyers for a branch of Groceryland, a large supermarket chain. The supermarket is getting into the business of franchising.

You have received strict instructions from head office that the key terms of such franchise agreements are non-negotiable. The terms on offer are: accounting and marketing support, limited access to the Groceryland's supplier network, and corporate branding, in exchange for €1,000 plus 5% of profits per month. You have a little flexibility with lesser matters connected with the contract.

You also have some leeway with the non-competition covenant. Your brief is to be flexible with the covenant only in order to rescue a deal which would otherwise collapse, and which the supermarket managers deem to be worth saving.

The initial terms of the covenant are: if the contract is terminated the franchisee is not allowed to engage in any retail or wholesale activity for 20 years.

Meet the supermarket managers to discuss your strategy for this particular negotiation.

# Photocopiable worksheet 6.1

**1** Read the case studies below (1–5). Decide which types of remedy (a–i), if any, each client might be entitled to.

|   |   |   |   |   |   |
|---|---|---|---|---|---|
| **a** | Expectation damages | **d** | Reliance damages | **g** | Punitive damages |
| **b** | General damages | **e** | Restitution damages | **h** | Right to rescind contract |
| **c** | Liquidated damages | **f** | Special damages | **i** | Right of repair |

**1** Your client recently invested in some software to help them track goods in their warehouses. Although your client thought it had bought some reliable software produced by a reputable company, it turned out that the supplier of the software, Pilfer Solutions, had installed a cheap pirate version of the program. The software has crashed several times already, and now it appears to have infected your client's whole system with a virus. To make matters worse, your client has had a letter from the lawyers of the multinational software company demanding that they stop using the pirate program immediately.

**2** Your client used to be a regular supplier of own-brand shampoo for Shoddies, a major chain of discount stores. Shoddies had demanded very short lead times, which meant that your client was obliged to keep large supplies of finished products and materials, including pre-printed shampoo bottles, in readiness for sudden orders. Your client had a five-year contract, which was cancelled for no apparent reason about six months ago, when there were still 18 months remaining. Your client now has about €300,000 worth of finished and part-finished products in its warehouse, which it cannot sell.

**3** Your client bought a packaging machine about two years ago from Two Bit Electronics. The machine has since completely broken down, and has been out of action for four weeks. This means that your client is running its factory at 50% capacity, and is rapidly losing both money and its reputation for reliability. The guarantee, which still has three years to run, states that only Two Bit is allowed to service the machine, but they have failed to show any interest in repairing it.

**4** Your client, a mobile phone network, was recently the main sponsor of a classical music concert, which had been organised by the local city council. The sponsorship deal was worth €6,000. Unfortunately, due to a mistake by a printing company, which was not noticed by the marketing team at the council, the date on all the promotional materials was wrong. As a result, fewer than 50 people attended the event, instead of the 500–800 your client had been led to expect by the council. Your client feels that its sponsorship money was wasted, and that its own reputation has suffered as a result of being associated with such incompetence.

**5** Your client is a medium-sized oil company, which has a network of 15 petrol stations around the country. Its 16th petrol station has just been built and was due to be opened last week, but due to a problem with the underground storage tanks, the building contractor, Slapdash Construction, has been unable to obtain a health and safety certificate. The contractor is working on the problem around the clock to get it resolved, but every day is costing your client a lot of money.

**2** Decide which case study these sentences might refer to.

    **a** **If** the breaching party **had performed** the contract, the injured party's reputation **would not have been** damaged.

    **b** The damages are calculated based on what the injured party **would have received had** the contract not **been breached**.

    **c** The injured party **could have done** more to mitigate its losses.

    **d** The supplier **should have sent** the proofs for checking before printing and distributing the materials.

**3** Choose one of the case studies. Make some sentences using the same structures. Invent any details which you don't know.

**4** Role-play an initial lawyer–client meeting to establish the facts of the case and to discuss what type of remedy might be available. Try to use your sentences from Exercise 3 in your meetings.

# Photocopiable worksheet 6.2

Change the words in brackets so that they make sense in the sentences. You may need to make some words negative. Be careful: one word does not need to be changed.

1   At the time of ................ (*contract*), parties to an ................ (*agree*) often want to calculate the damages one or both would incur upon breach of contract by the other.

2   By stipulating such damages before a breach, the ................ (*injure*) party can avoid the ................ (*substance*) costs which often arise and the ................ (*difficult*) of proving the amount of its loss.

3   Such clauses, when ................ (*reason*) designed to compensate a party for its ................ (*injure*) caused by a breach, are ................ (*enforce*).

4   On occasion, a ................ (*contract*) party may attempt to ensure that the other party will perform its promise by inserting a clause which imposes a ................ (*consider*) penalty for ................ (*perform*).

5   A penalty ................ (*provide*) is not intended to compensate the injured party for the expected loss ................ (*occasion*) by the breach.

6   A contractual penalty clause is intended as a ................ (*deter*) against a breach by specifying damages which the parties know would probably be much higher than could otherwise ................ (*ordinary*) be recovered by the ................ (*breach*) party.

7   A contractual penalty for breach is ................ (*enforce*) in many jurisdictions.

8   A court may require the ................ (*injure*) party to prove its loss in accordance with general principles ................ (*apply*) to damages for breach of contract.

9   ................ (*consequence*), knowing the ................ (*distinct*) between a provision for a penalty and for liquidated damages when drafting a damages clause may be critical to ................ (*enforce*).

10  The parties intended to ................ (*quantity*) the damages in advance of the ................ (*lose*).

11  The amount ................ (*stipulate*) in the provision is ................ (*reason*) in that it is not greatly ................ (*proportion*) to the presumed ................ (*injure*) or loss.

12  Elements a) and c) are ................ (*appear*) ................ (*contradict*).

13  More recent decisions have given little or no ................ (*weigh*) to the second element, i.e. the subjective ................ (*intend*) of the parties.

14  Rather, they take all three elements into account, along with other facts, such as the ................ (*relate*) ................ (*bargain*) power of the parties, in determining the ................ (*reasonable*) of the clause at issue.

15  ................ (*custom*), courts look to the time of contract to decide the reasonableness of stipulated damages.

16  It would be difficult for the ................ (*breach*) party to argue that the amount ................ (*forecast*) in the liquidated damages clause was ................ (*reason*).

17  The Uniform Commercial Code accepts a liquidated-damages clause if the amount stipulated was reasonable ................ (*consider*) the actual loss.

# Photocopiable worksheet 6.3

**1** Most of the punctuation has been removed from Reading C. Decide where to insert nine commas (,) and two semi-colons (;).

---

### FAILURE TO FINISH THE WORK ON TIME

It is mutually agreed by and between the parties hereto that time is of the essence and that in the event of the Contractor's failure to complete the contract within the time stipulated and agreed upon the Owner will be damaged thereby and because it is difficult to definitely ascertain and prove the amount of such damages inclusive of expenses for inspection necessary traveling expenses and other similar expenses it is hereby agreed that the amount of such damages shall be the liquidated sum of Two Thousand Dollars ($2,000.00) per calendar day for each day of delay in finishing the Work in excess of the number of working days prescribed and the Contractor hereby agrees that such sum shall be deducted from amounts due the contractor under the contract or if no amount is due the Contractor the Contractor hereby agrees to pay to the Owner as liquidated damages and not by way of penalty such total sum as shall be due for such delay calculated as aforesaid.

---

**2** Decide whether these sentences are true or false.

    **1** When it is correctly punctuated, the clause is easy to follow.

    **2** All verbs in the clause closely follow their subjects (e.g. *I signed the contract*).

    **3** All objects immediately follow their verbs (e.g. *I signed **the contract***).

    **4** The passive voice is not used needlessly (e.g. *The contract **was signed** by me*).

    **5** Infinitives are not split needlessly (e.g. *I want **to** eventually **sign** the contract*).

**3** Identify some of the problems with this clause. Can you suggest any ways to improve it?

---

### CONSEQUENTIAL DAMAGES RESULTING FROM LOSS OF PRODUCTION TIME

In the event manufacturing or otherwise processing of raw materials as described in exhibit 14 attached hereto become or threaten to become interrupted, and such interruption or threat thereof being shown to unquestionably have been caused solely by the Contractor, its subcontractors, employees, or agents, or employees thereof, while maintaining, repairing, utilising or otherwise occupying a facility and/or equipment in the aforesaid Premises belonging to the Company, the Contractor hereby agrees to fully and immediately reimburse the Company for all consequential damages resulting from such interruption, the amount thereof being calculated in accordance with the costing rates set forth in exhibit 12 attached hereto at the time of the incident, and the parties hereto hereby agree that in the event of a joint investigation by the parties set up according to principles set forth in exhibit 19 attached hereto determining that such interruption or threatened interruption occurred as a result of the joint fault or negligence of the parties hereto (Company and Contractor), their contractors, subcontractors, employees, or agents, or employees thereof then negotiations to establish a pro-rata formula by which to assess the distribution of such consequential damages incurred by the parties shall be undertaken by the parties hereto.

---

# Photocopiable worksheet 7.1

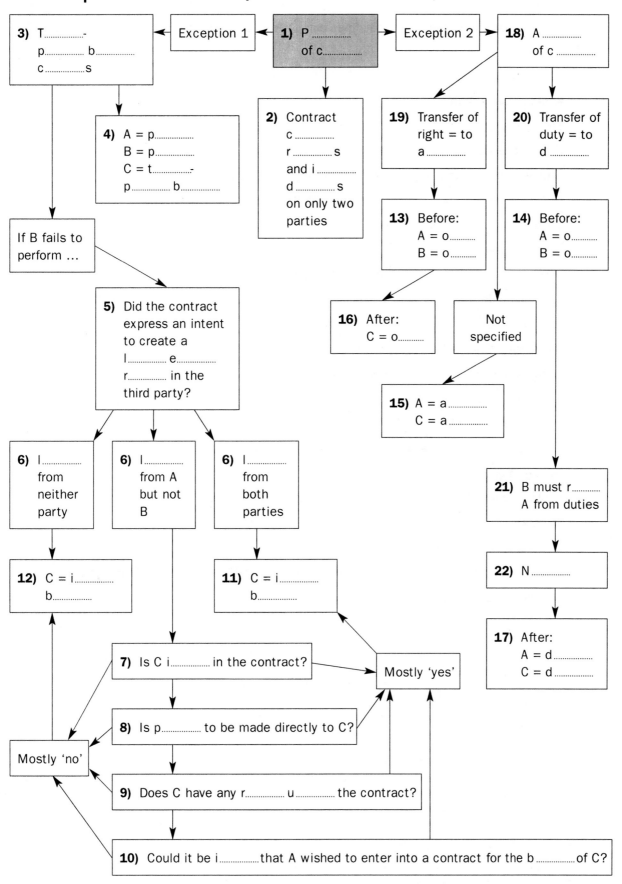

**3)** T.............-
p............. b.............
c............s

**Exception 1**

**1)** P.............
of c.............

**Exception 2**

**18)** A.............
of c.............

**4)** A = p.............
B = p.............
C = t.............-
p............. b.............

**2)** Contract
c.............
r.............s
and i.............
d.............s
on only two
parties

**19)** Transfer of
right = to
a.............

**20)** Transfer of
duty = to
d.............

If B fails to
perform ...

**13)** Before:
A = o..........
B = o..........

**14)** Before:
A = o..........
B = o..........

**5)** Did the contract
express an intent
to create a
l............. e.............
r............. in the
third party?

**16)** After:
C = o..........

Not
specified

**15)** A = a.............
C = a.............

**6)** I.............
from
neither
party

**6)** I.............
from A
but not
B

**6)** I.............
from
both
parties

**21)** B must r..........
A from duties

**12)** C = i.............
b.............

**11)** C = i.............
b.............

**22)** N.............

**17)** After:
A = d.............
C = d.............

**7)** Is C i............. in the contract?

Mostly 'yes'

**8)** Is p............. to be made directly to C?

Mostly 'no'

**9)** Does C have any r............. u............. the contract?

**10)** Could it be i............. that A wished to enter into a contract for the b............. of C?

# Photocopiable worksheet 7.2

Listen to the two parts of Listening A again. Then complete these sentences with one or two words in each gap.

---

**Keats v. Jones Corp**

Background to the case

Keats leased **1** ............ space from the Jones Corporation.

Last year, he tried to assign his interest in the lease to a **2** ............ .

Lease expressly allows **3** ............ , but only with the prior **4** ............ of Jones.

Contract also stipulates that Jones cannot unreasonably **5** ............ consent.

Jones requested:

- **6** ............ and ............ info. about prospective buyer;

- more detailed info. (e.g. photocopies of his **7** ............ , passport, work history)

Jones **8** ............ making a decision on the assignment.

Prospective buyer of the restaurant **9** ............ offer.

Keats is seeking damages from Jones for:

- **10** ............ of contract

- intentional **11** ............

Possible reason: personal **12** ............ between Keats and Jones.

Key arguments

Contract stipulation: Jones cannot '**13** ............ withhold consent'.

Evidence:

1 prospective buyer has excellent **14** ............;

2 expert on commercial **15** ............ transactions will testify that Jones had sufficient info.;

3 need to collect **16** ............ of animosity.

---

# Photocopiable worksheet 7.3

## Jones Corporation's lawyers

After losing the case against Mr Keats, you are not keen to go through another such experience. However, Keats is still trying to sell his restaurant business, and the latest buyer he has found, a fast-food chain called Ketchup's, would be completely inappropriate as a lessor in your premises, Jones Tower, a rather posh business centre. You suspect that Keats has set up the deal with Ketchup's purely to antagonise you.

The contract stipulates only that you cannot withhold your consent 'unreasonably', but does not specify what this means. Under normal circumstances, you might expect a court to use the 'reasonably prudent person' argument to suggest that any landlord in your position would also withhold consent. After all, if you allowed Ketchup's to set up in your premises the value of your property might decline. However, given your stormy history with Keats, you are concerned that Keats's lawyers may succeed in convincing the court that 'personal taste is not a proper criterion for withholding consent'.

Hold a meeting with all your colleagues to discuss your strategy. According to the letter from Keats's lawyers, time is of the essence, and they need a decision within five working days.

## Mr Keats and his lawyers

After your successful lawsuit against Jones Corporation, you are delighted with the damages you won, but still concerned about whether you can sell your restaurant business. Your previous buyers withdrew their offer when Jones started causing trouble, and most other potential buyers seem scared off by Jones. You have had only one sensible offer – from Ketchup's, a fast-food chain. This is bound to upset Jones, as they will hate the idea of such a restaurant in their posh business centre, Jones Tower. But you are desperate, and anyway you are convinced that Jones will not risk another court defeat. At least, this is what you have told Ketchup's. Unfortunately, three days after sending your request for Jones's consent to the sale, you have still heard nothing back. Your request stated clearly that time was of the essence, and that you needed an answer within five working days. You are starting to get nervous. To make matters worse, you have a meeting scheduled for today with Ketchup's, in which they will want to know what is going on.

## Corporate counsel for Ketchup's Fast-Food Restaurants

You represent Ketchup's, a rapidly expanding chain of fast-food restaurants. You have recently negotiated a deal with a Mr Keats to buy his restaurant business from him. Your bosses are very excited about this deal because it will give you space in the prestigious Jones Tower, a business centre, where many wealthy business people work.

You are concerned that Jones may attempt to block the sale on the grounds that Ketchup's is not 'in keeping' with the image of Jones Tower. However, Keats claims he is in a very strong position with regard to Jones, as he recently won substantial damages against them in a lawsuit. He is convinced that they will not try to block the deal. In any event, their contract with Keats states that they may not withhold consent 'unreasonably'.

Hold a meeting with Mr Keats and his lawyers to find out what is happening with his request for Jones's consent.

# Photocopiable worksheet 8.1

Use the words on the right to form one word that fits in the same numbered gap in the text.

An Alberta arbitration board has recently released a decision concerning the **1** ............. of an employee as a result of the contents of the employee's online blog site. In this case, an administrative employee in the Alberta Public Service (the "**2** .............") was dismissed after the employer became aware of the contents of her personal blog.

**1** DISMISS
**2** GRIEVE

The Grievor's blog contained **3** ............. comments about a number of her **4** ............. and management, **5** ............. to them as "imbeciles," "idiot savants," and "lunatic-in-charge." After an investigation, the Grievor was interviewed about her blog. **6** ............. the Grievor as largely **7** ............. , the employer terminated the Grievor's **8** ............. .

**3** FLATTER
**4** WORKER
**5** REFER
**6** PERCEIVE
**7** REPENT
**8** EMPLOY

The employer took the position that the **9** ............. of the blog postings and the Grievor's lack of remorse and **10** ............. as to why the blog had been so **11** ............. undermined the employment relationship **12** ............. , thereby **13** ............. the Grievor's termination. This was especially so, in the employer's view, in a department that handled sensitive cases and whose well-publicized values emphasized respect, **14** ............. , and co-operation.

**9** CONTAIN
**10** UNDERSTAND
**11** OFFEND
**12** REPAIR
**13** JUSTIFY
**14** FAIR

The Grievor's union, in **15** ............. the dismissal, argued that the employer had **16** ............. , that the Grievor's attempts at an **17** ............. had been **18** ............. by management, and that the Grievor had a previously **19** ............. record of six years' **20** ............. . As a remedy, the union **21** ............. reinstatement with appropriate **22** ............. . The employer replied that in a relatively small workplace, it would be very unfair to the Grievor's co-workers for the Grievor to be **23** ............. in her employment.

**15** CHALLENGE
**16** REACT
**17** APOLOGISE
**18** RAIL
**19** BLEMISH
**20** SERVE
**21** SEEK
**22** COMPENSATE
**23** STATE

In a 2–1 decision, the Arbitration Board denied the **24** ............. and **25** ............. the dismissal. The Board concluded that "while the Grievor has a right to create personal blogs and is entitled to her opinions about the people with whom she works, **26** ............. displaying those opinions may have consequences within an employment **27** ............. ." The Board was satisfied that the Grievor, in **28** ............. contempt for her managers, ridiculing her co-workers, and **29** ............. administrative processes, engaged in serious **30** ............. that irreparably severed the employment relationship, thereby justifying discharge.

**24** GRIEVE
**25** HOLD
**26** PUBLIC
**27** RELATE
**28** EXPRESS
**29** DENIGRATE
**30** CONDUCT

Employees cannot simply invoke **31** ............. of speech to publicly make **32** ............. comments online about co-workers or management or to disclose confidential information obtained in the course of employment.

**31** FREE
**32** DEROGATE

# Photocopiable worksheet 8.2

Read part of Reading D to complete some information in the table. Then work with a partner to complete the rest of the table. The shaded boxes are not answered directly in the text, but you may be able to guess what they contain.

| | Employment tribunals | Arbitration procedure | My jurisdiction |
|---|---|---|---|
| Date of introduction | 1 | 2 | |
| Voluntary or compulsory? | 3 | 4 | |
| Who hears the case? | 5 | 6 | |
| Cross-examination? | 7 | 8 | |
| Legal representatives? | 9 | 10 | |
| Intended to be ... | 11 | 12 | |
| What sorts of claims? | 13 | 14 | |
| Public or private hearings? | 15 | 16 | |
| How long? | 17 | 18 | |
| Adversarial or inquisitorial? | 19 | 20 | |
| Who covers costs? | 21 | 22 | |
| Principles underlying decisions | 23 | 24 | |
| Available remedies | 25 | 26 | |
| Award confidential? | 27 | 28 | |
| Scope for appealing or challenging award? | 29 | 30 | |
| Advantages for employers | 31 | 32 | |
| Advantages for employees | 33 | 34 | |

Now use the right-hand column to tell your partner about the situation in your jurisdiction.

# Photocopiable worksheet 8.3

## Employee 1

You are a window cleaner. A few weeks ago, you were forced to take a drugs test by your employer. When you failed the drugs test, they sacked you. You have now been advised that they violated your rights by forcing you to take the drugs test, so you have taken the case to an ACAS arbitration procedure.

## Employer 1

You own a facility management company. A few weeks ago, you forced one of your employees, a window cleaner, to take a drugs test. When he/she failed the drugs test, you sacked him/her. You have now been advised that you may have violated their rights by forcing them to take the drugs test and that the case has been taken to an ACAS arbitration procedure.

## Employee 2

You are a female lorry driver. You got your job only three months ago on the unofficial understanding that you would not become pregnant. In fact, you were already pregnant at the job interview, although you weren't sure at the time. When your employers found out a few weeks ago, they sacked you, claiming you had insulted a customer. This is completely untrue. You have now decided to take your former employer to an ACAS arbitration procedure.

## Employer 2

You own a transport company, which is struggling financially. A few months ago you recruited a female lorry driver. You gave her the job on the unofficial understanding that she would not become pregnant. In fact, she was already pregnant at the job interview. When you found out a few weeks ago, you sacked her, claiming she had insulted a customer. One of your friends has offered to pretend to be the insulted customer. She has now taken you to an ACAS arbitration procedure.

## Employee 3

You are a research chemist, working in the laboratory of a pharmaceutical company. A few weeks ago, they caught you with photocopies of confidential test results in your bag, which you were planning to sell to a rival company. They promptly sacked you. Now you have heard that they had no right to search your bags, and you have taken them to an ACAS arbitration procedure.

## Employer 3

You are a director of a pharmaceutical company. A few weeks ago, you caught one of your laboratory research chemists with photocopies of confidential test results in his/her bag, which you believe he/she was planning to sell to a rival company. You promptly sacked the chemist. Now the chemist has taken you to an ACAS arbitration procedure, claiming that you had no right to search his/her bags.

# Photocopiable worksheet 9.1

## Creating a vocabulary bank

**1** Open a new spreadsheet (e.g. on MS Excel). Write the following column headings in the top row: *Test*, *Priority*, *Answer*, *Target word*, *Explanation* and *Example*.

**2** In the *Target word* column, write ten items that you would like to learn. These may include difficult words, unusual uses of known words, idiomatic expressions, collocations, irregular past tenses, etc.

**3** In the *Explanation* and *Example* columns, enter a definition and/or a sample sentence for each target word. You may also add information in further columns such as *Translation* and *Pronunciation*.

**4** Write test questions in the *Test* column. These could be simply copied from the *Explanation* or *Example* columns (as long as you replace the target word with a space).

**5** Select all the cells, and allow text wrapping (on the Format menu select Format Cells, then Alignment, then Wrap text). Then adjust the column widths so that only the first three columns are visible when you open the document.

**6** If your document looks like this, save and close your vocabulary bank.

| | A | B | C |
|---|---|---|---|
| 1 | TEST | PRIORITY | ANSWER |
| 2 | Goods which can be moved, in contrast to real property | | |
| 3 | The Convention sets _____ rules that govern contracts for the international sale of goods. | | |
| 4 | The craftsman _____ his wares around all the villages | | |
| 5 | Warranties which are specifically stated either in writing or orally, as the case may be | | |
| 6 | A sale can be defined as the transfer of title _____ a good | | |
| 7 | What is the past of 'to deal'? | | |
| 8 | A statement of non-responsibility under given circumstances | | |
| 9 | What states what is not covered by a contract? | | |
| 10 | What is a warranty which is not explicitly stated but that is imposed by the law due to the nature of the transaction? | | |
| 11 | The Convention sets forth rules to _____ the development of international trade. | | |

## Using your vocabulary bank

**1** Open your vocabulary bank. Try to answer each *Test* question and type your answers in the *Answer* column.

**2** Scroll across to compare your answers with those in the *Target word* column. If your answer is correct, type '2' in the *Priority* column. If it is wrong, type '1'.

**3** Select all the cells and sort them according to their *Priority* (on the Data menu, choose Sort). You should now have all the difficult words at the top and the easier ones at the bottom. Save and close your vocabulary bank.

**4** Every day, add ten more target words to the top of your vocabulary bank. Test yourself daily on the priority-1 words, and weekly on the priority-2 words. If you remember priority-2 words repeatedly, change them to priority 3, to be tested monthly.

**5** At the end of a year, congratulate yourself if you have really learned 3,650 new words!

# Photocopiable worksheet 9.2

## Counsel for Volcano Heatproof Coatings

Your client, Volcano, manufactures heatproof coatings for use in heavy industrial processes. Earlier this year, Volcano sold ten 25-litre drums of very expensive Blasting Resin to Lightning Electrical Equipment (Lightning). Unfortunately, before Lightning could pay for the goods, they went bankrupt.

According to Volcano's contract with Lightning (part of which appears in Exercise 4.4), Volcano had the right to recover the goods from Lightning in such an event. However, when you and several Volcano employees went to the Lightning factory to recover the goods, you were told that the Blasting Resin had been transferred to a 400-litre storage tank, which included resin from previous deliveries and from another supplier which had already staked a claim to the resin. Lightning used this excuse to hold on to the resin.

Later you found out that the resin had been 'recovered' by one of these suppliers, Thunder Chemicals. Thunder is a sister company of Lightning. You immediately filed suit for breach of the ROT clause in the contract.

## Judge 1

You believe in justice first, technicalities second. If somebody has cheated, they should be punished, regardless of things like contracts.

## Judge 2

You believe in the letter of the law. If a lawyer has used a legal loophole to trick another party, you believe they should be celebrated for their ingenuity.

## Judge 3

You have been a judge for too long, and you have stopped caring about people's irritating disputes. The only thing you respect now is a talented lawyer.

## Counsel for Lightning Electrical Equipment

Your client, Lightning, has recently gone bankrupt. Lightning used to manufacture highly specialised lighting equipment. The manufacturing process required large quantities of Blasting Resin, which was stored in a 400-litre tank. Lightning bought Blasting Resin from two suppliers: Thunder Chemicals, a sister company, and Volcano Heatproof Coatings.

Just before Lightning's bankruptcy, Lightning received large deliveries of Blasting Resin from each of these suppliers, neither of which it was able to pay for. According to production records, the delivery of 250 litres from Volcano arrived first and was transferred into the storage tank, which already contained 25 litres from a previous delivery. 150 litres were then used in the manufacture of Dazzle Bulbs. The 200-litre delivery from Thunder then arrived, and was added to the tank. Finally, a further 150 litres was used to manufacture the next batch of Dazzle Bulbs.

When Lightning went bankrupt, both Volcano and Thunder tried to recover their resin. The company returned its remaining 75 litres of resin to Thunder, on the grounds that the 250 litres from Volcano had already been used up in the manufacture of the Dazzle Bulbs. But Volcano have taken you to court for breach of the ROT clause in the contract, which appears in Exercise 4.4.

# Photocopiable worksheet 9.3

Complete these six complex sentences from Reading B using the words in the box below each sentence.

**1** By .............. four .............. one .............. , the .............. has .............. the .............. of ..............
agreement .............. for .............. proceeds .............. sale .............. manufactured .............. to
.............. held .............. trust, .............. securing .............. manufacturer's .............. to ..............
seller.  ·

> a   an   be   court   effectiveness   goods   in   indebtedness
> majority   of   of   providing   the   the   the   thereby   to   upheld

**2** It .............. agreed .............. the .............. had .............. retained .............. to .............. steel
.............. since .............. steel .............. had .............. was .............. longer .............. in ..............
products; .............. steel .............. were .............. different .............. .

> ascertainable   it   no   not   physically   products   products
> property   Seller   supplied   that   the   the   the   the   title   was

**3** .............. Judge .............. first .............. , and .............. Court .............. Appeal, .............. held
.............. the .............. insofar .............. it .............. to .............. on .............. Seller ..............
proprietary .............. in .............. proceeds, .............. a .............. over .............. debts ..............
was .............. for .............. .

> a   and   as   at   book   charge   clause   confer   had   instance   interest
> non-registration   of   operated   that   the   the   the   the   void   was

**4** .............. drawing .............. distinction .............. relation .............. the .............. clause ..............
question, .............. Court .............. that .............. had .............. be .............. to .............. legal
.............. the .............. had .............. into.

> effect   entered   given   in   in   in   noted   particular
> parties   relationship   the   the   the   to   to

**5** In .............. end, .............. despite .............. upholding .............. Seller's .............. as ..............
the .............. of .............. clause, .............. Court .............. the .............. appeal ..............
an .............. ground.

> and   arguments   dismissed   effect   evidential   on
> Seller's   substantially   the   the   the   the   to

**6** However, .............. the .............. ultimate .............. , the .............. decision .............. a ..............
position .............. consequently .............. alter .............. balance .............. sellers ..............
secured .............. compete .............. priority.

> and   and   could   creditors   despite   failure   for
> majority's   seller's   Seller's   strengthens   the   where

# Photocopiable worksheet 10.1

🔊 **1** Listen to the presentation again and decide whether these statements are true or false.

**1** An easement is a right to use somebody else's property.

**2** Easement in gross, prescriptive easement and easement appurtenant are all types of temporary easement.

**3** A telecommunications provider might be given an easement in gross.

**4** Prescriptive easement is acquired by an open, notorious and continuous use.

**5** In the speaker's jurisdiction, if land has been used continuously by another party for 30 years, that party can claim prescriptive easement.

**6** An easement appurtenant is recorded when a property is divided into smaller lots.

**7** An easement by necessity is a type of prescriptive easement.

**8** A landlocked property (which does not have access to a public road) may be given an easement by necessity.

**2** The following notes were taken by one of the estate agents who attended the presentation on easements. Complete her notes using words and phrases from the box.

| | | | | | | |
|---|---|---|---|---|---|---|
| access | adjoining | appurtenant | gross | landlocked | necessity | Permanent |
| prescriptive | quasi | records | right | secretive | statutory | subdivision | visible |

Easements (= legal 1) ................. of another to use part of your property)

Temporary - e.g. 2) ................. during construction

3) ................. - three types:

   A  Easement in 4) .................

      • involve only one property

      • includes easements to 5) .................-public bodies (e.g. electric/phone company)

      • usually recorded in public 6) .................

   B  7) ................. easement (= right to use another's property)

      • acquired by open, notorious and continuous use

        - open = not 8) .................

        - notorious = clearly 9) .................

        - continuous (10) ................. period = 20 years)

   C  Easement 11) .................

      • benefits 12) ................. property (e.g. driveway/walkway)

      • usually recorded when a 13) ................. of property is made

      • important subtype: easement by 14) ................. (to reach 15) ................. property)

# Photocopiable worksheet 10.2

Put a word or phrase from the box in each space.

---

## STATUTORY CONDITIONS

**1** ..................... statutory conditions apply:

**1**  **Conditions of premises**
The landlord shall keep the premises in a good state of repair and fit for habitation **2** ..................... the tenancy and shall comply with any statutory enactment or law respecting standards of health, safety or housing.

**2(a)**  **Services**
**3** ..................... the landlord provides a service or facility to the tenant **4** ..................... reasonably related to the tenant's continued use and enjoyment of the premises **5** ..................... , **6** ..................... **7** ..................... , heat, water, electric power, gas, appliances, garbage collection, sewers or elevators, the landlord shall not discontinue providing that service.

**2(b)**  **Good behaviour**
A tenant shall conduct him/herself **8** ..................... interfere with the possession or occupancy of other tenants.

**3**  **Obligation of the tenant**
The tenant shall be responsible for the ordinary cleanliness of the interior of the premises and for the repair of damage **9** ..................... wilful or negligent act of the tenant or of any person **10** ..................... the tenant permits on the premises.

| |
|---|
| but not as to restrict the generality of |
| caused by |
| during |
| in such a manner as not to |
| such as |
| that is |
| the following |
| the foregoing |
| where |
| whom |

---

**4**  **Sub-letting premises**
The tenant may assign, sub-let or otherwise part with possession of the premises **11** ..................... the consent of the landlord **12** ..................... consent will not arbitrarily or unreasonably be withheld or charged for **13** ..................... the landlord has actually incurred expense **14** ..................... the grant of consent.

**5**  **Abandonment and termination**
**15** ..................... the tenant abandons the premises or terminates the tenancy **16** ..................... permitted, the landlord shall mitigate any damages **17** ..................... the abandonment or termination **18** ..................... a party to a contract is required by law to mitigate damages.

| |
|---|
| if |
| in respect of |
| otherwise than |
| in the manner |
| subject to |
| that may be caused by |
| to the extent that |
| unless |
| which |

---

**6**  **Entry of premises**
**19** ..................... an emergency, the landlord shall not enter the premises **20** ..................... the consent of the tenant **21** ..................... :
(a) notice of the termination of the tenancy has been given and the entry is at a reasonable hour **22** ..................... exhibiting the premises to prospective tenants or purchasers;
or
(b) the entry is made during daylight hours and written notice of the time of the entry has been given to the tenant at least twenty-four hours in advance of the entry.

**7**  **Entry doors**
**23** ..................... mutual consent, the landlord or the tenant shall not **24** ..................... occupancy by the tenant **25** ..................... the tenancy alter or **26** ..................... altered the lock or locking system on any door **27** ..................... gives entry to the premises.

| |
|---|
| cause to be |
| during |
| except by |
| except in the case of |
| for the purposes of |
| that |
| under |
| unless |
| without |

---

# Photocopiable worksheet 10.3

Put the verb in brackets into a suitable verb form. Some of the answers require verbs in the passive. Sometimes there is more than one possible answer.

**1** What steps must landlords ................... (*take*), in deference to their covenants of quiet enjoyment, when ................... (*comply*) with their repairing obligations under a lease?

**2** ................... (*be*) it enough for a landlord ................... (*take*) all reasonable precautions – or ................... (*the landlord require*) to take all possible precautions – to avoid ................... (*disturb*) its tenant?

**3** The landlord ................... (*bring*) in contractors ................... (*repair*) and clean the exterior of a building, which ................... (*let*) as a restaurant.

**4** The contractors ................... (*erect*) scaffolding and ................... (*fix*) sheeting to the exterior of the premises.

**5** The interior of the premises ................... (*become*) dusty and dark, and the restaurant ................... (*appear*) closed.

**6** The Appeal Court ................... (*say*) that, where the provisions of any contract ................... (*come*) into conflict, they are ................... (*interpret*) and applied ................... (*give*) proper effect, where possible, to each.

**7** The landlord's obligation ................... (*keep*) the building in repair ................... (*have*) to co-exist with the tenant's right to quiet enjoyment and vice versa.

**8** Neither obligation should ................... (*take*) priority over the other.

**9** It would ................... (*be*) possible ................... (*restrict*) the work to the days on which the restaurant ................... (*close*), but this would ................... (*be*) costly and impractical.

**10** The landlord ................... (*send*) the tenant a copy of the estimate for, and ................... (*agree*) to spread the cost of, the work.

**11** It ................... (*also postpone*) the start of the work to avoid ................... (*interfere*) with the tenant's busiest period and ................... (*arrange*) the work to meet the tenant's requirements in so far as it ................... (*can*).

**12** The landlord was under an obligation ................... (*take*) all reasonable steps – but not all possible precautions – ................... (*avoid*) disturbing the tenant, and ................... (*do*) so.

# Photocopiable worksheet 10.4

Match the legalese terms (1–8, 9–16, 17–24) with their definitions (a–h, i–p, q–x). Then write one in each gap in the sentences below them (A–H, I–P, Q–X).

| | | | |
|---|---|---|---|
| **1** whereof | | **a** | by which |
| **2** whereon | | **b** | in which |
| **3** whereto | | **c** | of which |
| **4** whereby | | **d** | on which |
| **5** whereas | | **e** | to which |
| **6** wherein | | **f** | with which |
| **7** whereupon | | **g** | while |
| **8** wherewith | | **h** | when |

**A** This fee tail shall allow the grantee to use the property until his death, ...................... said fee tail shall pass to his heirs.

**B** Your client signed an easement appurtenant ...................... it was expressly prohibited to restrict access to the driveway.

**C** A freehold estate refers to an estate in which ownership is for an indeterminate length of time, ...................... a leasehold is the term for the right to possession and use of land for a fixed period of time.

**D** The dispute concerned a piece of land ...................... the defendant's land shared a common border.

**E** An estate pur autre vie is a type of leasehold ...................... a party has the right to use land for the duration of another person's life.

**F** The landlord leased the tenant some land ...................... to graze his cows.

**G** The defendant was still not informed of the offence ...................... he had been accused.

**H** She had attempted to sell a plot of real estate ...................... she did not have good title.

| | | | |
|---|---|---|---|
| **9** heretofore | | **i** | by making this statement |
| **10** hereafter | | **j** | from now on in this document |
| **11** hereof | | **k** | from now on |
| **12** hereto | | **l** | below these words |
| **13** hereby | | **m** | in this document |
| **14** hereunder | | **n** | of this document |
| **15** herein | | **o** | up to now |
| **16** hereinafter | | **p** | to this document |

**I** Lessee ...................... agrees to indemnify, defend and hold Lessor harmless from any and all claims or assertions of every kind and nature.

**J** Lessee, upon payment of all of the sums referred to ...................... as being payable by Lessee, ...

**K** ... shall and may peacefully and quietly have, hold and enjoy said Premises for the term ...................... .

**L** This deed of conservation easement is made by Jack Gould (...................... 'Grantor') in favour of The Bird Conservation League ...

**M** The terms specified ...................... shall have the meanings set out opposite them.

**N** ...................... my client has always complied with all requests from the landlord, but he cannot accept the request to waive his right to quiet enjoyment.

**O** The aims of the Grantee are set out in the Mission Statement attached ...................... .

**P** I regret to inform you that ...................... I shall not be in a position to deal with your affairs as a lawyer.

# Photocopiable worksheet 10.4 [continued]

| | | | |
|---|---|---|---|
| **17** | therewith | **q** | of that thing |
| **18** | thereon | **r** | to that thing |
| **19** | thereof | **s** | from that thing |
| **20** | thereby | **t** | with that thing |
| **21** | thereafter | **u** | for that thing |
| **22** | thereto | **v** | from then on |
| **23** | therefrom | **w** | on that thing |
| **24** | therefor | **x** | by doing that |

**Q** Lessor and Lessor's agents shall have the right to enter the premises for the purpose of inspecting the Premises and all buildings and improvements ..................... .

**R** The easement shall exist in perpetuity unless both parties agree upon a discontinuation ..................... .

**S** The Grantor and any successors agree that they shall not erect any building upon said premises that will restrict access ..................... for all the above purposes.

**T** A conservation easement was placed on the land in 1972. ..................... no building was permitted on that land.

**U** Your client has consistently refused access to the radio mast on his land, ..................... breaching the terms of the easement in gross.

**V** The Grantor shall not engage in any activities prohibited in Section 48, and shall make every reasonable effort to act in accordance ..................... .

**W** When you place an order for goods, it is essential that payment ..................... is enclosed with the order.

**X** Any minerals or income deriving ..................... shall remain the property of the lessee.

# Photocopiable worksheet 11.1

Match the phrases on the left (1–16) with those on the right (a–p) to form collocations.

| | | | |
|---|---|---|---|
| **1** | an expansive | **a** | legal protection |
| **2** | the issues revolve | **b** | down into three main areas |
| **3** | rights are afforded | **c** | to relevant legislation |
| **4** | changes in this field raise | **d** | in an invention |
| **5** | IP rights are broken | **e** | of profits |
| **6** | a patent is a monopoly right | **f** | on the author's rights |
| **7** | patent law is regulated | **g** | that it provides an exclusive right |
| **8** | a right is granted pursuant | **h** | through legislation |
| **9** | a patent remains in | **i** | to include cybersquatting |
| **10** | similar to a patent in | **j** | from the relevant author |
| **11** | deception is deemed | **k** | topical debates |
| **12** | copyright subsists | **l** | area of the law |
| **13** | copyright work must originate | **m** | force for a statutory period |
| **14** | do not infringe | **n** | in enforcement actions |
| **15** | infringement may result | **o** | in original works |
| **16** | remedies include account | **p** | around the boundary lines |

# Photocopiable worksheet 11.2

Choose the best word to fill each gap from A, B, C or D below.

## The 'State Street' case expands patent protection to methods of doing business

In 1998, the United States Court of Appeals for the Federal Circuit handed **1** .............. a landmark decision in *State Street Bank and Trust Co. v. Signature Financial Group, Inc.* The 'State Street' case has attracted wide attention because it has opened up the patent system **2** .............. inventions which are not within traditional technologies.

The case involved a patent **3** .............. to Signature Financial Group which was called a 'Data-Processing System for Hub and Spoke Financial Services Configuration'. The data-processing system **4** .............. for complex calculations to be provided very quickly in relation to mutual funds (Spokes) pooled in an investment portfolio (Hub) which was organised as a partnership. The patent was **5** .............. by State Street Bank and Trust.

The lower court **6** .............. that the invention fell **7** .............. two exceptions to patentable **8** .............. matter: the mathematical-algorithm exception, and the business-method exception. The court **9** .............. that the data-processing system merely performed a series of mathematical functions and that the patent was further **10** .............. under 'the long-established principle that business "plans" and "systems" are not **11** .............. '.

However, on appeal, the Federal Circuit Court reasoned that the cases **12** .............. upon by the lower court were inappropriately applied to the case. It stated that the focus of what **13** .............. patentable subject matter should be the essential characteristics of it and, in particular, its practical **14** .............. . And, with regard **15** .............. the Hub and Spoke software in question, it produced a 'useful, concrete and tangible result'. The court ended by dismissing the 'ill-conceived' business-method exception to patentability in total.

| | | | | |
|---|---|---|---|---|
| **1** | **A** out | **B** over | **C** in | **D** down |
| **2** | **A** to | **B** on | **C** from | **D** with |
| **3** | **A** allocated | **B** provided | **C** addressed | **D** issued |
| **4** | **A** enabled | **B** ensured | **C** allowed | **D** permitted |
| **5** | **A** upheld | **B** challenged | **C** granted | **D** invaded |
| **6** | **A** held | **B** proscribed | **C** deemed | **D** told |
| **7** | **A** about | **B** by | **C** within | **D** between |
| **8** | **A** item | **B** topic | **C** subject | **D** object |
| **9** | **A** rejected | **B** reasoned | **C** reminded | **D** reckoned |
| **10** | **A** invalid | **B** obsolete | **C** unfit | **D** illegitimate |
| **11** | **A** protectable | **B** coverable | **C** enforceable | **D** patentable |
| **12** | **A** raised | **B** relied | **C** counted | **D** utilised |
| **13** | **A** means | **B** constitutes | **C** implies | **D** consists |
| **14** | **A** utility | **B** novelty | **C** obviousness | **D** patentability |
| **15** | **A** of | **B** on | **C** to | **D** by |

# Photocopiable worksheet 11.3

You are all lawyers and senior managers from a national office of Pirate Industries, a multinational corporation. Your bosses in the international headquarters are keen for you to enter the lucrative market for chocolate and ice cream, and they have identified the market leader, Soft & Sweet, as a soft target. They have instructed you to 'borrow' as much as possible of Soft & Sweet's IP: its patented inventions, its copyrighted works, its trade secrets and its trade marks. Pirate Industries is not interested in questions of morality, only short-term profitability.

Hold a meeting to discuss the issues on the agenda below. At the moment, you know little about the actions Soft & Sweet have taken to protect their IP, but you can assume that they have taken the usual precautions.

Use the following agenda to structure your meeting.

---

## EXTREMELY CONFIDENTIAL

### AGENDA

1  How can we undermine S&S's IP protection to take market share from them?

Patents:
- Computer-controlled refrigerated delivery vans
- Self-cleaning chocolate-mixing machines
- Others?

Copyright:
- 'Ode to chocolate' (poem by co-founder Susan Soft)
- *Soft & Sweet's Ice-cream Cookbook* (international bestseller)
- Others?

Trade secrets:
- Recipe for fat-free ice cream
- Supplier of 'extract of intangibility': mystery ingredient in Boom Bars
- Others?

Trade marks:
- Brand names, especially Boom Bar, Hub'n'Spoke Biscuits, Iced Cybersquat
- Soft & Sweet's famous 'two fat ladies' logo, plus logos for branded products
- Motto for Hub'n'Spoke biscuits: 'I could eat a bike'.

2  How can we protect such IP as our own?

3  How can we preserve our reputation as a caring company?

4  Any other business.

---

# Photocopiable worksheet 12.1

For each gap, choose the correct alternative: A, B, C or D.

1 .................... value received, the undersigned ('2 .................... ') promises to pay 3 .................... demand to the order 4 .................... Soderton National Bank ('5 .................... ') at its offices at 99 Hartsdale Avenue, Soderton, New York, the 6 .................... sum of ten thousand dollars ($10,000), together with 7 .................... at the rate and in the 8 .................... hereinafter provided 9 .................... on the outstanding principal 10 .................... from time to time until paid 11 .................... full.

| 1 | **A** As | **B** With | **C** For | **D** By |
|---|---|---|---|---|
| 2 | **A** Bearer | **B** Drawer | **C** Endorsee | **D** Maker |
| 3 | **A** under | **B** the | **C** when | **D** on |
| 4 | **A** of | **B** from | **C** by | **D** at |
| 5 | **A** Payee | **B** Drawee | **C** Holder | **D** Transferee |
| 6 | **A** total | **B** principal | **C** principle | **D** outstanding |
| 7 | **A** interest | **B** instalments | **C** accruals | **D** payments |
| 8 | **A** method | **B** order | **C** manner | **D** way |
| 9 | **A** on | **B** for | **C** of | **D** against |
| 10 | **A** thereof | **B** thereat | **C** hereat | **D** hereof |
| 11 | **A** off | **B** back | **C** in | **D** to |

Interest shall accrue 12 .................... the outstanding principal 13 .................... of this note commencing on the date hereof and continuing until 14 .................... of this note in full at a rate per 15 .................... equal to 6%. Interest-only payments shall be 16 .................... by Maker to Payee on or before the 1st day of each month.

Maker shall make all payments 17 .................... to Payee in US dollars.

The maturity of this note 18 .................... be accelerated by Payee in the 19 .................... Maker is in breach or 20 .................... of any of the terms, conditions, or covenants of any other agreement with Payee or its 21 .................... In the event of default in payment of any interest payments when 22 .................... hereunder, the whole 23 .................... of principal and interest shall become 24 .................... due and payable.

| 12 | **A** on | **B** under | **C** with | **D** for |
|---|---|---|---|---|
| 13 | **A** level | **B** rate | **C** balance | **D** remainder |
| 14 | **A** completion | **B** repayment | **C** reversion | **D** maturity |
| 15 | **A** yearly | **B** annum | **C** cent | **D** capita |
| 16 | **A** done | **B** given | **C** set forth | **D** made |
| 17 | **A** whereby | **B** hereunder | **C** heretofore | **D** wherefor |
| 18 | **A** could | **B** might | **C** should | **D** may |
| 19 | **A** event | **B** situation | **C** circumstances | **D** way |
| 20 | **A** dereliction | **B** defalcation | **C** default | **D** deficit |
| 21 | **A** allies | **B** affiliates | **C** accomplices | **D** auxiliaries |
| 22 | **A** requested | **B** urgent | **C** due | **D** mature |
| 23 | **A** amount | **B** quantity | **C** rest | **D** sum |
| 24 | **A** immediately | **B** instantly | **C** suddenly | **D** thereupon |

# Photocopiable worksheet 12.2

Legal English often contains very long and complex sentences, and lawyers need to work out (and remember) which sections relate to which other sections. One way to do this is to use brackets ( ) [ ] { }.

The following sentences from Reading C are long and complex. Show the relationships as in the example, and write a 'skeleton' of each sentence. You can invent your own system.

**1** The act [defines the terms ("record," "electronic record," and "electronic signature")] and [provides (as a general rule) that {electronic (records and signatures) satisfy legal requirements that (a record be in writing or signed)}].
**The act [defines the terms a, b and c] and [provides that …].**

.................................................................................................................................................................

.................................................................................................................................................................

**2** The UETA contains provisions governing provision or transmission of information in electronic form, attribution of electronic records and signatures, distributing risk of error in electronic transmissions, and retention of "original" electronic records.

.................................................................................................................................................................

.................................................................................................................................................................

**3** Other provisions govern automated electronic transactions or the use of so-called electronic "agents" and acceptance of electronic records and signatures by governmental agencies.

.................................................................................................................................................................

.................................................................................................................................................................

**4** As long as an entity has "control" of the transferable record, it is a holder of the record as defined by UCC § 1-201(20) and has the same rights and defenses as a holder of a negotiable instrument or document under UCC Articles 3, 7, and 9.

.................................................................................................................................................................

.................................................................................................................................................................

**5** A person has "control" over the record if "a system employed for evidencing the transfer of interests in the transferable record reliably established that person as the person to which the transferable record was issued or transferred."

.................................................................................................................................................................

.................................................................................................................................................................

**6** This requirement can be met by a system that creates, stores, and assigns the transferable record in a manner that satisfies six specific conditions listed in the UETA.

.................................................................................................................................................................

.................................................................................................................................................................

**7** Transactions existing or signed electronically that might be unenforceable under traditional principles of law may become enforceable when taking into account the UETA's provisions.

.................................................................................................................................................................

.................................................................................................................................................................

# Photocopiable worksheet 12.3

Put a word from the box into each numbered gap. Then complete the documents, using your own or invented personal details.

| | |
|---|---|
| accordance account annum behalf Certificate completion | |
| deposited Depositor evidenced interest maturity order penalty | |
| received substantial sum transferable withdraw | |

---

**Bill of Exchange**  No. _____

For _____  Date _____

At _____*sixty days sight*_____ of this_____*sole*_____Bill of Exchange

Pay to the **1** ................................ of _____

The **2** ................................ of _____

For value **3** ................................

To _____    For and on **4** ................................ of

_____    _____

_____    _____

---

## Pococurante Bank
## Certificate of Deposit

**5** ......................... number: _____

This is to certify that the **6** ......................... _____

of _____

has **7** ......................... the sum of _____

**8** ......................... no. _____

Date of deposit: _____    Date of **9** ......................... : _____

By this certificate, payment on the above stated deposit at an **10** ......................... rate of 12% per

**11** ......................... shall be made in full upon **12** ......................... of a 12-month time-fixed deposit.

If you **13** ......................... all or part of your deposit before it matures, a **14** ......................... interest

**15** ......................... . will be imposed. A personal time deposit **16** ......................... by this receipt is

not **17** ......................... except in **18** ......................... with the bank's rules and regulations.

_____                    _____
Deposit Manager                      General Manager

_____
Depositor

# Photocopiable worksheet 13.1

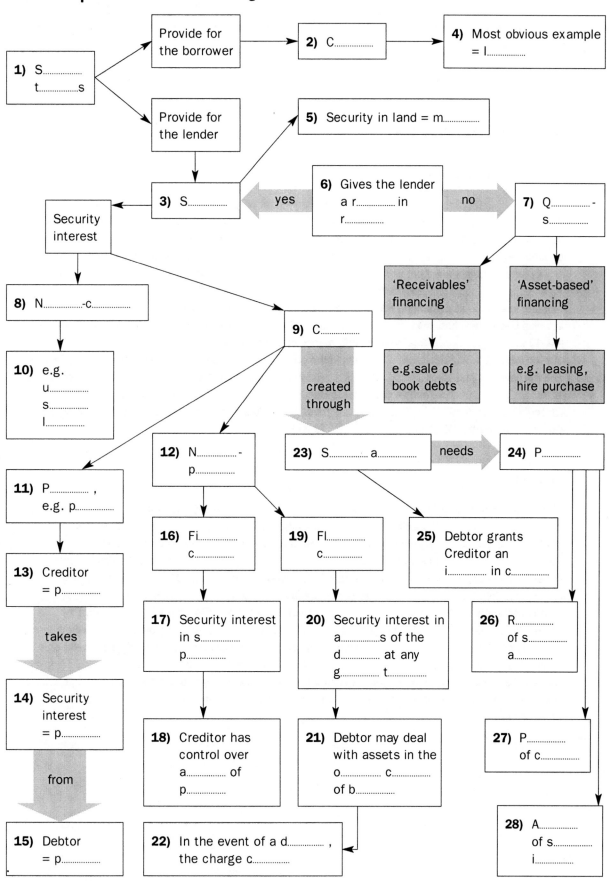

**1)** S............
t............s

**Provide for the borrower** → **2)** C............ → **4)** Most obvious example = I............

**Provide for the lender** → **5)** Security in land = m............

**3)** S............ ← yes — **6)** Gives the lender a r............ in r............ — no → **7)** Q............-s............

Security interest

**'Receivables' financing** → e.g. sale of book debts

**'Asset-based' financing** → e.g. leasing, hire purchase

**8)** N............-c............

**9)** C............

created through

**10)** e.g.
u............
s............
l............

**11)** P............ ,
e.g. p............

**12)** N............-
p............

**23)** S............ a............ — needs → **24)** P............

**25)** Debtor grants Creditor an i............ in c............

**13)** Creditor
= p............

takes

**16)** Fi............
c............

**19)** Fl............
c............

**26)** R............
of s............
a............

**14)** Security interest
= p............

from

**17)** Security interest in s............
p............

**20)** Security interest in a............s of the d............ at any g............ t............

**27)** P............
of c............

**18)** Creditor has control over a............ of p............

**21)** Debtor may deal with assets in the o............ c............ of b............

**15)** Debtor
= p............

**22)** In the event of a d............ , the charge c............

**28)** A............
of s............
i............

# Photocopiable worksheet 13.2

Complete the paragraphs using the correct form of the words in brackets. Sometimes you will have to use negative prefixes.

## SECURITY AGREEMENT

### SECURITY INTEREST

1 ................................. (*debt*) grants to Secured Party a security interest in all inventory, equipment, 2 .................................. (*apply*), furnishings and 3 .................................. (*fix*) now or hereafter placed upon the premises 4 ...............................(*locate*) at 99 Appleby Road, Baltimore, MD (the "Premises") or used in 5 .................................. (*connect*) 6 .................................. (*with*) and in which Debtor now has or hereafter acquires any right and the 7 .................................. (*proceed*) 8 .................................. (*from*). As 9 ...............................(*add*) collateral, Debtor assigns to Secured Party a 10 .................................. (*secure*) interest in all of its right, title and interest to any trade marks, trade names and contract rights in which Debtor now has or 11 .................................. (*after*) acquires. The Security Interest shall secure the 12 ...............................(*pay*) and performance of Debtor's 13 ..................................(*promise*) note of even date 14 .................................. (*with*) in the principal amount of twenty thousand ($20,000) Dollars and the payment and 15 .................................. (*perform*) of all other 16 .................................. (*liable*) and 17 .................................. (*oblige*) of Debtor to Secured Party of every kind and 18 .................................. (*describe*), direct or 19 .................................. (*direct*), absolute or contingent, due or to become due, now existing or hereafter 20 .................................. (*arise*).

### DEFAULT

The Debtor shall be in default under this 21 .................................. (*agree*) upon the 22 .................................. (*happen*) of any of the following: (a) any 23 ..................................(*represent*) in 24 .................................. (*connect*) with this Agreement on the part of the Debtor; (b) any 25 .................................. (*comply*) with or 26 .................................. (*perform*) of the Debtor's obligations under the Note or this Agreement; (c) if Debtor is involved in any financial 27 .................................. (*difficult*) as 28 .................................. (*evidence*) by (i) an assignment for the benefit of creditors, or (ii) an attachment or 29 .................................. (*receive*) of assets not dissolved within thirty days, or (iii) the 30 .................................. (*institute*) of 31 .................................. (*bankrupt*) proceedings, whether voluntary or 32 .................................. (*volunteer*), which is not dismissed within thirty days from the date on which it is filed. Upon 33 .................................. (*fault*) and at any time 34 .................................. (*after*), Secured Party may declare all obligations secured hereby immediately due and 35 .................................. (*pay*) and shall have the remedies of a Secured Party under the Uniform 36 .................................. (*commerce*) Code.

# Photocopiable worksheet 13.3

Some of these sentences are grammatically correct, and are used as they were in Listening B. Others contain grammar mistakes. Find the mistakes and correct them.

**1** Old Kellogg knows about what he's talking.

**2** He had some good stories to tell about cases what he worked on.

**3** On the whole, I'd have to say I learned a lot at that seminar.

**4** That's where things are going, if you will ask me.

**5** Can you fill me in on what he said?

**6** What he did was to give us the big picture, telling us about what the situation is in different countries.

**7** Then he talked about how are specific types of IP collateral perfected here in the US under the revised UCC.

**8** He started off by talking us about the importance of intellectual property as an asset.

**9** He said that for many companies, their intellectual property is their greatest asset.

**10** It makes sense, if you think about it.

**11** The main point he made was that the law is still anything but not settled.

**12** What was that he said about the UK?

**13** The law is still unclear about does this apply to a foreign company that has no presence in the UK.

**14** His point was that perfecting security interests internationally is a tricky business.

**15** You need to have someone who knows what they're doing in the countries in question.

**16** What he had to say about perfecting security interests in the US?

**17** Part of the problem is knowing where to file the security interest, whether on the state or the federal level.

**18** The key issue here seems to be whether the copyright is registered with the Copyright Office or not.

**19** Where I could get more information on what covered in the seminar was?

**20** Everything what you want to know is in there.

# Photocopiable worksheet 14.1

## Client 1

You have made a fortune through your empire of motorcycle couriers, which have a reputation for being the fastest in the country. You have offices in 40 towns and cities, and over 800 riders delivering packages on behalf of well-paying clients.

You are concerned that your insurance will not cover you in the event of a serious accident, as your drivers tend to drive in excess of legal speed limits.

Your assets include two houses and a luxury apartment in the capital, around half a million dollars' worth of shares, and a priceless collection of modern-art pieces.

## Client 2

You are a plastic surgeon, specialising in surgery for the rich and famous. Your work requires a steady hand and a great deal of concentration, both of which seem increasingly elusive as you get older.

You are concerned that you might one day accidentally disfigure a celebrity, and may be sued for malpractice. You have heard stories of insurers refusing to cover certain claims.

You have a large family home, two luxury cars and around $1 million in an investment account. You have considered setting up a trust in your children's names, but you don't really trust your children with your assets.

## Client 3

You are a property magnate, with 40 houses around the country, each of which you rent to tenants. All of the houses are fully owned by you.

You are especially concerned about fire insurance: you try to keep up to date with health and safety regulations, but with so many properties, you are worried that you may overlook something and then be unable to claim from your insurers.

You have two young sons who you would like to inherit your fortune, but are desperate to keep your estranged husband/wife as far away from your business affairs as possible.

## Client 4

You are a successful gangster who is planning to retire from a life of crime and abide by the law.

You have made a fortune through your criminal activities, such as kidnapping, blackmail and extortion, and you are keen to preserve your fortune from prosecutors.

You have over $4 million in various bank accounts, 12 properties in the capital city, four luxury cars and a very impressive collection of jewellery.

You would like to protect your assets by purely legal means.

## Lawyer 1

You are a specialist in advising clients on asset protection. Interview your clients in order to advise them. Think about:

- trusts
- transfer of assets to family members
- offshore investments

## Lawyer 2

You are an unscrupulous lawyer, specialising in charging huge fees for poor advice on asset protection, exposing them to criminal liability, and even persuading them to place assets under your control.

Convince your clients to follow your advice.

# Photocopiable worksheet 14.2

Discuss these questions with a partner. Then read the text to find which paragraph (1–9) relates to which question (a–i).

**a** What do insolvency practitioners actually do?

**b** What can an insolvency practitioner do to help in a formal insolvency?

**c** What arrangements can be used to make insolvency less destructive?

**d** What is the first step in becoming an insolvency practitioner?

**e** What percentage of insolvent companies can be rescued?

**f** What sorts of people do insolvency practitioners work closely with?

**g** How can clients be sure that an insolvency practitioner is competent?

**h** Would you enjoy working as an insolvency practitioner?

**i** How is the insolvency scene changing?

# Photocopiable worksheet 14.3

This letter was written in response to advertisement B in Reading D. It contains some mistakes (spelling, grammar, punctuation, style, content, layout). How could you improve it?

Dear Harold

I'm writting in a response to your advert at the website www.legalpositions.com. You say you are offering an exciting opportunity for an NQ Company Commercial Solicitor. I am a new-qualificated Company Commercial Solicitor and I want to join your team. I am enclosing my CV.

I am outgoing and reliable person. I love a challenge, what means that working for your firm will be a really good experience for me. I know a lot of about IT and e-commerce because I am buying a lot of computer games on Internet. I graduated three months ago. I worked in many big law firms. I specialy interested in international commercial law, it is field, that require much analitical thinking and attention to the details. Those are my qualities.

Please, interview me. I am person, what you look for. I'm look forward to hear you.

Yours faithfully

Vincent Fott

# Photocopiable worksheet 14.4

Complete the fragments below, which all come from Unit 14, with the prepositions from the box.

| | | | | | | | | | | | | | | |
|---|---|---|---|---|---|---|---|---|---|---|---|---|---|---|
| about | against | as | at | beyond | by | for | for | for | for | for | for | for | for | from |
| from | in | in | in | in | into | into | of | of | of | of | of | on | on | on | on | out | through |
| to | to | to | to | to | to | under | with | with | with | with | within | without | without | | |

**1** ... the defendant is justly indebted ..................... the plaintiff

**2** ... the attachment is not sought ..................... the purpose ..................... harassing the defendant

**3** ... specific grounds ..................... the writ exist under Section 61.002.

**4** ... the defendant is ..................... hiding so that the ordinary process of law cannot be served ..................... him

**5** ... the defendant has disposed ..................... or is about to dispose ..................... all or part of his property ..................... the intent to defraud his creditors

**6** ... the defendant is ..................... to convert all or part of his property ..................... money for the purpose of placing it ..................... the reach of his creditors

**7** ... the defendant owes the plaintiff ..................... property obtained ..................... the defendant ..................... false pretences.

**8** Insolvency practitioners can find themselves advising ..................... the viability of a business ...

**9** Insolvency practitioners deal ..................... hard-bitten businessmen with an eye ..................... a bargain.

**10** ..................... many cases, a positive approach ..................... the rescue of businesses and jobs can be taken ..................... the application of administrations.

**11** I was particularly happy to see that the position is open ..................... newly qualified lawyers.

**12** I would welcome the opportunity to work ..................... part of your successful team, to benefit ..................... your extensive experience, and to put my training ..................... practice ..................... your firm.

**13** My background, interests and skills are compatible ..................... the goals of your firm.

**14** A company is able to file ..................... Chapter 11 protection voluntarily and can do so regardless ..................... whether it can show that it is insolvent.

**15** Well, I see that my time is running ..................... and so I'd like to move ..................... my final point.

**16** Clients often ask 'How can I limit the exposure ..................... my business and personal assets ..................... the risks of my business?'

**17** A judgment lien applies if the plaintiff receives an award ..................... his favour.

**18** The judgment lien immediately attaches ..................... all real estate in your name.

**19** You cannot sell or refinance a property ..................... paying off the creditor, and he can foreclose ..................... the real estate and seize any accounts ..................... your name.

**20** Ed told us that there was a judgment ..................... him for $1.5 million.

**21** Had he not set up the plan, the plaintiff would have had a lien ..................... all of the client's real estate as security ..................... the judgment.

**22** Ed was able to negotiate ..................... a position of strength.

**23** ..................... two years after setting up the plan, my client was served ..................... a lawsuit.

**24** ..................... any assurance of payment, the plaintiff's attorney quickly lost interest and the case was settled ..................... under $2,000.

**25** I think insolvency work is like solving a puzzle in which people's livelihoods are ..................... stake.

# Photocopiable worksheet 15.1

These sentences contain many examples of active voice. Rewrite them, using passive voice, so that they sound more natural.

1   In America in the late 19<sup>th</sup> century, the owners of dominant companies in industries such as sugar, tobacco, steel and oil established a series of trusts to create a monopoly in their industries.

   ...........................................................................................................................................................................................

   ...........................................................................................................................................................................................

   ...........................................................................................................................................................................................

2   Some people acting on behalf of these trusts often coerced shareholders of other companies in the same sector into joining the trusts.

   ...........................................................................................................................................................................................

   ...........................................................................................................................................................................................

   ...........................................................................................................................................................................................

3   The shareholders transferred ownership of their shares. The shareholders received dividend-paying certificates in exchange.

   ...........................................................................................................................................................................................

   ...........................................................................................................................................................................................

   ...........................................................................................................................................................................................

4   The trusts grew so powerful that politicians agreed that somebody had to do something to bring them under control.

   ...........................................................................................................................................................................................

   ...........................................................................................................................................................................................

   ...........................................................................................................................................................................................

5   Before lawmakers introduced the Sherman Act, so-called barons had controlled whole industries.

   ...........................................................................................................................................................................................

   ...........................................................................................................................................................................................

   ...........................................................................................................................................................................................

6   'Muckraking' journalists led the campaign against Standard Oil, which the authorities finally brought before the courts 20 years later.

   ...........................................................................................................................................................................................

   ...........................................................................................................................................................................................

   ...........................................................................................................................................................................................

7   No one has ever calculated what advances people could have made by the market leader had the authorities allowed it to continue to increase its market share.

   ...........................................................................................................................................................................................

   ...........................................................................................................................................................................................

   ...........................................................................................................................................................................................

8   Regulators were investigating the firm for its alleged abuse of its dominant position.

   ...........................................................................................................................................................................................

   ...........................................................................................................................................................................................

   ...........................................................................................................................................................................................

# Photocopiable worksheet 15.1 [continued]

**9** Lawmakers introduced the Single European Market in 1993. Since then, it has protected the free flow of labour and capital within the EU.

.................................................................................................................................................................

.................................................................................................................................................................

.................................................................................................................................................................

**10** People have argued that antitrust laws have done more harm than good. Nobody can calculate how various factors would have affected markets if regulators had not enforced antitrust measures.

.................................................................................................................................................................

.................................................................................................................................................................

.................................................................................................................................................................

**11** People may bribe or even threaten small companies in order to persuade them to join cartels.

.................................................................................................................................................................

.................................................................................................................................................................

.................................................................................................................................................................

**12** Somebody needs to prevent this sort of coercive behaviour.

.................................................................................................................................................................

.................................................................................................................................................................

.................................................................................................................................................................

**13** The directors made the accountant conceal evidence of the collusion.

.................................................................................................................................................................

.................................................................................................................................................................

.................................................................................................................................................................

**14** Critics of regulation have pointed out that antitrust laws cannot defeat predatory pricing, but that people can rely on a truly free market to undermine such activities.

.................................................................................................................................................................

.................................................................................................................................................................

.................................................................................................................................................................

**15** The CEOs of the three companies agreed upon the cartel, and their companies entered into an unofficial agreement a few weeks later. Regulators only discovered the existence of the cartel when a former director, who the company had sacked, tipped off the OFT.

.................................................................................................................................................................

.................................................................................................................................................................

.................................................................................................................................................................

# Photocopiable worksheet 15.2

Look at the extracts below from Listening A. First, complete each gap using one word from the box. Then decide whether the speaker uses semi-informal (SI) or more formal (F) language. What do you notice? How could you make the semi-informal sentences more formal?

| down get get going guess have helped I'd in is make |
| newcomer other out over over themselves used |

1   The new cars aren't working ..................... as well as ..................... hoped, actually. (SI/F)

2   People just don't seem to be taking as many cab rides as they ..................... to – trying to cut .....................
    on their expenses, I ..................... . And the new subway connection to the airport hasn't ..................... us,
    either. (SI/F)

3   The problem ..................... , we've heard that a .....................'s planning to enter our market. (SI/F)

4   Well, these guys call ..................... the Orange Team or something, and all their cars are orange, and
    they've been advertising all ..................... the place ... (SI/F)

5   Don Belmont called me the ..................... day and said he wanted to meet and ..................... a beer. (SI/F)

6   I thought it was a good idea to ..................... together and talk things ..................... , you know, how
    business is ..................... and things like that. (SI/F)

7   And then Don started talking about prices, and if there wasn't something we could do to .....................
    it harder for these Orange boys to ..................... a foothold ..................... our territory. (SI/F)

| dirt for from in into left lower of |
| off on on on over still to to up |

8   Belmont suggested we cool ..................... our competition a little and agree ..................... some things, like
    territory and prices. (SI/F)

9   He said we should agree to ..................... our prices below those of the Orange Team, but also fix a
    certain lower limit that we both adhere ..................... , so that our losses wouldn't be too great. (SI/F)

10  I mean, there's no harm ..................... talking about things ..................... a beer, is there? (SI/F)

11  Even if you only discuss the idea of dividing ..................... territory or price-fixing with a competitor –
    that's what Mr Belmont's suggestion amounts ..................... , you know – even if the suggestion is
    never put ..................... practice, it is still an infringement ..................... the law. (SI/F)

12  Of course, it's very hard ..................... an evidentiary standpoint ..................... the case to be proven,
    but it's ..................... a violation. (SI/F)

13  Another suggestion he had was a discount ..................... airport trips, a special price, really
    ..................... cheap, that'd help us to hold ..................... to what's ..................... of the airport business. (SI/F)

# Photocopiable worksheet 15.3

These extracts from Listening B contain mistakes connected with the active and passive voices. Find the mistakes and correct them. Do not change the tenses or other structures. The first has been done for you as an example.

1   How ~~do~~ *are* mergers ~~evaluate~~ *evaluated*? Section 16 of the Act lays out the criteria to ~~employ~~ *be employed* in the merger evaluation process.

2   First, the investigators, and, where appropriate, the Tribunal, must be considered the impact of the merger on competition.

3   It's a sophisticated analysis in which a range of factors must consider.

4   The nature of the product, the state of international trade in the product, past inter-firm relations, and the prospect that, in the absence of the merger, one of the firms may be failed are some of the factors that have to account for.

5   Once this analysis does, it's possible that a merger that leads to a large market share might approve, whereas one that results in substantially smaller market shares might reject.

6   If the first question answers in the affirmative, that is, if it finds that the merger will impede competition, the investigators and tribunal must ask whether there are not efficiency gains from the merger that may be counter-balanced the negative impact on competition.

7   ... don't simply assert it, and don't simply be claimed that because there are significantly bigger firms in the same industry elsewhere in the world that this somehow means that the continued existence of your firm demands that you permit to merge.

8   Your problem with efficiency defences is that they need to evaluate up front before the merger has consummated.

9   An anti-competitive merger may permit in the face of strong public-interest reasons in favour of the merger; by the same token, a merger that judges to have no negative impact on competition may disallow on public-interest grounds.

10  It eases somewhat by the fact that the Act specifies the public-interest grounds that may consider, but it will always be a difficult judgment call.

11  On the contrary, it recognises that these transactions are frequently an aspect of corporate restructuring that's inevitable and productive. I would expect the vast majority of mergers to easily approve.

12  But mergers that devise for dominating markets will be fallen foul of the Act.

# Photocopiable worksheet 16.1

Complete this diagram of Reading B with words from the text. The words are numbered in the order they first appear in the text. The first letter of each word is given.

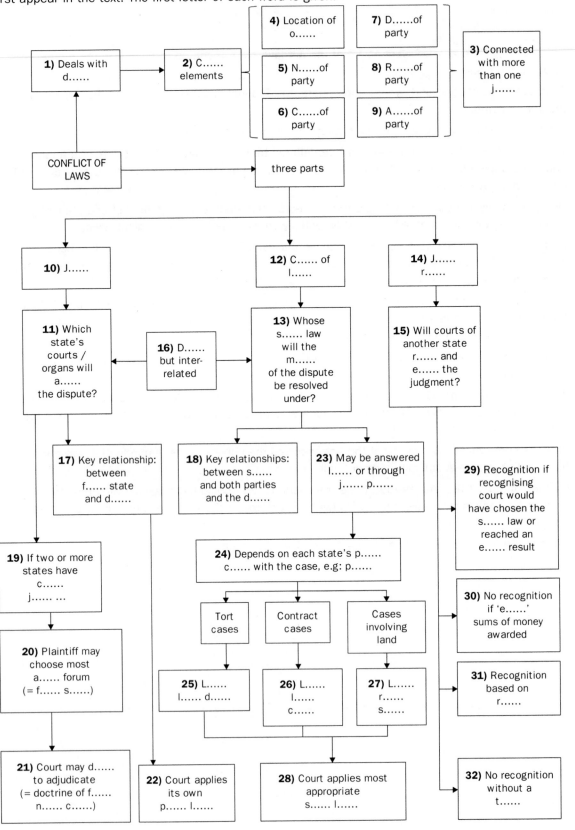

**1)** Deals with d......

**2)** C...... elements

**4)** Location of o......

**5)** N......of party

**6)** C......of party

**7)** D......of party

**8)** R......of party

**9)** A......of party

**3)** Connected with more than one j......

CONFLICT OF LAWS

three parts

**10)** J......

**12)** C...... of l......

**14)** J...... r......

**11)** Which state's courts / organs will a...... the dispute?

**16)** D...... but inter-related

**13)** Whose s...... law will the m...... of the dispute be resolved under?

**15)** Will courts of another state r...... and e...... the judgment?

**17)** Key relationship: between f...... state and d......

**18)** Key relationships: between s...... and both parties and the d......

**23)** May be answered l...... or through j...... p......

**29)** Recognition if recognising court would have chosen the s...... law or reached an e...... result

**19)** If two or more states have c...... j......  ...

**24)** Depends on each state's p...... c...... with the case, e.g: p......

Tort cases

Contract cases

Cases involving land

**30)** No recognition if 'e......' sums of money awarded

**20)** Plaintiff may choose most a...... forum (= f...... s......)

**25)** L...... l...... d......

**26)** L...... l...... c......

**27)** L...... r...... s......

**31)** Recognition based on r......

**21)** Court may d...... to adjudicate (= doctrine of f...... n...... c......)

**22)** Court applies its own p...... l......

**28)** Court applies most appropriate s...... l......

**32)** No recognition without a t......

# Photocopiable worksheet 16.2

**1** Complete these extracts from Listening A using the correct form of the words in brackets.

   **1** The cornerstone of international commercial arbitration is its ………… nature. (*consent*)

   **2** The parties to an international contract may – to an extent – design the manner in which the arbitral ………… are conducted. (*proceed*)

   **3** In drafting the clause, there are a few ………… requirements that must be met. (*mandate*)

   **4** These provisions should be clear and ………… . (*equivocate*)

   **5** A clause may be ………… with a wide variety of other provisions. (*supplement*)

   **6** Each clause should be carefully tailored to the ………… of a given situation, taking into account the likely types of dispute, the needs of the parties' ………… and the ………… laws. (*exigent*, *relate*, *apply*)

   **7** The ICC suggests the following sample arbitration clause for ………… in international contracts. (*include*)

   **8** The term *all disputes* encompasses all types of ………… , without ………… . (*controversial*, *except*)

   **9** The phrase *in connection with* creates a broad form clause that will cover ………… claims such as tort and fraud in the ………… . (*contract*, *induce*)

**10** This can be an important issue, because the recent ………… to the rules of the ICC have been ………… . (*amend*, *substance*)

**11** The parties may wish to adopt the rules in ………… at the time of ………… because these are the rules they know, and future rule changes may have ………… effects. (*exist*, *contract*, *predict*)

**12** While allowing the parties ………… to choose which version of the rules they prefer, the rules of the ICC contain a default provision stating that in the ………… of an agreement to the contrary, the arbitration shall be conducted according to the rules in effect on the date of the ………… of the arbitral proceeding. (*express*, *absent*, *commence*)

**13** In some cases the ICC has refused to administer an arbitration because of ………… made by the parties' agreement to particular rules. (*alter*)

**14** The ICC has refused to set in motion arbitration proceedings when arbitral clauses provided that the ICC Court could not ………… arbitrators' fees or ………… the draft award. (*determination*, *scrutiny*)

**15** Any alteration of the ICC rules may be ………… if the ICC will otherwise refuse to ………… the arbitration. (*regard*, *administration*)

**2** Write the words you wrote in the gaps above in the correct column of this table, according to their stress pattern.

| ●● | ●●● | ●●●● | ●●●● |
|---|---|---|---|
| | | | |

| ●●● | | ●●●● | ●●●●● |
|---|---|---|---|
| | | | |

# Photocopiable worksheet 16.3

Choose the best word to fill each gap from A, B, C or D below.

## Article 31

In legal proceedings **1** ..................... out of carriage under this Convention, the plaintiff may **2** ..................... an action in any court or tribunal of a contracting country designated by agreement between the parties and, in addition, in the courts or tribunals of a country within **3** ..................... territory: (a) the defendant is **4** ..................... resident, or has his principal place of business, or the branch or agency through which the contract of carriage was **5** ..................... , or (b) the place where the goods were **6** ..................... over by the carrier or the place designated for delivery is situated.

Where in **7** ..................... of a claim referred to in paragraph 1 of this article an action is **8** ..................... before a court or tribunal competent under that paragraph, or where in respect of such a claim a judgment has been **9** ..................... by such a court or tribunal, no new action shall be started between the same parties on the same grounds unless the judgment of the court or tribunal **10** ..................... which the first action was brought is not enforceable in the country in which the **11** ..................... proceedings are brought.

When a judgment entered by a court or tribunal of a contracting country in any such action **12** ..................... is referred to in paragraph 1 of this article has become enforceable in that country, it **13** ..................... also become enforceable in each of the other contracting States, as soon as the formalities required in the country **14** ..................... have been complied **15** ..................... . These formalities shall not permit the **16** ..................... of the case to be re-opened.

| 1 | **A** arising | **B** appearing | **C** occurring | **D** proceeding |
|---|---|---|---|---|
| 2 | **A** call | **B** set | **C** take | **D** bring |
| 3 | **A** whose | **B** that | **C** which | **D** said |
| 4 | **A** often | **B** regularly | **C** ordinarily | **D** typically |
| 5 | **A** opened | **B** entered | **C** stated | **D** made |
| 6 | **A** looked | **B** taken | **C** held | **D** brought |
| 7 | **A** regard | **B** respect | **C** light | **D** spite |
| 8 | **A** pending | **B** hanging | **C** waiting | **D** rendering |
| 9 | **A** inserted | **B** deemed | **C** advised | **D** entered |
| 10 | **A** behind | **B** below | **C** before | **D** beneath |
| 11 | **A** clear | **B** clean | **C** fresh | **D** pure |
| 12 | **A** what | **B** as | **C** so | **D** like |
| 13 | **A** has | **B** had | **C** can | **D** shall |
| 14 | **A** concerned | **B** relevant | **C** appropriate | **D** applied |
| 15 | **A** to | **B** with | **C** against | **D** on |
| 16 | **A** values | **B** basis | **C** merits | **D** trial |

9 780521 279